WEAPONS AND TACTICS

Tim Cooke

Gareth Stevens
Publishing

Please visit our website, www.garethstevens.com. For a free color catalog of all our high-quality books, call toll free 1-800-542-2595 or fax 1-877-542-2596.

Library of Congress Cataloging-in-Publication Data
Cooke, Tim, 1961-
  Weapons and tactics / Tim Cooke.
        p. cm. — (American Civil War: the right answer)
  Includes index.
ISBN 978-1-4339-7552-3 (pbk.)
ISBN 978-1-4339-7553-0 (6-pack)
ISBN 978-1-4339-7551-6 (library binding)
1. United States—History—Civil War, 1861-1865—Equipment and supplies—Juvenile literature.
2. United States. Army—Weapons systems—History—19th century—Juvenile literature. 3.
United States. Army—Drill and tactics—History—19th century—Juvenile literature. 4.
Confederate States of America. Army—Weapons systems—Juvenile literature. 5.   Confederate
States of America. Army—Drill and tactics—Juvenile literature.   I. Title.
  E491.C86 2013
  973.7'13—dc23

                                                                            2012008403

Published in 2013 by
Gareth Stevens Publishing
111 East 14th Street, Suite 349
New York, NY 10003

© 2013 Brown Bear Books Ltd.

For Brown Bear Books Ltd:
Editorial Director: Lindsey Lowe
Managing Editor: Tim Cooke
Children's Publisher: Anne O'Daly
Art Director: Jeni Child
Designer: Karen Perry
Picture Manager: Sophie Mortimer
Production Director: Alastair Gourlay

Picture Credits:
Front Cover: Library of Congress

Interior: all Library of Congress except, Medford Historical Society Collection: 40; National
Archives: 9, 11, 12t, 14, 21, 22, 28, 29, 32, 33, 35, 41; Robert Hunt Library: 27.

All Artworks © Brown Bear Books Ltd.

Manufactured in the United States of America
1 2 3 4 5 6 7 8 9   12 11 10

CPSIA compliance information: Batch #BRS12GS: For further information contact Gareth Stevens, New York, New York
at 1-800-542-2595.

Contents

Introduction

The Civil War is sometimes described as the first modern war. New weapons appeared that changed the nature of fighting. They forced generals to come up with new tactics.

Commanders on both sides had learned the same ways to maneuver units on the battlefield. But the introduction of rifled muskets that shot further and more accurately, and that could be loaded faster, made tactics such as bayonet charges suicidal. Generals had to work out new ways to make their attacks.

There were similar advances in artillery and in naval warfare. The Union manfactured cannons and mortars to use to besiege enemy cities. The Confederates produced the world's first armored warship, or ironclad. But the Union could build more ironclads and won the naval war.

Industrial warfare

The Union enjoyed the same advantage when it came to other weapons. In a conflict that relied on mass production, the Union's industrial strength put it far ahead. Even where the Confederates had an advantage, the resources of the North overcame it. At the start of the war, for example, the Confederate cavalry was seen as being superior because many of their recruits were horsemen. But the Union cavalry soon improved to match it.

About this book

This book describes the weapons used to fight the war and how tactics changed as a result. Boxes in the margins help you get more out of your reading. **Comment** boxes highlight specific information and explain its importance. **Ask Yourself** boxes suggest questions for you to consider. There are no right or wrong answers; the questions are meant to help you think about the subject. Other boxes explain difficult words or ideas. The book finishes with a glossary and a list of resources for further information. There is also an index that you can use to find facts fast.

↻ A Union artillery battery prepares to fire during the Siege of Petersburg in 1864.

Artillery

Two types of artillery were common in the Civil War. Fixed heavy artillery was used in fortifications and in sieges. On the battlefield, artillery was more mobile and so was used to support the troops.

T he most common guns used by both Union and Confederate armies in the Civil War were smoothbore muzzle-loaded cannons. Other weapons were breech-loading guns, rifled guns, and mortars.

⌒ A Confederate artillery battery. Each gun had up to seven men to load and fire it.

New field gun

The Model 1857 12-pounder (5.4 kg) Napoleon, named for the French emperor Napoleon III, was the most widely used gun of the war. A muzzle-loaded smoothbore, it had a bronze barrel 5 feet 6 inches (168 cm) long. With a range of up to 1,600 yards (1,463 m), it could fire four different types of projectile.

At the start of the war, U.S. arsenals still stored Model 1841 six-pounder (2.7 kg) cannons. When the Confederates captured federal arsenals in 1861, they seized the six-pounders. But the guns did not have the range or power of the Napoleon. By July 1862, the main Confederate gun foundry, the Tredegar Works in Richmond, Virginia, was producing 12-pounders. The Confederacy would produce more than 450 Napoleons during the war; but the Union made 1,127.

Types of ammunition

Different types of shot were used for various purposes. Solid shot—like cannonballs—was the most accurate. It was fired against masses of enemy troops at long range. The balls were made of cast iron; each weighed 12 pounds (5.4 kg).

The second type of shot required a fuse. It included shrapnel and explosive shells. They were hollow and filled with a type of gunpowder. Shrapnel was used against soldiers, but explosive shells were used to blow up buildings.

Canister shot was used at ranges of up to 350 yards (320 m). The gun fired a container full of iron shot. The container split apart, turning the artillery piece into a giant shotgun.

◑ The Napoleon was loaded through the muzzle. Muzzle-loaders were quicker to fire than the new breech-loading guns, which were rarely used in the Civil War.

New technology

Rifled artillery soon appeared. They had a spiraled groove cut into the inside of the barrel that made the shell spin in the air. That gave the guns a greater range and made them more accurate than smoothbores. They were made of iron because it lasted longer than bronze. Union rifled weapons were the 3-inch (7.6 cm) Ordnance Rifle and the 10-pounder (4.5 kg) Parrott gun. By 1863, the Confederates were producing similar but inferior weapons.

Other artillery

The most powerful guns were the heavy artillery. They were made of iron; by the end of the war, most were rifled. Siege guns, such as the 30-

To fire artillery, a rope or lanyard was pulled out of the gun. This ignited a friction primer filled with gunpowder in the rear of the gun.

⮑ *Union artillery at a dock in May 1863. The supplies include solid shot (foreground), coehorn mortars (middle), and Parrott guns (background).*

pounder (13.6 kg) Parrott, traveled with a marching army. Anything bigger was mounted on a carriage (to control the massive recoil). Coastal artillery pieces, for use against shipping, were the biggest guns. The Union Rodman gun had a barrel nearly 16 feet (4.9 m) long and a range of over 3 miles (5 km).

The Union army used mortars during sieges. They launched shells in a high arc from a short, stubby barrel. The largest mortars could be mounted on railroad cars. A smaller bronze mortar, the coehorn, was used at the Siege of Petersburg, Virginia, in 1864 and 1865.

⌒ *Confederate troops stand near a mortar at Pensacola, Florida.*

THE RIGHT ANSWER

?

The Union army had more artillery than the Confederate army. Was that why they won?

The Union army had the great advantage of the factories and industries of the North. Unlike the South, where the economy was based on agriculture, the North could manufacture artillery and ammunition. The North also had ample supplies of iron and bronze. Much iron came from melted-down railroad track. Meanwhile, the South had only one ironworks. The North therefore had a vast advantage in artillery production over the South throughout the war. That alone did not win the war, however. The Union also had more troops and other resources at its disposal.

Cavalry

During the Civil War, the number of cavalry regiments increased dramatically on both sides. The Union total grew from 5 to 170; the Confederate cavalry regiments numbered over 130.

🔊 *Union cavalry officers near Petersburg, Virginia, in August 1864.*

The Confederate cavalry was initially made up of men who had been used to handling horses in their prewar lives. Many Union cavalrymen, who often came from more urban backgrounds, did not have the same experience of horses. Throughout the war, cavalry units on both sides—particularly on the Confederate side—were often understrength.

Horses

Southern troopers supplied their own mounts. This worked well at the start of the war when there were plenty of horses. As the fighting went on and losses grew, Confederates could find fewer horses, and their cavalry shrank. The Union War Department had set up the Cavalry Bureau to buy horses in July 1863. It supplied more than 150,000 horses to the Union army.

Cavalry tactics and weapons

The three main weapons used by the cavalry were the saber, the carbine, and the pistol. The saber was a sword with a 3-foot-long (90 cm) curved blade. It was the main cavalry weapon at the start of the war.

The introduction of the breech-loading carbine changed cavalry tactics as the war went on. Early in the war, the Confederate cavalry commander J.E.B. Stuart's saber-carrying 1st Virginia Cavalry defeated the 11th New York Zouaves at the First Battle of Bull Run (Manassas) on July 21, 1861. But rifled muskets accurate at ranges of up to 300 yards (275 m) turned any similar cavalry attack into a suicide charge.

The Confederates preferred to use large-caliber pistols like the six-shot Colt Navy, while the Union cavalry still used sabers for close combat.

◐ A Union Army of the Potomac blacksmith at work during the Siege of Petersburg (1864–1865).

Cavalry raids

By 1862, the role of the cavalry had changed in both armies. The Union cavalry was still a young and

➲ *A Union cavalry officer at winter quarters near Brandy Station, 1863–1864.*

↻ *Alfred Pleasonton (right) and George A. Custer, two Union cavalry commanders, in April 1863.*

inexperienced force. Its role was to guard supply lines and camps. The superior Confederate cavalry began to carry out large-scale raids and reconnaissance operations. Cavalry units from both sides also served behind the lines as guerrilla fighters. While raids behind enemy lines boosted morale, however, they distracted from the task of watching enemy movements. This failure had serious consequences for the Union at Chancellorsville in May 1863 and for the Confederates at Gettysburg. Such failures added to the cavalry's poor reputation among the infantry of both sides.

A tactical change

During 1863, things changed. The Confederate cavalry, lacking new recruits, horses, and weapons, started to decline. The Union cavalry, meanwhile, was growing and taking on a more offensive role as mounted infantry. Their horses gave them more mobility, while the carbine, especially the Spencer, gave them the firepower to attack Confederate infantry on foot.

Two brigades of John Buford's 1st U.S. Cavalry Division used these tactics to hold off two Confederate divisions on the first day of the Battle of Gettysburg on July 1, 1863. From behind a stone wall, the cavalrymen fought for two hours until infantry arrived. They ensured that the Army of the Potomac kept the high ground that would prove decisive to the battle's outcome.

ASK YOURSELF

Did the use of the carbine by Union cavalry suggest that they were more adaptable to using new technology than the Confederates?

The battle began when two detachments of cavalry blundered into one another.

THE RIGHT ANSWER

?

How important was the contribution made by the cavalry on both sides to outcome of the war?

The cavalry was vital. When war began, the U.S. Army had 176 cavalry officers. The majority—104—chose to join the Confederacy. The U.S. Army decided that cavalry were an unnecessary luxury. The Battle of First Bull Run proved otherwise. As the war went on, the Union invested more in the cavalry; the investment paid off at Gettysburg and elsewhere. Used well, the cavalry were the eyes of the army; they kept commanders informed of enemy movements and provided cover for infantry. The cavalry also covered disrupted communications and supply lines.

Fortifications

The Civil War began at Fort Sumter in Charleston Harbor in 1861. Fortifications continued to play an important role in the war, with trenches around towns and armies besieged behind enemy lines.

◐ *The Siege of Petersburg saw trench building evolve as the long battle went on.*

Fort Sumter in Charleston Harbor, South Carolina, and Fort Pulaski off Savannah, Georgia, were examples of a new kind of sea fort built to withstand heavy pounding from the guns of warships out at sea. When war broke out, the Confederacy also built semipermanent forts at strategic points on its vast network of navigable rivers. The rivers provided routes for commerce and trade but also a potential invasion route into the South for Union gunboats.

More fortifications

The sheer size of the territory over which the 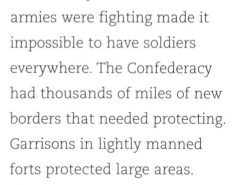 armies were fighting made it impossible to have soldiers everywhere. The Confederacy had thousands of miles of new borders that needed protecting. Garrisons in lightly manned forts protected large areas.

As more cities came under attack, fortifications were

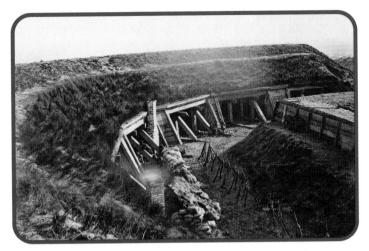

⤷ **Fort Fisher guarded the Southern port of Wilmington, North Carolina. The sand of its fortifications simply absorbed the impact of cannonballs.**

constructed to defend them. Early on, the Union War Department built over 20 miles (32 km) of trenches and 68 artillery forts to prevent a Confederate attack on Washington, D.C. The Union army besieged and captured Confederate cities, including Atlanta, Charleston, New Orleans, Vicksburg, and the capital, Richmond.

A new warfare

The introduction of the latest infantry weapons such as rifled guns to the battlefield changed the way the war was fought. Fieldwork fortifications such as trenches and earthworks became more essential for cover from enemy fire. Any protected defensive position could turn an assault into a bloodbath. A sunken road and wooden fence near Sharpsburg, Maryland, became known as Bloody Lane after an afternoon of fierce fighting at Antietam in September 1862. A stone wall along Marye's Heights gave enough

At Vicksburg, Mississippi, a Union force of more than 70,000 men and 200 guns attacked civilians as well as soldiers between May and July 1863.

ASK YOURSELF

How did advances in gun technology alter the way in which Civil War armies fought?

By 1864, soldiers were using new methods of fighting. If they stopped for more than one day, they built trenches for protection.

protection to 6,000 Confederates to fight off attacks by 40,000 Union troops in the Battle of Fredericksburg in Virginia in December 1862.

Defensive obstacles

To protect their positions and make it more difficult for the enemy to approach, troops placed obstacles in front of their earthworks. They included chevaux-de-frise, a screen of logs fitted with pointed stakes. Gabions, or wicker baskets packed with earth, were used to protect dugouts, or "bombproofs," from attack. Union general Ambrose E. Burnside is said to have ordered wire entanglements to be strung at ground level to trip up attackers: an early forerunner of barbed-wire and razor-wire fences.

↻ A reinforced dugout, known as a bombproof, built by Union soldiers at the Siege of Petersburg, Virginia, in 1864.

Trenches

The nature of fighting changed during the Civil War. Soldiers

FORT SEDGWICK

no longer spent their days marching behind regimental colors and firing volleys by rank. Instead, they spent days and days building and repairing trenches—of which there might be miles and miles in any one position. The hours of boredom and manual labor were only broken up by the terrifying business of dodging the sharpshooter's bullet or the endless rain of mortar shells that were fired from close range and fell down out of the sky.

↳ *A drawing of a Union camp on the battlefield at Cold Harbor in June 1864. The fortifications were built from anything the soldiers found.*

ASK YOURSELF

Civilians were also subject to mortar bombardment. What might the experience have been like?

THE RIGHT ANSWER

?

Would it be fair to describe the Civil War as the first modern war?

Over the course of the Civil War, the way armies fought changed significantly. Advances in weapons technology meant that guns could be fired more quickly and more times before they needed to be reloaded. This meant that exposed soldiers could be more easily hit. Hiding behind some protection—any protection—became vital for survival. Troops needed to shelter as they moved around the battlefield, so trenches were dug. In both the destructive firepower of the weapons and the importance of trenches, the war predicted the nature of warfare in the 20th century.

Guerrilla Warfare

Across the Confederacy, in Union border states, and in Indian Territory, cavalry raiders, partisans, and armed criminal bands brought death and terror to civilian communities.

↻ *Confederate partisan raider John S. Mosby and his men attack a civilian wagon train in September 1863.*

The term "guerrilla" comes from the Spanish word for "little war." It refers to tactics such as raids and ambushes, rather than set-piece battles.

Three distinct groups used guerrilla tactics in the Civil War. The first group were regular cavalrymen like Confederate general Nathan B. Forrest. They often made hit-and-run raids on camps and depots behind enemy lines.

The second group were so-called partisan rangers. These armed gangs were backed by the Confederate government, but they operated independently. They often attacked nonmilitary targets. Between their raids, they hid away their weapons and uniforms.

The largest group of guerrillas were criminal gangs that operated without any authorization. They usually wore civilian clothing and concealed their weapons. They sabotaged trains and ambushed isolated enemy troops. They also attacked and killed civilians.

A necessary evil?

Both governments thought that guerrilla tactics were acceptable if combatants clearly identified themselves. But those who did not were treated as bandits and murderers. If caught, they were subject to military trial and execution.

But Union and Confederate troops often operated just within the law: They took hostages, burned houses, and seized goods. Such methods often served to make guerrillas on the other side more angry and dangerous.

Missouri's guerrillas

Charles R. Jennison, William C. Quantrill, and Champ Furguson were guerrillas who fought mainly in Missouri. The state probably saw the

The most famous partisan rangers were John S. Mosby's 43rd Partisan Battalion, who carried out raids in northern Virginia.

ASK YOURSELF

Were guerrillas much worse than the regular soldiers? If your house is burned down, does it matter who did it?

↻ Antislavery guerrillas known as Jayhawkers attack civilians in Missouri. The state suffered a high level of guerrilla warfare.

In this drawing by Adalbert Volck, Southern guerrillas try to recruit farmers to join their band in 1863.

most widespread and intensive guerrilla struggle. Jennison and his Jayhawkers were Union supporters. They used the war as a chance to retaliate against the "border ruffians" who had tried and failed to make Kansas a slave state.

The Union declared Quantrill an outlaw, but the Confederate army made him a captain. He and his men, including the outlaws Frank and Jesse James, killed any Union soldiers or Jayhawkers they captured. On August 21, 1863, Quantrill's men attacked the antislavery town of Lawrence, Kansas. His men murdered more than 150 people and destroyed 200 buildings.

Jennison and Quantrill each led a large body of followers. Champ Furguson led small groups of "bushwhackers" from Tennessee in the

In the years before the war, Kansas had seen so much violence between pro- and antislavery settlers that it was named "Bleeding Kansas."

Cumberland highlands. He had a reputation for cruelty and is thought to have killed more than a hundred men. The postwar U.S. government executed him as an outlaw.

A guerrilla war

In early 1865, it became clear that the Confederates would soon lose the war. Some Southerners wanted the struggle to be carried on via large-scale guerrilla warfare. Union commanders such as Ulysses S. Grant and William T. Sherman feared such a possibility, but it was never a serious option.

◑ *Partisan leader John S. Mosby operated behind enemy lines in northern Virginia.*

THE RIGHT ANSWER

?

Was the contribution made by the different guerrilla groups effective in the Civil War?

As defeat loomed, some Confederates wanted to prolong the war through guerrilla warfare. Some fought on for a short time, but Confederate general Robert E. Lee warned against such action. There were simply not enough men for an effective campaign. During the war, guerrilla bands had succeeded in terrifying local communities. The brutality of Furguson, who murdered Union soldiers as they lay sick in their hospital beds, added to the fear the guerrillas could inspire. But their overall impact was limited. They never had enough manpower, weapons, or opportunity.

Infantry Tactics

Infantry tactics changed over the course of the war. The introduction of new weapons such as the rifled musket, with its greater range and increased accuracy, changed the battlefield.

Most Union and Confederate generals attended the same military schools and served in the U.S. Army before the war. They tended to use similar battle tactics. Their field officers, who led the troops into battle, were mostly volunteers. They learned maneuvers from books such as Hardee's *Tactics*, which was used by officers on both sides of the conflict.

The aim of infantry tactics was to be able to maneuver units of troops into a position where they could deploy on the battlefield as quickly

⟳ *The 96th Pennsylvania Infantry drills in a camp in 1861. Drilling taught troops how to deploy rapidly in battle.*

⟳ Union troops launch a bayonet charge at the Battle of Fair Oaks (Seven Pines), Virginia, in June 1862. Such forms of attack soon became out of date.

and efficiently as possible. They then had to be able to direct the maximum amount of musket fire onto the enemy or charge with bayonets to drive the enemy from the field.

To achieve this, infantry companies were trained to march in column, usually four men across. They then worked in coordinated units on the battlefield. They drilled often in training to make the movements second nature in battle.

Means of attack

The most common method of infantry attack was to advance lines of men, one after the other, in waves about 25 yards (23 m) apart. The first wave bore the brunt of the attack and shielded the following units. The speed of the attack depended on the distance to be covered.

The U.S. Army had successfully used the wave technique during the Mexican War (1846–1848), but by 1861 it was becoming outdated. The main

ASK YOURSELF

Why did soldiers need to be able to carry out maneuvers without thinking too much about them?

reason for this was that the infantry were no longer facing an enemy armed with the inaccurate smoothbore flintlock musket. In the 1860s, the rifled musket was introduced. It had a range of 500 yards (450 m), nearly 10 times that of the smoothbore.

Because of the new weapons, the Civil War was notable for a series of bloody frontal assaults. They included the Union charges on Marye's Heights during the Battle of Fredericksburg in December 1862 and Pickett's Charge on the third day of Gettysburg in July 1863.

The rifled musket made a bayonet charge suicidal. Standing in line without cover led to huge casualties.

The need for cover

By 1864, bitter experience had forced soldiers to change the way they fought. From then on, infantry attacks were made in short rushes.

⟳ Union sailors practice fencing. Many soldiers carried swords for close-quarter fighting.

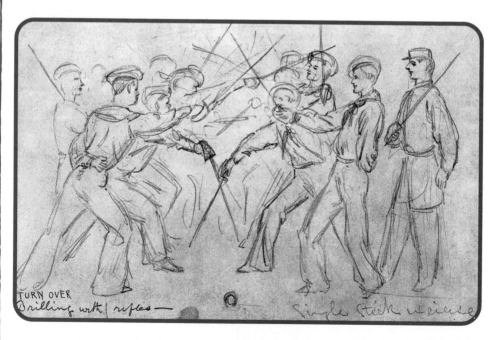

Soldiers gave each other covering fire as they ran from one safe place to another. In defense, avoiding enemy fire became the first priority. If troops stopped marching for a day or more, they dug trenches to cover them from enemy fire.

The Union VI Corps holds its formation as it fights in dense undergrowth at the Battle of the Wilderness.

Union general Jacob D. Cox summed up after the war, "One rifle in the trench was worth five in front of it." This way of thinking became the basis of the tactics that would dominate infantry warfare in the next 50 years.

ASK YOURSELF

If all the soldiers were in the safety of trenches and were not moving daily, how might that change the nature of battles?

THE RIGHT ANSWER

?

Did Civil War generals experiment with new tactics as new weapons were introduced?

The Civil War coincided with technological advances that altered forever how wars were fought. The type of infantry advance that had been perfected in Europe in the Napoleonic Wars of the early 1800s, and which had been used as recently as the Mexican War of 1846–1848, were now outdated. As rifles fired further and more accurately, tactics changed to take this into account. Marching in formation in open spaces became suicidal. However, some generals were slow to appreciate the changes, resulting in the doomed frontal charges that characterized some battles.

Naval Warfare

Naval warfare was at a point of change during the Civil War. New technology was being developed, with steam-powered ironclad vessels and sea mines (called torpedoes) used for the first time.

At the start of the war, the Union navy's commanders had three objectives. They wanted to protect the Union's merchant ships, blockade Confederate ports, and take control of the South's many waterways. The Confederate navy's aim was to stop them.

◑ *The ironclads* USS *Monitor (left) and CSS Virginia clash at the Battle of Hampton Roads on March 9, 1862.*

Union blockade

Before the war, the United States had just 90 warships, of which few were serviceable. By December 1864, its navy consisted of more than 600 ships, including 236 steam-powered vessels constructed during the war.

Many of the ships were used to blockade the South's ports and reduce its ability to export its cotton. Maintaining the blockade was a challenge because the Confederate coastline was roughly 3,000 miles (4,830 km) long. The Confederates used fast ships known as blockade-runners to

COMMENT

At the start of the war, the Union was able to build ships quickly because of its manufacturing base and wealth.

challenge the blockade. Although most of them succeeded, the Confederacy had few blockade-runners. As a result, the Union blockade worked.

Different defenses

Southern ports were defended by Confederate forts, ships, and sea mines, which were known as "torpedoes" in the Civil War. The older forts had been built with thick masonry walls and were vulnerable to the new generation of large explosive shells. The Confederates discovered that earthwork forts were easier to build and absorbed shell fire better.

The ships that defended Confederate harbors were armored rams. They rammed an enemy ship as well as firing on it with cannons. Both sides used these rams during the war.

The Union blockade halted Southern trade. The South could no longer supply the world with cotton, so its main source of income dried up.

↻ *Union warships sail past Confederate guns at Port Hudson on the Mississippi River in 1863.*

🎧 *A sailor poses by a Dahlgren gun on deck. Its carriage and rope helped contain the recoil of the heavy gun.*

Confederate warships also sank a large number of Union merchant ships. U.S. maritime trade did not recover for many years.

Torpedoes were the final part of Confederate harbor defenses. They were watertight cylinders, packed with black explosive powder and attached to cables. When an enemy ship came close, shore observers would detonate the mine using an electric current. The torpedo was the most effective weapon: During the war, Confederate torpedoes sank 29 Union warships, far more than were lost to ramming or gunfire.

Battle of the ironclads

In the war, the Union built nearly 60 ironclad vessels. Launched in May 1862, these new vessels, with their 4.5-inch-thick (11 cm) armor plating, served throughout the war. They played a notable part in the long, but finally unsuccessful, attempt to capture Charleston, South Carolina, in 1863.

The most famous Union ironclad was the USS *Monitor*, launched in January 1862. It fought in the world's first duel between armored warships in a famous engagement with the CSS *Virginia*, on March 9, 1862, at Hampton Roads, Virginia. The *Monitor* influenced the design of most subsequent Union ironclads, but there was one drawback: Their low hulls meant they sank easily in heavy seas. Hampton Roads was an important duel. It showed the way forward for naval warfare.

○ **The USS Onondaga was the first double-turreted ironclad in the Union navy. It guarded Union troops on the James River.**

Without the Union navy, the Union army might not have won the war. With control of the seas and rivers, the Union armies were able to move deep into the South to achieve victory.

THE RIGHT ANSWER

?

Did the two American navies lead the world in naval technology in the 1860s?

Although neither the *Monitor* nor the *Virginia* won a clear victory at Hampton Roads, the contest was of great interest to other navies. It was clear what a threat an ironclad now posed. Not only did the ship have metal cladding, it also had an armored turret that could turn its two 11-inch (28 cm) Dahlgren guns in any direction. This innovation would be adopted by warships across the world as a standard design feature. The smaller river gunboat was another much-copied innovation. It was a small vessel, mounted with cannons, that could sail shallow rivers.

Reconnaissance

Successful reconnaissance will find out what the enemy is doing and what the terrain is like. The Civil War was often fought on unmapped territory, so reconnaissance was vitally important.

The Civil War was fought in countryside that was known well only to the local people who lived there. Most of it was semiwilderness, which meant that armies had no idea most of the time where they were. At the same time, they were trying to find and fight their enemy.

⚓ *Confederate cavalry commander J.E.B. Stuart leads his troops on his three-day reconnaissance in June 1862.*

Failures of reconnaissance

On April 6, 1862, the Battle of Shiloh started when 9,000 Confederates launched a surprise attack on the Union camp of General Ulysses S. Grant. Grant's troops were caught off guard. By the end of the day, they had been pushed back to Pittsburg Landing on the Tennessee River and were close to defeat, although they recovered the next day.

The Confederates were able to surprise the Union forces for a second time on May 2, 1863.

confederate general Robert E. Lee sent Thomas J. "Stonewall" Jackson and 28,000 men on a flanking march to attack the Union right flank at the Battle of Chancellorsville in Virginia. The entire force—almost two-thirds of Lee's army—found its way through 12 miles (20 km) of forest. In the late afternoon, Jackson attacked, taking the Union XI Corps completely by surprise. The Union soldiers fled. They only avoided defeat because Jackson stopped the attack at nightfall.

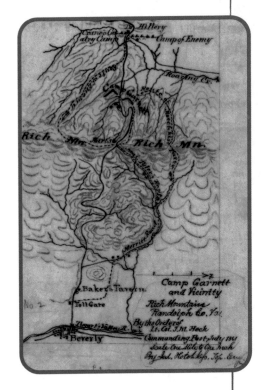

🎧 *Union and Confederate positions at Rich Mountain, Virginia, as drawn by Confederate mapmaker Jedediah Hotchkiss.*

The cavalry's role

Cavalrymen were the soldiers most heavily involved in reconnaissance as they could cover large distances on horseback. Riders would scout forward of the main army to seek out the enemy, sometimes with the help of local guides or spies.

The largest cavalry reconnaissance of the war took place in June 1862 during the Peninsular Campaign. J.E.B. Stuart led a Confederate force of 1,200 men in a three-day ride around General George B. McClellan's Union army. Stuart gave Lee precise information about the location of McClellan's men, which proved invaluable when Lee began a counterattack ten days later.

ASK YOURSELF

Can you think of modern equivalents for the cavalryman riding ahead to find out information?

Army commanders relied completely on the reconnaissance work of the cavalry. A failure to find the enemy could result in defeat. At Gettysburg, in July 1863, the Union cavalry was the first to the battlefield and took up a good defensive position on Cemetery Hill. That position helped the Union to finally win the battle. One reason for the Confederate defeat at Gettysburg was the failure of Stuart's cavalry to reconnoiter in front of Lee's army. Lee therefore had no idea that General George G. Meade had concentrated the Army of the Potomac on the high ground above Gettysburg.

↻ Both sides experimented with using hot-air balloons for reconnaissance.

On the battlefield

Infantry soldiers carried out reconnaissance on the battlefield. Small groups of men, sometimes acting independently, would move ahead of the main battle line to find out what was happening. They could then give advance warning of an oncoming attack.

This was vital, because the gunpowder used in the weapons of the day created a smoky atmosphere. During fierce firefights, visibility fell to only a few hundred feet.

Signalers

Signalers played an important role. Once the enemy was located, it was important to let the commanding generals know as quickly as possible. Although fast dispatch riders were often employed, it was increasingly common to see men of the signal corps on the front line. They sent back information using a semaphore system of flags, colored lights, or signal flares.

☞ *Soldiers pose at a Union signal tower on Elk Mountain, overlooking the battlefield of Antietam, Maryland, in September 1862.*

ASK YOURSELF

How dangerous was it for the signalmen to do their job? They had to be fully visible—which meant enemy snipers could see them, too.

THE RIGHT ANSWER

?

Reconnaissance was a crucial part of the Civil War. Why was it so important?

You could not fight a battle if you could not find the enemy. The role of reconnaissance was to try to locate the enemy before the enemy was able to locate you. This required great skill in moving around. Civil War America was largely uncharted territory. It had many forests and semiwilderness with no roads. They had to be cut through this terrain. Unmarked rivers and swamps had to be explored and negotiated. A good reconnaissance man could map new territory and record it for his commanding officers to use as they planned their line of attack. His role was crucial.

Siege Warfare

Siege warfare had been perfected in Europe over 200 years. It played an important role in the Civil War, with the Union laying siege to Confederate fortifications and cities.

⌒ *Union gunboats bomb Port Hudson during the siege in May 1863.*

The aim of a siege was to force the besieged to surrender or starve. It was a slow business.

Once an army had surrounded the city or fort, they would put in place siege artillery. These were heavy guns that could fire 32-lb (14.5 kg) shot or shell up to 2,000 yards (1,828 m). The mortar was developed specifically for sieges. It fired shells in a high arc that passed straight over enemy defenses to land inside a fort or city. There was no defense against mortar fire.

Trenches

Artillery was just part of siege warfare. As a bombardment continued, the besieging infantry dug entrenchments. They began with a ring of trenches, or parallel; trenches were then dug in front of them to create a second parallel. Digging was slow, hard work and went on 24 hours a day. As they dug, the soldiers were usually fired on by enemy snipers and artillery.

Blowing a hole

To make a gap or breach in the defense lines, the attacking army dug a tunnel beneath them. They filled the tunnel with gunpowder, then blew it up. The Union army did this at Vicksburg in June 1863 and again in July 1864 at Petersburg, Virginia. The latter explosion blew such a huge crater in the Confederate defenses that the Union forces became trapped inside it. The Confederates attacked, killing 4,000 Union men in what became known as the Battle of the Crater.

☙ *Union mortars at the Siege of Yorktown, Virginia, in April 1862. Mortars were used to hit the earthworks and fortifications around towns.*

⌒ General Lee (right, with telescope) examines Union trenches at Vicksburg.

To defend themselves from Union army tunnels, the Southerners often dug countermines. These tunnels went under the Union tunnel, which could then be collapsed or blown up.

But it was usually hunger, not encirclement or even the continual bombing, that led defenders to surrender. At Vicksburg, the besieged Confederates had only mule and rat meat to eat by the time the city surrendered on July 4, 1863.

The final siege

Trench lines at Petersburg extended 30 miles (48 km) from the eastern edge of Richmond, Virginia, toward Petersburg.

The Siege of Petersburg lasted 10 months, only ending in April 1865 because Confederate general Robert E. Lee was running low on supplies. Lee's Army of Northern Virginia had built its own huge trench system around Petersburg that had successfully kept Grant and the Army of the

Potomac at bay since June 1864. Now Lee took the decision to try and break out from his trench lines to secure access to his only source of resupply, a railroad line that ran to the west.

Lee knew his army would grow weaker as Grant's grew stronger. Any new Union attack would finish off the Confederate army if it stayed where it was. So Lee ordered his men to leave Petersburg and led them westward toward the rail station near Appomattox, where he was finally forced to surrender on April 9, 1865.

More than perhaps any other Civil War battle, the Siege of Petersburg anticipated the trench warfare widely used in World War I (1914–1918).

> The citizens of Petersburg suffered just as much as the soldiers during the lengthy siege.

ASK YOURSELF

Were Confederate generals wrong to tie up so many men in sieges rather than letting them fight on the battlefield?

THE RIGHT ANSWER

?

The Confederate strategy of using fortifications to defend Southern territory failed. Why?

The South set out to use fortified positions to defend territory it claimed belonged to the Confederacy rather than the United States. Fewer men were needed to defend fortifications than to fight on the battlefield, and the South lacked men. But, no matter how strong the Confederate fortifications were or how difficult terrain was to cross, the Union army was always better equipped and better manned. Once the Union army was entrenched, it could play a waiting game. It waited for the Confederates to run out of supplies, which they inevitably did.

Strategy and Tactics

Both the Union and the Confederacy used diplomatic, political, and economic strategies to reinforce their campaigns on the battlefield and their efforts to defeat their enemy.

Strategy and tactics are key to the outcome of any war. Strategy refers to how to direct military operations and movements to achieve an overall goal (victory). Tactics describes moves taken to carry out a plan on the battlefield.

↻ *A drawing by Alfred Waud of the 1st Maine Cavalry in June 1863. The new repeating rifles made battle tactics, such as cavalry charges, out of date.*

Different strategies

Both sides failed in their diplomatic endeavors to engage Europe on their side in the war. They both turned to different strategies. The Union "Anaconda Plan" proposed, among other things, a naval blockade of Southern ports. Meanwhile, Confederate president Jefferson Davis encouraged planters to withhold cotton from British and French mills to encourage their fleets to sail to Southern ports and end the blockade. The strategy failed: Britain and France were not that reliant on Southern cotton.

↻ Union forces destroy a railroad bridge over the Chickahominy River in June 1862. Cutting railroads was a key tactic.

Military strategies

Union generals soon realized that the blockade would not win the war alone. They would have to invade the South and seize its territory to win the war; the Confederate generals had just to defend their land. The two strategies manifested themselves in a series of battles that were each indecisive, but that together wore down the enemy. Two examples were Confederate general Robert E. Lee's success in the Seven Days' Battles and Union general Ulysses S. Grant's pursuit of Lee through Virginia in the spring of 1864.

With increasing success, the Union used a strategy of making Confederate civilians suffer in order to undermine their will to fight on. The Union achieved this by blockading the Southern ports and by splitting the Confederacy, east from west, by capturing the Mississippi River.

Lincoln's 1863 Emancipation Proclamation won the diplomatic war. No European power would support a fight to protect slavery.

ASK YOURSELF

Why do you think people in the South put up with all the shortages they suffered in the war?

Union strategy also involved capturing the South's few industrial sites. Nashville, New Orleans, Atlanta, and Richmond were the focus of many of their military campaigns.

After the failure of "cotton diplomacy," the Confederates adopted a military strategy to win the war. This involved defending every inch of their territory, whether it was necessary or not. Soldiers were spread across the South and concentrated wherever a specific Union threat existed. The strategy proved unsuccessful, however. It allowed Union forces to pick and choose their targets. For example, Mobile, Alabama, had a large garrison that saw no action until relatively late in the war.

The Confederacy depended on the goodwill of its citizens. Each state governed itself and had to be treated as such.

Undermining morale

The Confederates hoped to turn the Northern public against the war by inflicting heavy losses on the Union armies. To this end, Lee repeatedly attacked the Army of the Potomac. Raids into Northern territory were designed to damage morale. They failed after Atlanta, Georgia, fell and Northerners reelected Lincoln in fall 1864.

◑ *Confederate artillery and earthworks at Petersburg, Virginia. The Confederates only had to fight defensively, which could have given them an advantage.*

New tactics

The improved accuracy of rifled weapons meant the infantry learned to take cover. Cavalry no longer charged at infantry with sabers drawn. Instead, they fought as dismounted skirmishers, with pistols and carbines. Union gunboats helped in battles and dominated Southern rivers. The Union always had the advantage in numbers. Confederate efforts to compensate by using skirmishing tactics were ineffective.

⌒ *Confederates destroyed this railroad as they retreated from Atlanta, Georgia, in September 1864 as part of their "scorched-earth" tactic.*

THE RIGHT ANSWER

?

Since the Union won the Civil War, does that prove it had the better strategies and tactics?

Overall, the Union probably did have superior strategies and tactics to the South. Just as important, though, it also had better resources and more manpower. Confederate president Jefferson Davis made an error in assuming that cotton was indispensable to other countries, and his strategy failed accordingly. When Europe failed to behave as he hoped, the Confederacy was isolated. With its smaller forces and inferior equipment, it was always fighting for survival. Southern citizens showed great bravery in withstanding the Union assault but eventually gave in.

Weapons and Firearms

During the Civil War, weapons were changing fast. The improvements revolutionized how battles were fought and changed the tactics used by both Union and Confederate commanders.

⌒ *Outnumbered, Confederates at the Third Battle of Winchester in 1864 were forced to retreat.*

The infantryman's single-shot rifle-musket was the most commonly used weapon of the Civil War.

To load and fire the musket took 20 separate movements. The soldier poured black powder into the barrel, inserted a Minié bullet, rammed the ball home, cocked the hammer, and put a percussion cap in place.

Although the drill was complicated, it was practiced so often that it became second nature to most infantrymen. But the stress and fear of battle inevitably led to mistakes. Infantrymen might leave a ramrod in the barrel, causing an explosion, while others replaced the percussion cap without realizing that their weapon had not fired. After the Battle of Gettysburg, it was discovered that as many as 18,000 discarded muskets had more than one round in them.

Different tactics

As the war continued and weapons technology improved, the tactic of arranging troops in tight standing formations to advance together and fire on command risked high casualties. Infantry now advanced in smaller units. They took advantage of the land for cover, firing, then kneeling or lying down to reload to avoid enemy fire.

The new rifles were loaded from the end of the barrel. They needed a bullet small enough to slip down inside the barrel that then expanded to touch its sides when fired. A Frenchman, Captain Minié, developed a conical lead bullet with a hollow base. As the rifle fired, the expanding gases of the exploding powder pushed out the sides of the bullet so they gripped the rifling in the barrel and began to spin. The Minié bullet, or Minnie ball, was widely used in the war.

The addition of a spiral groove or rifling inside the barrel made the bullet spin. This increased the rifle's accuracy and range.

⟳ *Hand-to-hand fighting with bayonets at Frayser's Farm on June 30, 1862, during the Seven Days' Campaign.*

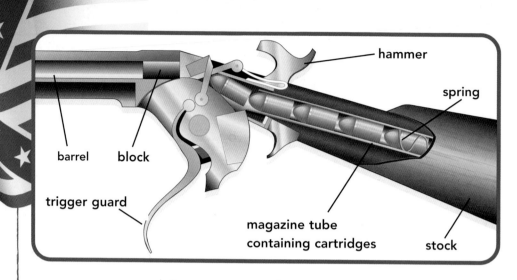

hammer

spring

barrel   block

trigger guard

magazine tube
containing cartridges

stock

⊙ The internal mechanism of the Spencer repeating rifle. It could fire up to eight rounds before it needed to be reloaded. The Spencer was a breechloader that replaced the rifle-musket.

Shortage of weapons

Both sides had to import rifles from Europe to meet demand. Some imports, such as the British Model 1853 Enfield, were better than others.

At the start of the war, the Confederacy had only about 150,000 rifle-muskets, most seized from Union arsenals. By the First Battle of Bull Run (Manassas) in July 1861, new volunteers were being asked to supply their own weapons, such as shotguns and hunting rifles. In the state of Tennessee, a law allowed troops to seize firearms from private homes.

Both sides used old weapons. Bowie knives with long blades were used by the South, while the Union even tried using lances.

Other weapons

Every rifle-musket was issued with a bayonet. The bayonets for the Springfield and Enfield rifles were about 18 inches (45 cm) long with a spike-shaped triangular blade. Imported rifles, such as the Belgian Pattern 1842 and the British Brunswick Rifle, carried broad-bladed sword-bayonets up to 2 feet (60 cm) long. The function of the bayonet changed as the rifle-musket became more widely used. Bayonets had been used to kill the enemy in infantry charges, but the long range of the rifle-musket made such charges suicidal. Bayonets played a less

important role in battles as the war went on. The cavalry saber was gradually phased out and replaced by the revolver and carbine.

ASK YOURSELF

If bayonet charges had become so dangerous, why would soldiers bother to carry a bayonet?

⟳ "California Joe" was one of Berdan's Sharpshooters, a Union unit known for its marksmanship.

THE RIGHT ANSWER

?

The Civil War has been called the first modern war. Why might that be so?

The Civil War saw a major change in the way wars were fought. Infantry charges became too dangerous in the face of new breech-loading, repeating rifles. Instead, infantrymen started to advance in small groups and under cover; they often crouched down rather than standing up. Today, that is still the preferred method of advance. Hand-to-hand combat also became outdated, and with it, weapons like bayonets. During sieges, mortars were launched to land on the enemy at a distance. They were forerunners of the long-range guided missiles of today.

Glossary

arsenal: A place where weapons are made and stored.

artillery: Heavy guns such as cannons and mortars that are used to attack enemy defenses.

battery: A group of heavy guns or artillery pieces.

bayonet: A sharp blade fixed to the muzzle of a rifle.

blockade: A system of ships that intercept vessels in order to prevent a country or other body from being able to trade.

bombardment: A sustained artillery attack on a target.

breechloader: A gun that is loaded through a hole at the back of the barrel.

cavalry: Part of the army that fights on horseback.

flank: The side of a military unit or position.

fortifications: Strong defenses, such as walls or trenches.

guerrilla warfare: Warfare that is carried on by ambushes and raids, rather than by set battles or fighting.

infantry: Soldiers who are trained to fight on foot.

ironclad: A warship that has a protective covering of iron armor.

mortar: A heavy gun that fires shells in a high arc, so that they can pass over walls and other defenses.

muzzle-loader: A gun that is loaded through the end of the barrel.

reconnaissance: Observation of enemy positions.

siege: An attack that cuts off a military position or city to force it to surrender.

strategic: A word that describes something that is important to achieving an overall goal, even if it may not be very important on its own.

tactical: A word that describes a short-term plan on the battlefield, such as capturing a particular position.

torpedo: A floating bomb, today known as a mine.

Further reading

Abnett, Dan. *The Monitor vs. the Merrimac: Ironclads at War* (Graphic Battles of the Civil War). Rose Publishing Group, 2006.

Beller, Susan Provost. *Billy Yank and Johnny Reb* (Soldiers on the Battlefront). Twenty-First Century Books, 2007.

Brager, Bruce L. *Petersburg* (Sieges That Changed the World). Chelsea House Publishers, 2003.

Doeden, Matt. *Weapons of the Civil War* (Blazers). Capstone Press, 2008.

Fein, Eric. *Weapons, Gear, and Uniforms of the Civil War.* (Edge Books). Capstone Press, 2012.

Katcher, Philip. *Confederate Cavalrymen of the Civil War* (Soldier's Life). Heinemann Library, 2003.

Katcher, Philip. *Union Cavalrymen of the Civil War* (Soldier's Life). Heinemann Library, 2003.

Lieurance, Suzanne. *Weapons and Strategies of the Civil War* (The American Civil War). Myreportlinks.com, 2004.

Ollhoff, Jim. *Weapons* (The Civil War). ABDO and Daughters, 2012.

Stanchak, John E. *Civil War* (DK Eyewitness Books). DK Publishing, 2011.

Websites

History Place interactive timeline of the Civil War.
http//www.historyplace.com/civilwar

Smithsonian Institution page with resources on the Civil War.
http//www.civilwar.si.edu

A site supporting the PBS film *The Civil War*, directed by Ken Burns.
http//www.pbs.org/civilwar

About.com gallery of the most significant weapons of the war.
http://militaryhistory.about.com/od/smallarms/ig/Civil-War-Weapons-Gallery/

Index

Prenatal Cocaine Exposure

Edited by

Richard J. Konkol, M.D., Ph.D.
Department of Neurology
Oregon Health Sciences University
Portland, Oregon

George D. Olsen, M.D.
Department of Physiology and Pharmacology
Oregon Health Sciences University
Portland, Oregon

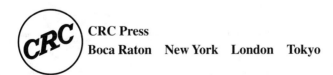

CRC Press
Boca Raton   New York   London   Tokyo

Acquiring Editor: Paul Petralia
Cover Design: Shayna Murry
Marketing Manager: Becky McEldowney
Project Editor: Gail Renard
Manufacturing Assistant: Sheri Schwartz

Library of Congress Cataloging-in-Publication Data

Prenatal cocaine exposure / edited by Richard J. Konkol, George D. Olsen.
    p. cm.
    Includes bibliographical references and index.
    ISBN 0-8493-9465-1
    1. Cocaine—Toxicology   2. Fetus—Effect of drugs on.
3. Children of prenatal substance abuse. I. Konkol, Richard J.
II. Olsen, George D.
    [DNLM: 1. Prenatal Exposure Delayed Effects. 2. Cocaine—adverse
effects. 3. Substance effects—in pregnancy 4. Fetus—drug
effects. WQ 210 P9237 1996]
    RG627.6.N37P74   1996
    618.3'.268—dc20   96-48362
                                                                        CIP

The Editors

Richard J. Konkol, M.D., Ph.D., received his medical degree from Georgetown University and his Ph.D. in neuroanatomy from the University of Iowa. Postgraduate medical training in pediatrics, pediatric neurology, and epilepsy were done at the Boston Children's Hospital Medical Center at the Harvard Medical School. He also trained with Dr. George Breese in developmental neuropharmacology at the University of North Carolina in Chapel Hill. He is currently Professor of Neurology and Chief of the Division of Pediatric Neurology at Oregon Health Sciences University. His diverse background provides a unique vantage point to view the overlapping areas of bench research and clinically related studies focused on the prenatally drug-exposed infant.

He has published over 50 papers including clinical studies and animal models to investigate a variety of problems encountered in pediatric neurology, such as seizures and disruptive behavior. A particular emphasis has been on the pharmacology and role of central monoaminergic neurotransmitters. This effort is targeted on a multidisciplinary approach to defining a biological basis for the cocaine-exposed baby "syndrome" in conjunction with an animal model, exploring the role of cocaine metabolites on epileptogenesis and behavior alteration.

George D. Olsen, M.D., is a graduate of Dartmouth College and Dartmouth and Harvard Medical Schools. He is Professor of Pharmacology, Medicine and Pediatrics at the Oregon Health Sciences University in Portland, Oregon. Dr. Olsen is a diplomate of the American Board of Clinical Pharmacology. His research interests include the pharmacokinetics of drugs of abuse in the maternal–fetal unit, development of the control of breathing, the physiological effects of drug dependence, and the relationship of *in utero* drug exposure to neonatal development.

His scientific publications include 50 original articles, the most recent of which concern the neonatal consequences of prenatal exposure to cocaine or morphine in an animal model of drug dependence.

Contributors

Jeffrey R. Buchhalter, MD, PhD
Associate Professor of Neurology
and Pediatrics
Department of Neurology
Oregon Health Sciences University
Portland, Oregon

Claudia A. Chiriboga, MD, MPH
Assistant Professor of
Neurology and Pediatrics
Neurological Institute
Columbia-Presbyterian Medical Center
and Harlem Hospital Center
New York, New York

Harry T. Chugani, MD
Professor of Pediatrics, Neurology,
and Radiology
Director, PET Center
Wayne State University
Detroit, Michigan

Delia A. Dempsey, MD
Clinical Instructor
Department of Pediatrics
Department of Medicine —
Division of Clinical Pharmacology
University of California
San Francisco, California

J. Christopher Glantz, MD
Assistant Professor of Obstetrics
and Gynecology
Department of Obstetrics and
Gynecology
Division of Maternal-Fetal Medicine
University of Rochester
School of Medicine and Dentistry
Rochester, New York

William V. Good, MD
Professor of Ophthalmology
and Pediatrics
Department of Ophthalmology
University of Cincinnati
Cincinnati, Ohio

Donna Ferriero, MD
Associate Professor of Neurology
Department of Neurology
University of California
San Francisco, California

Beatrice Latal Hajnal, MD
Instructor in Neurology
University of California
San Francisco, California

John A. Harvey, PhD
Professor of Pharmacology
The Medical College of Pennsylvania
and Hahnemann University
Philadelphia, Pennsylvania

Sarah N. Jacobson
Department of Neurology
San Francisco General Hospital
Medical Center
University of California
San Francisco, California

Richard J. Konkol, MD, PhD
Professor of Neurology
Department of Neurology
Oregon Health Sciences University
Portland, Oregon

Barry E. Kosofsky, MD, PhD
Assistant Professor of Neurology
Department of Neurology
Massachusetts General Hospital
Harvard Medical School
Boston, Massachusetts

Jane A. Madden, PhD
Professor
Department of Neurology
The Medical College of Wisconsin
Research Service, VA Medical Center
Milwaukee, Wisconsin

George D. Olsen, MD
Professor of Pharmacology
Department of Physiology and
  Pharmacology
Oregon Health Sciences University
Portland, Oregon

Anthony G. Romano, PhD
Department of Pharmacology
Medical College of Pennsylvania
  and Hahnemann University
Philadelphia, Pennsylvania

Peter C. Schalock
Department of Physiology and
  Pharmacology
Oregon Health Sciences University
Portland, Oregon

Guy Schuelke, PhD
Department of Neurology
The Medical College of Wisconsin
Milwaukee, Wisconsin

Michael D. Schreiber, MD
Associate Professor of Pediatrics
Department of Pediatrics
Pritzker School of Medicine
University of Chicago
Chicago, Illinois

Linda Patia Spear, PhD
Department of Psychology
Binghamton University
State University of New York
Binghamton, New York

Aaron S. Wilkins
Laboratory of Molecular and
  Developmental Neuroscience
Massachusetts General Hospital
Boston, Massachusetts

James R. Woods, Jr., MD
Professor of Obstetrics and Gynecology
Department of Obstetrics
  and Gynecology
University of Rochester
School of Medicine and Dentistry
Rochester, New York

Foreword

This volume addresses the timely problem of maternal cocaine abuse and its adverse effect on the infants of these mothers.* Concern about cocaine during the '80s and '90s is the lineal descendant of the focus on alcohol abuse in the '60s and '70s. It is now quite clear that alcohol has a highly significant adverse effect on brain and somatic development (the fetal alcohol syndrome), while there would seem to be less symptomatology during late pregnancy and the neonatal period. On the other hand, it would seem that cocaine exerts its most dramatic adverse effects during late pregnancy and the neonatal period (CVAs, neonatal hypertonia, and seizures), while its dysgenetic effects may be less severe. In fact, this issue is one of the salient points considered in this book. The presentations deal with both the clinical observations and results from the experimental models such as species, dose, etc. Basic issues of the chemistry and pharmacology of cocaine round out this comprehensive and authoritative presentation.

The format is a series of chapters that consist of in-depth reviews of an aspect of the topic, each with an extensive bibliography. This leads to some minor overlap which I believe is an advantage for the usual reader who does not read such a book from cover to cover, but tends to be selective of topics of interest at the moment. At the same time, the authors have taken care to cite the appropriate chapter that treats another subject in greater depth. A significant point that is made repeatedly is the healthy regard for the many issues that are not currently understood.

In closing, it seems that society is often its own worst enemy and falls prey to its own indiscretions. Substance abuse is certainly a major issue in this regard, and especially frustrating because all of its adverse consequences are preventable. We cannot blame the lawmakers—because legislation will not solve the problem. The solution lies within us, although how it may come about is a totally perplexing question. Meanwhile, medicine must do its best to deal with the consequences—hence this book.

Charles F. Barlow, M.D.
Neurologist-in-Chief, Emeritus
Department of Neurology
Harvard Medical School

* Konkol, R.J., Editorial: *Is there a cocaine baby syndrome? J. Child Neurol.* 9, 225, 1994

Acknowledgments

In addition to the contributing authors, many others have added their support both directly and indirectly to the development of this book. Among these others are: Julie Doerr, PhD, Jennifer Kron, Michael McNealy, Dean Rein, Janet Cadey, Sarah Dean, Penny Nemeth, RN, CPN, Ruth Heimler, MD, Dave Roerig, PhD, David Walsh, MD, John R. Sty, MD, Robert Wells, Ronald Tikofosky, PhD, Laine Murphy, MD, PhD, Brian Erickson, MD, Sabiha Keskin, MD, Robert Hellman, MD, Robert Snodgrass, MD, Joseph Volpe, MD, Elizabeth Bendeich, DDS, PhD, Debra Olsen, Suzi Kohls, S. Budden MD, and L. Cass Terry, MD, PhD. We are appreciative of the grants from The National Institute of Drug Abuse and Sigma Tau Corporation for supporting the September 30, 1994, symposium, from which the concept for this book grew.

Dedicated to our children
— Jon, Margaret, Derrick, Sonja, and James —
and all the children, in the hope that our efforts today will improve their future.

R.J.K.
G.D.O.

CONTENTS

Prenatal Cocaine Exposure:
An Overview

The popular media and initial clinical reports have focused on the catastrophic outcomes of infants exposed to cocaine prenatally. Cocaine has been said to be the cause of a wide range of clinical problems, including microcephaly, growth retardation, malformations, strokes, seizures, and a variety of behavior changes. Clinical disturbances in the neonate due to prenatal drug exposure are thought to represent a risk factor for continuing behavioral disturbances and learning disabilities in the older child. However, a firm scientific basis for many of the initial ominous conclusions is now questioned. Most of these children are also exposed to confounding influences which cloud characterization of the specific effect of cocaine on development.[1]

Current surveys indicate that high-risk, drug-exposed pregnancies will continue. While studies of infants exposed to drugs are provocative, there is a publication bias for those reporting dramatic positive effects.[2] In contrast, animal studies allow a more direct examination of drug action but may not reflect the multifactorial nature of influences impinging on human fetal development.[3] Clinicians, then, are faced with the prospect of making assessments and clinical decisions without benefit of an adequate understanding of the underlying pathophysiological mechanisms, while scientists may be unaware of the clinical context in which drug exposure occurs.

The recent expansion of the clinical and scientific literature on cocaine exposure provides an opportunity for a book reviewing both animal and clinical studies evaluating the prenatal factors which may predict the outcome of cocaine-exposed infants. A review of drug exposure patterns for women of childbearing age by Claudia Chiriboga will describe methods of ascertaining confounding factors and outline clinical associations linked to prenatal cocaine use. Associate editor George Olsen lays a foundation emphasizing cocaine molecular genetics, pharmacokinetics, elimination, and drug interactions related to cocaine. An analysis of cocaine's impact on the physiology of the fetal-maternal unit from the obstetrical point of view, by Christopher Glantz and James Woods, summarizes a large body of knowledge derived from a laboratory which has made a significant contribution to this field.

Reports of the vascular effects of cocaine have frequently appeared, while our understanding of the mechanisms of vascular reactivity has recently expanded. This information suggests alternate possibilities for prognosis and management. Jeffrey Buchhalter reviews the literature addressing the possibility of cocaine-induced strokes in neonates. Jane Madden and Mike Schreiber then analyze the vascular mechanisms of cocaine and its metabolites, while Richard Konkol and Guy Schuelke discuss the role of cocaine metabolites as demonstrated in laboratory studies and relate these to possible implications for the clinical setting. A review of clinical pharmacokinetics by Delia Dempsey and associates critically discusses what is currently known about cocaine and its metabolites and their possible relationship to some neonatal syndromes. The often neglected characterization of cocaine's effects on the developing visual system is succinctly reviewed by Good and associates.

Long-term cocaine-related behavior and learning studies after *in utero* cocaine exposure, derived from the laboratories of Barry Kosofsky and John Harvey, correlate animal learning experiments with possible clinical behavioral outcomes. Linda Spear's analysis of the developmental effects of cocaine, based on a variety of models, summarizes her extensive contribution to the study of long-term neurobehavioral functioning. Lastly, the hope for advanced technology to reveal the effect of cocaine on the developing brain will be foreshadowed by Harry Chugani, who presents preliminary findings in the drug-exposed human infant using the state-of-the-art functional brain imaging technique, positron emission tomography.

In summary, this book includes selected basic animal and clinical studies on prenatal cocaine exposure for the purpose of integrating recent information and providing a basis for informed clinical decisions. The comparability of cocaine-related effects across species suggests a specific role for cocaine in the alteration of development. The multitude of studies reviewed indicates that neonatal physiological and behavioral changes may be explained by several mechanisms which have implications for treatment and long-term outcome. Several chapters emphasize the potential impact of cocaine metabolites as a unique theme to be explored further in the laboratory and clinic. It is hoped that this book will facilitate the exchange and sharing of scientific and clinical data on the effects of drugs in development and be of interest to pediatricians, medical specialists, basic scientists, educators, and policy makers, evaluating the effects of xenobiotics on the developing brain.

Richard J. Konkol
George D. Olsen
Portland, Oregon
December 1995

REFERENCES

1. Konkol, R.J., Is there a cocaine baby syndrome?, *J Child Neurology,* 9, 225, 1994.
2. Koren, G., Shear, H., Graham, K., and Einarson, T., Bias against the null hypothesis: the reproductive hazards of cocaine, *Lancet*, 2, 1440, 1989.
3. Olsen, G.D., Potential mechanisms of cocaine-induced developmental neurotoxicity: A mini review, *Neurotoxicology*, 16, 159, 1995.

Chapter 1

Cocaine and the Fetus: Methodological Issues and Neurological Correlates

Claudia A. Chiriboga, MD, MPH

1.0 INTRODUCTION

In the 1980s a drop in cocaine prices coupled with the introduction of "crack" cocaine fueled an unprecedented degree of cocaine abuse. During the peak of the cocaine epidemic 30% of adults between the ages of 19 and 28 years reported using cocaine at least once.[1] Although cocaine use declined abruptly in 1987, it is still a major public health problem, as an unfortunately high level of abuse continues unabated. Infants born to women using crack/cocaine, the so-called "crack/cocaine babies," have been stigmatized by the media because of their potential burden to society. The pendulum of the medical and lay press has swung away from its initially fatalistic outlook that doomed such children from birth to the current nihilistic climate that tends to minimize any possible cocaine effects, despite the lack of solid information on the long-term consequences of fetal cocaine exposure.

Efforts to determine whether prenatal exposure to cocaine damages the human nervous system are fraught with methodological difficulties. Unlike the experimental model where variables are fixed by the investigator, the clinical setting is laden by the many factors that act in concert to influence the fetal or postnatal environment. Although epidemiological methods offer some control over these extraneous or "confounding" variables, the erratic high-risk behaviors associated with drug use introduce additional elements that make inferences in clinical studies regarding cocaine-related associations more vulnerable to bias, e.g., selection bias resulting from a high level of attrition. This chapter focuses on the methodological problems that have arisen in the clinical research of fetal cocaine exposure and provides a broad overview of the salient clinical findings associated with cocaine exposure (Table 1.1), with the exception of strokes and seizures, which are discussed elsewhere.

1.1 BACKGROUND

Cocaine is obtained from *Erythroxylon coca*, a plant indigenous to the mountainous regions of South America. For centuries the natives of this region have used coca leaves in religious rituals or for its medicinal properties to treat a variety of ailments, notably fatigue and mountain sickness. In these settings coca is administered by either chewing on coca leaves or by preparing an infusion of coca leaves, coca tea.

0-8493-9465-1/96/$0.00+$.50

Table 1.1 Fetal Cocaine Effects and Associations

Pregnancy
  Spontaneous abortions
  Abruptio placentae
  Stillbirths
  Premature delivery
Growth
  Low birth weight
  Intrauterine growth retardation
  Small head size
Infections
  Perinatal HIV
  Congenital syphilis
Malformations
  Urogenital
  Brain
    Midline defects (agenesis of corpus callosum, septo-optic dysplasia)
    Skull defects, encephaloceles
  Ocular
  Vascular disruption (limb reduction, intestinal atresia)
  Cardiac
Neurodevelopmental findings
  Neonates
  Impaired organizational state
  Hypertonia, tremor
  Strokes, porencephaly
  Seizures
  Brainstem conduction delays
  Sudden infant death syndrome
  Infants and children
  Hypertonia in infancy
  Abnormal behaviors (?)

(Adapted with permission from Chiriboga, C.A., Abuse of children: Pediatric AIDS, fetal alcohol syndrome, fetal cocaine effects, and the battered child syndrome, in *Merritt's Textbook of Neurology*, 9th ed., Baltimore, Williams & Wilkins, Lea & Febiger, 1995.)

In the United States, legal cocaine use was barred following the Harrison Narcotic Act in 1914. Thereafter, because of its high cost, illegal cocaine use continued mostly among the affluent. In recent times, however, cocaine has become much less expensive and widely available. This combination of factors has resulted in an alarming increase in cocaine use by the less affluent, especially among individuals of lower socioeconomic status. Thus, cocaine traffic has flourished in inner cities, bringing with it the infamous "drug dealer," as well as escalating violence.[2] Regrettably, no geographical area in the United States has been totally immune to its spread.

The two most common forms of cocaine used by addicts on the street are cocaine hydrochloride, a water soluble salt, and crack/cocaine, a free-base alkaloid. Cocaine hydrochloride can be used by either snorting a line, applying it to various mucosal membranes (oral or genital), or injecting it intravenously. Crack/cocaine is volatile and is administered by smoking.

1.2 PHARMACOLOGY

Cocaine is a highly psychoactive substance with numerous effects[3]: it inhibits postsynaptic reuptake of catecholamines, leading to an increase in postsynaptic norepinephrine and epinephrine, which produce hypertension and tachycardia and have vasoconstrictive effects; it increases postsynaptic dopamine levels, which is thought to mediate cocaine addiction at the mesolimbic and mesocortical levels; it inhibits tryptophan reuptake, thus altering serotonin pathways, which presumably mediate cocaine effects on sleep; and it blocks sodium ion permeability, thus acting as a local anesthetic agent. In addition to the multiple effects exerted by the parent compound, cocaine breaks down into active metabolites (e.g., benzoylecgonine, benzoylnorecgonine) of similar or yet more powerful pharmacological activity. Many of these substances are independently neurotoxic and may be responsible for perceived cocaine effects.[4,5]

Cocaine and its metabolites readily pass the placenta, achieving variable levels in the fetus.[6] The mechanism by which cocaine affects the fetus is not fully known, but is postulated to result from either a direct effect to the fetus or an indirect effect mediated through the maternal autonomic and cardiovascular system, especially at the level of the uterus.[7]

1.3 ADDICTION

A discussion of the biological and psychological basis of cocaine addiction is warranted to gain a better understanding of the behavioral correlates associated with cocaine use. In adults, cocaine use produces a state of euphoria characterized by increased energy and enhanced alertness. According to classical and operational conditioning theory, the degree of euphoria is a prominent positive reinforcer. The level of euphoria in turn is predicated on the speed of delivery and cerebral concentrations attained by cocaine. Because crack/cocaine is smoked, this preparation delivers the highest levels of cocaine to the brain in the most expedient fashion,[8] thus producing a more intense euphoria than other methods of delivery, i.e., snorting or injecting. This intense sensation, described by addicts as a "rush" of pleasure, gradually gives way to dysphoria, an equally intense but opposite sensation that is described as a "crash" from cocaine. Dysphoria is characterized by a strong craving for the drug, a depressed state, and hypersomnia; it acts as a powerful negative reinforcer.

Converging lines of evidence support a dopaminergic hypothesis of cocaine addiction related to a mesocortical limbic reward system. Experimentally different animal species will self-administer cocaine, dopamine (DA), and D2 receptor agonists such as apomorphine, but not D1 receptor, serotonin, or noradrenergic agonists.[9,10] This response is mitigated by co-administration of D2 receptor blockers. Ablation studies of the medial prefrontal region with 6-hydroxydopamine, which selectively decreases dopamine levels, results in a decrease in the cocaine maintained response, which can be reinstated by replacing dopamine, but not serotonin for cocaine.[11] Fluctuations in postsynaptic levels of dopamine in this brain region are postulated to account for the reinforcing properties of cocaine.[12]

Despite lacking the severe physical symptoms that are associated with opiate or sedative withdrawal, abrupt cessation of cocaine use generates an unwavering craving for the drug. The overpowering grip of cocaine addiction is evident in experimental models in which animals allowed to self-administer cocaine will do so compulsively and at the expense of food intake and to the point of toxicity or death.[9] Crack/cocaine produces high cerebral concentrations rapidly, hence it elicits a strikingly powerful addiction that tends to render crack-addicted women unable to abstain or curtail its use during pregnancy despite the hazards posed to their fetuses and at the risk of losing custody of their offspring. The human correlates of such addiction-related behaviors during pregnancy have obvious detrimental consequences to the fetus.

1.4 METHODOLOGICAL ISSUES

1.4.1 Prevalence

The prevalence of cocaine use during pregnancy varies across the U.S. ranging from less than 1% to 18%.[13-19] Population-based rates are influenced by a number of demographic factors, namely race, urban dwelling, and socioeconomic status, as well as by the method of ascertaining cocaine use (see section 1.4.2). Rates are lowest in smaller cities and among private patients[13,15] and highest in inner-cities among ward patients.[16-19] For example, in New York City the prevalence of cocaine use among parturients was 5%,[18] based on urine toxicology results gathered from birth certificates, while in two private Denver hospitals it was less than 0.5%, based on anonymous urine testing.[15] Although drug use in general is distributed equally across racial lines, urban blacks are more likely to use cocaine than other drugs.[13]

Estimated prevalence of cocaine use is influenced by the method of ascertaining use. Rates of cocaine use among women giving birth in two urban hospitals ranged from 9 to 13% using urine toxicology testing,[16-19] but rates reached 18% using both self report and urine testing.[19] Highest rates were found with meconium testing, which was positive for cocaine in 31% of women delivering in a high-risk urban population,[14] and 3.4% on random testing in an urban sample more representative of the community.[20]

Poor prenatal care and syphilis are the risk factors associated with the highest rates of cocaine use during pregnancy. About 30 to 50% of urban women who lack prenatal care will have a positive urine toxicology for cocaine at the time of delivery;[18,21] rates reach 70 to 80% with the use of meconium or hair analysis.[21] The profile that emerges of women most likely to use cocaine during pregnancy points to those living in inner cities who are single, black, older, of low socioeconomic status, and have syphilis, HIV, and poor prenatal care.

1.4.2 Ascertainment

1.4.2.1   Self Report

Self report during interview and urine toxicological testing are the traditional methods of ascertaining drug and alcohol use. The information gleaned from structured interviews allows researchers to quantify and assess patterns of drug use over time, especially during the first trimester. However, self report of cocaine use is not a reliable method for ascertaining drug use, as most studies show that of women who, on interview, deny using cocaine during pregnancy, about 25% have positive urine toxicologies.[19] Thus, estimates of drug use, especially during pregnancy, remain problematic, mostly because of poor exposure recall and questions regarding maternal veracity. The latter stems from the stigma and legal consequences attached to drug use during pregnancy, such as loss of child custody. For example, in New York State children who test positive for cocaine are placed in foster care custody unless the mothers make adequate efforts to rehabilitate. Consequently, ascertainment of fetal drug exposure based solely on self report leads to substantial misclassification of exposure status that tends to obscure the strength of associations between exposure and outcome and consequently may bias study findings.

1.4.2.2 Urine Toxicology

Urine toxicology assays can confirm drug use, but because cocaine is rapidly metabolized, this method informs solely about recent use. Cocaine can be detected in urine for 6 to 8 hours, and cocaine metabolites can be detected up to 6 to 8 days.[22] However, in exceptional cases of prolonged heavy cocaine use, metabolites have been detected in urine up to 22 days after use.[23] Even though urine toxicology is indicative of recent exposure, paradoxically this method tends to ascertain women who are heavy drug users and are, therefore, probably not representative of the general population. This is because women who use cocaine regularly are more likely to test positive at the time of delivery than women who use cocaine sporadically or quit early in pregnancy. With certain exceptions (e.g., *abruptio placentae*), most adverse effects in infants with cocaine-positive urine toxicology are not likely to be the result of a single exposure at the time of birth, and instead probably reflect a pattern of high use throughout most of the pregnancy. An additional limitation of using urine toxicology to assess cocaine use in clinical research settings is that it does not allow quantification of use.

1.4.2.3 Hair Radioimmunoassay

New methods of drug ascertainment, hair radioimmunoassay and meconium analysis, have emerged that allow determining more remote use of drugs, including marijuana, narcotics, and cocaine. So far, however, few studies have been published using these newer, more accurate methods of ascertainment. Hair radioimmunoassay determines the past use of a number of drugs, including marijuana, narcotics, and cocaine.[24] Analysis of each 1.5 cms of maternal hair informs on drugs used during the previous 3 months. With a sufficiently long hair sample, the entire pregnancy can be screened for drug use. Hair that has been treated chemically or physically altered may provide less reliable estimates of exposure. External contamination of the hair sample by the environment is readily avoided by thorough washings of the sample prior to processing.

1.4.2.4   Meconium Analysis

Meconium develops at about 18 weeks of gestational age. Thereafter, it acts as a reservoir of drugs used by the mother. The analysis of meconium specimens collected during the first 2 days of life permits determining chronic drug exposure during the latter half of fetal life.[25] Unlike hair analysis, meconium analysis does not inform on the timing of *in utero* exposure. It does, however, afford a reliable estimate of cumulative exposure to cocaine and its various metabolites, including cocaethylene, which is formed by the combined use of cocaine and alcohol. This pharmacologically active metabolite then concentrates in meconium tenfold.[26] Thus, measures of coca-ethylene in meconium promise to enhance the ascertainment of concomitant alcohol use, which is a vexing confounder of cocaine studies.

Both hair analysis and meconium analysis use cocaine metabolites as surrogates for cocaine exposure. Since chronic exposure to cocaine during fetal life results in exposure to both the parent compound and its metabolites, neither hair nor meconium analysis can be used to discern which of these substances is responsible for the deleterious effects to the fetus. Attempts to correlate blood levels of cocaine or cocaine metabolites with concurrent neurobehaviors are flawed as there is little assurance that current behaviors reflect ongoing exposures. Animal studies assessing chronic fetal exposure to specific cocaine metabolites are better suited to elucidate these questions.

1.4.3 Other Associations and Risk Factors

1.4.3.1   Infections

Systemic Infections. In addition to any specific cocaine effects, cocaine-exposed infants are at increased risk because of behaviors related to drug abuse. Women who use cocaine intravenously are at risk for systemic and cutaneous infection,[27] including hepatitis B, subacute bacterial endocarditis, brain abscesses, HIV infection, and AIDS. They also tend to exchange sex for drugs (although most would deny this constitutes prostitution), thereby increasing their risks for sexually transmitted diseases.

Human Immunodeficiency Virus (HIV). The use of cocaine intravenously poses a substantial risk for HIV infection, as contaminated needles are a well-described mode of transmission. Nonparenteral cocaine use, however, is becoming an increasingly important HIV risk factor due to the exchange of sex for drugs. Women who are unemployed and use crack have nearly a 3.5 increased risk of being HIV seropositive than employed women who use crack,[28] suggesting that female crack addicts use sex to pay for their cocaine habit.

Although a connatal form of pediatric-AIDS or neuro-AIDS has thus far not been documented, high rates of neurological abnormality are reported in the U.S. among children born HIV antibody-positive, even among those who lose passively acquired maternal antibodies (seroreverters). These high rates are in part attributable to cocaine exposure, as evidenced by a controlled study in which cocaine-positive urine toxicology, but not HIV infection, was significantly associated with hypertonia at 6 months of age.[29] In the same cohort, HIV antibody status at birth appeared to correlate with the level of cocaine exposure; among cocaine-positive children those who were HIV antibody positive (HIV infected and seroreverters) showed significantly higher rates of neurological abnormalities than those who were HIV antibody negative; while among cocaine-negative children, rates were similar between these two groups,[30] suggesting that HIV positivity among drug using women may be a proxy for higher levels of cocaine exposure.

Congenital Syphilis. The cocaine epidemic coincided with a rise in the incidence of syphilis,[31-34] which in certain urban centers reached epidemic proportions. For instance, the rate of congenital syphilis in New York City increased from 1.2 cases per 1000 births in 1982 to 5.8 cases per 1000 births in 1988.[31] In controlled analyses the odds of cocaine exposure were increased fourfold among infants with congenital syphilis.[32] Syphilis is also linked to poor prenatal care. In one study, poor prenatal care achieved the highest adjusted odds ratio associated with congenital syphilis (OR = 11.0), while cocaine use achieved the second highest adjusted odds ratio (OR = 4.9).[33]

1.4.3.2   Maternal Nutrition

The adverse impact of poor maternal nutrition on fetal well being is well documented. Picone et al. showed that poor maternal weight gain (≤15 lbs.) was significantly associated with lower birth weights, ponderal indices, growth rates and shorter gestations, as well as with a reduction in placental weight, even when controlling for gestational age.[35] Total placental DNA was 14% lower among women with low weight gain during pregnancy, a phenomenon that is not observed with exposure to maternal cigarette smoking or illicit substances. Another nutritional factor affecting the offspring of drug-using women is the lack of nutritional supplements, which accounts for an additional 40 or 60 grams decrement in newborn weight.[36]

Poor maternal weight gain exerts a significant and independent effect on neonatal neurobehavioral status. Using the Brazelton Newborn Assessment Scales (BNBAS) poor maternal weight gain was associated with impaired habituation, orientation, and regulation of state. Low weight gain in the second trimester was related to impaired motor performance, visual habituation, orientation, and reflexes.[35] In another study, nutritional variables predicted poor performance on the Brazelton including poor habituation, motor, orientation, reflex score, and autonomic responses.[37]

Experimental studies show that cocaine administration during pregnancy is associated with decreased nutritional intake. When allowed equal food access, pregnant dams that are administered cocaine eat less and gain less weight than control dams.[38] Low nutritional intake among cocaine addicts arises from economic factors, as meager resources are spent in procuring cocaine rather than food, and also from cocaine's ability to suppress appetite. The lower levels of serum folate and ferritin found in cocaine positive pregnant women as compared with controls attest to the poor nutritional status of drug users.[39]

In experimental models, maternal caloric intake may be controlled, albeit imperfectly, by pair feeding so that nutritional intake is comparable between exposed and control dams. However, in the clinical arena the chaotic lifestyles led by cocaine addicts make it increasingly difficult to control for nutrition, as erratic eating habits and poor recall make 24-hour nutritional assessments unreliable. To further complicate matters, the association between cocaine use and poor prenatal care results in an unmonitored pregnancy in which most women are unaware of their baseline weights and of their weight gain during pregnancy. Thus, the impact of nutritional factors on fetal outcome remains largely unknown in neonatal cocaine studies.

1.4.3.3   Polysubstance Use

Women who use cocaine are more likely to use multiple drugs, smoke cigarettes, and drink alcohol. Polydrug use is, thus, a major confounder of fetal cocaine effects. Many of the adverse outcomes related to cocaine exposure, such as low birth weight, intrauterine growth retardation, malformations, and neurobehavioral abnormalities, are not unique to cocaine and have been described with prenatal exposure to other substances of abuse.[40] Some of the more significant outcomes associated with abused substances are described below.

Cigarette Smoking. Cigarette smoking correlates with drug and alcohol use and is also reported to affect fetal growth, neonatal neurobehaviors, and subsequent development. It is a major cause of low birth weight babies, with the offspring of women who smoke cigarettes weighing on average 150 to 250 grams less than infants of women who do not smoke.[41] *In utero* exposure to cigarette smoke is reported to impair neonatal habituation, orientation, consolability, autonomic regulation, and orientation to sound.[35] Exposure is also associated with a heightened startle response and tremor.

Of late, small but detectable effects of heavy maternal cigarette smoking have been noted on developmental quotients and subsequent behaviors.[42-43] Infants exposed prenatally to more than 10 cigarettes per day had a 4 point lower IQ than control infants after controlling for postnatal smoke and other factors.[42] Behavioral effects were significantly increased among infants of heavy smokers, as reflected by an overall composite behavioral score; yet the incidence of specific behavioral disorders was not increased.[43]

Alcohol. Alcohol, which is frequently used in combination with cocaine, has numerous effects[44-49] that tend to confound cocaine studies. At the upper extreme of the alcohol exposure spectrum lies the fetal alcohol syndrome, a constellation of signs and symptoms seen with both heavy chronic and binge drinking that is characterized by impaired growth (either prenatal or postnatal), CNS abnormalities, and a typical dysmorphic fascies.[45] Infants with FAS are commonly mentally retarded and microcephalic. At the lower end of the spectrum are fetal alcohol effects, a term that does not refer to a diagnostic entity per se, as effects cannot be distinguished at the individual level, but to effects identified in prospective studies, such as impaired fetal growth — both somatic and cerebral — teratogenesis, and cognitive differences.[40]

The teratogenicity of alcohol exposure *in utero* has been clearly established: over 30% of offspring of heavy drinkers have minor or major congenital anomalies compared to 9% in infants of abstinent women,[48] and infants with FAS commonly have multiple congenital anomalies. Neurological malformations include Klippel–Feil anomaly, agenesis of the corpus callosum, and neural tube defects. Neuropathologically, children with FAS show abnormalities in neuronal and glial migration.[50] The degree of teratogenicity displayed by alcohol is not equaled by any other substance discussed herein.

Because alcohol lacks a stable assay by which to measure exposure during pregnancy, alcohol studies rely solely on structured interview. Quantification of use is hampered by poor exposure recall, as well as by a reluctance to admit use in light of the public awareness of the hazards of alcohol use during pregnancy. All of these factors can lead to misclassification of alcohol exposure and consequently bias study results.

Marijuana. Used by one in three of women of childbearing age, marijuana is one of the most popular psychoactive substances used in the United States. The effects of fetal marijuana exposure on neonatal outcome are relatively minor, with only minimal effects on gestational age and inconsistent effects on fetal growth reported.[51-53] In a controlled study growth effects were noted in the offspring of women who had a positive urine assay for marijuana at delivery. Yet no effects were found in those who reported use of marijuana during pregnancy but had negative urine assays, suggesting that effects occur only with heavier exposures.[19] Fetal marijuana exposure induces a proportional or symmetric pattern of intrauterine growth retardation (IUGR) in which fat deposition is spared and lean body mass is decreased.[54] This finding is consistent with prolonged hypoxia *in utero,* not a nutritional deficiency.

Marijuana-induced teratogenicity is unproven. Although Hingson et al. described a fivefold increased rate of fetal alcohol syndrome-like features among marijuana-exposed offspring,[51] this was not corroborated by a later study that used computerized morphometric assessments to determine such features.[55] Other studies have also described no association between prenatal marijuana and minor physical anomalies.[56,57]

Reported adverse marijuana-related effects on neonatal neurobehavior encompass a dose-related diminution in neonatal light response and an increase in startle response and tremor.[52] Children of marijuana users were also found to have slightly longer latencies for the major wave form components of the visual evoked response, suggesting dysmaturity of the visual pathways.[58] The long-term effects of prenatal marijuana on cognitive and language development have not been established in analyses that controlled for prenatal and postnatal environmental factors.[59] Marijuana exposure via maternal breast milk in the first postpartum month was noted at age 12 months to have a negative effect on motor, but not mental, development.[60]

Opiates. Heroin and methadone may be harmful to the fetus. Low birth weight (LBW) has been reported with *in utero* exposure to either substance. Some studies show growth effects to be long term, with "catch-up" growth occurring after age 4 months and coinciding with abatement of neurobehavioral signs and symptoms.[61] Controlled studies, however, have found no differences in birth weight after adjusting for health and biological factors. Heroin, because of its parenteral route of administration, poses a substantial risk for HIV infection. Sudden infant death syndrome (SIDS) is also strongly linked with opiate exposure. Compared to infants without fetal drug exposure, infants exposed to methadone showed a 3.7-fold increased risk, and those exposed to heroin showed a 2.3-fold increased risk of SIDS.[62]

The most conspicuous neurobehavioral abnormality associated with exposure to opiates is the neonatal withdrawal syndrome. Of varying severity, withdrawal occurs in 50 to 80% of infants born to opiate-dependent mothers. Withdrawal is characterized by signs and symptoms in three domains: central nervous system, gastrointestinal, and autonomic/metabolic. Central nervous system signs are hypertonicity, tremor, hyperreflexia, irritability, sleep disturbances, and occasionally seizures. Gastrointestinal dysfunction encompasses poor feeding, frantic suck, vomiting, and diarrhea. Autonomic disturbances include fever, sweating, nasal stuffiness, mottling, and tachypnea. Onset of withdrawal usually begins within 48 to 72 hours of birth. Withdrawal-like symptoms described to persist for several months after birth have been termed, perhaps inappropriately, "subacute withdrawal"; these findings resolved by 6 months.[63]

Although early studies noted numerous cognitive, neurological, and behavioral impairments,[63-65] controlled studies have not substantiated this claim.[66,67] Most of the opiate effects on subsequent cognitive function have been mediated by associated risk factors, such as poor prenatal care, maternal intelligence, and aversive behaviors,[66] or the presence of withdrawal.[65]

1.4.3.4   Low Birth Weight

Low birth weight is common among cocaine-exposed infants and can result from either prematurity or intrauterine growth retardation (IUGR). Prematurity is a well-established risk factor for cerebral palsy, developmental delay, behavioral impairments, and learning difficulties.[68-70] Impaired fetal growth also poses a risk to neurodevelopment. IUGR stems from numerous causes, such as exposure to cigarettes, alcohol, and illicit substances, and maternal malnutrition. Regardless of its etiology, infants who are small for dates (SGA) are at risk for cognitive and neurological impairments in later life compared to infants who are appropriate for dates, especially if fetal brain growth is proportionately impaired (symmetric or proportional SGA).[71] Drillien reported high rates of neurological impairments among SGA infants, which resolved by age 12 months in 80% of affected children; the remaining children were diagnosed with cerebral palsy. She also noted lower developmental quotients among neurologically abnormal children as compared with neurologically intact LBW infants.[70] Because of their impact on neurological, behavioral, and cognitive function, prematurity and IUGR/SGA are important factors to consider in cocaine-related studies.

1.5 COCAINE-RELATED EFFECTS

1.5.1 Neonatal Effects

1.5.1.1   Withdrawal-Like Symptoms and Other Neurobehaviors

Early studies reported a transient withdrawal syndrome related to fetal cocaine exposure. Bingol et al. described irritability, crying, and a vigorous suck in 10% of exposed infants.[72] Others reported infants as tremulous, hypertonic, with abnormal sleep patterns, and poor feeding.[73-75] Because infants scored in the mildly elevated range when assessed with neonatal abstinence scales, findings were interpreted by some as indicative of a withdrawal syndrome. Other studies have failed to note evidence of withdrawal.[76-79] Instead infants were depressed and exhibited poor state and impaired orientation.[76] Most of these infants were examined shortly after birth, and cocaine exposure was assessed by urine toxicology.

The timing of the neonatal assessment may explain these seemingly contradictory findings. Neuspiel et al. found significant differences in motor clusters between cocaine-exposed and unexposed infants when the Brazelton Neonatal Behavioral Assessment Scales (BNBAS) was administered at 11 to 30 days after birth.[78] Yet no differences were noted on any of the clusters when the BNBAS was administered within 72 hours of birth, suggesting that neurobehavioral abnormalities may be late in emerging. Moreover, reports by other investigators describing cocaine-related hypertonia persisting into the second year of life makes withdrawal an even less likely explanation.[30]

These divergent results can be reconciled by dividing neurobehaviors into two types based on the onset of symptoms: 1) an early depressed state occurring immediately after birth and resolving within 3 to 4 days, and 2) a late-emerging excitable phase with variable onset ranging from 3 to 30 days. The early depressed state usually coincides with recent cocaine exposure[80] and may be the neonatal equivalent of the crash-like withdrawal observed in adult cocaine addicts. The late excitable phase with its variable onset and prolonged duration is not a withdrawal syndrome, but probably reflects a direct cocaine effect on the developing brain.

Other abnormal neurobehaviors reported among cocaine-exposed infants are increased rates of stress-related behaviors[79] and hypertonic tetraparesis.[81] Neurobehavioral abnormalities have also been noticed prior to birth with organizational and regulatory behavioral states abnormalities observed prenatally in 13 of 20 cocaine-exposed fetuses by ultrasonic techniques.[82] A major study flaw was the lack of control subjects and that examiners were not blinded to exposure status. In most neurobehavioral studies, infants were selected primarily from high-risk populations, and small sample size prevented controlling for confounding variables. A study based on a nonselected cohort that was more representative of the community failed to identify neurobehavioral effects in cocaine-exposed infants with the Brazelton scale after controlling for confounders.[78]

1.5.1.2   Intrauterine Growth

High rates of low birth weight (LBW) and intrauterine growth retardation (IUGR) are reported among infants with positive urine toxicologies at the time of birth,[19,72-76,82-84] but not in those exposed exclusively in the first trimester.[77] IUGR adopts a symmetric pattern with measures of body composition revealing reduced body fat and leanness which is consistent with a nutritional deficiency.[54] In a prospective study involving 1226 mothers, cocaine positivity on urine toxicology accounted for a 93 gram decrease in birth weight, a 0.5 cm decrement in length, and 0.43 cm head size difference compared to nonusers.[19] The latter was impaired independent of birth weight and gestational age. Fetal brain growth may be even more impaired than somatic growth.[85] The relevance of this effect is evident in a study by Chasnoff, in which cognitive differences in toddlers were indirectly mediated through cocaine effects on brain growth.[86]

1.5.1.3   Malformations

Cocaine has been linked to numerous congenital malformations, some of which are ascribed to vascular disruption resulting from cocaine-induced vasoconstriction occurring during different periods of organogenesis. Genitourinary anomalies include hydronephrosis, prune belly syndrome, and masculinization of external genitalia.[87-90] A controlled study reported a 4.4-fold increased risk of urinary anomalies associated with cocaine exposure, but no increased risk of genital anomalies.[90] This finding was confirmed by a large-scale epidemiological study, which reported an association between urogenital malformations and cocaine exposure in the first trimester.[91]

Although limb reduction deformities and intestinal atresia and infarction are reported among cocaine-exposed infants,[92-94] a population-based study found no significant increase in the prevalence of vascular disruption defects coinciding with the cocaine epidemic.[95] The heart may also be susceptible to cocaine-related vascular disruption as suggested by an autopsy describing a cocaine-positive fetus with a single cardiac ventricle that was secondary to a coronary thrombus.[96] Most cases of single ventricle, however, are probably unrelated to cocaine exposure.[97] The risk ratio of cardiac anomalies was elevated 3.7-fold among cocaine-positive infants compared to control,[98] but the study did not account for confounding factors.

Cocaine has been implicated in the genesis of brain and eye malformations. Early in the epidemic, Bingol et al. reported skull defects, exencephaly, encephaloceles, and delayed ossification.[72] Others noted a 12% rate of cerebral malformations among cocaine-exposed infants, comprised mostly of encephaloceles and skull defects.[99] In a referral sample to a neurophthalmologist, Dominguez et al. described high rates of strabismus, nystagmus, and hypoplastic discs.[100] Most infants also had cerebral malformations, strokes, or porencephaly. Many were exposed to illicit substances other than cocaine; only two infants with malformations were exposed exclusively to cocaine: one case of agenesis of the corpus callosum and one of septo-optic dysplasia. Other ocular anomalies noted among cocaine-exposed infants are delayed visual maturation, optic nerve hypoplasia, and persistent eyelid edema.[101] Tortuous abnormally dilated iris vessels[102] and a persistent hyperplastic primary vitreous with retinopathy of prematurity-like findings[103] have also been linked to fetal cocaine exposure. Finally, other investigators in comparisons of 40 cocaine-positive infants with controls have found no differences in rates of congenital anomalies, optic disc and nerve abnormalities, or scleral and retinal hemorrhage.[104] However, their small sample might have provided insufficient power to detect such an association.

In rodents, high doses of cocaine can induce urogenital, cardiac, cerebral, and limb reduction anomalies. Mahalik reported a high incidence of malformations induced by cocaine in CF-1 mice, which mirrored those reported in human infants, namely skeletal defects, exencephaly, ocular malformations, hydronephrosis, and delayed ossification.[105] Nevertheless, the teratogenic potential for cocaine effects in animal studies is inconsistent and occurs with doses much larger than those encountered in clinical settings.

The teratogenicity of cocaine in humans, with the exception of urogenital malformations, has yet to be established by large-scale epidemiological studies. Most reports on cocaine-related malformations are case reports or series, where ascertainment bias is surely operant as cases are collected in a nonblinded, nonsystematic fashion based on exposure status; the few population-based studies have not controlled for the effects of fetal alcohol exposure, a well-known teratogen. The influence of confounders on cocaine-related teratogenic effects is exemplified in a study by Zuckerman in which cocaine-exposed infants had significantly higher rates (14%) of 3 minor or 1 major congenital anomalies compared to cocaine-unexposed infants (8%), that disappeared after controlling for confounders, including alcohol.[19]

One of the problems in making causal associations between cocaine and malformations in nonpopulation-based studies is that both cocaine use and malformations of any type are common in clinical practice. The high frequency of both cases and exposure makes associations between the two likely to result from chance and nullifies the rare disease assumption, which is the basis for the approximation of the odds ratio to the risk ratio, thus, raising questions regarding the validity of the odds ratio in case-controlled cocaine studies.[106]

1.5.1.4   SIDS and Other Effects

Studies on sudden infant death syndrome (SIDS) and fetal cocaine exposure have yielded somewhat discrepant results. Several studies have reported an association between prenatal cocaine exposure and SIDS,[62,107,108] although others have failed to do so.[109] The rarity of SIDS may have made findings unstable, especially in smaller studies. A large population-based study found a 1.6-fold elevation in the risk of SIDS linked to cocaine, which reached statistical significance, but was much lower than that noted with fetal opiate exposure.[62]

In pneumographic studies involving term infants, those with cocaine exposure exhibited increased episodes of longest apnea, bradycardia, and less periodic breathing than control infants.[110] A cocaine effect on the norepinephrine system at the level of the locus coerulus, which is responsible for arousal from sleep-related apnea, has been invoked in the genesis of SIDS.[111]

Adverse cocaine effects on the auditory system have also been described, with separate reports showing prolonged interpeak latencies I through V on brain stem auditory evoked responses among cocaine-exposed infants that persisted up to 3 months.[112,113] An increased startle response was also reported among cocaine-exposed neonates.[114] Collectively, these studies would suggest that cocaine may affect the central pathways of the developing brain at the level of the brainstem.

1.5.2 Long Term Neurodevelopment

The mechanism(s) by which fetal cocaine exposure affects the developing brain is not known. Neither is it known whether effects are related to cocaine or to one of its metabolites. Postulated mechanisms of action include hypoxia, direct toxicity, cortical dysgenesis, and alterations of monoaminergic (norepinephrine, dopamine, and serotonin) or other neural pathways. Evidence for the latter mechanism derives from experiments showing a prolonged effect of cocaine on the developing rat brain producing lasting neurochemical changes in the dopaminergic system in the brain coupled with both late and early behavioral abnormalities.[115] Dopaminergic involvement is also suggested in clinical settings where newborn infants exposed to cocaine showed lower cerebrospinal fluid levels of homo-vanillic acid than did unexposed controls.[116]

Anecdotally, cocaine-exposed children seem to suffer from neurobehavioral abnormalities. Sleep disturbances, especially night terrors or inverted sleep patterns, unexplained unconsolable daytime crying, and excessive startle response are commonly observed in a subset of cocaine-exposed infants and young children. In an uncontrolled study, high rates of autism and developmental abnormalities were reported among cocaine-exposed infants referred to a developmental clinic.[117]

1.5.2.1 Cognitive Effects

Few prospective studies have dealt with cocaine exposure and long-term neurodevelopment.[30,86,118] Most have involved infants or toddlers and two reports refer to the same cohort of children. One of the latter involved comparisons between 3 groups of 2-year-old children: a cocaine/polydrug exposed, a no-cocaine/polydrug exposed, and a drug-negative control group.[86] No significant differences in mean development scores were noted between the two drug-exposed groups; nonetheless, compared to controls, the polydrug- (with and without cocaine) exposed groups had a significantly larger proportion of children scoring in the abnormal range. Fetal cocaine exposure was the best predictor of depressed head size, which in turn mediated effects on cognition. The other study, which involved the same cohort at age 3 years, identified via path analysis both a direct and indirect drug effect on cognitive function; indirect effects were mediated through head size, perseverance at a task, and home environment.[118] One study limitation that resulted from analyzing all illicit drugs as a single exposure category was that it did not distinguish individual cocaine effects from other drug effects.

1.5.2.2   Neurological Effects

A prospective study that focused on neurological function reported high rates of hypertonia associated with fetal cocaine exposure among children at risk for HIV.[30] Rates of hypertonia, shown in Figure 1.1, were maximal at age 6 months and resolved in most children by age 2 years, arms first and legs last.[30] A diagnosis of hypertonic tetraparesis (HTP) was more strongly associated with cocaine-positivity than were all types of hypertonia combined: 27% of 51 cocaine-positive infants compared with 9% of 68 cocaine-negative infants (chi-square, $p = 0.006$; OR = 4.0, 95% CI = 1.5-10.8). Cocaine exposure remained significantly associated with hypertonia in logistic regression models that controlled for 11 variables, including gestational age, birth weight, head circumference, HIV infection, and opiate withdrawal. The adjusted odds of hypertonia associated with cocaine was 3.4 at age 6 months, 5.4 at age 12 months, and 8.7 at age 18 months. Development quotients were similar between cocaine-exposed and unexposed children, but among the cocaine-exposed group a diagnosis of hypertonic tetraparesis (HTP) at age 6 months appeared to be a marker for later developmental impairments (Figure 1.2).

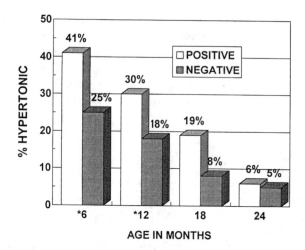

FIGURE 1.1 Percent of children with hypertonia of any type according to age and presence of cocaine in urine toxicology (positive and negative). (*) = p ≤0.05.

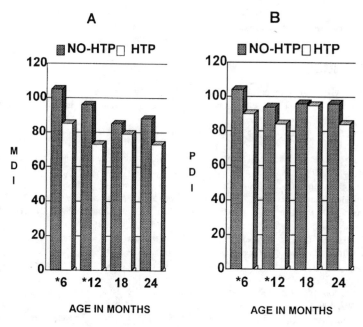

FIGURE 1.2 Developmental index scores at age 6 months among 41 cocaine-positive children and presence of hypertonic tetraparesis (HTP). Analysis excludes HIV-infected children. Panel A shows mental development index (MDI), and panel B shows psychomotor development index (PDI). (*) = p ≤0.05.

1.5.2.3 Behavioral Effects

Whether fetal cocaine exposure results in behavioral abnormalities is not known. Anecdotally, cocaine-exposed children appear to show high rates of attention deficit disorder, but few, if any studies, focus on cocaine-related behaviors. Infants with polydrug exposure, including cocaine, exhibited significantly lower scores on the Fagan Test of Infant Intelligence, a structured test of visual memory.[119] Differences in attention and distractibility between groups were also noted. Although this test is a good predictor of later intelligence, it is less apt at predicting subsequent behaviors. To date, the cohorts reported are much too young for behavioral estimates to be made reliably. Studies in older children are therefore needed to address this question.

1.6 SUMMARY

Clinical studies of cocaine effects on the exposed offspring are hindered by numerous factors that confound outcome. Of concomitant exposures, alcohol, with its well-established effects on teratogenesis, brain growth, and cognition, is perhaps the most important confounder. A plethora of neonatal studies supports a cocaine effect on fetal growth, whereas the teratogenic effect of cocaine, especially in the brain, is far from established. Cocaine-related effects on cognition have not been documented, but long-term neurodevelopment studies are scarce. Cocaine effects on neurological function are transient, disappearing by the second year of life, and may predispose infants to cognitive impairments. No study has yet assessed the impact of cocaine on subsequent behavior and learning.

REFERENCES

1. O'Malley, P.M., Johnston, L.D., and Bachman, J.G., Quantitative and qualitative changes in cocaine use among American high school seniors, college students and young adults, *NIDA Res. Monogr.*, 110, 19, 1991.
2. Brust, J.C.M., *Neurological Aspects of Substance Abuse,* Butterworth-Heinemann, Boston, 1993, Chap. 4.
3. Johanson, C.E. and Fischman, M.W., The pharmacology of cocaine related to its abuse, *Pharmacol. Rev.*, 41, 3, 1989.
4. Kurth, C.P. Monitto, C., Albuquerque, M.L., Feuer, P., Anday, E., and Shaw, L., Cocaine and its metabolites constrict cerebral arterioles in new born pigs, *J. Pharmacol. Exp. Ther.*, 265, 587, 1993.
5. Konkol, R.J., Erickson, B.A., Doerr, J.K., Hoffman, R.G., and Madden J.A., Seizures induced by cocaine metabolite benzoylecgonine in rats, *Epilepsia,* 33, 420, 1992.
6. Schenker, S., Yang, Y., Johnson, R.F., et. al., The transfer of cocaine and its metabolites across the term human placenta, *Clin. Pharmacol. Ther.,* 53, 329, 1993.
7. Woods, J.R., Plessinger, M.S., and Clark, K.E., Effects of cocaine on uterine blood flow, *JAMA,* 257, 957, 1987.
8. Woolverton, W.L., and Johnson, K.M., Neurobiology of cocaine abuse, *Trends Pharmacol. Sci.,* 13, 193, 1992.
9. Deneau, G.A., Yanagita, T., and Seevers M.H., Self administration of psychoactive substances by monkeys, *Psychopharmacologia*, 16, 30, 1969.
10. Fischman, M.W., Behavioral pharmacology of cocaine, *J. Clin. Psychiatry,* 49 Supp, 7, 1988.
11. Goeder, N.E. and Smith, J.E., Reinforcing properties of cocaine in the medial prefrontal cortex: primary action of presynaptic dopaminergic terminals, *Pharmacol. Biochem. Behav.,* 25, 191, 1986.
12. Dackis, C.A. and Gold, M.S., New concepts in cocaine addiction: the dopamine depletion hypothesis, *Neurosci. Biobehav. Rev.,* 9, 469, 1985.
13. Vaughn, A.J., Carzoli, R.P., Sanchez-Ramos, L., Murphy, S., Khan, N., and Chiu T., Community wide estimation of illicit drug use in delivering women: prevalence, demographic and associated risk factors, *Obstet. Gynecol.,* 82, 92, 1993.

14. Ostrea, E.M., Brady, M.J., Gause, S., Raymundo, A.L., and Stevens M., Drug screening of newborns by meconium analysis: a large scale, prospective, epidemiological study, *Pediatrics*, 89, 107, 1992.

15. Burke, M.S. and Roth, D., Anonymous screening in private obstetric population, *Obstet. Gynecol.*, 81, 354, 1993.

16. McCalla, S., Minkoff, H.L., Feldman, J., Delke, I., Salwin, M., Valencia, G., and Glass, L., The biological and social consequences of perinatal cocaine use in an inner city population: results of an anonymous cross-sectional study, *Am. J. Obstet. Gynecol.*, 164, 625, 1991.

17. Bateman, D.A., Ng, S.K., Hansen, C.A., and Heagarty, M.C., The effect of intrauterine cocaine exposure in newborns, *Am. J. Public Health*, 83, 190, 1993.

18. Habel, L., Kaye, K., and Lee, J., Trends in the reporting of drug use and infant mortality among drug-exposed infants in New York City, *Women and Health*, 16,41, 1990,

19. Zuckerman, B., Frank, D.A., Hingson, R., et al., Effects of maternal marijuana and cocaine on fetal growth, *N. Engl. Med.*, 320, 762, 1989.

20. Rosengren, S.S., Meconium testing for cocaine metabolite, *Am. J. Obstet. Gynecol.*, 68, 1449, 1993.

21. DiGregorio, G.J., Ferko, A.P., Barbieri, E.J., et al., Detection of cocaine usage in pregnant women by urinary EMIT drug screen and GC-MS analyses, *J. Anal. Toxicol.*, 18, 247, 1994.

22. Ambre, J.J., Ruo, T., Smith, G.L., Smith, G.L., Backes, D., and Smith, C.M., Ecgonine methyl ester, a major metabolite of cocaine, *J. Anal. Toxicol.*, 6, 26, 1982.

23. Weiss, R.D. and Gawin, F.H., Protracted elimination of cocaine metabolites in long-term, high dose cocaine abuser, *Am. J. Med.*, 85, 879, 1988.

24. Graham, K., Koren, G., Klein, J., et al., Determination of gestational cocaine exposure by hair analysis, *JAMA*, 262, 3328, 1989.

25. Ostrea, E.M. Jr., Brady, M.J., Parks, P.M., Asensio, D.C., and Naluz, A., Drug screening of meconium in infants of drug-dependent mothers: an alternative to urine testing, *J. Pediatr.*, 115, 474, 1989.

26. Lewis, D.E., Moore, C.M., and Leiken, J.B., Cocaethylene in meconium specimens, *J. Toxicol. Clin. Toxicol.*, 32, 697, 1994.

27. Shepherd, S.M., Druckenbrod, G.C., and Haywood, Y.C., Other infectious complications in intravenous drug users. The compromised host, *Emerg. Med. Clin. North. Am.*, 8, 683, 1990.

28. Lindsay, M.K., Peterson, H.B., Boring, J., Gramling, J., Willis, S., and Klein, L., Crack/cocaine as a risk factor for Human Immunodeficiency Virus Infection type I among inner city parturients, *Obstet. Gynecol.*, 80, 981, 1992.

29. Chiriboga, C.A., Vibbert, M., Malouf, R., Suarez, M., Abrams, E., Heagarty, M.C., Brust, J.C.M., and Hauser, W.A., Children at risk for HIV infection: neurological and developmental abnormalities, (abstract) *Ann. Neurol.*, 34, 500, 1993.

30. Chiriboga, C.A., Vibbert, M., Malouf, R., et al., Neurological correlates of fetal cocaine exposure: transient hypertonia of infancy and early childhood, *Pediatrics*, 96, 1070, 1995.

31. Webber, M.P. and Hauser, W.A., Secular trends in New York City Hospital discharges of diagnosis of congenital syphilis and cocaine dependency, *Public Health Rep.*, 108, 279, 1993.

32. Greenberg, M.S., Singh, T., Htoo, M., and Schultz, S., The association between congenital syphilis and cocaine/crack in New York City: a case control study, *Am. J. Public Health*, 81, 1316, 1991.

33. Webber, M.P., Lambert, G., Bateman, D.A., and Hauser, W.A., Maternal risk factors for congenital syphilis. A case-control study, *Am. J. Epidemiol*, 137, 415, 1993.

34. Rawstron, S.A., Jenkins, S., Blanchard, S., Li, P.N., and Bromberg, K., Maternal and congenital syphilis in Brooklyn, NY. Epidemiology transmission and diagnosis, *Am. J. Dis. Child*, 147, 727, 1993.

35. Picone, T.A., Allen, L.H., Olsen, P.N., et al., Pregnancy outcome in North American women. II Effects of diet, cigarette smoking, stress and weight gain on placentas, and on neonatal physical and behavioral characteristics, *Am. J. Clin. Nutr.*, 36, 1214, 1982.

36. Moro, J.O., de Paredes, B., Wagner, M., et al., Nutritional supplementation and outcome of pregnancy. I Birth weight, *Am. J. Clin. Nutr.*, 32, 455, 1979.

37. Oyemade, U.J., Cole, O.J., Johnson, A.A. et al., Prenatal predictors of performance on the Brazelton Neonatal Assessment Scales, *J. Nutr.*, 124, 1000s, 1994.

38. Church, M.W., Overbeck, G.W., and Andrzejczak, A.L., Prenatal cocaine exposure in Long-Evans Rat: I. Dose dependent effects on gestation, mortality and postnatal maturation, *Neurotoxicol. Teratol.*, 12, 327, 1990.

39. Knight, E.M., James, H., Edwards, C.H., et al., Relationship of serum illicit drug concentrations during pregnancy to maternal nutritional status, *J. Nutr.*, 124, 973S, 1994.

40. Chiriboga, C.A., Fetal effects, in *Neurological Complications of Drug and Alcohol Abuse*, Brust. J.C.M. (Ed.), *Neurologic Clinics*, 11, 707, 1993.

41. Abel, E.L., Smoking during pregnancy: a review of effects on growth and development of offspring, *Human Biol.*, 52, 593, 1980.

42. Olds, D.L., Henderson, C.R., and Tatelbaum, R., Intellectual impairment in children of women who smoke cigarettes during pregnancy, *Pediatrics*, 93, 221, 1994.

43. Ferguson, D.M., Horwood, L.J., and Lynskey, M.T., Maternal smoking before and after pregnancy: effects on behavioral outcomes in middle childhood, *Pediatrics*, 92, 815, 1993.

44. Lemoine, P., Haronsseau, H., Borteryu, J.P., et al., Les infants de parent alcooliques: Anomalies observe a propopos de 127 cas, *Ouest Med.*, 25, 476, 1968.

45. Clarren, S.K. and Smith, D.W., The fetal alcohol syndrome, *N. Engl. J. Med.*, 298, 1063, 1978.

46. Abel, E.L. and Sokol R.J., Incidence of fetal alcohol syndrome and economic impact of FAS-related anomalies, *Drug and Alcohol Dep.*, 19, 51, 1987.

47. Wright, J.T., Barrison, I.G. and Lewis, I.G., et al., Alcohol consumption, pregnancy and low birth weight, *Lancet*, 1, 663, 1983.

48. Sokol, R.J., Miller, S.I., and Reed, G., Alcohol abuse during pregnancy: an epidemiologic study, *Alcoholism: Clin. Exp. Res.*, 4, 135, 1980.

49. Hanson, J.W., Streissguth, A.P., and Smith, D.W., The effect of moderate alcohol consumption during pregnancy on fetal growth and morphogenesis, *J. Pediatrics*, 92, 457, 1978.

50. Clarren, S.K., Alvord, E.C., Sumi, M., et al., Brain malformations related to prenatal exposure to ethanol, *J. Pediatr.*, 92, 64, 1977.

51. Hingson, R., Alper, T.T., Day, N., et al., Effects of maternal drinking and marijuana use on fetal growth and development, *Pediatrics*, 70, 539, 1982.

52. Fried, PA., Postnatal consequences of maternal marijuana use during pregnancy: consequences for the offspring, *Seminars in Perinatol.*, 15, 280, 1991.

53. Day, N., Sambamoorthi, U., and Taylor, P., et al., Prenatal marijuana use and neonatal outcome, *Neurotoxicol. Teratol.*, 13, 329, 1990.

54. Frank, D.A., Bauchner, H., Parker, S. et al., Neonatal body proportionality after in -utero exposure to cocaine and marijuana, *J. Pediatr*, 117, 662, 1990.

55. Astley, S.J., Clarren, S.K., and Little, R.E., et al., Analysis of facial shape in children gestationally exposed to marijuana, alcohol, and/or cocaine, *Pediatrics*, 89, 67, 1992.

56. Linn, S., Schoenbaum, S., Monson, R., and Rosner, R., Stubblefield P.R., and Yan K., The association of marijuana use with the outcome of pregnancy, *Am. J. Public Health*, 73, 1161, 1983.

57. O'Connell, C.M. and Fried, P.A., An investigation of prenatal cannabis exposure and minor physical anomalies in a low risk population, *Neurobehav. Toxicol. Teratol.*, 6, 345, 1984.

58. Tansley, B.W., Fried, P.A., and Mount, H.T.J., Visual processing in children prenatally exposed to marijuana and nicotine: a preliminary report, *Can. J. Public Health*, 77, 72, 1986.

59. Fried, P.A. and Watkinson, B., 12- and 24-month neurobehavioral follow-up of children prenatally exposed to marijuana, cigarettes and alcohol, *Neurobehav. Teratol.*, 10, 305, 1988.

60. Little, R.E., Anderson, K.W., Ervin, C.H., et al., Maternal alcohol use during breast feeding and infant mental and motor development at one year, *N. Engl. J. Med.*, 32, 425, 1989.

61. Chasnoff, I.J., Hatcher, R., and Burns, W.J., Polydrug- and methadone-addicted newborns: a continuum of impairment?, *Pediatrics*, 70, 210, 1982.

62. Kandall, S.R., Gaines, J., and Habel, L., et al., Relationship of maternal substance abuse to subsequent infant death syndrome in offspring, *J. Pediatr.*, 123, 120, 1993.

63. Wilson, G.S., Desmond, M.M., and Verniaud, W.M., Early development of infants of heroin-addicted mothers, *Am. J. Dis. Child*, 126, 457, 1973.

64. Rosen, T.S. and Johnson, H.L., Children of methadone maintained mothers: follow-up to 18 months of age, *J. Pediatr.*, 101, 192, 1982.

65. Marcus, J., Hans, S.L., and Jeremy, R.J., A longitudinal study of offspring born to methadone-maintained women. III. Effects of multiple risk factors on development at 4, 8 and 12 months, *Am. J. Drug Abuse,* 10, 195, 1984.
66. Bauman, P. and Levine, S., The development of children of drug addicts, *Int. J. Addict.,* 21, 849, 1986.
67. Hans, S.L., Developmental consequences of prenatal exposure to methadone, *Ann. N.Y. Acad. Sci.,* 562, 195, 1989.
68. Nelson, K.B. and Broman, S.H., Perinatal risk factors in children with serious motor and mental handicaps, *Ann. Neuro.,* 2, 371, 1977.
69. Hunt, J.V., Tooley, W.H., and Harvin, D., Learning disabilities in children with birth weights < 1500 grams, *Semin. Perinatol.,* 6, 280, 1992.
70. Drillien, C.M., Abnormal neurological signs in the first year of life in low-birthweight infants: possible prognostic significance, *Dev. Med. Child Neurol.,* 14, 575, 1972.
71. Villar, J., Smerigilio, V., and Martorell, R., et al., Heterogenous growth and mental development of intrauterine growth-related infants during the first 3 years of life, *Pediatrics,* 89, 67, 1984.
72. Bingol, N., Fuchs, M., and Diaz, V., et al., Teratology of cocaine use, *J. Pediatr.,* 110, 93, 1987.
73. Oro, A.S. and Dixon, S.D., Perinatal cocaine and methamphetamine exposure: Maternal and neonatal correlates, *J. Pediatr.,* 111, 571, 1987.
74. Ryan, L., Erlichs, T., and Finnegan, L., Cocaine abuse in pregnancy: effects on the fetus and newborn, *Neurotox. Teratol.,* 9, 295, 1987.
75. Fulroth, R.F., Phillips, B., Durand, B., and Durand, D.J., Perinatal outcome of infants exposed to cocaine and/or heroin in utero, *Am. J. Dis. Child,* 243, 905, 1989.
76. Chasnoff, I.J., Burns, W.J., and Scholl, S.H., et al., Cocaine use in pregnancy, *N. Engl. J. Med.,* 313, 666, 1985.
77. Chasnoff, I.J., Griffith, D.R., MacGregor, S.N., Dirkes, K., and Burns K.S., Temporal patterns of cocaine use in pregnancy, *JAMA,* 261, 171, 1989.
78. Neuspiel, D.R., Hamel, C., Hochberg, E., et al., Maternal cocaine use and infant behavior, *Neurotoxicol. Teratol.,* 13, 1990.
79. Eisen, L.N., Field, T.M., Bandstra, E.S., et al., Perinatal cocaine effects on neonatal stress behavior and performance on the Brazelton Scale, *Pediatrics,* 88, 477, 1991.
80. Konkol, R.J., Murphey, L.J., Ferriero, D.M., and Demsey, D.A., Olsen G.D., Cocaine metabolites in the neonate: potential for toxicity, *J. Child Neurol.,* 9, 242, 1994.
81. Chiriboga, C.A., Bateman, D., Brust, J.C.M., and Hauser, W.A., Neurological findings in cocaine-exposed infants, *Pediatr. Neurol.,* 9, 115, 1993.
82. Hume, R.F., O'Donnell, K.J., Stanger, C.L., In-utero cocaine exposure: Observations of fetal behavioral state may predict neonatal outcome, *Am. J. Obstet Gynecol,* 161, 685, 1989.
83. Gillogley, K.M., Evans, A.T., Hansen, R.L., et al., The perinatal impact of cocaine, amphetamine, and opiate use detected by universal intrapartum screening, *Am. J. Obstet Gynecol,* 163, 1535, 1990.
84. Handler, A., Kristen, N., Davis, F., et al., Cocaine use during pregnancy: perinatal outcomes, *Am. J. Epidemiol.,* 133, 818, 1991.
85. Little, R.E. and Snell, L.M., Brain growth among fetuses exposed to cocaine in utero: asymmetrical growth retardation, *Obstet. Gynecol.,* 77, 361, 1991.
86. Chasnoff, I.J., Griffith, D.R., and Freier, C., et al., Cocaine/polydrug use in pregnancy, *Pediatrics,* 89, 284, 1992.
87. Chasnoff, I.J., Chisum, G.M., and Kaplan, W.E., Maternal cocaine use and genitourinary tract malformations, *Teratology,* 37, 201, 1988.
88. Bingol, N., Fuchs, M., and Diaz, V., et al., Teratology of cocaine use, *J. Pediatr.,* 110, 93, 1987.
89. Greenfield, S.P., Rutigliano, E., and Steinhardt, G., and Elders J.S., Genitourinary tract malformations and maternal cocaine abuse, *Urology,* 37, 455, 1991.
90. Chavez GAF., Mulinare J., and Cordero J.F., Maternal cocaine use during early pregnancy as a risk factor for congenital urogenital anomalies, *JAMA,* 262, 795, 1989.
91. Centers for Disease Control, Urogenital anomalies in the offspring of women using cocaine during early pregnancy, *MMWR,* 38, 536, 1989.
92. Hoyme, H.E., Lyons, Jones, K., and Dixon, S.D., Prenatal cocaine exposure and fetal vascular disruption, *Pediatrics,* 85, 743, 1990.

93. Hannig, V.A. and Phillips, J.A., Maternal cocaine abuse and fetal abnormality: evidence for teratogenic effects of cocaine, *South Med. J.,* 84, 498, 1991.

94. Steinbaum, K.A. and Badell, A., Physiatric management of two neonates with limb deficiencies and prenatal cocaine exposure, *Arch. Phys. Med. Rehabil.,* 73, 385, 1992.

95. Martin, M.L., Koury, M.J., Corderos, J.F., and Waters, G.D., Trends in rate of multiple vascular disruption, Atlanta. Is there evidence for a cocaine epidemic?, *Teratology,* 45, 647, 1992.

96. Shepard, T.H., Fantel, A.G., and Kapur, R.P., Fetal coronary thrombosis as a cause for single ventricle, *Teratology,* 43, 113, 1991.

97. Martin, M.L. and Khoury, M.J., Cocaine and single ventricle: a population study, *Teratology,* 46, 267, 1992.

98. Lipschultz, S.E., Frassica, J.J., and Orau, E.J., Cardiovascular abnormality in infants prenatally exposed to cocaine, *J. Pediatr.,* 118, 44, 1991.

99. Heier, L.A., Carpanzano, C.R., and Mast, J., et al., Maternal cocaine abuse: the spectrum of radiologic abnormalities in the neonatal CNS, *AJNR,* 12, 951, 1991

100. Dominguez, R., Vila-Coro, A.A., and Slopis, J.M., et al., Brain and ocular abnormalities in infants with in-utero exposure to cocaine and other street drugs, *AJDC,* 145, 688, 1991.

101. Good, W.V., Ferriero, D.M., Golabi, M., and Kobori, J.A., Abnormalities of the visual system in infants exposed to cocaine, *Ophthalmology,* 99, 341, 1992.

102. Isenberg, S., Spierrer,A., and Inekelis, S., Ocular signs of cocaine intoxication in neonates, (Letter) *Am. J. Ophthal.,* 103, 350, 1987.

103. Teske, M. and Trese, M., Retinopathy of prematurity like fundus and persistent hyperplastic primary vitreous associated with maternal cocaine use, *Am. J. Ophthal.,* 103, 719, 1987.

104. Stafford, J.R., Rosen, T.S., Zaider, M., and Merriam, J.C., Prenatal cocaine exposure and the developing human eye, *Ophthalmology,* 101, 301, 1994.

105. Mahalik, M., Gautierri, R., and Maun, D., Teratogenic potential of cocaine hydrochloride in CF-12 mice, *J. Pharm. Sci.,* 111, 703, 1980.

106. Kleinbaum, D.G., Kupper, L.L., and Morgenstern, H., *Epidemiological Research. Principles and quantitative methods,* Van Norstrand Reinhold, New York, 1982, 211.

107. Durand, D.J., Espinoza, A.M., and Nickerson, B.G., Association between prenatal cocaine exposure and sudden infant death syndrome, *J. Pediatr.,* 117, 909, 1990.

108. Davidson, S.L., Bautista, D., Chan, L., Derry, M., Lisbin, A., Durfee, M.J., Mills, K.S.C., and Keens, T.G., Sudden infant death syndrome in infants of substance-abusing mothers, *J. Pediatr.,* 117, 876, 1990.

109. Bauchner, H., Zuckerman, B., and McClain, M., et al., Risk of sudden infant death syndrome among infants with in utero cocaine exposure, *J. Pediatr.,* 113, 831, 1988.

110. Silvestri, J.M., Long, J.M., Weese-Mayer, D.E., and Barkov, G.A., Effects of prenatal cocaine on respiration, heart rate and sudden infant death syndrome, *Pediatr. Pulmonol.,* 11, 328, 1991.

111. Gingras, J.L. and Weese-Mayer, D., Maternal cocaine addiction II: an animal model for the study of brainstem mechanisms operative in sudden infant death syndrome, *Med. Hypotheses,* 33, 231, 1990.

112. Salamy, A., Eldredge, L., Anderson, J., et al., Brainstem transmission time in infants exposed to cocaine in-utero, *J. Pediatrics,* 117, 627, 1990.

113. Shi, L., Cone-Wesson, B., Reddix, B., Effects of maternal cocaine use and the neonatal auditory system, *Int. J. Pediatr. Otorrhinlaryngo,* 15, 245, 1988.

114. Anday, E.K., Cohen, M.E., and Kelley, N.E., et al., Effects of in utero cocaine exposure on startle and its modification, *Dev. Pharmacol. Ther.,* 12, 137, 1989.

115. Dow-Edwards, D.L., Long term neurochemical and neurobehavioral consequences of cocaine use during pregnancy. *Ann. N.Y. Acad. Sci.,* 562, 280, 1989.

116. Needleman, R., Zuckerman, B.S., and Anderson, G., et al., CSF monoamine precursors and metabolites in human neonates following in-utero cocaine exposure, *Pediatric Res.,* 31,13A, 1992.

117. Davis, E., Fenoy, I., and Laraque, D., et al., Autism and developmental abnormalities in children with perinatal cocaine exposure, *J. Nation. Med. Assoc.,* 84, 315, 1992.

118. Azuma, S. and Chasnoff, I.J., Outcome of children prenatally exposed to cocaine and other drugs: a path analysis of three year data, *Pediatrics*, 92, 396, 1993.
119. Struthers, J.M. and Hansen R. L., Visual recognition memory in drugs exposed in infants, *J. Dev. Behav. Pediatr.*, 13, 108, 1992.

Chapter 2

Cocaine Pharmacology and Drug Interaction in the Fetal-Maternal Unit

George D. Olsen, MD and Peter C. Schalock

2.0 INTRODUCTION

The developmental pharmacology and toxicology of cocaine are of interest and concern at the present time due to the increased use of cocaine in women of childbearing age[1] and the reports of obstetrical, fetal, and neonatal morbidity in cocaine users.[2-3] Gestational effects of cocaine have been difficult to study because cocaine acts at multiple sites and by several mechanisms. In addition, many of cocaine's metabolites are biologically active. Confounding variables such as ethanol and tobacco use are also common in drug abusers, and the degree of cocaine exposure is often difficult to document in this population. Consequently, there is an important role for animal studies. However, species selection is difficult because of differing sensitivities to the drug and differing degrees of physiological maturation at birth. Direct fetal effects, as well as indirect effects as a result of drug-induced changes in maternal physiology, add to the complications. In the developing neonate, neuroplasticity may alter, and consequently obscure, cocaine's true effects upon neurological development. Finally, studies in nonpregnant animals may be misleading because at least two investigators have reported that pregnant animals are more sensitive to cocaine's effects. The threshold for cocaine-induced convulsions decreases in the rat[4] and cardiovascular toxicity is increased in sheep[5-6] during pregnancy. Many of the above-mentioned problems have been reviewed recently by one of us.[7]

Ultimate solutions to the understanding of cocaine's effects in the maternal-fetal unit involve interdisciplinary approaches, with *in vivo* and *in vitro* studies where appropriate, interspecies comparisons, and a better understanding of each animal model used. (Most likely, there is not one animal model that is appropriate in all respects for the observed clinical problems of cocaine abuse during pregnancy.) The application of sensitive and reproducible analytical techniques to document human drug exposure during development[8-10] will improve the objectivity in the assessment of human data. In evaluating the consequences of cocaine exposure, it is necessary to avoid either an exaggeration of cocaine's effects during development, which occurred in the early years of the cocaine epidemic,[11-13] or an underestimation of the seriousness and consequences of prenatal cocaine exposure.

The epidemiology of cocaine use during pregnancy is discussed in more detail by Dr. Chiriboga in Chapter 1 of this volume. In spite of the wide range in the prevalence rates reported for cocaine use by pregnant women, the fact is that too many babies in the United States are being exposed to this drug.[1] It is a public health problem that continues to be a concern for families and the health care team.

2.1 COCAINE STRUCTURE AND CHEMISTRY

Cocaine (ecgonine methyl ester benzoate) is a small molecular weight compound of 303.35 Daltons.[14] It is lipid soluble with a octanol/buffer partition coefficient of 8 to 10 at pH 7.4[15-17] and therefore easily crosses biological membranes, including the placenta and blood brain barrier of all species.[7,18] There are three thermodynamically favored points in the molecule (Figure 2.1) where chemical bonds can be broken in biological systems to form active metabolites. The N-methyl group on the ecgonine portion is removed enzymatically in the liver[19-21] resulting in norcocaine which is also a lipid-soluble compound. Hydrolysis of one or both of the ester bonds in cocaine produces hydrophilic metabolites: enzymatic and spontaneous removal of the methyl group from the carboxyl group of ecgonine gives benzoylecgonine, and enzymatic loss of the benzoic acid moiety from the hydroxyl group of ecgonine results in ecgonine methyl ester.[8,22-23] Hydrolysis of cocaine can occur in many tissues including the placenta.[24] The methyl group on the ecgonine portion can be exchanged for an ethyl group in the presence of ethanol.[25-27] This enzymatic transesterification results in cocaethylene. Cocaethylene can in turn undergo N-demethylation to form norcocaethylene. Both norcocaine and norcocaethylene are further hydrolyzed to benzoylnorecgonine. Methyl ester cleavage converts ecgonine methyl ester or ecgonine ethyl ester to ecgonine.

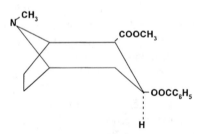

FIGURE 2.1   Structure of cocaine.

The nitrogen atom in norcocaine and norcocaethylene can undergo further oxidation reactions which produces metabolites usually considered to be minor and of no consequence. However, under special circumstances these reactive metabolites may be produced in the liver in large enough quantity to do damage to that organ.[28] For the toxic effects, large doses of the precursor drug are needed; enzymes have to be induced with pretreatment using an inducing drug such as phenobarbital; and there is species-dependent specificity, with the rodent being very susceptible in this regard.[29]

In recent years, a great deal of attention has been devoted to the chemical form in which cocaine is taken by humans. Both the hydrochloride salt of cocaine, which is the protonated form, and cocaine base ("crack") are abused. The main difference between the two compounds is that when heated to high temperatures (above 90°C), such as are achieved during smoking, cocaine HCl degrades rapidly, whereas cocaine base is volatile and the molecule stays intact.[14] Once either form is absorbed into the body it exists in both the protonated and the base forms, the exact ratio of the two forms depending upon the pH and temperature of the biological fluid since cocaine is a weak organic base with a pKa of 8.6 at 37°C[30] and 8.8 at 25°C.[31]

2.2 PHARMACOKINETICS

The amount of cocaine absorbed when administered depends upon its chemical form (salt versus base), the route of administration, the purity, and the dose. The latter two variables are usually not known for street drugs. Smoking of "crack" has become popular in recent years because smoking avoids the use of a contaminated needle and the dangers thereof; the lung offers a large absorptive surface for rapid and efficient uptake into the arterial blood stream; and the drug reaches the brain faster because it bypasses the systemic venous circulation. There is also less time for the drug to undergo enzymatic or spontaneous degradation in plasma or other tissues.

Distribution of cocaine, as stated above, includes placental transfer, although the hydrophilic metabolites such as benzoylecgonine do not cross the placenta (and presumably the blood brain barrier) as rapidly as cocaine.[21] Cocaine and its metabolites can also access amniotic fluid.[32] Amniotic fluid, as a potential reservoir for cocaine, is discussed in more detail by Glantz and Woods in Chapter 3 of this volume. Cocaine and metabolites also enter into meconium.[8-10,33-35]

Biotransformation of cocaine has been introduced and discussed briefly above. N-demethylation occurs in the cytochrome P-450 system of the liver. Hydrolysis takes place in many tissues including the plasma and the liver.[32] There is an indication that an unidentified soluble metabolite of cocaine can inhibit cocaine N-demethylation, which may explain why in most species norcocaine is a minor metabolite of cocaine. Another explanation for the small amount of norcocaine detected in biologic fluids is the rapid hydrolysis of norcocaine to benzoylnorecgonine.[32,36]

Very little cocaine (2%) is excreted unchanged in the urine.[21,37] It is so lipid soluble that most of the cocaine filtered at the glomerulus is passively reabsorbed. The more polar metabolites are not reabsorbed and therefore are readily found in the urine. Benzoylecgonine, in fact, is the form of cocaine sought in urine screens for cocaine abuse.[38]

The elimination of cocaine in mammals is rapid, with a half-life of about one hour in the human[39] and as fast as five minutes in the pregnant sheep.[40] Most species studied, including the rat[41] and guinea pig,[36] have a half-life similar to the human. Publications on cocaine kinetics up to 1989 have been reviewed by Shuster.[42] With an elimination half-life under one hour, cocaine will not accumulate in the body with intermittent dosing unless it is sequestered by ion trapping in an area such as the amniotic fluid where there is little enzymatic degradation and the pH is acidic enough to prevent rapid spontaneous disintegration. It is important here to distinguish pharmacokinetics from toxicokinetics. It is quite conceivable that longer elimination half-lives occur when large doses of cocaine are consumed because of saturation of enzymes that eliminate cocaine. The hydrophilic metabolites of cocaine have a longer half-life, approximately one order of magnitude longer than cocaine, and therefore do accumulate in the body. They continue to be excreted into the urine for days or weeks after the last dose of cocaine.[8]

2.3 PHARMACODYNAMICS

Cocaine and norcocaine have local anesthetic affects due to inhibition of the voltage gated sodium ion channel.[43] This effect requires high tissue concentrations of cocaine, which are achieved only with the concentrated solution used in local anesthesia. At lower concentrations, cocaine and norcocaine also inhibit the dopamine, norepinephrine, and serotonin transporters.[44-45] Less well known is that cocaine causes release of epinephrine and norepinephrine from the adrenal medulla.[46-49] Benzoylecgonine and benzoylnorecgonine are known to chelate Ca^{2+} [50] and cause stimulation[15] and seizures.[51-52] The actions of cocaine and its metabolites are discussed in greater detail in the section on mechanisms of neurotoxicity and in Chapter 6 by Konkol and Schuelke.

2.4 INTERACTION WITH ETHANOL

Interaction of cocaine with other drugs of abuse is a topic of scientific and practical importance. Only the interaction with ethanol is discussed here because of the common co-abuse of the two drugs and because of the current interest in cocaethylene, the metabolite that forms in the presence of the two drugs. It has been estimated that 80% of cocaine users also consume ethanol.[53] The metabolite, cocaethylene, has been reported in the human.[25-26,54-55] The only experimental *in vivo* data on cocaethylene formation are in male volunteers.[56-57] The data indicate that the concentration of cocaethylene in plasma is significantly less than cocaine and that the concentration of cocaine is increased by the co-administration of ethanol, perhaps due to inhibition of the formation of benzoylecgonine. Cocaethylene crosses the perfused placenta, as would be expected.[58] It is active in several test systems[28,59-61] and is more lethal than cocaine in mice with a 30% lower LD_{50}.[60] In spite of this intriguing information, there are no published studies of the *in vivo* or *in vitro* pharmacokinetics or production of cocaethylene in the maternal-fetal unit of any species.

2.5 MECHANISMS OF COCAINE NEUROTOXICITY
DURING DEVELOPMENT

There are many reports of neurobehavioral and neurostructural effects of cocaine upon the developing brain. The neurobehavioral effects of cocaine are discussed in detail in Chapter 10 by Dr. Spear. The potential mechanisms for these effects were recently published in a review,[7] which suggested a number of possible sites of action and mechanisms for alleged cocaine-induced developmental neurotoxicity. Topics covered were the voltage-gated sodium ion channel, monoamine transporters, epinephrine release, vasoconstriction, calcium ion chelation, superoxide formation, enzyme inhibition, neurotrophic activity, cortical architecture, immediate early genes, and glycosphingolipid composition of neural membranes. Of these topics no new information is available on the sodium ion channel development, epinephrine release, vasoconstriction, enzyme inhibition, neurotrophic activity, cortical architecture, or glycosphingolipid composition of neurons in relation to cocaine exposure during gestation. There are two new areas of interest, cell death or damage and neuronal growth inhibition, which are not covered in that review[7] and which are included below following the discussion of some of the other categories.

Cocaine has a reversible local anesthetic effect mediated by inhibition of the voltage-gated sodium ion channel. Although the sodium ion channel is essential for neuronal function and may be affected during development by cocaine exposure, there is no evidence for such a developmental effect. It is doubtful that cocaine concentrations in the brain would reach levels that would affect the function of this channel.

There is no new information on epinephrine release. Nevertheless, it bears repeating that cocaine-initiated epinephrine release induces hyperglycemia[48] experimentally and that hyperglycemia in turn may potentially enhance ischemia-reperfusion injury in the brain.[62-63] The release of catecholamines also would have cardiovascular effects.

Vasoconstriction of the uterine vessels and the cerebral circulation remain prominent mechanisms in the theories of cocaine-induced fetal neurotoxicity. Decreased blood flow would lead to fetal hypoxia and tissue damage. Glantz and Woods (Chapter 3), and Madden and Schreiber (Chapter 5) discuss the vascular effects of cocaine in more detail in this volume.

Cocaine exposure *in vivo* can induce cytochrome P-450 mediated N-demethylation *in vitro* in hepatic microsomal preparations. However, in the process of incubation there is formed a soluble metabolite that inhibits continued N-demethylation.[20-21] It is not known whether these phenomena have overall pharmacokinetic consequences *in vivo*.

Although cocaine has been found in one study to increase total and neutral glycosphingolipids,[64] this observation has not been explored further. Changes in these compounds would alter neural membrane structure and perhaps function. The neural membranes contain receptors, effectors, and channels that are important for normal function.

Monoamines and their transporters are of continued interest in cocaine research. Cocaine inhibits the presynaptic uptake of dopamine, norepinephrine, and serotonin by binding to the transporter for each of these compounds. In the rat brain, specific binding sites on these transporters can be demonstrated with low concentrations of cocaine (10nM). They are present by day 15 of gestation and reach adult levels by gestational day 20 (term 21 days).[65] There are other cocaine-induced changes in the monoaminergic systems. Tyrosine hydroxylase, an enzyme necessary for the synthesis of dopamine and norepinephrine, is increased in the fetal rat brain following chronic cocaine exposure, but dopamine concentrations are not altered.[66] Another chronic cocaine study in neonatal rats suggests that there are transiently altered dopamine receptors or transduction mechanisms due to a decrease in the cataleptic response to haloperidol, a dopamine$_2$ receptor antagonist.[67] It should be noted that haloperidol also blocks the dopamine$_1$ and the serotonin$_2$ receptors, and therefore, this drug is not absolutely selective.

The role of cocaine in calcium metabolism remains an area of investigation. In the single cardiomyocyte preparation, cocaine reduces the free concentration of Ca^{2+} in the cytosol following electrical stimulation.[68] The mechanism of the change in concentration is not known. Unfortunately, nerve cell cytosol Ca^{2+} has not been examined using the same techniques.

Oxygen free radical production is increased by cocaine and cocaethylene exposure in rat hepatocytes and hepatic microsomes, but not the rat brain microsomes.[69-70] It is possible that liver damage, which is not a recognized adverse effect of cocaine abuse for the maternal-fetal unit, could be induced via this mechanism by cocaine or cocaethylene. Brain toxicity is unlikely due to a direct effect of cocaine or cocaethylene upon the formation of reactive oxygen metabolites, however, indirect brain injury due to oxygen radicals is conceivable because of the ability of cocaine and metabolites to constrict cerebral vessels.[71-74] For example, cocaine and cocaethylene reduce fetal sheep carotid artery blood flow when the ewe is given 1.0 mg/kg of either drug.[75] The reduced blood flow would cause hypoperfusion and hypoxia followed by reperfusion and generation of superoxides.

Several recent papers suggest that the expression of immediate early genes (IEGs) is changed by acute and chronic cocaine exposure. IEGs are a class of genes which respond to environmental signals such as neurotransmitters and growth factors. The products of some of these genes go on to act as transcription factors for the late response genes.[76] The IEGs may play a critical role in mediating stimulus-induced neuronal plasticity and have been implicated in behavioral tolerance and sensitization to cocaine.[76] In this regard, cocaine is capable of causing a brief rise in mRNA of the effector IEG protein arc (activity-regulated, cytoskeleton-associated) in the striatum.[77] This protein is associated with the actin cytoskeleton in the cell body and dendrites of striatal neurons. In another study using *in-situ* hybridization,[78] the cellular phenotype in the striatum which showed increased c-fos activity after acute cocaine administration was neurons containing substance P, but not enkephalin. When IEG expression was studied in the withdrawal period, reductions of zif268 and c-fos were noted.[79] This reduction lasted several hours after a single dose. If multiple cocaine doses were given, a reduction of these mRNAs was seen for several days, suggesting chronic cocaine exposure is capable of significantly lowering mRNA levels.

Cytotoxic effects of benzoylecgonine on neuronal and glial cells have been examined using cell cultures.[80] Upon addition of benzoylecgonine in concentrations as low as 10 μM, there was a cessation of cellular processes followed by cell death in these cultures. The cell death was dependent upon the concentrations of benzoylecgonine used. However, since the concentration of benzoylecgonine in fetal brain is less than 10 μM in animal studies,[81] this mechanism may not be relevant to the reported neurotoxic effects of cocaine. In contrast, no irreversible neuronal damage in the adult rat brain was observed after cocaine administration of 40 mg/kg intraperitoneally once daily for 5 days or for 5 days a week for 3 months.[82] The study uses an *in vivo* model of cocaine administration, whereas the Lin and Leskawa paper[80] uses an *in vitro* model with benzoylecgonine only. These differences, plus the fact that brain levels of benzoylecgonine probably do not reach 10 μM in the *in vivo* model, may explain the disparate results. It should be noted that concentration of benzoylecgonine may vary with species, dose, and developmental factors.

The effects of cocaine on neuronal growth and differentiation were examined *in vitro*, using PC-12 cells.[83] Cocaine was used in concentrations ranging from 0.01 µM to 10 µM. It was found that cocaine had a statistically significant inhibitory effect upon neuronal cells when exposed to neural growth factor at 20 ng/ml. Cocaine inhibited insulin-like growth factor (IGF-1) stimulated thymidine incorporation as well as reducing neuronal differentiation at cocaine concentrations commonly found in the cocaine user. The effects seen were concentration dependent.

In an *in vivo* study on the effects of cocaine on the fetal brain, cocaine inhibited forebrain cell growth during the second postnatal week, which was the period in which cell size rose most rapidly.[84] Acute administration of 30 mg/kg subcutaneously to pregnant rats in late gestation also caused transient increases in fetal brain ornithine decarboxylase activity. The effects were considered minor compared to previous work of the author showing more profound effects of nicotine on the same parameters.

2.6 COCAINE AND VENTILATORY CONTROL

An increased risk of the sudden infant death syndrome (SIDS) is associated with gestational use of drugs of abuse. The strongest association is with tobacco use. Narcotic use is also linked to SIDS. The association between cocaine abuse and SIDS is weaker. Some studies have found an increased risk, while others have not. The evidence has been reviewed in several recent articles.[85-88]

One of the theories of the pathophysiology of SIDS is that the underlying problem of this disorder is abnormal ventilatory control. In the case of cocaine abuse during gestation, the hypothesis is that prenatal exposure to cocaine induces an alteration in the neural control of breathing. The classical methods for examining the control of breathing are to test the ventilatory response to hypercapnia and/or hypoxia. Rabbit, guinea pig, and rat models using these methods are discussed below.

Weese-Mayer and her collaborators[89-90] examined several levels of hypoxic challenge in neonatal rabbits exposed *in utero* to cocaine in two different studies. Cocaine exposure did not affect room air ventilation. The normal neonatal ventilatory response to hypoxia was eliminated by cocaine exposure in the last two thirds of gestation, whereas exposure from day 7 to 15 of gestation (term 32 days) increased the ventilatory response to hypoxia. However, in the latter study the ventilatory response to severe and prolonged hypoxia, although increased, was not sufficient to maintain normal blood oxygen saturation or heart rate, both declined. These abnormalities suggest that cocaine may alter total body oxygen consumption and/or cardiovascular function and that the increased ventilation is insufficient to overcome these alterations. Since these studies are not longitudinal, it is not known if the abnormalities are reversible.

Olsen and Weil[91] examined the ventilatory response to hypercapnia in the neonatal guinea pig. Cocaine exposure in the last half of gestation increased neonatal ventilation while breathing either room air or elevated gas mixtures with elevated CO_2 content. The alterations in breathing were due primarily to increases in tidal volume. The changes were observed by day 3 after birth and persisted until day 14. Since oxygen consumption and blood gases were not measured, it is not known whether the increased ventilation represents hyperpnea or hyperventilation.

In addition to the above studies, recent abstracts using the rabbit model[92] and a rat model[93] indicate that there are alterations in ventilatory control induced by prenatal cocaine exposure. Gingras has also reported[94] that human newborns exposed *in utero* to cocaine have abnormal hypoxic arousal response and an abnormal hypercarbic ventilatory response compared to control infants.

2.7 SUMMARY

Developmental exposure to cocaine and its metabolites, although an important public health problem, has been difficult but rewarding to study. Much has been learned about cocaine pharmacodynamics and pharmacokinetics and about neurological development. The emphasis on active metabolites, species differences, and the special changes in drug response with pregnancy has increased our understanding of fetal and maternal cocaine pharmacology. The search for knowledge has brought together chemists, clinicians, neuroscientists, and pharmacokineticists who are learning from each other. Work still to be accomplished includes the task to precisely define the specific developmental deficits and to correlate these deficits with specific neuroanatomical, physiologic, and molecular actions of cocaine. What is learned about cocaine will certainly be very useful in approaching the study of other drugs of abuse used during pregnancy.

REFERENCES

1. Day, N. L., Cottreau, C. M., and Richardson, G. A., The epidemiology of alcohol, marijuana and cocaine use among women of childbearing age and pregnant women, *Clin. Obstet. Gynecol.*, 36, 232, 1993.
2. Volpe, J. J., Effects of cocaine use on the fetus, *N. Engl. J. Med.*, 327, 399, 1992.
3. Chiriboga, C. A., Fetal effects: neurological complications of drug and alcohol abuse, *Neuro. Clin.*, 11, 707, 1993.
4. Morishima, H. O., Masaoka, T., Hara, T., Tsuji, A., and Cooper, T. B., Pregnancy decreases the threshold for cocaine-induced convulsions in the rat, *J. Lab. Clin. Med.*, 122, 748, 1993.
5. Woods, J. R. Jr., and Plessinger, M. A., Pregnancy increases cardiovascular toxicity to cocaine, *Am. J. Obstet. Gynecol.*, 162, 529, 1990.
6. Plessinger, M. A. and Woods, J. R. Jr., Progesterone increases cardiovascular toxicity to cocaine in nonpregnant ewes, *Am. J. Obstet. Gynecol.*, 163, 1659, 1990.
7. Olsen, G. D., Potential mechanisms of cocaine-induced developmental neurotoxicity: A mini-review, *Neurotoxicol.*, 16, 159, 1995.
8. Konkol, R. J., Murphey, L. J., Ferriero, D. M., Dempsey, D. A., and Olsen, G. D., Cocaine metabolites in the neonate: potential for toxicity, *J. Child Neurol.*, 9, 242, 1994.
9. Rosengren, S. S., Longobucco, D. B., Bernstein, B. A., Fishman, S., Cooke, E., Boctor, F., and Lewis, S. C., Meconium testing for cocaine metabolite: prevalence, perceptions, and pitfalls, *Am. J. Obstet. Gynecol.*, 168, 1449, 1993.
10. Dusick, A. M., Covert, R. F., Schreiber, M. D., Yee, G. T., Moore, C. M., and Tebbett, I. R., Risk of intracranial hemorrhage and other adverse outcomes after cocaine exposure in a cohort of 323 very low birth weight infants, *J. Pediatr.*, 122, 438, 1993.
11. Mayes, L. C., Granger, R. H., Bornstein, M. H., and Zuckerman, B., The problem of prenatal cocaine exposure: a rush to judgment, *JAMA*, 267, 406, 1992.
12. Zuckerman, B. and Frank, D. A., "Crack kids": not broken, *Pediatrics*, 89, 337, 1992.
13. Hutchings, D. E., The puzzle of cocaine's effects following maternal use during pregnancy: are there reconcilable differences?, *Neurotoxicol. Teratol.*, 15, 281, 1993.
14. Budavari, S., *The Merck Index*, 11th Ed., Merck and Co., Inc., Rahway, 1989, 383.

15. Misra, A. L., Nayak, P. K., Bloch, R., and Mulé, S. J., Estimation and disposition of [3H]ben-zoylecgonine and pharmacological activity of some cocaine metabolites, *J. Pharm. Pharmacol.*, 27, 784, 1975.

16. Nayak, P. K., Misra, A. L., and Mulé, S. J., Physiological disposition and biotransformation of [^{3}H] cocaine in acutely and chronically treated rats, *J. Pharmacol. Exp. Ther.*, 196, 556, 1976.

17. Hansch, C., Björkroth, J. P., and Leo, A., Hydrophobicity and central nervous system agents: on the principle of minimal hydrophobicity in drug design, *J. Pharmaceut. Sci.*, 76, 663, 1987.

18. Olsen, G. D., Placental permeability for drugs of abuse and their metabolites, in *Membranes and Barriers: Targeted Drug Delivery*, Rapaka, R. S., Ed., National Institutes on Drug Abuse, Research Monograph 154, 1995, 152.

19. Inaba, T., Cocaine: Pharmacokinetics and biotransformation in man, *Can. J. Physiol. Pharmacol.*, 67, 1154, 1989.

20. Sandberg, J. A., Murphey, L. J., and Olsen, G. D., *In vitro* hepatic biotransformation of cocaine in maternal and fetal guinea pigs: Induction of cocaine N-demethylation with cocaine pre-treat-ment, *Drug Metab. Dispos.*, 21, 390, 1993.

21. Sandberg, J. A., Murphey, L. J., and Olsen, G. D., Pharmacokinetics and metabolism of cocaine in maternal and fetal guinea pigs, *Neurotoxicol.*, 16, 169, 1995.

22. Inaba, T., Stewart, D. J., and Kalow, W., Metabolism of cocaine in man, *Clin. Pharmacol. Ther.*, 23, 547, 1978.

23. Stewart, D. J., Inaba, T., Lucassen, M., and Kalow, W., Cocaine metabolism: Cocaine and norco-caine hydrolysis by liver and serum esterases, *Clin. Pharmacol. Ther.*, 25, 464, 1979.

24. Roe, D. A., Little, B. B., Bawdon, R. E., and Gilstrap III, L. C., Metabolism of cocaine by human placentas: Implications for fetal exposure, *Am. J. Obstet. Gynecol.*, 163, 715, 1990.

25. Dean, R. A., Christian, C. D., Sample, R. H. B., and Bosron, W. F., Human liver cocaine esterases: ethanol-mediated formation of ethylcocaine, *Fed. Am. Soc. Exp. Biol. J.*, 5, 2735, 1991.

26. Dean, R. A., Harper, E. T., Dumaual, N., Stoeckel, D. A., and Bosron, W. F., Effects of ethanol on cocaine metabolism: formation of cocaethylene and norcocaethylene, *Toxicol. Appl. Pharma-col.*, 117, 1, 1992.

27. Boyer, C. S. and Petersen, D. R., Enzymatic basis for the transesterification of cocaine in the presence of ethanol: evidence for the participation of microsomal carboxylesterases, *J. Pharmacol. Exp. Ther.*, 260, 939, 1992.

28. Roberts, S. M., Roth, L., Harbison, R. D., and James, R. C., Cocaethylene hepatotoxicity in mice, *Biochem. Pharmacol.*, 43, 1989, 1992.

29. Benuck, M., Reith, M. E. A., and Lajtha, A., Presence of the toxic metabolite N-hydroxy-norcocaine in brain and liver of the mouse, *Biochem. Pharmacol.*, 37, 1169, 1988.

30. Skou, J. C., Local anaesthetics. III, Distribution of local anesthetics between the solid phase/aque-ous phase of peripheral nerves, *Act. Pharmacol. Toxicol.*, 10, 297, 1954.

31. Truant, A. P. and Takman, B., Differential physical-chemical and neuropharmacologic properties of local anesthetic agents, *Anesth. Analgesia*, 38, 478, 1959.

32. Sandberg, J. A. and Olsen, G. D., Cocaine and metabolite concentrations in the fetal guinea pig after chronic maternal cocaine administration, *J. Pharmacol. Exp. Ther.*, 260, 587, 1992.

33. Murphey, L. J., Olsen, G. D., and Konkol, R. J., Quantitation of benzoylnorecgonine and other cocaine metabolites in meconium by high-performance liquid chromatography, *J. Chromatogr.*, 613, 330, 1993.

34. Browne, S., Moore, C., Negrusz, A., Tebbett, I., Covert, R., and Dusick A., Detection of cocaine, norcocaine and cocaethylene in the meconium of premature neonates, *J. Forensic. Sci.*, 39, 1515, 1994.

35. Lewis, D. E., Moore, C. M., and Leikin, J. B., Cocaethylene in meconium specimens, *J. Toxicol. Clin. Toxicol.*, 32, 697, 1994.

36. Sandberg, J. A. and Olsen, G. D., Cocaine pharmacokinetics in the pregnant guinea pig, *J. Pharmacol. Exp. Ther.*, 258, 477, 1991.

37. Kogan, M. J., Verebey, K. G., DePace, A. C., Resnick, R. B., and Mulé, S. J., Quantitative determination of benzoylecgonine and cocaine in human biofluids by gas-liquid chromatography, *Anal. Chem.*, 49, 1965, 1977.

38. Hamilton, H. E., Wallace, J. E., Shimek, Jr., E. L., Land, P., Harris, S. C., and Christenson, J. G., Cocaine and benzoylecgonine excretion in humans, *J. Forensic. Sci.*, 22, 697, 1977.

39. Barnett, G., Hawks, R., and Resnick, R., Cocaine pharmacokinetics in humans, *J. Ethnopharmacol.*, 3, 353, 1981.

40. DeVane, C. L., Burchfield, D. J., Abrams, R. M., Miller, R. L., and Braun, S. B., Disposition of cocaine in pregnant sheep, *Dev. Pharmacol. Ther.*, 16, 123, 1991.

41. DeVane, C. L., Simpkins, J. W., Miller, R. L., and Braun, S. B., Tissue distribution of cocaine in the pregnant rat, *Life Sci.*, 45, 1271, 1989.

42. Shuster, L., Pharmacokinetics, metabolism, and disposition of cocaine, in *Cocaine Pharmacology, Physiology and Clinical Strategies,* Lakowski, J. M., Galloway, M. P., and White, F. J., Eds., CRC Press, Boca Raton, 1992, Chap. 1.

43. Just, W. W. and Hoyer, J., The local anesthetic potency of norcocaine, a metabolite of cocaine, *Experientia*, 33, 70, 1977.

44. Hawks, R. L., Kopin, I. J., Colburn, R. W., and Thoa, N. B., Norcocaine: A pharmacologically active metabolite of cocaine found in the brain, *Life Sci.*, 15, 2189, 1974.

45. Ritz, M. C., Cone, E. J., and Kuhar, M. J., Cocaine inhibition of ligand binding at dopamine, norepinephrine and serotonin transporters: A structure-activity study, *Life Sci.*, 46, 635, 1990.

46. Chiueh, C. C. and Kopin, I. J., Centrally mediated release by cocaine of endogenous epinephrine and norepinephrine from the sympathoadrenal medullary system of unanesthetized rats, *J. Pharmacol. Exp. Ther.*, 205, 148, 1978.

47. Kuhn, F. E., Johnson, M. N., Gillis, R. A., Visner, M. S., Schaer, G. L., Gold, C., and Wahlstrom, S. K., Effect of cocaine on the coronary circulation and systemic hemodynamics in dogs, *J. Am. Coll. Cardiol.*, 16, 1481, 1990.

48. Owiny, J. R., Sadowsky, D., Jones, M. T., Reimers, T. J., and Nathanielsz, P. W., Effect of maternal cocaine administration on maternal and fetal glucose, lactate, and insulin in sheep, *Obstet. Gynecol.*, 77, 901, 1991.

49. Stambler, B. S., Komamura, K., Ihara, T., and Shannon, R. P., Acute intravenous cocaine causes transient depression followed by enhanced left ventricular function in conscious dogs, *Circulation*, 87, 1687, 1993.

50. Misra, A. L. and Mulé, S. J., Calcium-binding property of cocaine and some of its active metabolites -formation of molecular complexes, *Res. Commun. Chem. Pathol. Pharmacol.*, 11, 663, 1975.

51. Konkol, R. J., Erickson, B. A., Doerr, J. K., Hoffman, R. G., and Madden, J. A., Seizures induced by the cocaine metabolite benzoylecgonine in rats, *Epilepsia*, 33, 420, 1992.

52. Konkol, R. J., Kesken, S., and Buchhalter, J.R., Neuroactive properties of common long-lasting cocaine metabolite, benzoylnorecgonine, *Pediatric Neurology,* 11:99, 1994.

53. Grant, B. F. and Harford, T. C., Concurrent and simultaneous use of alcohol with cocaine: results of national survey, *Drug Alcohol Depend.*, 25, 97, 1990.

54. Rafla, F. K. and Epstein, R. L., Identification of cocaine and its metabolites in human urine in the presence of ethyl alcohol, *J. Anal. Toxicol.*, 3, 59, 1979.

55. Bailey, D. N., Serial plasma concentrations of cocaethylene, cocaine, and ethanol in trauma victims, *J. Anal. Toxicol.*, 17, 79, 1993.

56. Farré, M., DeLaTorre, R., Llorente, M., Lamas, X., Ugena, B., Segura, J., and Cami, J., Alcohol and cocaine interactions in humans, *J. Pharmacol. Exp. Ther.*, 266, 1364, 1993.

57. McCance-Katz, E. F., Price, L. H., McDougle, C. J., Kosten, T. R., Black, J. E., and Jatlow, P. I., Concurrent cocaine-ethanol ingestion in humans: pharmacology, physiology, behavior, and the role of cocaethylene, *Psychopharmacol.*, 111, 39, 1993.

58. Schenker, S., Yang, Y., Johnson, R. F., Downing, J. W., Schenken, R. S., Henderson, G. I., and King, T. S., The transfer of cocaine and its metabolites across the term human placenta, *Clin. Pharmacol. Ther.*, 53, 329, 1993.

59. Hearn, W. L., Flynn, D. D., Hime, G. W., Rose, S., Cofino, J. C., Mantero-Atienza, E., Wetli, C. V., and Mash, D. C., Cocaethylene: a unique cocaine metabolite displays high affinity for the dopamine transporter, *J. Neurochem.*, 56, 698, 1991.

60. Hearn, W. L., Rose, S., Wagner, J., Ciarleglio, A., and Mash, D. C., Cocaethylene is more potent than cocaine in mediating lethality, *Pharmacol. Biochem. Behav.*, 39, 531, 1991.

61. Katz, J. L., Terry, P., and Witkin, J. M., Comparative behavioral pharmacology and toxicology of cocaine and its ethanol-derived metabolite, cocaine ethyl-ester (cocaethylene), *Life Sci.*, 50, 1351, 1992.

62. Hsu, S.S.-F., Meno, J. R., Gronka, R., Kushmerick, M., and Winn, H. R., Moderate hyperglycemia affects ischemic brain ATP levels but not intracellular pH, *Am. J. Physiol.*, 266, H258, 1994.

63. Zhou, J., Meno, J. R., Hsu, S.S.-F., and Winn, H. R., Effects of theophylline and cyclohexyladenosine on brain injury following normo- and hyperglycemic ischemia: A histopathologic study in the rat, *J. Cereb. Blood Flow Metab.*, 14, 166, 1994.

64. Leskawa, K. C., Jackson, G. H., Moody, C. A., and Spear, L. P., Cocaine exposure during pregnancy affects rat neonate and maternal brain glycosphingolipids, *Brain Res. Bull.*, 33, 195, 1994.

65. Meyer, J. S., Shearman, L. P., Collins, L. M., and Maguire, R. L., Cocaine binding sites in fetal rat brain: implications for prenatal cocaine action, *Psychopharmacology*, 112, 445, 1993.

66. Meyer, J. S. and Dupont, S. A., Prenatal cocaine administration stimulates fetal brain tyrosine hydroxylase activity, *Brain Res.*, 608, 129, 1993.

67. Meyer, J. S., Robinson, P., and Todtenkopf, M.S., Prenatal cocaine treatment reduces haloperidol-induced catalepsy on postnatal day 10, *Neurotoxicol. Teratol.*, 16, 193, 1994.

68. Renard, D. C., Delaville, F. J., and Thomas, A. P., Inhibitory effects of cocaine on Ca^{2+} transients and contraction in single cardiomyocytes, *Am. J. Physiol.*, 266, H555, 1994.

69. Boelsterli, U. A., Wolf, A., and Göldlin, C., Oxygen free radical production mediated by cocaine and its ethanol-derived metabolite, cocaethylene, in rat hepatocytes, *Hepatology*, 18, 1154, 1993.

70. Lloyd, R. V., Shuster, L., and Mason, R. P., Reexamination of the microsomal transformation of N-hydroxynorcocaine to norcocaine nitroxide, *Mol. Pharmacol.*, 43, 645, 1993.

71. Madden, J. A. and Powers, R. H., Effect of cocaine and cocaine metabolites on cerebral arteries *in vitro*, *Life Sci.*, 47, 1109, 1990.

72. Wang, A-M., Suojanen, J. N., Colucci, V. M., Rumbaugh, C. L., and Hollenberg, N. K., Cocaine and methamphetamine-induced acute cerebral vasospasm: An angiographic study in rabbits, *Am. J. Neuroradiol.*, 11, 1141, 1990.

73. Kurth, C. D., Monitto, C., Albuquerque, M. L., Feuer, P., Anday, E., and Shaw, L., Cocaine and its metabolites constrict cerebral arterioles in newborn pigs, *J. Pharmacol. Exp. Ther.*, 265, 587, 1993.

74. Madden, J. A., Konkol, R. J., Keller, P. A., and Alvarez, T. A., Cocaine and benzoylecgonine constrict cerebral arteries through different mechanisms, *Life Sci.*, 56, 679, 1995.

75. Covert, R. F., Schreiber, M. D., Tebbett, I. R., and Torgerson, L. J., Hemodynamic and cerebral blood flow effects of cocaine, cocaethylene and benzoylecgonine in conscious and anesthetized fetal lambs, *J. Pharmacol. Exp. Ther.*, 270, 118, 1994.

76. Hughes, P. and Dragunow, M., Induction of immediate-early genes and the control of neurotransmitter-regulated gene expression within the nervous system, *Pharmacol. Rev.*, 47, 133, 1995.

77. Fosnaugh, J. S., Bhat, R. V., Yamagata, K., Worley, P. F., and Baraban, J. M., Activation of arc, a putative "effector" immediate early gene, by cocaine in rat brain, *J Neurochem*, 64, 2377, 1995.

78. Kosofsky, B. E., Genova, L. M., and Hyman, S. E., Substance P phenotype defines specificity of c-fos induction by cocaine in developing rat striatum, *J. Comp. Neurol.*, 351, 41, 1995.

79. Ennulat, D. J., Babb, S. M., and Cohen, B. M., Persistent reduction of immediate early gene mRNA in rat forebrain following single or multiple doses of cocaine, Brain Research, *Mole. Brain. Res.*, 26, 106, 1994.

80. Lin, Y. and Leskawa, K. C., Cytotoxicity of the cocaine metabolite benzoylecgonine, *Brain Res.*, 643, 108, 1994.

81. Spear, L. P., Frambes, N. A., and Kirstein, C. L., Fetal and maternal brain levels of cocaine and benzoylecgonine following subcutaneous administration of cocaine during gestation in rats, *Psychopharmacol.*, 97, 427, 1989.

82. Goodman, J. H. and Sloviter, R. S., Cocaine neurotoxicity and altered neuropeptide Y immunoreactivity in the rat hippocampus: a silver degeneration and immunocytochemical study, *Brain Res.*, 616, 263, 1993.

83. Zachor, D., Cherkes, J. K., Fay, C. T., and Ocrant, I., Cocaine differentially inhibits neuronal differentiation and proliferation *in vitro*, *J. Clin. Invest.*, 93, 1179, 1994.

84. Seidler, F. J. and Slotkin, T. A., Prenatal cocaine and cell development in rat brain regions: effects on ornithine decarboxylase and macromolecules, *Brain Res. Bull.*, 30, 91, 1993.

85. Kandall, S. R. and Gaines, J., Maternal substance use and subsequent sudden infant death syndrome (SIDS) in offspring, *Neurotoxicol. Teratol.*, 13, 235, 1991.

86. Kandall, S. R., Gaines, J., Habel, L., Davidson, G., and Jessop, D., Relationship of maternal substance abuse to subsequent sudden infant death syndrome in offspring, *J. Pediatr.*, 123, 120, 1993.

87. Olsen, G. D. and Weil, J. A., Neonatal ventilatory changes following *in utero* cocaine exposure: A minireview of the guinea pig and rabbit models, *Neurotoxicol.*, 16, 153, 1995.

88. Olsen, G. D. and Murphey, L. J., Effects of morphine and cocaine on breathing central in neonatal animals: A minireview in, *Biological Mechanisms and Perinatal Exposure to Abused Drugs*, Thadani, P. V., Ed., National Institute on Drug Abuse, Research Monograph 158, 1995, 22.

89. Weese-Mayer, D. E., Klemka-Walden, L. M., Barkov, G. A., and Gingras, J. L., Effects of prenatal cocaine on the ventilatory responses to hypoxia in newborn rabbits, *Dev. Pharmacol. Ther.*, 18, 116, 1992.

90. Weese-Mayer, D. E. and Barkov, G. A., Effect of cocaine in early gestation: Physiologic responses to hypoxia in newborn rabbits, *Am. Rev. Respir. Dis.*, 148, 589, 1993.

91. Olsen, G. D. and Weil, J. A., *In utero* cocaine exposure: Effect on neonatal breathing in guinea pigs, *J. Pharmacol. Exp. Ther.*, 261, 420, 1992.

92. Gingras, J. L., Dalley, L., and Leatherman, N., Prenatal cocaine exposure affects postnatal ventilatory response to chemical stimuli, *Am. J. Respir. Crit. Care Med.*, 151, A635, 1995.

93. Graham, C. J., Rao, R., Sica, A. S., Greenberg, H. E., and Scharf, S. M., Effect of intrauterine cocaine exposure on postnatal ventilatory control, *Am. J. Respir. Crit. Care. Med.*, 151, A635, 1995.

94. Gingras, J. L., Muelenaer, A., Dalley, L. B., and O'Donnell, K. J., Prenatal cocaine exposure alters postnatal hypoxic arousal responses and hypercarbic ventilatory responses but not pneumocardiograms in prenatally cocaine-exposed term infants, *Pediatr. Pulmonol.*, 18, 13, 1994.

Chapter 3

OBSTETRICAL PATHOPHYSIOLOGY OF COCAINE

J. Christopher Glantz, MD, and James R. Woods, Jr., MD

3.0 INTRODUCTION

Throughout its history, cocaine has been used for both licit and illicit purposes. Cocaine was isolated in the 1800s from the leaves of the Erythroxylon coca plant. Freud popularized its medicinal use as a stimulant, and used it himself. Cocaine is now a schedule II drug, and its medical utility in recent years is relegated to topical anesthesia. Its illicit use in the United States has markedly escalated in the past decade and far outstrips its legal use. Up to 60 tons of cocaine, worth $55 billion, are estimated to enter the country each year.[1] Over 20 million people have tried it; over 4 million use it regularly; and thousands try it for the first time every day.[1] Because of its ease of use, low cost, and quick "high," "crack" cocaine has become especially popular in the past decade. Many of these users are in the reproductive age range, and therefore cocaine use during pregnancy has become an obstetrical problem.

3.1 PHARMACOLOGY OF COCAINE

Cocaine, or benzoylmethylecgonine, is an alkaloid of the local anesthetic "caine" group of drugs. Cocaine hydrochloride is a white, water-soluble powder which can be injected, ingested, or absorbed across mucus membranes such as the nasal mucosa, vagina, or rectum. Because it is heat labile, cocaine hydrochloride cannot be smoked. Administration is most commonly through the nasal mucosa, for which bioavailability is 60 to 80%.[2-4] The plasma half-life of cocaine in humans is approximately 60 ± 30 minutes.[3,5] Approximate doses range from 20 mg I.V. to 100 mg nasal, with resultant serum levels between 125 and 475 ng/ml.[1,3,6] Because of tolerance with chronic use, higher doses become necessary to achieve the same euphoric effect.

Cocaine hydrochloride can be put into alkaline solution and extracted, yielding the freebase or "crack." Crack cocaine is colorless, water insoluble, heat-stable to 98°C, and can be smoked to gain rapid access to the blood through the lungs, quickly achieving high concentrations in the brain. Whether used in the form of cocaine or "crack," catabolism proceeds via hydrolysis (spontaneously and through plasma pseudocholinesterases) to benzoylecgonine, ecgonine, and ecgonine methyl ester, and by hepatic N-demethylation to norcocaine (Figure 3.1).[7] Hepatic esterase and nonhepatic cytochrome P-450 play minor roles in cocaine metabolism. Cocaine and its metabolites are excreted in the urine, in which they are detectable for 3 to 7 days, depending on the sensitivity of the assay.[8] To a lesser extent, they are also excreted into the bile. Cocaine is also incorporated into hair; strands of hair can be cut into segments and assayed, giving a chronological diary of chronic cocaine use.[9] Transplacental passage occurs and does not appear to be flow-limited.[10] Placental esterases may metabolize some cocaine, limiting its delivery to the fetus.[11] There is evidence from human placental perfusion studies that placental tissue may retain cocaine, which could either protect the fetus or serve as a depot for prolonged, slow release.[12] The fetus does metabolize cocaine, but the resulting proportions of metabolites are different than in the adult.[13,14] These differences may be due to placental metabolism, ion trapping by acidic fetal blood, differential rates of metabolite transfer across the placenta, or immaturity of fetal enzyme systems.

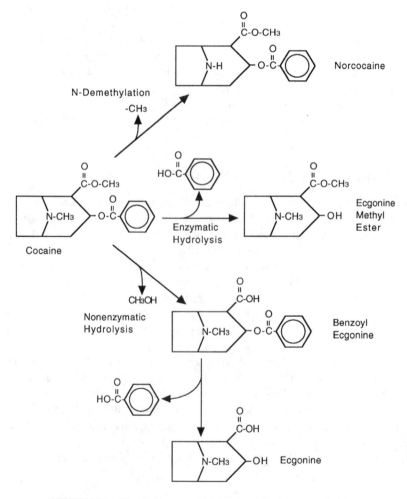

FIGURE 3.1 Chemical structures of cocaine and primary metabolites.

3.1.1 Mechanisms of Action

Cocaine's stimulant actions are due to its ability to block reuptake of catecholamines by the neuronal endplate, thereby prolonging catecholamine effect (Figure 3.2). Heart rate and blood pressure rise due to adrenergic stimulation and vasoconstriction. Increased muscular activity produces heat and may lead to hyperthermia. Cocaine's euphoric effects appear to be due to its ability to prolong dopamine's action on neurons in the medial forebrain bundle projecting from the ventral tegmentum to the striatum, limbic system, and cortex, stimulating pleasure centers in these areas.[15] Dopamine antagonists will reduce this effect. Prolonged use of cocaine can deplete dopamine, resulting in tolerance and dysphoria, necessitating use of higher doses of cocaine to achieve the previous degree of effect.[1]

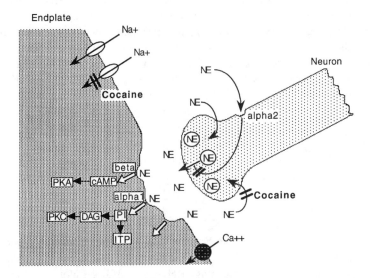

FIGURE 3.2 Cocaine's mechanisms of action. Cocaine inhibits reuptake of norepinephrine into the neuron (right lower) and also blocks the sodium channel (left upper). NE = norepinephrine; circles in neuron = vesicles containing norepinephrine; Na+ = sodium; Ca++ = calcium; ovals on endplate = sodium channels; circles on endplate = calcium channels; beta = beta adrenergic receptor; alpha = alpha adrenergic receptor; cAMP = cyclic adenosine monophosphate; PKA = protein kinase A; PKC = protein kinase C; PI = phosphatidyl inositol; ITP = inositol triphosphate; DAG = diacyl glycerol.

Cocaine also blocks the sodium channel, preventing conduction of impulses through nerves and excitable tissues. In higher doses, this can lead to central nervous system dysfunction or cardiac arrhythmias.

The psychological effects of cocaine are similar to those of amphetamines. Onset of action occurs within minutes of injection or inhalation. This is the "rush"—the euphoria produced by sudden, high concentrations of cocaine in the brain. Nasal administration results in a lesser effect due to slower absorption secondary to mucosal vasoconstriction. Routes of administration of cocaine that result in rapid onset of effect also result in quicker resolution of effect, leading to more frequent use to maintain the euphoria. Mood is intensely elevated, appetite decreased, energy and alertness increased, sexual feelings accentuated, and social inhibitions decreased.[16] Insomnia, anxiety, and irritability may occur. Larger doses or bingeing can cause disinhibition, impaired judgment, impulsivity, and excessive psychomotor activity.[17] When the effect wears off, the user may "crash" and become lethargic, somnolent, and depressed, with persistent dysphoria. Withdrawal may be manifested by anergia, anhedonia, and depression, all of which can last for weeks or months.[17] Bromocriptine or tricyclic antidepressants may help the withdrawal phase,[1] but the craving for cocaine often persists even after the withdrawal symptoms have abated.

3.2 MEDICAL COMPLICATIONS ASSOCIATED WITH COCAINE

Cocaine is associated with numerous medical complications. Anosmia, rhinitis, and nasal septal perforation can occur from vasospasm and ischemic necrosis following nasal administration. Intravenous use with contaminated syringes entails risks of abscesses, septicemia, hepatitis, human immune deficiency virus infection, and endocarditis. Death can occur, even with relatively low serum cocaine levels,[18] from cardiac arrhythmias, hypertension, coronary spasm with myocardial infarction, aortic rupture, convulsions, respiratory arrest, hyperthermia, intracranial hemorrhage, or pulmonary edema.[19] Maternal deaths have occurred from ruptured intracranial aneurysm[20] or massive overdose.[21,22] Cardiomyopathy has been described with cocaine use,[23] as have contraction bands within the myocardium which are thought to result from episodes of ischemic necrosis.[24] Cocaine's toxic effects are due to both central and peripheral actions.[1] Diazepam and sedatives have proved useful in combating toxic cocaine reactions.

3.3 COCAINE USE DURING PREGNANCY

A number of studies have examined the prevalence of cocaine use during pregnancy. Some rely on elicited history, some on antenatal urine screening, and some on neonatal urine or meconium screening. Relying on history alone is notoriously inaccurate, because approximately 50% of positive cocaine screens during pregnancy occur in women who deny cocaine use.[25-29] Although Chasnoff et al. reported similar incidences of illicit drug use among patients receiving prenatal care at public health clinics compared with patients from private offices (15.8% and 11.6%, respectively), the incidence of cocaine use in his study was 5% in the public group and 1.5% in the private group.[30] Three studies utilizing urine cocaine screening of private[30,31] and military[32] pregnant women showed prevalences of 1 to 1.4% and 1.6%, respectively, compared with rates of up to 62% in unregistered populations.[30] Most studies of mixed populations report prevalences between 6.3% and 17% with higher rates in black, single, unemployed, unregistered, and lower socioeconomic class women.[25,27,29,33-39]

Even 10 years ago, it was unclear whether cocaine had important obstetric implications. In 1985, the authors of a small pilot study of 8 infants born to mothers who used cocaine during pregnancy concluded by tentatively stating, "The fact that no evident, potentially life-threatening symptomatology was noted in this group of eight infants lends some initial comfort…" However, even in this preliminary study, 2 infants were small for gestational age, another was born at 33 weeks, 1 had sacral exosotosis, and 2 had capillary hemangiomata.[40] That same year, Chasnoff et al. reported a greater incidence of a history of spontaneous abortion in 23 pregnant women using cocaine when compared with 30 pregnant women not using cocaine.[41] There were four placental abruptions in the cocaine group compared with no placental abruptions in the noncocaine group. In that study there were no differences in neonatal gestational age, birth weight, or head circumference between the groups. Subsequently, numerous studies have repeatedly linked adverse perinatal outcomes with the antenatal use of cocaine.

3.3.1 Selected Obstetrical Complications Associated with Cocaine

Many of the adverse obstetrical outcomes associated with cocaine use are related to the cardiovascular activity of cocaine. The pathophysiology frequently can be explained by a combination of vasoconstriction, hypertension, hypoperfusion, and ischemia. Placental abruption and fetal anomalies are two such outcomes associated with antenatal cocaine abuse.

3.3.1.1   Placental Abruption

Placental abruption is reported to be associated with cocaine use.[42,43] The incidence of abruption is increased in women with hypertension; cocaine elevates blood pressure, providing a potential mechanism for this increased risk. Although a meta-analysis in 1991 did not demonstrate a significant increase in risk of placental abruption associated with the antenatal use of cocaine,[44] a recent review of published reports of adverse obstetrical outcomes associated with cocaine concluded that the incidence of abruption was increased as much as fivefold in pregnant women using antenatal cocaine when compared to pregnant women not exposed to cocaine.[45] However, 5 of 13 reports included in that review did not find significant increases in abruption, and in one study of patients with known cocaine use during pregnancy, a positive screen during labor itself did not increase the risk of abruption when compared with a negative screen.[46] Because of these discrepant findings, the precise magnitude of the abruption risk associated with cocaine use is unclear.

Cocaine use has been associated with placental pathology such as decidual vascular thickening, villous ischemic infarction, and intervillous hemorrhage,[47] although no characteristic abnormalities were noted in another series.[48] While there do not appear to be specific placental abnormalities pathognomonic for cocaine, Chasnoff et al. concluded that cocaine use during early pregnancy may cause uteroplacental vascular changes that may interfere with the normal implantation process and predispose to abruption later in pregnancy, whether or not cocaine has been used at the actual time of abruption.[49]

3.3.1.2   Fetal Anomalies

Fetal anomalies have been associated with prenatal cocaine exposure. Cocaine-related hypoxia, hyperthermia, or vasospasm with hemorrhage and vascular disruption in the fetus have been found to result in atresias and limb reductions in animal models.[50,51] Webster and Brown-Woodman demonstrated a dose-dependent embryopathic effect of cocaine administered to day 16 pregnant rats (Figure 3.3).[50] The effect consisted of hemorrhage and edema in the extremities, leading to necrosis and reduction defects within 48 hours of cocaine administration. When cocaine was administered before day 14, these effects were not seen. The authors proposed that the teratogenic effects were due to uterine artery vasoconstriction, with subsequent fetal hypoxia and ischemia. It is also possible that the effects were due to transplacental passage of cocaine into the fetus, causing severe fetal vascular spasm with resultant local ischemia. In humans, genitourinary,[52] limb reduction,[53,54] cardiovascular,[55,56] and gastrointestinal anomalies[49,54] have been reported. Differences in methodology and in definitions of major and minor anomalies make it difficult to compare studies. For example, in a retrospective case-control study, Chavez found an odds ratio of 4.4 for urinary tract (but not genital) anomalies associated with cocaine use in early pregnancy.[57] However, Rosenstein found only one renal anomaly out of 100 ultrasonographically screened neonates born to cocaine users. Although there was no control group, the authors concluded that routine ultrasound of cocaine-exposed neonates was not indicated because the risk of renal anomalies was not higher than that of the general population (approximately 1%).[58]

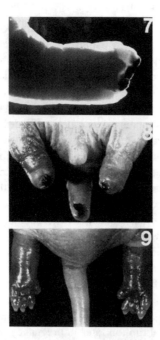

FIGURE 3.3 Top (7): Right hindlimb of a 21-day rat fetus 4 days after maternal administration of 2 doses of 50 mg/kg cocaine. Note distal hemorrhage in digits 2 through 4. Middle (8): Bilateral hindlimbs of a 21-day rat fetus 5 days after maternal administration of 2 doses of 50 mg/kg cocaine. Both hindlimbs lack footplates, and there is eschar on the limbs and tail. Bottom (9): Bilateral hindlimbs of a 21-day rat fetus 7 days after maternal administration of 2 doses of 50 mg/kg cocaine. Note reduction of the 3rd digit of the fetus' left limb. (From Webster W. S., Brown-Woodman, P. D. C., Cocaine as a cause of congenital malformations of vascular origin: Experimental evidence in the rat, *Teratology*, 41, 689, 1990. Copyright © 1990. Reprinted by permission of Wiley-Liss, a subsidiary of John Wiley & Sons.)

Bingol reported three major neonatal skull defects out of 50 pregnancies during which the mother had used cocaine, compared with no defects in a control group.[4] Abnormal intracranial anatomy has been noted in several studies of neonates exposed prenatally to cocaine. Dixon reported a 39% incidence of neonatal CT or MRI abnormalities in infants with antenatal cocaine exposure, most commonly areas of deep hemorrhagic infarction and cystic lesions.[59] Using similar methodology and matching for gestational ages, Heier demonstrated a 17% incidence of cortical infarction in infants exposed to cocaine compared with 2% in the control infants.[60] These lesions presumably represent the direct result of cocaine-induced episodes of vasospasm, hypertension, hemorrhage, or hypoxia. Van de Bor et al. used Doppler to compare intracranial arterial flow velocities of neonates with positive urine cocaine screens with those of neonates with negative screens.[61] The cocaine-positive neonates had increased flow on post-delivery day 1, but not on day 2, consistent with a transient effect of cocaine. It is possible that this increased flow may predispose to hemorrhage in the fragile fetal germinal matrix or other parts of the developing brain.

In summary, the precise risk of fetal anomalies with cocaine is difficult to ascertain with certainty, but is probably increased in the fetus exposed to antenatal cocaine.[62]

Other perinatal complications associated with maternal cocaine abuse include premature rupture of the membranes, preterm labor and delivery, low birth weight, small for gestational age, fetal distress, low Apgar scores, and fetal demise.[45] The common element in these complications is the relation to cocaine's adrenergic and vasoactive effects: vasoconstriction, hypertension, decreased perfusion, and decreased oxygenation.

3.3.2 Maternal-Fetal Response to Catecholamines and Cocaine

3.3.2.1 Adrenergic Mechanisms and Receptors

In addition to its ability to inhibit catecholamine reuptake in the synaptic cleft and to potentiate catecholamine activity, cocaine increases concentrations of circulating epinephrine and norepinephrine as much as twofold.[63,64] In the cardiovascular system, norepinephrine is the predominant catecholamine within the synapse, although cocaine facilitates release of epinephrine and norepinephrine from the adrenal glands as well.[65] In vascular smooth muscle, norepinephrine primarily binds to $alpha_1$ receptors, causing vasoconstriction, increased systemic vascular resistance, hypertension, and decreased perfusion. Presynaptic $alpha_2$ receptor binding of norepinephrine decreases subsequent release of catecholamine from the synaptic terminal, and serves as a negative feedback mechanism to limit the postsynaptic effect of cocaine.[66] In the myocardium, stimulation of $beta_1$ receptors normally causes tachycardia and increased inotropy, via activation of cyclic AMP and protein kinase. Cocaine prolongs the action of synaptic norepinephrine on these adrenergic receptors, and also potentiates the pressor, chronotropic, and inotropic responses to infused norepinephrine by limiting reuptake and delaying its metabolism.[67]

Although the uterus is functionally denervated during pregnancy, alpha adrenergic receptors are present within the vessels and myometrium.[68] Estrogen causes an increase in number of alpha adrenergic receptors in the rabbit uterus, as measured by tritium-labeled dihydroergocryptine binding.[69] Because of the presence of functional alpha$_1$ receptors in the uterine vasculature, infusions of norepinephrine decrease uteroplacental flow by causing vasoconstriction of the uterine arteries, as measured by electromagnetic flow transducers or by injected microspheres in pregnant sheep (Figure 3.4).[70-72] Graded mechanical reductions in uteroplacental blood flow result in proportional increases in fetal hypoxia and acidosis.[73]

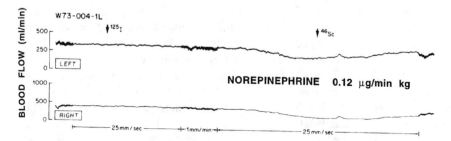

FIGURE 3.4 Continuous flowmeter recording of the right and left uterine arteries in a day-133 ewe carrying a singleton gestation on the left. The times of isotope-labeled microsphere infusion and systemic infusion of 0.12 µg/min/kg norepinephrine are noted. Decreased blood flow is apparent bilaterally after norepinephrine infusion. (From Rosenfeld, C. R., West, J. W., Circulatory response to systemic infusion of norepinephrine in the pregnant ewe, *Am. J. Obstet. Gynecol.*, 127, 376, 1977. With permission.)

3.3.2.2   Influence of Anesthesia and the Central Nervous System

In the intact animal, central nervous system responses to cocaine may influence local effects. Increased or decreased central nervous system outflow determines how much neurotransmitter is actively released from distal nerve terminals, and thus influences cocaine's effect. Conflicting results have been reported in animal studies. Ganglionic blocking agents have been reported in several studies to attenuate the pressor response to intravenous cocaine in conscious dogs and rats.[74-76] These studies are consistent with central nervous system activation by cocaine, leading to increased adrenergic peripheral cardiovascular response.

In a study of 36 male Sprague-Dawley rats, intravenous cocaine caused hypertension in all animals, but decreased cardiac output in 17.[77] In a subset of rats manifesting decreased cardiac output, renal sympathetic nerve activity tended to briefly increase after administration of cocaine, and then decrease. In a subset of rats without change in cardiac output, only a decrease in renal nerve activity was generally noted. Perfused hearts from both groups showed similar responses to cocaine, and there were no differences in resting autonomic tone or cocaine metabolism between the two groups. The authors concluded that differential cardiovascular responsiveness to cocaine is mediated by transient central sympathoexcitation, but the ultimate effect of cocaine is inhibition of sympathetic outflow. The pressor response appeared to be local, and differences could not be attributed to altered cardiac sensitivity to the local effects of cocaine, or to differences in metabolic transformation. It was not clear how sympathoexcitation led to decreased cardiac output in that study.

Other studies have not linked cocaine to central nervous system sympathetic activation. In anesthetized rabbits, renal nerve activity decreased after administration of 1 mg/kg intravenous cocaine,[78] as did cardiac sympathetic nerve activity in anesthetized dogs and in anesthetized, decerebrate cats after administration of intravenous cocaine.[79,80] In contrast to the studies in conscious dogs and rats,[74-76] the ganglionic blocker hexamethonium did not antagonize the pressor and chronotropic effects of intravenous cocaine in conscious monkeys.[81] These latter findings lead to the conclusion that cocaine decreases central nervous system outflow, and that cardiovascular activation by cocaine is due to peripheral actions rather than to those of the central nervous system. Because nerve activity measurements require anesthesia, such measurements may not be representative of the response of the unanesthetized animal, as emphasized by Wilkerson.[75] Differences in anesthesia and species may account for some of the different findings reported in these studies. While the central nervous system may mediate some of cocaine's effects, its precise role remains unclear.

3.3.3 *In Vivo* Cocaine Studies

To investigate the hypothesis that cocaine-related adrenergic vasoconstriction of the uteroplacental vasculature could explain many of the untoward perinatal outcomes associated with antenatal cocaine abuse, studies have been conducted using pregnant ewes prepared with maternal and fetal vascular catheters and maternal electromagnetic flow probes on the uterine arteries. In 1986, Moore et al. reported that bolus intravenous infusions of 0.5 and 1.0 mg/kg cocaine given to pregnant ewes raised maternal mean arterial pressure by 32% and 37%, respectively. Fetal mean arterial pressure rose by 12.6% after 1.0 mg/kg cocaine had been administered to the ewe. Uterine blood flow decreased by 36% and 42%, respectively, for 15 minutes after the two doses (Figure 3.5). In addition, cocaine-induced uterine artery vasoconstriction was not blocked by the infusion of therapeutic doses of phentolamine, an alpha receptor antagonist. The authors concluded that cocaine may have vascular effects at sites other than the alpha receptors.[63] Dolkart et al. reported the inability of phenoxybenzamine (another alpha receptor antagonist) to completely block the reduction in uterine blood flow following maternal cocaine administration, despite phenoxybenzamine's complete eradication of the maternal and fetal systemic hypertensive responses to cocaine.[82] They also concluded that part of cocaine's effect on the uteroplacental vasculature was due to activity outside the alpha adrenergic system.

Prostaglandins have been implicated as potential mediators of cocaine's actions. Certain prostaglandins, such as thromboxane A_2, cause vasoconstriction, while other prostaglandins, such as prostacyclin, cause vasodilatation. In human placental explants, cocaine increased production of thromboxane and decreased the production of prostacyclin in a dose-dependent manner (Figures 3.6 and 3.7).[83] Cocaine decreases the production of prostacyclin metabolites in human umbilical artery strips,[84] and concentrations of prostaglandins $F_{2\alpha}$ and E_2 in the amniotic fluid are increased in women testing positive for cocaine during labor when compared with cocaine-negative laboring women.[85] Cocaine's effect on placental and endothelial

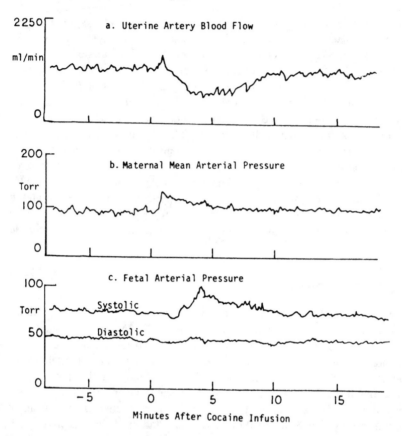

FIGURE 3.5 Maternal and fetal cardiovascular responses to 0.5 mg/kg cocaine infusion in the pregnant ewe. Uterine artery blood flow decreased, while maternal and fetal arterial pressures increased. (From Moore, T. R., Sorg, J., Miller, L., Key, T. C., Resnik, R., Hemodynamic effects of intravenous cocaine on the pregnant ewe and fetus, *Am. J. Obstet. Gynecol.,* 155, 883, 1986. With permission.)

prostaglandin production could explain the inability of alpha receptor antagonists to completely block cocaine's vasoconstrictive effect.

Dopamine also causes uterine artery vasoconstriction and reduced blood flow in gravid baboons,[86] but its relation to cocaine has not been studied during pregnancy. Dopamine receptor antagonists have been reported to attenuate the effect of cocaine on plasma catecholamine concentrations in conscious rats, but did not affect pressor and chronotropic responses to cocaine.[74] It is uncertain whether dopaminergic mechanisms play a role in the obstetrical pathophysiology of cocaine.

In pregnant baboons prepared with catheters and flow probes similar to those used in sheep, Morgan et al. administered maternal boluses of 0.1 mg/kg and 0.3 mg/kg intravenous cocaine.[87] They noted maternal mean arterial pressure increases of 7.3% and 12%, respectively, and uterine blood flow decreases of 13.1% and 22.7%, respectively. The primate cardiovascular response pattern to cocaine appears to be similar to that noted in sheep, although the baboon appears to be more sensitive to cocaine than is the sheep.

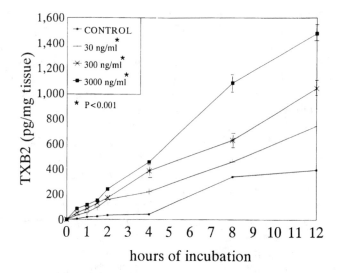

FIGURE 3.6 *In vitro* effect of cocaine on human placental thromboxane A2 production, measured as a stable metabolite thromboxane B2 (pg/mg tissue). Data shown are mean ± SE (SE not shown if <10). At each time point, each concentration of thromboxane B2 was significantly different at each concentration of cocaine and from control. (From Monga, M., Chmielowiec, S., Andres, R. L., Troyer, L. R., Parisi, V. M., Cocaine alters placental production of thromboxane and prostacyclin, *Am. J. Obstet. Gynecol.,* 171, 965, 1994. With permission.)

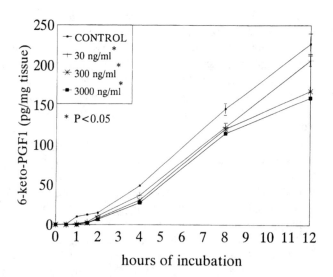

FIGURE 3.7 *In vitro* effect of cocaine on human placental PGI2 production, measured as a stable metabolite 6-keto-PGF1α (pg/mg tissue). Data shown are mean ± SE (SE not shown if <5). At each time point, each concentration of 6-keto-PGF1α was significantly different from control at each concentration of cocaine. (From Monga, M., Chmielowiec, S., Andres, R. L., Troyer, L. R., Parisi, V. M., Cocaine alters placental production of thromboxane and prostacyclin, *Am. J. Obstet. Gynecol.* 171, 965, 1994. With permission.)

Using the catheterized pregnant sheep model in 1987, Woods et al. reported that maternal intravenous bolus infusions of 0.5, 1.0, and 2.0 mg/kg cocaine raised mean uterine vascular resistance by 52%, 96%, and 168%, while decreasing uterine blood flow 24%, 34%, and 47%.[88] Maternal mean arterial blood pressure rose during the bolus infusions (Figure 3.8), but maternal blood gas values were unchanged. The fetal responses to the 1.0 and 2.0 mg/kg maternal cocaine boluses were tachycardia, elevated mean arterial pressure, and a decrease in P_{O2} (Figures 3.9 and 3.10). There were no significant changes in fetal P_{CO2} or pH.

The fetal responses to maternal cocaine could be due to several mechanisms. Decreased uteroplacental perfusion could produce fetal hypoxemia, leading to reflex release of catecholamines from the fetal chromaffin tissue. This hypoxemia-catecholamine response has been observed in fetal sheep.[89] The fetus responds to adrenergic stimulation; Padbury et al. infused epinephrine and norepinephrine into catheterized fetal sheep and demonstrated increased systolic and diastolic blood pressures.[90] Cocaine crosses the placenta to achieve fetal concentrations equal to maternal cocaine concentrations at 1 to 2 minutes, declining to 12% to 14% of maternal concentrations at 5 minutes (Figure 3.11).[10,63] Transplacental cocaine could also potentiate fetal adrenergic activity directly by inhibition of catecholamine reuptake. In the study of Woods et al.,[88] when the fetus was exposed to cocaine directly through the fetal catheter (0.5, 1.0, or 2.0 mg/kg estimated fetal weight), there were no significant changes in fetal blood gas values. Fetal mean arterial pressure immediately rose, and there was a delayed rise in fetal heart rate (Figure 3.12). There were no significant maternal effects from direct fetal cocaine administration.

To explain these findings, Chan et al. catheterized fetal sheep and then administered 0.5 mg/kg and 1.0 mg/kg boluses of intravenous cocaine directly to the fetuses.[91] Fetal plasma norepinephrine concentrations rose rapidly, simultaneous with an increase in systolic blood pressure (Figure 3.13). No significant changes in P_{O2}, and pH were observed. Epinephrine levels increased more slowly than norepinephrine and were accompanied by a slight increase in fetal heart rate that was not statistically significant. These findings were similar to those of Woods et al.: direct administration of cocaine to the fetus caused immediate hypertension, delayed tachycardia, but not hypoxia. These findings indicate that, following maternal exposure to cocaine, fetal hypoxemia is secondary to decreased uterine perfusion rather than to a direct effect on the fetal cardiovasculature.

Following maternal exposure to cocaine, the fetal cardiovascular response appears to be secondary to a combination of hypoxemia plus the fetal adrenergic effects of transplacental cocaine. Skillman et al. progressively clamped uterine arteries in pregnant ewes and measured fetal P_{O2}.[73] Mechanical reductions in uterine flow of 24%, 49%, and 63% resulted in decreases in fetal P_{O2} of -2.4 mm Hg, -7.9 mm Hg, and -8.2 mm Hg, respectively. Mean fetal arterial pressure rose slightly in the latter two groups with uterine flow reductions of 49% and 63%. In the study by Woods et al.,[88] the 47% reduction in uterine blood flow observed with 2.0 mg/kg intravenous cocaine resulted in a similar decline in fetal P_{O2} to that observed after a 49% mechanical reduction of uterine artery flow in Skillman et al.'s study.[73]

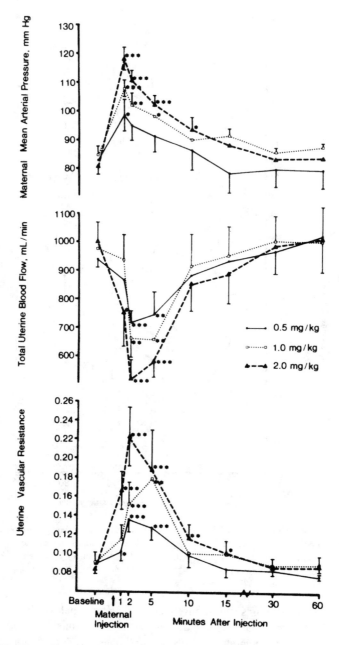

FIGURE 3.8 Maternal mean arterial pressure (top), total uterine blood flow (middle), and uterine vascular resistance (bottom) following maternal administration of cocaine to the ewe. For significant changes from preinjection baseline, single asterisks indicate p<0.05, double asterisks p<0.01, and triple asterisks p<0.001. (From Woods, J. R., Plessinger, M. A., Clark, K. E., Effect of cocaine on uterine blood flow and fetal oxygenation, *JAMA*, 257, 957, 1987. Copyright © 1987, American Medical Association. With permission.)

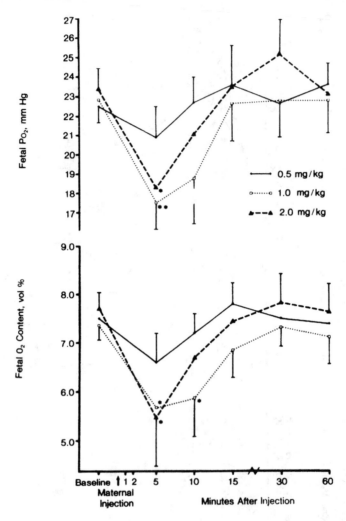

FIGURE 3.9   Fetal oxygen pressure (PO$_2$) (top) and oxygen (O$_2$) content (bottom) following maternal administration of cocaine to the ewe. For significant changes from preinjection baseline, single asterisks indicate p<0.05, and double asterisks p<0.01. (From Woods, J. R., Plessinger, M. A., Clark, K. E., Effect of cocaine on uterine blood flow and fetal oxygenation. *JAMA*, 257, 957, 1987. Copyright © 1987, American Medical Association. With permission.)

However, the fetal hypertensive response secondary to maternal cocaine was approximately twofold greater than that noted after mechanical reduction in uterine blood flow, even though both methods produced approximately 50% reductions in uterine blood flow. Cocaine induces maternal uterine artery vasoconstriction, which leads to fetal hypoxemia and hypertension. But cocaine exerts an additive direct effect on the fetus via transplacental passage to release fetal catecholamines or to block reuptake of released catecholamines, thereby potentiating their actions. Generally, fetal hypoxemia produces hypertension and reflex bradycardia. Fetal tachycardia

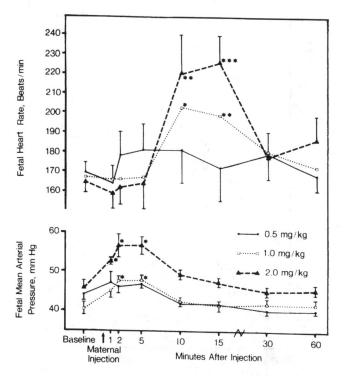

FIGURE 3.10 Fetal heart rate (top) and mean arterial pressure (bottom) following maternal administration of cocaine to the ewe. For significant changes from preinjection baseline, single asterisks indicate p<0.05, double asterisks p<0.01, and triple asterisks p<0.001. (From Woods, J. R., Plessinger, M. A., Clark, K. E., Effect of cocaine on uterine blood flow and fetal oxygenation, *JAMA*, 257, 957, 1987. Copyright © 1987, American Medical Association. With permission.)

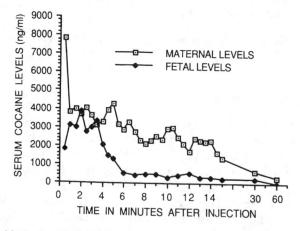

FIGURE 3.11 Maternal and fetal serum cocaine levels obtained every 30 to 60 seconds for 15 minutes and then at 30 and 60 minutes following IV injection of 2.0 mg/kg cocaine to the ewe. (Reprinted with permission from Woods, J. R., Plessinger, M. A., Scott, K., Miller, R. K., Prenatal cocaine exposure to the fetus: A sheep model for cardiovascular evaluation, *Ann. NY Acad. Sci.*, 562, 267, 1989.)

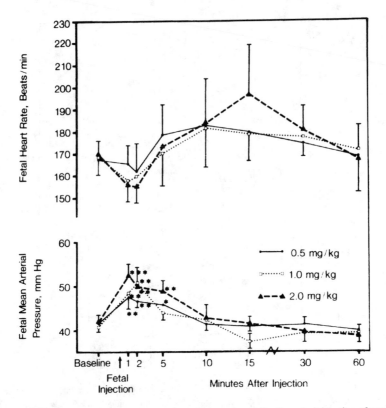

FIGURE 3.12 Fetal heart rate (top) and mean arterial pressure following administration of cocaine to the sheep fetus. For significant changes from preinjection baseline, single asterisks indicate p<0.05, double asterisks p<0.01, and triple asterisks p<0.001. (From Woods, J. R., Plessinger, M. A., Clark, K. E., Effect of cocaine on uterine blood flow and fetal oxygenation. *JAMA*, 257, 957, 1987. Copyright © 1987, American Medical Association. With permission.)

and disproportionate pressor responses following maternal cocaine administration provide clear evidence of cocaine's direct actions in the fetal circulation.

3.3.4 Amniotic Fluid and Cocaine

The amniotic fluid may serve as a reservoir for cocaine and its metabolites, prolonging their biologic activities in the fetus past that expected on the basis of serum half-lives. Cocaine and benzoylecgonine have been detected in human amniotic fluid following maternal cocaine use.[92,93] In pregnant guinea pigs receiving daily subcutaneous cocaine from days 50 through 59, amniotic fluid cocaine concentrations at the end of the exposure period were 3 to 4 times higher than fetal plasma cocaine concentrations.[14] In addition, the *in vitro* half-life of cocaine in amniotic fluid was 30 times longer than the *in vivo* plasma half-life. This raises the possibility that the fetus may either ingest cocaine by swallowing amniotic fluid, or absorb cocaine through the skin or mucosa in contact with the amniotic fluid.

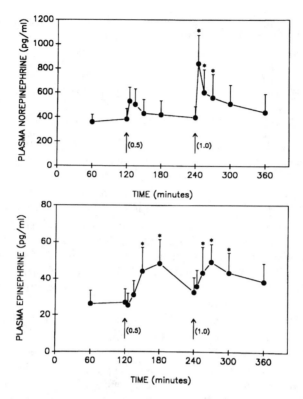

FIGURE 3.13 Fetal sheep plasma norepinephrine (upper panel) and epinephrine (lower panel) levels before and after intravenous cocaine infusions (0.5 and 1.0 mg/kg). Asterisk indicates $p<0.05$ from baseline. (From Chan, K., Dodd, A., Day, L., et al., Fetal catecholamine, cardiovascular, and neurobehavioral responses to cocaine, *Am. J. Obstet. Gynecol.*, 167, 1616, 1992. With permission.)

To determine whether amniotic fluid cocaine can enter the fetus, pregnant sheep and their fetuses were catheterized and osmotic pumps loaded with cocaine were placed in the amniotic sac.[94] Esophageal ligation was performed on a subset of fetal sheep. Samples of fluid and plasma were taken over 7 days and assayed for cocaine and metabolites. In the amniotic fluid, concentrations of ecgonine methyl ester were highest, followed by cocaine and benzoylecgonine. In the fetuses, cocaine, norcocaine, and benzoylecgonine concentrations were all approximately 3% those of the amniotic fluid, regardless of whether or not esophageal ligation had been performed. Norcocaine was detectable in fetal meconium. Cocaine concentrations in the amniotic fluid were approximately 40% of those measured in plasma from pregnant sheep 5 minutes after receiving a 1 mg/kg bolus intravenous infusion of cocaine in a prior study.[10] The cocaine concentrations in fetal plasma from absorption of amniotic fluid cocaine were approximately 8% of those measured in fetal blood 5 minutes after intravenous bolus maternal administration of 1 mg/kg cocaine. The authors concluded that there is passage of cocaine and metabolites from the amniotic fluid into the fetus, but that fetal swallowing is not required for such to occur. Cocaine may pass transcutaneously into the fetus from the amniotic fluid, especially in early pregnancy before cutaneous keratinization has occurred. Fetal cocaine concentrations achieved in that experimental setting were lower than those following acute maternal intravenous administration, but were still significant.

3.4 HORMONAL MODULATION OF COCAINE EFFECT

3.4.1 Cocaine Metabolism During Pregnancy

Cocaine is metabolized by a combination of hydrolysis and, to a lesser extent, N-demethylation. Hydrolysis occurs either spontaneously or through the action of plasma esterases, and demethylation through the action of hepatic cytochrome P-450. In rat liver cell cultures, hepatic demethylation accounts for approximately 20% of cocaine's metabolism.[95] Hepatic cytochrome P-450 concentrations have been reported to decline by 25% during pregnancy in the rat,[96] and tissue concentrations of norcocaine in the pregnant rat range between 0.5% to 20% that of cocaine.[97] In human males, conversion of cocaine to norcocaine is less than in rats, between 2.6% to 6.2%.[98] This difference may be due to low levels of plasma esterases in rats when compared with plasma esterases in humans, leading to greater demethylation in the rat and greater hydrolysis in humans.[95]

Plasma cholinesterase activity is decreased during human pregnancy when compared to the nonpregnant state[99,100] and so cocaine might be expected to be more slowly metabolized during pregnancy. Unfortunately, supportive experimental evidence is lacking, and there is great variation among species in which the effects of pregnancy have been studied. Also, results obtained using *in vitro* plasma may indicate slower cocaine metabolic rates than those observed *in vivo*, possibly reflecting tissue metabolism and redistribution in the whole animal. Comparison of reports using *in vitro* methods with those using whole animals must be made with caution.[101]

In experiments with sheep, serum cocaine concentrations five minutes after 1 and 2 mg/kg bolus infusions of cocaine were higher in pregnant than in nonpregnant sheep.[102] The authors postulated that possible differences in cocaine metabolism might account for this difference. In Sprague-Dawley female rats given continuous intravenous cocaine infusions, convulsions, hypotension, and death occurred at lower total doses in pregnant rats when compared with nonpregnant rats.[103] However, serum cocaine levels at the moment those events occurred were not different between groups. The authors concluded that pregnancy enhances the systemic toxicity of cocaine, as lower total doses were required to achieve toxic plasma concentrations. The same group reported somewhat different results in a second study, in which cocaine concentrations in pregnant rats were actually lower at the time of convulsions and circulatory collapse than those of nonpregnant rats.[104] Unlike humans, pregnant rats in that study had higher cholinesterase levels than nonpregnant rats, so the significance of these findings for our understanding of human pregnancy is unclear. In a study by Kambam et al. using male Sprague-Dawley rats, administration of a pseudocholinesterase inhibitor (to impair hydrolysis) prior to an intraperitoneal dose of cocaine actually *reduced* the incidence of cardiorespiratory toxicity.[105] Intraperitoneal or intravenous administration of cocaine results in rapid achievement of high cocaine concentrations. Under these circumstances, cholinesterase may not have time to act before toxic cocaine levels are achieved, but this does not explain a protective effect of a cholinesterase inhibitor. Significant differences among species that make comparisons and generalizations regarding cocaine metabolism during pregnancy tenuous.

A theoretical explanation for the results of Kambam et al. would be that esterase converts cocaine to a metabolite that has greater toxicity in the rat than cocaine itself. Benzoylecgonine, ecgonine methyl ester, ecgonine, norcocaine, and cocaethylene are all cocaine metabolites with cardiovascular activity. Benzoylecgonine, ecgonine methyl ester, and ecgonine are products of hydrolysis (benzoylecgonine via nonenzymatic hydrolysis, and the latter two primarily via plasma esterase[106]), and have longer half-lives than cocaine (approximately 1 hour for cocaine, and 4 to 6 hours for the metabolites).[107] However, the cardiovascular effects of these metabolites are variable and not necessarily greater than the effects of cocaine itself. Norcocaine's ability to inhibit ^{3}H-norepinephrine by synaptosomes is comparable to cocaine's, whereas this ability is less for benzoylecgonine and ecgonine.[108] In rats, norcocaine infusions of 4.5 mg/kg resulted in patterns of tachypnea and convulsions similar to those observed after the same dose of cocaine.[109] Porcine esterase inhibition with tetraisopropyl pyrophosphamide decreased plasma ecgonine methyl ester concentrations while elevating concentrations of benzoylecgonine.[110] Benzoylecgonine causes hypertension in pregnant sheep, fetal lambs, and in rats, but does not alter ovine uterine artery blood flow or fetal P_{O2}.[77,111] Benzoylecgonine and ecgonine are more potent than cocaine in constricting isolated adult cat cerebral arteries,[112] but less potent *in vivo* in cerebral arterioles of anesthetized neonatal piglets.[113] In this latter study, norcocaine's ability to potentiate norepinephrine and constrict piglet cerebral arterioles was similar to cocaine's, but benzoylecgonine's and ecgonine's abilities to potentiate norepinephrine were much less than cocaine's. In another study, intraventricular administration of norcocaine to catheterized, conscious Wistar-Kyoto rats did not alter blood pressure, whereas intraventricular administration of cocaine produced a pressor response.[114] Central administration of cocaine or norcocaine to anesthetized rats resulted in hypotension in that same study. Although cocaine's primary metabolites all possess adrenergic and vasoactive properties, differences in species, preparations, routes of administration, and anesthetics limit the generalizability of these studies.

Cocaine is highly protein bound in the human,[2,115] although possibly less so in other species.[14] Protein binding is often reduced during pregnancy, and this could result in elevated free cocaine concentrations with increased bioactivity. This effect has been variable with other drugs in the "caine" family of local anesthetics. Bupivacaine is 73% bound to protein in nonpregnant sheep but only 51% protein bound in pregnant sheep,[116] and a constant infusion of bupivacaine at 0.5 mg/kg/minute caused cardiovascular collapse at a lower mean dose and lower total serum concentration in pregnant sheep when compared with nonpregnant sheep.[117] However, mepivacaine and lidocaine do not appear to have increased cardiovascular toxicity during pregnancy, so not all local anesthetics are equally affected by the changes occurring during pregnancy.[118]

Pregnancy is not thought to be associated with altered adrenergic sensitivity in most studies, although the data are not entirely consistent. Systemic responses to infusions of norepinephrine were similar in pregnant and nonpregnant women in a study by Chesley et al.,[119] and *in vitro* alpha adrenergic reactivity to norepinephrine does not differ in systemic vessels from pregnant and nonpregnant ewes.[120] In a study by Barton et al., in which electromagnetic flow probes were used to measure uterine artery blood flow in pregnant and nonpregnant sheep, responses to infused epinephrine and norepinephrine were similar.[121] In contrast, McLaughlin et al. studied sheep responses to sequential infusions of methoxamine, phenylephrine, and norepinephrine.[122] Pregnancy was associated with decreased norepinephrine sensitivity, increased phenylephrine sensitivity, and no change in methoxamine sensitivity. The different responses may have been due to differences in reuptake properties among the three agonists, rather than due to differences in adrenergic receptor sensitivity.

In a small series of pregnant sheep, Woods et al. noted fatal complications in 3 of 5 sheep receiving a 3 mg/kg intravenous cocaine bolus.[10] The complications included placental abruption, pulmonary artery rupture, and cardiac arrhythmias. Similar cardiovascular complications had been noted in nonpregnant sheep, but with higher cocaine doses of 10 to 15 mg/kg. Woods and Plessinger then monitored the responses of pregnant and nonpregnant ewes to intravenous bolus infusions of 1 to 2 mg/kg cocaine.[123] In the first 5 minutes following injection, mean arterial pressure in the pregnant ewes increased 29.6% and 48.7%, respectively, compared to respective increases of 15.6% and 27.7% in nonpregnant ewes. In a subsequent study, cocaine infusion increased systemic vascular resistance to a greater degree in pregnant sheep than in nonpregnant sheep.[102] Morishima et al. infused cocaine into catheterized pregnant and nonpregnant rats, and measured serum concentrations of cocaine.[124] Cocaine concentrations resulting in comparable changes in heart rate and cardiac output between the two groups were lower in pregnant rats. Pregnancy appears to augment the cardiovascular response to cocaine.

3.4.2 Progesterone and Cocaine

Progesterone concentrations are high during pregnancy and have been reported to augment toxicity of certain local anesthetics. When rabbit vagus nerve, Purkinje fibers, and right ventricular muscle were studied *in vitro*, nerve conduction was depressed by bupivacaine to a greater extent after pretreatment with progesterone when compared with untreated animals.[125-127] This is consistent with a local effect of progesterone, in that the nature of the *in vitro* experiments eliminated serum metabolism, protein binding, and blood pH changes as variables. However, progesterone pretreatments did not alter the response to lidocaine. Whether the effect of pregnancy and progesterone on cocaine is analogous to bupivacaine, or whether it is like lidocaine and mepivacaine, was not addressed in these reports.

Progesterone receptors have been localized to aortic media smooth muscle in the baboon, and to a lesser extent in myocardial and interstitial cells.[128] Administration of estrogen increases the progesterone receptor content in these tissues.[129] In humans, progesterone receptors have been identified in aortic smooth muscle and myocardium, but not in vessels of the uterus, breast, kidney, or gastrointestinal tract.[130] To determine whether the rise in progesterone might explain cocaine's increased toxicity during pregnancy, Plessinger and Woods catheterized oophorectomized nonpregnant sheep and administered intramuscular progesterone at a dose of 10 mg/kg/day for 3 days.[131] During these 3 days, adrenergic receptor sensitivity was monitored using daily challenges with intravenous norepinephrine. Additionally, daily bolus infusions of 1 mg/kg and 2 mg/kg cocaine were administered. Progesterone treatment did not modify alpha adrenergic receptor sensitivity as measured by cardiovascular response to norepinephrine. In contrast, the hypertensive and chronotropic responses to cocaine increased twofold and threefold, respectively, when compared to responses observed before the initial dose of progesterone had been administered (Figure 3.14). Increased cardiovascular toxicity associated with pregnancy appears to be due to an effect of progesterone on the action of cocaine, but does not involve a change in alpha adrenergic receptor sensitivity.

Sharma et al. studied the responses to cocaine of *in vitro* posterior papillary muscles from pregnant, nonpregnant, and nonpregnant/progesterone-treated rats.[132] Muscles from pregnant and progesterone-treated rats manifested a decreased positive inotropic response to increasing cocaine concentrations when compared to muscles from nonpregnant control rats, and cessation of muscle function in the muscles from pregnant and progesterone-treated rats occurred at cocaine concentrations 10- to 100-fold lower than those required for cessation of function in the control muscles. In muscles from rats receiving concurrent treatments with both progesterone and RU-486 (a progesterone receptor antagonist), positive and subsequent negative inotropic effects with increasing cocaine doses were similar to controls.[133] These results are consistent with increased cocaine cardiotoxicity from progesterone, but could not be confirmed in another study, nor could a mechanism be determined from these reported effects.[134] Estrogen has also been reported to mediate pregnancy-enhanced cardiotoxicity of cocaine, in isolated perfused rat hearts.[135] In those experiments, progesterone did not alter the response to cocaine. Whichever hormone is responsible, this increased toxicity does not result in a decrease in the LD50 in pregnant or progesterone-treated nonpregnant rats receiving intraperitoneal boluses of cocaine, when compared with nonpregnant rats. The clinical significance of these findings remains uncertain.[136]

In summary, there is evidence in the sheep and rat that cocaine's cardiotoxic effects are increased during pregnancy. This increase appears to be primarily due to increased progesterone concentrations, but estrogen may also have a role. The biochemical mechanism for this effect is unknown, and the clinical significance in humans is uncertain.

3.5 COCAINE'S EFFECT ON THE MATERNAL MYOMETRIUM

3.5.1 Myometrial Adrenergic Response

Sympathetic denervation of the uterus normally occurs during pregnancy. Investigators using electron microscopy have shown that nerve varicosities are rarely observed in term human myometrium, in contrast to their presence in myometrium from nonpregnant humans.[68] Indirect immunofluorescence revealed a paucity of fibers in myometrial strips obtained from pregnant uteri when compared with strips from nonpregnant uteri.[137] Despite denervation, the pregnant uterus does retain alpha and beta adrenergic receptors.[138,139] Beta$_2$ receptors predominate over beta$_1$. Stimulation of beta receptors in the myometrium activates adenyl cylase, raising

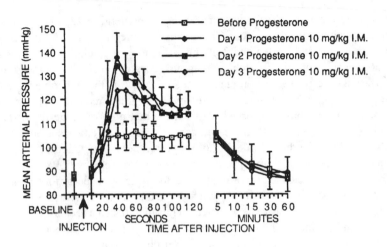

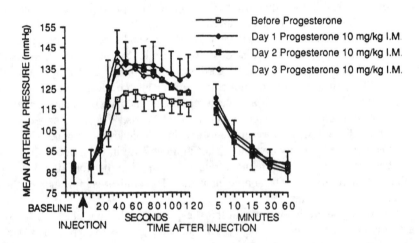

FIGURE 3.14 Responses of oophorectomized sheep mean arterial pressure to intravenous bolus injections of 1.0 mg/kg (top) and 2.0 mg/kg (bottom) cocaine, before and after 1, 2, and 3 days of 10 mg/kg intramuscular progesterone treatments. Values are means ± SEM. The maximum increase in mean arterial pressure after injection of cocaine was significantly above baseline in every case shown (p<0.05). With the exception of the 2-day progesterone treatment group receiving 2.0 mg/kg cocaine, sheep treated with progesterone had significantly higher maximal mean arterial pressure responses to cocaine than did sheep not treated with progesterone (p<0.05). (From Plessinger, M. A., Woods, J. R., Progesterone increases cardiovascular toxicity to cocaine in nonpregnant ewes, *Am. J. Obstet. Gynecol.*, 163,1659, 1990. With permission.)

intracellular levels of cyclic AMP. Cyclic AMP then activates a protein kinase that phosphorylates myosin light-chain kinase, decreasing its ability to phosphorylate and activate myosin. Unphosphorylated myosin does not bind ATP, and the muscle fiber cannot contract.[138] Epinephrine, a predominantly beta agonist, decreases uterine activity when infused into pregnant women.[140] Synthetic beta adrenergic agonists have been used to inhibit uterine contractions during preterm labor.

There are both alpha$_1$ and alpha$_2$ receptors in a 3-to-2 ratio in the human pregnant uterus.[139] Myometrial alpha$_2$ receptors are not involved in negative feedback pathways, as they are in neurons. Instead, both types of alpha receptors mediate contractility in human myometrium. Both types of receptors appear to function through depression of intracellular cyclic AMP concentrations—possibly through an effect on phosphodiesterase—but alpha$_2$ effects predominate.[139] It is not clear whether phospholipase C, phosphatidyl inositol, and inositol triphosphate play a role in mediating alpha receptor activity in the myometrium as they do in some other cells.[141] Norepinephrine, a predominantly alpha agonist, increases uterine activity (albeit incoordinate) when infused into pregnant women.[140] Norepinephrine increases prostaglandin $F_{2\alpha}$ and E_2 production by human myometrial strips, whereas epinephrine decreases their production while augmenting the prostacyclin metabolite 6-keto-prostaglandin $F_{1\alpha}$.[142] Because prostaglandins cause myometrial contractions, adrenergic-mediated prostaglandin production may help explain the effects of alpha and beta stimulation upon myometrial contractility.

In rats, estrogen increases the number of myometrial alpha receptors and results in a predominance of alpha over beta receptors. When progesterone treatments follow the estrogen treatments, beta receptor response increases above that of alpha response, even though progesterone treatment does not increase the beta receptor concentration above that following estrogen alone.[69] Progesterone appeared to augment beta receptor sensitivity. In rabbits, Riemer et al. and Roberts et al. reported that estrogen treatment increased the number of alpha$_2$ receptors to a greater degree than alpha$_1$.[69,143] Despite this, adrenergic sensitivity increased only to alpha$_1$ stimulation, and this increased sensitivity persisted after the receptor number had normalized. Contractile responses appear to be mediated by increased sensitivity of alpha$_1$ receptors, rather than by increases in receptor numbers.[143] Hoffman et al. also used rabbit myometrium and reported that estrogen increased the numbers of alpha$_2$ but not alpha$_1$ receptors.[144] Contractile responses were mediated by alpha$_1$ but not alpha$_2$ receptor stimulation. In contrast to Roberts, estrogen did not increase alpha$_1$ sensitivity; the reasons for the differences are unclear.

3.5.2 Myometrial Response to Cocaine

Preterm labor is common in pregnant women who use cocaine.[45] The myometrium is sensitive to adrenergic stimulation, and because cocaine prolongs the stimulatory effect of catecholamines on adrenergic receptors, cocaine's relation to uterine contractility has been studied. Daniel and Wolowyk reported that cocaine caused myometrial contractures *in vitro* in rabbits, but that alpha adrenergic antagonists did not block the effect.[145] Intravenous bolus administration of cocaine increases myometrial activity in the gravid baboon,[146] but not in pregnant ewes.[147] In a study by Monga et al. using *in vitro* human term myometrial strips, cocaine augmented myometrial contractility (Figure 3.15).[148] The same group reported similar results using myometrium from Sprague-Dawley rats, and found that adrenergic blockade did not completely inhibit this effect (Figure 3.16).[149] Cocaine may have a direct effect on myometrial contractility that is not associated with adrenergic receptors.

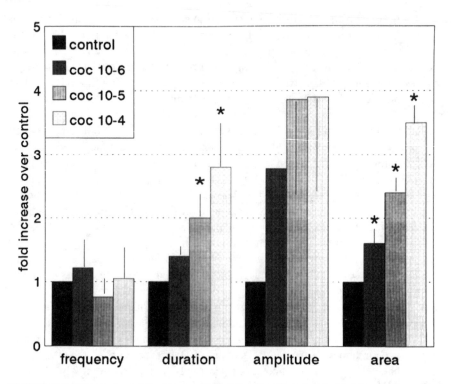

FIGURE 3.15 Effect of cocaine on contractile activity of myometrium isolated from term pregnant women at cesarean section. Data shown as mean ± SE relative to control. Asterisk p<0.001. (From Monga, M., Weisbrodt, N. W., Andres, R. L., Sanborn, B. M., The acute effect of cocaine exposure on pregnant human myometrial contractile activity, *Am. J. Obstet. Gynecol.*, 169, 782, 1993. With permission.)

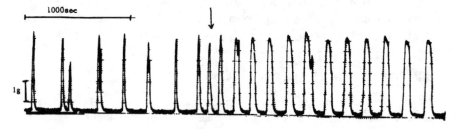

FIGURE 3.16 Effect of 10^{-5} molar cocaine on spontaneous contractile activity of myometrium isolated from a virgin Sprague-Dawley rat. Arrow indicates addition of cocaine. (From Monga, M., Weisbrodt, N. W., Andres, R. L., Sanborn, B. M., Cocaine acutely increases rat myometrial contractile activity by mechanisms other than potentiation of adrenergic pathways, *Am. J. Obstet. Gynecol.*, 169, 1502, 1993. With permission.)

Hurd et al. reported that cocaine alone had no effect on contractility in myometrial strips from rabbits, but when administered concurrently with epinephrine, cocaine increased epinephrine sensitivity by 51% and the maximal response by 33% (Figure 3.17).[150] DL-propranolol increased the epinephrine response by focusing adrenergic stimulation onto alpha receptors, but blocked cocaine's effect. D-propranolol alone (a stereoisomer lacking beta adrenergic antagonist activity, but retaining propranolol's membrane-stabilizing properties) did not affect the epinephrine response but still blocked cocaine's effect. The authors concluded that cocaine augments the alpha adrenergic contractile response by a mechanism that is blocked by the non-beta-adrenergic effects of propranolol, possibly at the level of the cell membrane itself.

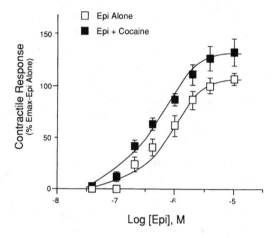

FIGURE 3.17 Concentration-response curve for uterine strips (from day-27 pregnant rabbits) exposed to epinephrine with and without 30 micromolar cocaine. Data expressed as percentage of maximal response to epinephrine alone (mean ± SE). (From Hurd, W. W., Robertson, P. A., Riemer, R. K., Goldfien, A., Roberts, J. M., Cocaine directly augments the alpha-adrenergic contractile response of the pregnant rabbit uterus, *Am. J. Obstet. Gynecol.* 164, 182, 1991. With permission.)

Analogous to catecholamine uptake by nerve terminals, human myometrium takes up catecholamine, and this extraneuronal reuptake is partially blocked by cocaine in a manner similar to that in the synapse.[151] Hurd et al. reported that cocaine, but not benzoylecgonine, decreases beta receptor binding in human term myometrium without affecting alpha receptor binding.[152] Although this could explain the contractile response to cocaine as mediated by preferential stimulation of alpha receptors, high *in vitro* concentrations of cocaine were used in that study, and the clinical relevance is uncertain.

As is frequently the case, variation among animal species makes interpretation of data derived from different animal experiments difficult to extrapolate to humans. Preterm labor and delivery is common in pregnant women who use cocaine. Although the data from animal experiments are not completely consistent, they indicate that cocaine potentiates catecholamine effects by prolonging alpha adrenergic receptor stimulation, decreasing beta adrenergic receptor binding, and inhibiting extraneuronal catecholamine uptake, all of which increase myometrial contractility. Cocaine also increases contractility by direct or nonadrenergic mechanisms, possibly mediated by prostaglandins. The increased incidence of preterm labor and delivery in cocaine users is both plausible and consistent with several known mechanisms of action of cocaine.

3.6 SUMMARY

Cocaine is associated with many adverse obstetrical outcomes, most of which can be related to cocaine's adrenergic effects on the cardiovasculature, myometrium, and the fetus. Maternal hypertension may predispose to placental abruption, cardiac arrhythmias and ischemia, or intracranial hemorrhage. Maternal vasospasm and decreased uteroplacental perfusion may lead to fetal hypoxia, growth disturbances, anomalies, distress, or death (Figure 3.18). The amniotic fluid serves as a reservoir for cocaine and its metabolites, prolonging fetal exposure and possibly increasing fetal risks. Alpha adrenergic stimulation of the myometrium increases the risk of preterm labor and delivery, and there may be direct effects of cocaine on the myometrium as well. Hormonal changes that occur during pregnancy, particularly involving progesterone, may further augment cocaine's toxic effects.

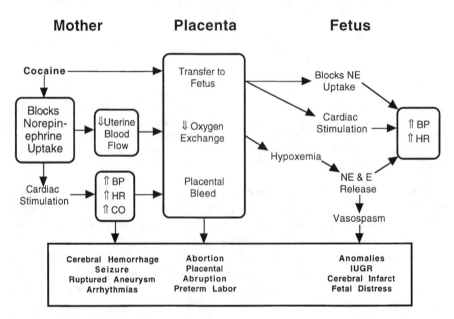

FIGURE 3.18 Maternal, placental, and fetal actions of cocaine, with potential consequences. NE = norepinephrine, E = epinephrine, BP = blood pressure, HR = heart rate, CO = cardiac output, IUGR = intrauterine growth restriction. (From Plessinger, M. A., Woods, J. R., The cardiovascular effects of cocaine use in pregnancy, *Repro. Toxicol.*, 5, 99, 1991. With kind permission from Elsevier Science Ltd., The Boulevard, Langford Lane, Kidlington 0X5 1 GB, UK.)

REFERENCES

1. Gold, M. S. and Giannini, A. J., Cocaine and cocaine addiction, in *Drugs of Abuse*, Giannini, A. J., Slaby, A. E., Eds. Medical Economics Books, Oradell, 1989, 83.
2. Gilman, A., Rall, T., Nies, A., and Taylor, P. The Pharmacologic Basis of Therapeutics. (8th ed.), Pergamon Press, New York, 1990, 1672.

3. Jeffcoat, R. A., Perez-Reyes, M., Hill, J. M., Sadler, B. M., and Cook, C. E., Cocaine dispostition in humans after intravenous injection, nasal insufflation (snorting), or smoking, *Drug Metab. Disp.*, 17(2), 153, 1989.

4. Bingol, N., Fuchs, M., Diaz, V., Stone, R. K., and Gromisch, D. S., Teratogenicity of cocaine in humans [published erratum appears in *J. Pediatr.*, 1987 Mar;110(3):350], *J. Pediatr.*, 110(1), 93, 1987.

5. Inaba, T., Cocaine: Pharmacokinetics and biotransformation in man, *Can. J. Physiol. Pharmacol.*, 67, 1154, 1989.

6. Van Dyke, C., Barash, P. G., Jatlow, P., and Byck, R., Cocaine: Plasma concentrations after intranasal application in man, *Science*, 191, 859, 1976.

7. Ritchie, J. M. and Greene, N. M. Local anesthetics (Chapter 15), in *The Pharmacologic Basis of Therapeutics*, 8th ed., Gilman, A. G., Rall, T. W., Nies, A. S., Taylor, P., Ed., Pergamon Press, New York, 1990, 311.

8. Hamilton, H. E., Wallace, J. E., and Shimek, E. L. Cocaine and benzoylecgonine excretion in humans, *J. Forensic Sci.*, 22, 697, 1977.

9. Forman, R., Schneiderman, J., Klein, J., Graham, K., Greenwald, M., and Koran, G., Accumulation of cocaine in maternal and fetal hair: the dose response curve, *Life Sci.*, 50, 1333, 1992.

10. Woods, J. R., Plessinger, M. A., Scott, K., and Miller, R. K., Prenatal cocaine exposure to the fetus: A sheep model for cardiovascular evaluation, *Ann. NY Acad. Sci.*, 562, 267, 1989.

11. Roe, D. A., Little, B. B., Bawdon, R. E., and Gilstrap, L. C., Metabolism of cocaine by human placentas: implications for fetal exposure, *Am. J. Obstet. Gynecol.*, 163(3), 715, 1990.

12. Simone, C., Derewlany, L. O., Oskamp, M., Knie, B., and Koren, G., Transfer of cocaine and benzoylecgonine across the perfused human placental cotyledon, *Am. J. Obstet. Gynecol.*, 170(5), 1404, 1994.

13. Plessinger, M. A. and Woods, J. R., The cardiovascular effects of cocaine use in pregnancy, *Repro. Toxicol.*, 5(2), 99, 1991.

14. Sandberg, J. A. and Olsen, G. D. Cocaine and metabolite concentrations in the fetal guinea pig after chronic maternal cocaine administration, *J. Pharmacol. Exp. Ther.*, 260(2), 587, 1992.

15. Bozarth, M. A., New perspectives on cocaine addiction: recent findings from animal research, *Can. J. Physiol. Pharmacol.*, 67, 1158, 1989.

16. Jaffe, J., Drug addiction and drug abuse, in *The Pharmacologic Basis of Therapeutics*, 8th ed., Gilman, A., Rall, T., Nies, A., Taylor, P., Eds. Pergamon Press, New York, 1990, 522.

17. Rosenak, D., Diamant, Y. Z., Yaffe, H., and Hornstein, E. Cocaine: maternal use during pregnancy and its effect on the mother, fetus, and the infant, *Obstet. Gynecol. Surv.*, 45(6), 348, 1990.

18. DiMaio, V. J. and Garriott, J. C., Four deaths due to intravenous injection of cocaine, *Forensic Sci. Internat.*, 12, 119, 1978.

19. Bates, C. K., Medical risks of cocaine use, *West. J. Med.*, 148, 440, 1988.

20. Henderson, C. E., and Torbey, M., Rupture of intracranial aneurysm associated with cocaine use during pregnancy, *Am. J. Perinatol.*, 5(2), 142, 1988.

21. Greenland, V., Delke, I., and Minkoff, H., Vaginally administered cocaine overdose in a pregnant woman. *Obstet. Gynecol.*, 74(3), 476, 1989.

22. Burkett, G., Bandstra, E. S., Cohen, J., Steele, B., and Palow, D., Cocaine-related maternal death, *Am. J. Obstet. Gynecol.*, 163(1), 40, 1990.

23. Peng, S. K., French, W. J., and Pelikan, P. C. D., Direct cocaine cardiotoxicity demonstrated by endomyocardial biopsy, *Arch. Pathol. Lab. Med.*, 113, 842, 1989.

24. Karch, S. B. and Billingham, M. E. The pathology and etiology of cocaine-induced heart disease, *Arch. Pathol. Lab. Med.*, 112, 225, 1988.

25. Spence, M. R., Williams, R., DiGregorio, G. J., Kirby-McDonnell, A., and Polansky, M., The relationship between recent cocaine use and pregnancy outcome, *Obstet. Gynecol.*, 78(3), 326, 1991.

26. Cohen, H. R., Green, J. R., and Crombleholme, W. R., Peripartum cocaine use: estimating risk of adverse pregnancy outcome, *Int. J. Obstet. Gynecol.*, 35(1), 51, 1991.

27. Gillogley, K. M., Evens, A. T., Hanson, R. L., Samuels, S. J., and Batra, K. K., The perinatal impact of cocaine, amphetamine, and opiate use detected by universal intrapartum screening, *Am. J. Obstet. Gynecol.*, 163(5), 1535, 1990.

28. Neerhof, M. G., MacGregor, S. N., Retzky, S. S., and Sullivan, T. P., Cocaine abuse during pregnancy: Peripartum prevalence and perinatal outcome, *Am. J. Obstet. Gynecol.,* 161(3), 633, 1989.

29. Zuckerman, B., Frank, D. A., Hingson, R., Amaro, H., Levenson, S. M., Kayne, H., Parker, S., Vinci, R., Aboagye, K., Fried, L. E., Cabral, H., Timperi, R., and Bauchner, H., Effects of maternal marijuana and cocaine use on fetal growth, *N. Engl. J. Med.,* 320(12), 762, 1989.

30. Chasnoff, I. J., Landress, H. J., and Barrett, M. E., The prevalence of illicit-drug or alcohol use during pregnancy and discrepancies in mandatory reporting in Pinellas county, Florida, *N. Engl. J. Med.,* 322, 1202, 1990.

31. Matera, C., Warren, W. B., Moomjy, M., Fink, D. F., and Fox, H. E., Prevalence of use of cocaine and other substances in an obstetric population, *Am. J. Obstet. Gynecol.,* 163(3), 797, 1990.

32. Brunader, R. E., Brunader, J. A., and Kugler, J. P. Prevalence of cocaine and marijuana use among pregnant women in a military health care setting, *J. Am. Board. Fam. Pract.,* 4(6), 395, 1991.

33. Frank, D. A., Zuckerman, B. S., Amaro, H., Aboagye, K., Bauchner, H., Cabral, H., Fried, L., Hingson, R., Kayne, H., Levenson, S. M., Parker, S., Reece, H., and Vinci, R., Cocaine use during pregnancy: prevalence and correlates. *Pediatrics,* 82(6), 888, 1988.

34. Cartwright, P. S., Schorge, J. D., and McLaughlin, F. J., Epidemiologic characteristics of drug use during pregnancy: experience in a Nashville hospital, *South. Med. J.,* 84(7), 867, 1991.

35. Schutzman, D. L., Frankenfield-Chernicoff, M., Clatterbaugh, H. E., and Singer, J., Incidence of intrauterine cocaine exposure in a suburban setting, *Pediatrics,* 88(4), 825, 1991.

36. George, S. K., Price, J., Hauth, J. C., Barnette, D. M., and Preston, P., Drug abuse screening of childbearing-age women in Alabama public health clinics, *Am. J. Obstet. Gynecol.,* 165(4), 924, 1991.

37. Oro, A. S. and Dixon, S. D., Perinatal cocaine and methamphetamine exposure: maternal and neonatal correlates, *J. Pediatr.,* 111(4), 571, 1987.

38. Reddin, P., Schlimmer, B., and Mitchell, C., Cocaine and pregnant women: a hospital study, *Iowa Med.,* 81(9), 374, 1991.

39. Minkoff, H. L., McCalla, S., Delke, I., Stevens, R., Salwen, M., and Feldman, J. The relationship of cocaine use to syphilis and human immunodeficiency virus among inner city parturient women, *Am. J. Obstet. Gynecol.,* 163(2), 521, 1990.

40. Madden, J. D., Payne, T. F., and Miller, S. Maternal cocaine abuse and effect on the newborn, *Pediatrics,* 77(2), 209, 1986.

41. Chasnoff, I. J., Burns, W. J., Schnoll, S. H., and Burns, K. A., Cocaine use in pregnancy, *N. Engl. J. Med.,* 313(11), 666, 1985.

42. Townsend, R. R., Laing, F. C., and Brooke, J., Placental abruption associated with cocaine abuse, *Am. J. Roentgenol.,* 150, 1339, 1988.

43. Acker, D., Sachs, B. P., Tracey, K. J., and Wise, W. E., Abruptio placentae associated with cocaine use, *Am. J. Obstet. Gynecol.,* 146(2), 220, 1983.

44. Lutiger, B., Graham, K., Einarson, T. R., and Koren, G., Relationship between gestational cocaine use and pregnancy outcome: A meta-analysis, *Teratology,* 44, 405, 1991.

45. Glantz, J. C. and Woods, J. R., Cocaine, heroin, and phencyclidine: obstetric perspectives, *Clin. Obstet. Gynecol.,* 36(2), 279, 1993.

46. Mastrogiannis, D. S., Decavalas, G. O., Verma, U., and Tajani, N., Perinatal outcome after recent cocaine usage, *Obstet. Gynecol.,* 76(1), 8, 1990.

47. Page, D. V., Brady, K., and Ward, S. The placental pathology of substance abuse, *Mod. Pathol.,* 2(1), 69, 1989.

48. Gilbert, W. M., Lafferty, C. M., Benirschke, K., and Resnik, R. Lack of specific placental abnormality associated with cocaine use, *Am. J. Obstet. Gynecol.,* 163(3), 998, 1990.

49. Chasnoff, I. J., Griffin, D. R., MacGregor, S., Dirkes, K., and Burns, K. A., Temporal patterns of cocaine use in pregnancy, *JAMA,* 261(12), 1741, 1989.

50. Webster, W. S. and Brown-Woodman, P. D. C., Cocaine as a cause of congenital malformations of vascular origin: Experimental evidence in the rat, *Teratology,* 41, 689, 1990.

51. Jones, K. L., Developmental pathogenesis of defects associated with prenatal cocaine exposure: Fetal vascular disruption, *Clinics in Perinatol.,* 18(1), 139, 1991.

52. Chasnoff, I. J., Chisum, G. M., and Kaplan, W. E., Maternal cocaine use and genitourinary tract malformations, *Teratology,* 37(3), 201, 1988.

53. Hanning, V. L. and Phillips, J. A. Maternal cocaine abuse and fetal anomalies: evidence for teratogenic effects of cocaine, *South. Med. J.,* 84(4), 498, 1991.

54. Hoyme, H. E., Jones, K. L., Dixon, S. D., Jewett, T., Hanson, J. W., Robinson, L. K., Msall, M. E., and Allanson, J. E., Prenatal cocaine exposure and fetal vascular disruption, *Pediatrics,* 85(5), 743, 1990.

55. Lipshultz, S. E., Frassica, J. J., and Orav, E. J., Cardiovascular abnormalities in infants prenatally exposed to cocaine, *J. Pediatr.,* 118(1), 44, 1991.

56. Little, B. B., Snell, L. M., Klein, V. R., and Gilstrap, L. C., Cocaine abuse during pregnancy: Maternal and fetal implications, *Obstet. Gynecol.,* 73, 157, 1989.

57. Chavez, G. F., Mulinare, J., and Cordero, J. F., Maternal cocaine use during early pregnancy as a risk factor for congenital urogenital abnormalities, *JAMA,* 262, 795, 1989.

58. Rosenstein, B. J., Wheeler, J. S., and Heid, P. L., Congenital renal abnormalities in infants with in utero cocaine exposure, *J. Urol.,* 144, 110, 1990.

59. Dixon, S. D. and Bejar, R., Brain lesions in cocaine and methamphetamine exposed neonates, *Pediatr. Res.,* 23(4), 405, 1988.

60. Heier, L. A., Carpanzano, C. R., Mast, J., Brill, P. W., Winchester, P., and Deck, M. D., Maternal cocaine abuse: the spectrum of radiologic abnormalities in the neonatal CNS, *Am. J. Neuroradiol.,* 12(5), 951, 1991.

61. van de Bor, M., Walther, F. J., and Sims, M. E., Increased cerebral blood flow velocity in infants of mothers who abuse cocaine, *Pediatrics,* 85(5), 733, 1990.

62. Gingras, J. L., Weese-Mayer, D. E., Hume, R. F., and O'Donnell, K. J., Cocaine and development: mechanisms of fetal toxicity and neonatal consequences of prenatal cocaine exposure, *Early Human Dev.,* 31, 1, 1992.

63. Moore, T. R., Sorg, J., Miller, L., Key, T. C., and Resnik, R., Hemodynamic effects of intravenous cocaine on the pregnant ewe and fetus, *Am. J. Obstet. Gynecol.,* 155(4), 883, 1986.

64. Bayorth, M. A., Zukowska-Grojec, Z., and Kopin, I. J., Effect of desipramine and cocaine on plasma norepinephrine and pressor response to adrenergic stimulation in pithed rats, *J. Clin. Pharmacol.,* 23, 24, 1983.

65. Chiueh, C. C. and Kopin, I. J., Centrally mediated release by cocaine of endogenous epinephrine and norepinephrine from the sympathoadrenal medullary system of unanesthetized rats, *J. Pharmacol. Exp. Ther.,* 205(1), 148, 1978.

66. Wilkerson, D. R. Cardiovascular effects of cocaine: enhancement by yohimbine and atropine. *J. Pharmacol. Exp. Ther.,* 248(1), 57, 1989.

67. Levy, M. N. and Blattberg, B. The influence of cocaine and desipramine on the cardiac responses to exogenous and endogenous norepinephrine, *Eur. J. Pharmacol.,* 48, 37, 1978.

68. Morizaki, N. Morizaki, J., Hayashi, R. H., and Garfield, R. E., A functional and structural study of the innervation of the human uterus, *Am. J. Obstet. Gynecol.,* 160(1), 218, 1989.

69. Roberts, J. M., Insel, P. A., and Goldfien, A., Regulation of myometrial adrenoreceptors and adrenergic response by sex steroids, *Mol. Pharmacol.,* 20, 52, 1981.

70. Greiss, F. C., Differential reactivity of the myoendometrial and placental vasculatures: Adrenergic responses, *Am. J. Obstet. Gynecol.,* 112(1), 20, 1972.

71. Greiss, F. C. J. and Van Wilkes, D., Effects of sympathomimetic drugs and angiotensin on the uterine vascular bed, *Obstet. Gynecol.,* 23(6), 925, 1964.

72. Rosenfeld, C. R. and West, J. W., Circulatory response to systemic infusion of norepinephrine in the pregnant ewe, *Am. J. Obstet. Gynecol.,* 127(4), 376, 1977.

73. Skillman, C. A., Plessinger, M. A., Woods, J. R., and Clark, K. E., Effect of graded reductions in uteroplacental blood flow on the fetal lamb, *Am. J. Physiol.,* 249, H1098, 1985.

74. Kiritsy-Roy, J. A., Halter, J. B., Gordon, S. M., Smith, M. J., and Terry, L. C., Role of the central nervous system in hemodynamic and sympathoadrenal responses to cocaine in rats, *J. Pharmacol. Exp. Ther.,* 255(1), 154, 1990.

75. Wilkerson, R. D., Cardiovascular effects of cocaine in conscious dogs: Importance of fully functional autonomic nervous system, *J. Pharmacol. Exp. Ther.,* 246, 466, 1988.

76. Tella, S. R., Korupolu, G. R., Schindler, C. W., and Goldberg, S. R., Pathophysiological and pharmacological mechanisms of acute cocaine toxicity in conscious rats, *J. Pharmacol. Exp. Ther.,* 262(3), 936, 1992.

77. Branch, C. A., and Knuepfer, M. M., Causes of differential cardiovascular sensitivity to cocaine. II: Sympathetic, metabolic and cardiac effects, *J. Pharmacol. Exp. Ther.,* 271(2), 1103, 1994.

78. Rhee, H. M., Valentine, J. L., and Lee, S. Y., Toxic effects of cocaine to the cardiovascular system in conscious and anesthetized rats and rabbits: Evidence for a direct effect on the myocardium, *Neurotoxicology,* 11, 361, 1990.

79. Gantenberg, N. S., and Hageman, G. R., Cocaine depresses cardiac sympathetic efferent activity in anesthetized dogs, *J. Cardiovasc. Pharmacol.,* 17(3), 434, 1991.

80. Raczkowski, V. C. F., Hernandez, Y. M., Erzouki, H. K., Abrahams, T. P., Mandal, A. K., Hamosh, P., Friedman, E., Quest, J. A., Dretchen, K. L., and Gillis, R. A., Cocaine acts in the central nervous system to inhibit sympathetic neural activity, *J. Pharmacol. Exp. Ther.,* 257(1), 511, 1990.

81. Tella, S. R., Schindler, C. W., and Goldberg, S. R., The role of central and autonomic neural mechanisms in the cardiovascular effects of cocaine in conscious squirrel monkeys, *J. Pharmacol. Exp. Ther.,* 252(2), 491, 1990.

82. Dolkart, L. A., Plessinger, M. A., and Woods, J. R., Effect of alpha$_1$ receptor blockade upon maternal and fetal cardiovascular responses to cocaine, *Obstet. Gynecol.,* 75, 745, 1990.

83. Monga, M., Chmielowiec, S., Andres, R. L., Troyer, L. R., and Parisi, V. M., Cocaine alters placental production of thromboxane and prostacyclin, *Am. J. Obstet. Gynecol.,* 171(4), 965, 1994.

84. Cejtin, H. E., Parsons, M. T., and Wilson, L., Cocaine abuse and its effect on umbilical artery prostacyclin production, *Prostaglandins,* 40, 249, 1990.

85. Ahluwalia, B. S., Clark, J. F., Westney, L. S., Smith, D. M., James, M., and Rajguru, S., Amniotic fluid and umbilical artery levels of sex hormones and prostaglandins in human cocaine users, *Repro. Toxicol.,* 6, 57, 1992.

86. Fishburne, J. I., Dormer, K. J., Payne, G. G., Gill, P. S., Ashrafzadeh, A. R., and Rossavik, I. K., Effects of amrinone and dopamine on uterine blood flow and vascular responses in the gravid baboon, *Am. J. Obstet. Gynecol.,* 158(4), 829, 1988.

87. Morgan, M. A., Silavin, S. L., Randolph, M., Payne, G. G., Sheldon, R. E., Fishburne, J. I., Wentworth, R. A., and Nathanielsz, P. W., Effect of intravenous cocaine on uterine blood flow in the gravid baboon, *Am. J. Obstet. Gynecol.,* 164(4), 1021, 1991.

88. Woods, J. R., Plessinger, M. A., and Clark, K. E., Effect of cocaine on uterine blood flow and fetal oxygenation, *JAMA,* 257(7), 957, 1987.

89. Phillippe, M., Fetal catecholamines, *Am. J. Obstet. Gynecol.,* 146, 840, 1983.

90. Padbury, J. F., Ludlow, J. K., Ervin, M. G., Jacobs, H. C., and Humme, J. A., Thresholds for physiological effects of plasma catecholamines in fetal sheep, *Am. J. Physiol.,* 252, E530, 1987.

91. Chan, K., Dodd, A., Day, L., Kullama, L., Ervin, M. G., Padbury, J., and Ross, M. G., Fetal catecholamine, cardiovascular, and neurobehavioral responses to cocaine, *Am. J. Obstet. Gynecol.,* 167(6), 1616, 1992.

92. Jain, L., Meyer, W., Moore, C., Tebbett, I., Gauthier, D., and Vidyasager, D., Detection of fetal cocaine exposure by analysis of amniotic fluid, *Obstet. Gynecol.,* 81(5), 787, 1993.

93. Moore, C. M., Brown, S., Negrusz, A., Tebbett, I., Meyer, W., and Jain, L., Determination of cocaine and its major metabolite, benzoylecgonine, in amniotic fluid, umbilical cord blood, umbilical cord tissue, and neonatal urine: A case study, *J. Analytic Toxicol.,* 17, 62, 1993.

94. Mahone, P. R., Scott, K., Sleggs, G., D'Antoni, T., and Woods, J. R., Cocaine and metabolites in amniotic fluid may prolong fetal drug exposure, *Am. J. Obstet. Gynecol.,* 171(2), 465, 1994.

95. Stewart, D. J., Inaba, T., and Kalow, W., N-Demethylation of cocaine in the rat and in isolated rat hepatocytes: Comparison with aminopyrine demethylation, *J. Pharmacol. Exp. Ther.,* 207(1), 171, 1978.

96. Neale, M. G., and Parke, D. V., Effects of pregnancy on the metabolism of drugs in the rat and rabbit, *Biochem. Pharmacol.,* 22, 1451, 1973.

97. DeVane, C. L., Simpkins, J. W., Miller, R. L., and Braun, S. B., Tissue distribution of cocaine in the pregnant rat, *Life Sci.,* 45(14), 1271, 1989.

98. Inaba, T., Stewart, D. J., and Kalow, W., Metabolism of cocaine in man, *Clin. Pharmacol. Ther.,* 23(5), 547, 1978.

99. Shnider, S. M., Serum cholinesterase activity during pregnancy, labor, and the puerperium, *Anesthesiology,* 26(3), 335, 1965.

100. Pritchard, J. A. Plasma cholinesterase activity in normal pregnancy and in eclamptogenic toxemia. *Am. J. Obstet. Gynecol.,* 70, 1083, 1955.

101. Sandberg, J. A., and Olsen, G. D., Cocaine pharmacokinetics in the pregnant guinea pig, *J. Pharmacol. Exp. Ther.*, 258(2), 447, 1991.

102. Woods, J. R., Scott, K. J., and Plessinger, M. A., Pregnancy enhances cocaine's actions on the heart and within the peripheral circulation, *Am. J. Obstet. Gynecol.*, 170(4), 1027, 1994.

103. Morishima, H. O., Hara, T., Cooper, T. B., and Miller, E. D., Pregnancy enhances acute intoxication by cocaine in the rat, *Anesthesiology*, 71(3A), A894, 1989.

104. Morishima, H. O., Masaoka, T., Tetsuaki, H., Tsuji, A., and Cooper, T. B., Pregnancy decreases the threshold for cocaine-induced convulsions in the rat, *J. Lab. Clin. Med.*, 122, 748, 1993.

105. Kambam, J. R., Naukam, R., and Berman, M. L., Inhibition of pseudocholinesterase activity protects from cocaine-induced cardiorespiratory toxicity in rats, *J. Lab. Clin. Med.*, 119(5), 553, 1992.

106. Stewart, D. J., Inaba, T., Lucassen, M., and Kalow, W., Cocaine metabolism: Cocaine and norcocaine hydrolysis by liver and serum esterases, *Clin. Pharmacol. Ther.*, 25(4), 464, 1979.

107. DeVane, C. L., Burchfield, D. J., Abrams, R. M., Miller, R. L., and Braun, S. B., Disposition of cocaine in pregnant sheep I. Pharmacokinetics, *Dev. Pharmacol. Ther.*, 16, 123, 1991.

108. Hawks, R. L., Kopin, I. J., Colburn, R. W., and Thoa, N. B., Norcocaine: A pharmacologically active metabolite of cocaine found in brain, *Life Sci.*, 15(12), 2189, 1974.

109. Borne, R. F., Bedford, J. A., Buelke, J. L., Craig, C. B., Hardin, T. C., Kibbe, A. H., and Wilson, M. C., Biological effects of cocaine derivatives I: Improved synthesis and pharmacologic evaluation of norcocaine, *J. Pharmaceut. Sci.*, 66(1), 119, 1977.

110. Kambam, J., Mets, B., Hickman, R. M., Janicki, P., James, M. F., Fuller, B., and Kirsch, R. E., The effects of inhibition of plasma cholinesterase and hepatic microsomal enzyme activity on cocaine, benzoylecgonine, ecgonine methyl ester, and norcocaine blood levels in pigs, *J. Lab. Clin. Med.*, 120(2), 323, 1992.

111. Covert, R. F., Schreiber, M. D., Tebbett, I. R., and Torgerson, L. J., Hemodynamic and cerebral blood flow effects of cocaine, cocaethylene and benzoylecgonine in conscious and anesthetized fetal lambs, *J. Pharmacol. Exp. Ther.*, 270(1), 118, 1994.

112. Madden, J. A. and Powers, R. H., Effect of cocaine and cocaine metabolites on cerebral arteries *in vitro*, *Life Sci.*, 47(13), 1109, 1990.

113. Kurth, C. D., Monitto, C. L., Albuquerque, M. L., Feuer, D. P., Anday, E. K., and Shaw, L., Effect of cocaine and cocaine metabolites on the cerebral microvasculature in piglets, *Anesthesiology*, 77(3A), A1039, 1992.

114. Barber, D. A. and Tackett, R. L., Hemodynamic effects of centrally administered norcocaine in the rat, *Life Sci.*, 51(16), 1269, 1992.

115. Edwards, D. J. and Bowles, S. K., Protein binding of cocaine in human serum, *Pharmaceut. Res.*, 5(7), 440, 1988.

116. Santos, A. C., Pederson, H., Harmon, T. W., Morishima, H. O., Finster, M., Arthur, G. R., and Covino, B. G., Does pregnancy alter the systemic toxicity of local anesthetics?, *Anesthesiology*, 70(6), 991, 1989.

117. Morishima, H. O., Pederson, H., Finster, M., Hiraoka, H., Tsuji, A., Feldman, H. S., Arthur, G. R., and Covino, B. G., Bupivacaine toxicity in pregnant and nonpregnant ewes, *Anesthesiology*, 63(2), 134, 1985.

118. Morishima, H. O., Finster, M., Arthur, R., and Covino, B. C., Pregnancy does not alter lidocaine toxicity, *Am. J. Obstet. Gynecol.*, 162(5), 1320, 1990.

119. Chesley, L. C., Talledo, E., Bohler, C. S., and Zuspan, F. P., Vascular reactivity to angiotensin II and norepinephrine in pregnant and nonpregnant women, *Am. J. Obstet. Gynecol.*, 91(6), 837, 1965.

120. Assali, N. S., Nuwayhis, B., Brinkman, C. R., Tabsh, K., Erkkola, R., and Ushioda, E., Autonomic control of the pelvic circulation: *In vivo* and *in vitro* studies in pregnant and nonpregnant sheep, *Am. J. Obstet. Gynecol.*, 141, 873, 1981.

121. Barton, M. D., Killam, A. P., and Meschia, G., Response of ovine uterine blood flow to epinephrine and norepinephrine, *Proc. Soc. Expt. Biol. Med.*, 145, 996, 1974.

122. McLaughlin, M. K., Keve, T. M., and Cooke, R., Vascular catecholamine sensitivity during pregnancy in the ewe, *Am. J. Obstet. Gynecol.*, 160(1), 47, 1989.

123. Woods, J. R. and Plessinger, M. A., Pregnancy increases cardiovascular toxicity to cocaine, *Am. J. Obstet. Gynecol.*, 162(2), 529, 1990.

124. Morishima, H. O., Cooper, T. B., Hara, T., and Miller, E. D., Pregnancy alters the hemodynamic responses to cocaine in the rat, *Dev. Pharmacol. Ther.,* 19, 69, 1992.

125. Datta, S., Lambert, D. H., Gregus, J., Gissen, A. J., and Covino, B. G., Differential sensitivities of mammalian nerve fibers during pregnancy, *Anesth. Analges.,* 62, 1070, 1983.

126. Flanagan, H. L., Datta, S., Lambert, D. H., Gissen, A. J., and Covino, B. G., Effect of pregnancy of bupivacaine-induced conduction blockade in the isolated rabbit vagus nerve, *Anesth. Analges.,* 66, 123, 1987.

127. Moller, R. A., Datta, S., Fox, J., Johnson, M., and Covino, B. G., Effects of progesterone on the cardiac electrophysiologic action of bupivacaine and lidocaine, *Anesthesiology,* 76, 604, 1992.

128. Sheridan, P. J., and McGill, H. C., The nuclear uptake and retention of a synthetic progestin in the cardiovascular system of the baboon, *Endocrinology,* 114(6), 2015, 1984.

129. Lin, A. L., Gonzalez, R., Carey, K. D., and Shain, S. A., Estradiol-17β affects estrogen receptor distribution and elevates progesterone receptor content in baboon aorta, *Arteriosclerosis,* 6, 495, 1986.

130. Ingegno, M. D., Money, S. R., Thelmo, W., Greene, G. L., Davidan, M., Jaffe, B. M., and Pertschuk, L. P., Progesterone receptors in the human heart and great vessels, *Lab. Invest.,* 59(3), 353, 1988.

131. Plessinger, M. A. and Woods, J. R., Progesterone increases cardiovascular toxicity to cocaine in nonpregnant ewes, *Am. J. Obstet. Gynecol.,* 163(5), 1659, 1990.

132. Sharma, A., Plessinger, M. A., Sherer, D. M., Liang, C. S., Miller, R. K., and Woods, J. R., Pregnancy enhances cardiotoxicity of cocaine: Role of progesterone, *Toxicol. App. Pharm.,* 113, 30, 1992.

133. Sharma, A., Plessinger, M. A., Miller, R. K., and Woods, J. R., Progesterone antagonist mifepristone (RU-486) decreases cardiotoxicity of cocaine, *Proc. Soc. Expt. Biol. Med.,* 202, 279, 1993.

134. Glantz, J. C. and Woods, J. R., Does progesterone potentiate the *in vitro* effect of cocaine on papillary myocardium in Long-Evans rats? *Reprod. Toxicol.,* 9(6), 563, 1995.

135. Kurtzman, J. T., Thorp, J. M., Spielman, F. J., Perry, S., Mueller, R. A., and Cefalo, R. A., Estrogen mediates the pregnancy-enhanced cardiotoxicity of cocaine in the isolated perfused rat heart, *Obstet. Gynecol.,* 83, 613, 1994.

136. Glantz, J. C. and Woods, J. R. J., The cocaine LD50 in Long-Evans rats is not altered by pregnancy or progesterone, *Neurotox. Teratol.,* 16(4), 297, 1994.

137. Wikland, M., Lindblom, B., Dahlstrom, A., and Haglid, K. G., Structural and functional evidence for the denervation of human myometrium during pregnancy, *Obstet. Gynecol.,* 64(4), 503, 1984.

138. Huszar, G. and Roberts, J., Biochemistry and pharmacology of the myometrium and labor: Regulation at the cellular and molecular levels, *Am. J. Obstet. Gynecol.,* 142(2), 225, 1982.

139. Berg, G., Andersson, R. G. G., and Ryden, G., α-Adrenergic receptors in human myometrium during pregnancy, *Am. J. Obstet. Gynecol.,* 154(5), 601, 1986.

140. Zuspan, F. P., Cibils, L. A., and Pose, S. V., Myometrial and cardiovascular responses to alterations in plasma epinephrine and norepinephrine, *Am. J. Obstet. Gynecol.,* 84(7), 841, 1962.

141. Berridge, M. J., Inositol triphosphate and diacylglycerol: two interacting second messengers, *Ann. Rev. Biochem.,* 56, 159, 1987.

142. Quaas, L. and Zahradnik, H. P., The effects of α- and β-adrenergic stimulation on contractility and prostaglandin (prostaglandins E2 and F2α and 6-keto-prostaglandin F1α) production of pregnant human myometrial strips, *Am. J. Obstet. Gynecol.,* 152(7), 852, 1985.

143. Riemer, R. K., Goldfien, A., and Roberts, J. M., Rabbit myometrial adrenergic sensitivity is increased by estrogen but is independent of changes in alpha adrenoceptor concentration, *J. Pharmacol. Exp. Ther.,* 240(1), 44, 1987.

144. Hoffman, B. B., Lavin, T. N., Lefkowitz, R. J., and Ruffolo, R. R., Alpha adrenergic receptor subtypes in rabbit uterus: Mediation of myometrial contraction and regulation by estrogens, *J. Pharmacol. Exp. Ther.,* 219(2), 290, 1981.

145. Daniel, E. E. and Wolowyk, M., The contractile response of the uterus to cocaine, *Can. J. Physiol. Pharmacol.,* 44, 721, 1966.

146. Morgan, M. A., Wentworth, R. A., Silavin, S. L., Jenkins, S. L., Fishburne, J., Jr., and Nathanielsz, P. W., Intravenous administration of cocaine stimulates gravid baboon myometrium in the last third of gestation, *Am. J. Obstet. Gynecol.,* 170(5 Pt 1), 1416, 1994.

147. Owiny, J. R., Myers, T., Massmann, G. A., Sadowsky, D. W., Jenkins, S., and Nathanielsz, P. W., Lack of effect of maternal cocaine administration on myometrial electromyogram and maternal plasma oxytocin concentrations in pregnant sheep at 124-146 days' gestational age, *Obstet. Gynecol.*, 79(1), 81, 1992.

148. Monga, M., Weisbrodt, N. W., Andres, R. L., and Sanborn, B. M., The acute effect of cocaine exposure on pregnant human myometrial contractile activity, *Am. J. Obstet. Gynecol.*, 169(4), 782, 1993.

149. Monga, M., Weisbrodt, N. W., Andres, R. L., and Sanborn, B. M., Cocaine acutely increases rat myometrial contractile activity by mechanisms other than potentiation of adrenergic pathways, *Am. J. Obstet. Gynecol.*, 169(6), 1502, 1993.

150. Hurd, W. W., Robertson, P. A., Riemer, R. K., Goldfien, A., and Roberts, J. M., Cocaine directly augments the alpha-adrenergic contractile response of the pregnant rabbit uterus, *Am. J. Obstet. Gynecol.*, 164(1 Pt 1), 182, 1991.

151. Hurd, W. W., Smith, A. J., Gauvin, J. M., and Hayashi, R. H., Cocaine blocks extraneuronal uptake of norepinephrine by the pregnant human uterus, *Obstet. Gynecol.*, 78(2), 249, 1991.

152. Hurd, W. W., Gauvin, J. M., Dombrowski, M. P., and Hayashi, R. H. Cocaine selectively inhibits beta-adrenergic receptor binding in pregnant human myometrium, *Am. J. Obstet. Gynecol.*, 169(3), 644, 1993.

Chapter 4

Does Prenatal Cocaine Exposure Cause Strokes in Neonates? — Clinical Evidence

Jeffrey R. Buchhalter, MD, PhD

4.0 INTRODUCTION

It is reasonably well established that acute exposure to cocaine in adults results in cerebral ischemic infarctions, intraparenchymal and subarachnoid hemorrhage.[1-3] Proposed "vascular" mechanisms include vasospasm, vasculitis, and hypertension.[4,5] The cause and effect relationship between drug and stroke is supported by the temporal relationship and lack of other likely etiologies.

The relationship of *in utero* exposure to cocaine and postpartum abnormalities is less clear. These proposed sequelae include: reduced somatic and brain growth, dysmorphic features, sudden infant death syndrome, and urogenital malformations. Proposed abnormalities affecting the nervous system include: seizures, strokes, and structural malformations including cerebral atrophy, abnormalities of midline development (agenesis of corpus callosum and septum pellucidum, septo-optic dysplasia, schizencephaly), and abnormalities of neuronal migration and differentiation.[6] It has been suggested that a vascular pathophysiology underlies these multiple abnormalities.[7,8] Recent reviews of the difficulties in demonstrating that prenatal cocaine exposure results in these postnatal effects emphasized that these infants are subject to multiple risk factors (e.g., malnutrition, alcohol, infection) which could result in somatic and brain abnormalities.[9,10]

This review will focus exclusively on reports of strokes (ischemic and hemorrhagic) in human neonates exposed to cocaine *in utero*. Evidence from studies using commonly accepted indicators of cerebral ischemia will be considered, i.e., brain ultrasound (US), computed tomography (CT), magnetic resonance imaging (MRI), and single photon computed tomography (SPECT). Preliminary studies utilizing positron emission tomography are presented elsewhere in this volume. The review will be organized by whether or not the data indicate that *in utero* cocaine exposure resulted in cerebrovascular complications.

4.1 EVIDENCE SUGGESTING PRENATAL COCAINE EXPOSURE CAUSES STROKES

In 1986 Chasnoff et al.[11] reported a case of a neonate who was the product of a full-term pregnancy during which his mother reported use of intranasal cocaine during the first 5 weeks and last 3 days of gestation. Variable decelerations, thick meconium, and Apgars of 1 and 7 (at 1 and 5 minutes, respectively) suggested perinatal distress. At 16 hours of life right-sided seizures prompted an evaluation in which a CT revealed an acute infarction consistent with left middle cerebral artery occlusion. Urine was positive for cocaine in the mother at the time of delivery and in the infant at 24 hours of life. The authors noted that this case did not prove a causal relationship between the intrauterine exposure and subsequent infarction.

The next case report (1989) described a hemorrhage in the caudothalamic groove of a term neonate with cocaine exposure throughout intrauterine life.[12] The hemorrhage was detected by cranial US at 96 hours of life. No coagulation or metabolic studies were performed. Other than meconium staining, tremors, and irritability, no serious clinical sequelae were apparent. Due to the US appearance, it was suggested that the hemorrhage occurred *in utero*.

Dixon and Bejar[13] performed a prospective, controlled study of term infants with positive urine toxicology for cocaine (n=74) and compared this group with term ill neonates (n=87) and healthy controls (n=19). All children had brain US on or before day 3 of life. A variety of cerebrovascular lesions was found in significantly greater numbers in the cocaine-exposed and ill (predominantly hypoxia-ischemia) groups which included: white matter abnormalities; intraventricular, subarachnoid and subependymal hemorrhage; and ventricular enlargement. However, as there was no significant difference in the representation of these abnormalities between the first two groups, it was concluded that there was no *specificity* for these types of lesions in cocaine-exposed infants.

Hoyme et al.[14] reported 10 children ascertained from 5 genetics and dysmorphology clinics who by history were exposed to cocaine throughout pregnancy (with or without other drug exposures) and had a variety of congenital malformations. Four of the children had a gestation of less than 36 weeks. One infant had an intracranial hemorrhage without indication of location or detection technique and another had bilateral infarctions by cranial US.

Dominguez et al.[6] reported 10 infants identified by presentation with strabismus before 6 months of age (n=7) or with abnormal neurological findings in the neonatal period (n=3). Nine of the 10 were the products of full-term gestations. Seven infants had intrauterine cocaine exposure. Abnormalities found in the cocaine-exposed children via CT and/or MRI included dysgenesis of the corpus callosum (n=1), septo-optic dysplasia with schizencephaly (n=1), porencephaly with (n=2) and without (n=2) midline abnormalities and bilateral cerebral infarcts (n=1).

Singer et al.[15] analyzed data from a prospective, longitudinal study of very low birth weight (<1500 grams) infants. Forty-one cocaine-exposed infants were identified by a combination of maternal history and/or urine screening and compared to a similar number of nonexposed infants controlled for race, socioeconomic status, maternal age, and bronchopulmonary dysplasia status. Fifty-four percent of cocaine-exposed infants had an IVH compared to 29% in the nonexposed group, a statistically significant difference. It was noted that exposure to other drugs (alcohol, tobacco, and marijuana) was also greater in the cocaine-exposed group.

Dogra et al.[16] prospectively identified 42 weight appropriate for gestational age (AGA) infants, 27 to 41 weeks gestation, with a maternal history of cocaine abuse during pregnancy. These infants had "no evidence of hypoxia or respiratory distress at birth." Seventy-five percent of these neonates were positive for cocaine metabolites within 48 hours of birth. The control group was composed of 34 well AGA infants who were negative for cocaine metabolites. All neonates had cranial US within 72 hours of birth. No abnormalities were found in the control group. Focal echolucenies were present in 25% and caudate echogenicity was present in 7% of the cocaine-exposed group. Neither gestational age nor presence of metabolites in urine correlated with US abnormalities.

4.2 EVIDENCE AGAINST PRENATAL COCAINE EXPOSURE CAUSING STROKES

Link et al.[17] retrospectively identified 21 full-term infants with evidence of intrauterine cocaine exposure by maternal history and/or urine toxicology. Infants were studied at 30 days to 12 months of age. No abnormalities were noted in the 8 infants who were studied with MRI. Difficulties with the interpretation of these data include the retrospective nature of the study, lack of control groups, uncertainty regarding duration of intrauterine exposure, and the small number of infants studied. Of note, all were developmentally normal.

Frank et al.[18] reported in abstract form 140 full-term neonates exposed to cocaine *in utero* and a control group matched for age and low socioeconomic status. Cranial ultrasound performed within the first week of life revealed lesions consistent with ischemia in approximately 60% in both groups. Thus, abnormalities were common in these inner city populations, but not over-represented in the cocaine-exposed group.

McClenan et al.[19] retrospectively identified premature infants (≤37 weeks) admitted to a neonatal intensive care unit who had cranial US within the first week of life and who had a history of intrauterine cocaine exposure. When the infants were stratified into risk of intraventricular hemorrhage by risk factor(s), gestational age, 5-minute Apgar score, and pneumothorax, no increased risk was found in the infants exposed to cocaine.

Dusick et al.[20] studied 323 very low birth weight neonates (≤1400 grams) identified in a prospective, consecutive fashion. *In utero* cocaine exposure was ascertained by a variety of methods including: maternal history, infant and maternal urine toxicology, and meconium examination. Eighty-six infants were classified as cocaine-exposed, 146 not exposed, and 91 were not assigned (early death or missed toxicology testing). No significant difference in the incidence of intraventricular hemorrhage (36% versus 35%) or periventricular leukomalacia was reported.

Konkol et al.[21] reported 21 infants with gestational ages 34 to 40 weeks and without significant hypoxic-ischemic encephalopathy who were cocaine exposed as evidenced by positive cord blood or meconium toxicology. SPECT was performed between 1 and 9 days of life and was normal in all children. Fifteen of these infants were also studied with MRI or CT. All were normal except one child with evidence of delayed myelination.

4.3 SUMMARY

The literature addressing the issue of intrauterine exposure leading to cerebrovascular events, strokes, is composed of case reports, prospective and retrospective studies. Identification of affected pregnancies has included maternal report as well as maternal and/or infant blood, urine, and meconium toxicology. Duration of exposure to cocaine and other drugs of abuse, alcohol, and tobacco are impossible to know with certainty. The studied infants have been from term or preterm pregnancies with weights that are appropriate for gestational age and from the very low birth weight groups. Comparison groups have either been absent or derived from healthy and ill populations of similar socioeconomic status. Although several imaging techniques have been used, cranial US has been the most popular. Thus, it is not surprising that a definitive answer is not available for any of the potential subpopulations. In the most comparable controlled, prospective studies involving large cohorts of very low birth weight preterm infants, different results were found. The authors of the study indicating that intrauterine cocaine exposure leads to a higher incidence of intraventricular hemorrhage[15] suggest that inclusion of infants on the basis of positive meconium toxicology only "... may have affected outcome findings" in the negative study.[20] However, sufficient information is not available regarding the dose-duration-effect of cocaine and its metabolites to understand how inclusion of a group identified by positive meconium, but not by urine or blood, could influence the occurrence of stroke.

Further studies are clearly needed to define the cerebrovascular effects of *in utero* exposure to cocaine.

REFERENCES

1. Levine, S. R., Brust, J. C., Futrell, N., et al., A comparative study of the cerebrovascular complications of cocaine: alkaloidal versus hydrochloride — a review, *Neurology,* 41, 1173, 1991.
2. Rowbotham, M. C. and Lowenstein, D. H., Neurologic consequences of cocaine use, *Ann. Rev. Med.,* 41, 417, 1990.
3. Daras, M., Tuchman, A. J., and Marks, S., Central nervous system infarction related to cocaine abuse, *Stroke,* 22, 1320, 1991.
4. Brown, E., Prager, J., Lee, H. Y., and Ramsey, R. G., CNS complications of cocaine abuse: prevalence, pathophysiology, and neuroradiology, *Am. J. Roentgenol.,* 159, 137, 1992.
5. Fredericks, R. K., Lefkowitz, D. S., Challa, V. R., and Troost, B. T., Cerebral vasculitis associated with cocaine abuse, *Stroke,* 22, 1437, 1991.
6. Dominguez, R., Aguirre Vila-Coro, A., Slopis, J. M., and Bohan, T. P., Brain and ocular abnormalities in infants with in utero exposure to cocaine and other street drugs [see comments], *Am. J. Dis. Child.,* 145, 688, 1991.
7. Webster, W. S. and Brown-Woodman, P. D., Cocaine as a cause of congenital malformations of vascular origin: experimental evidence in the rat, *Teratology,* 41, 689, 1990.
8. Volpe, J. J., Effects of cocaine on the fetus, *N. Engl. J. Med.,* 327, 399, 1992.
9. Konkol, R. J., Is there a cocaine baby syndrome? *J. Child. Neurol.,* 9, 225, 1994.
10. Frank, D. A., Bresnahan, K., and Zuckerman, B. S. Maternal cocaine use: impact on child health and development, *Adv. Ped.,* 40, 65, 1993.
11. Chasnoff, I. J., Bussey, M. E., Savich, R., and Stack, C. M., Perinatal cerebral infarction and maternal cocaine use, *J. Ped.,* 108, 456, 1986.
12. Spires, M. C., Gordon, E. F., Choudhuri, M., Maldonado, E., and Chan, R., Intracranial hemorrhage in a neonate following prenatal cocaine exposure, *Pediatr. Neurol.,* 5, 324, 1989.

13. Dixon, S. D. and Bejar, R., Echoencephalographic findings in neonates associated with maternal cocaine and methamphetamine use: incidence and clinical correlates, *J. Ped.,* 115, 770, 1989.

14. Hoyme, H. E., Jones, K. L., Dixon, S. D., et al., Prenatal cocaine exposure and fetal vascular disruption [see comments], *Pediatrics,* 85, 743, 1990.

15. Singer, L. T., Yamashita, T. S., Hawkins, S., Cairns, D., Baley, J., and Kliegman, R. Increased incidence of intraventricular hemorrhage and developmental delay in cocaine-exposed, very low birth weight infants, *J. Ped.,*124, 765, 1994.

16. Dogra, V. K., Shyken, J. M., Menon, P. A., Poblete, J., Lewis, D., and Smeltzer, J. S., Neurosonographic abnormalities associated with maternal history of cocaine use in neonates of appropriate size for their gestational age, *Am. J. Neuroradiol.,* 15, 697, 1994.

17. Link, E. A., Weese-Mayer, D. W., and Byrd, S. E., Magnetic resonance imaging in infants exposed to cocaine prenatally: a preliminary report, *Clin. Ped.,* 30, 506, 1991.

18. Frank, D. A., McCarten, K., Cabral, H., Levenson, S. M., and Zuckerman, B. S., Cranial ultrasound in term newborns: failure to replicate excess abnormalities in cocaine exposed, *Ped. Res.,* 247A, 1992 (Abstract).

19. McLenan, D., Ajayi, O. and Pildes, R. S., Cocaine and intraventricular hemorrhage (IVH), *Ped. Res.,* 212A, 1992 (Abstract).

20. Dusick, A. M., Covert, R. F., Schreiber, M. D., et al., Risk of intracranial hemorrhage and other adverse outcomes after cocaine exposure in a cohort of 323 very low birth weight infants, *J. Ped.,* 122, 438, 1993.

21. Konkol, R. J., Tikofsky, R. S., Wells, R., et al., Normal high-resolution cerebral ^{99m}TC-HMPAO SPECT scans in symptomatic neonates exposed to cocaine, *J. Child. Neurol.,* 9, 278, 1994.

Chapter 5

Vascular Complications and Mechanisms Related to Cocaine

Jane A. Madden, PhD, and Michael D. Schreiber, MD

5.0 VASCULAR SYNDROMES ASSOCIATED WITH COCAINE ABUSE

5.0.1 General

There is growing evidence that occasional, or even first-time cocaine use can have significant toxic effects. Numerous clinical and basic studies have shown that cocaine as well as its metabolites can adversely affect the cerebral, coronary, and pulmonary circulations in both humans and animals.

5.0.2 Syndromes Peculiar to the Fetus and Newborn

Of particular interest is the effect that cocaine has on the fetus and newborn. Cocaine use during pregnancy has increased to epidemic proportions and, in certain populations, over 20% of pregnant women abuse cocaine.[1-3] The placenta offers the fetus little protection from cocaine exposure as cocaine freely diffuses across the placenta with little significant metabolism.[4] Data from our own patient population document an abuse rate greater than 35% in mothers delivering prematurely.[5] Reported perinatal effects of *in utero* cocaine exposure include neurovascular[6-10] and neurobehavioral complications,[11,12] prematurity,[13,14] intrauterine growth retardation,[5] and possible fetal malformations.[15,16]

This review will describe the effects of cocaine and its metabolites in various circulatory beds of adult and immature humans and animals. It will also consider some of what is known and hypothesized about possible mechanisms responsible for these effects.

5.1 CIRCULATIONS AFFECTED BY COCAINE

5.1.1 Cerebral

Cocaine appears to have a particularly potent effect on the cerebrovasculature. Evidence demonstrating this is provided by the numerous articles linking cocaine abuse with depressed cerebral blood flow, migraine-like headaches, cerebral vaso-constriction, and cerebrovascular accidents.[17-28] Cocaine-associated strokes, which may be either hemorrhagic or ischemic, can occur regardless of the route of cocaine administration.[18] Strokes are seen most often in young adults,[18] however, infants born of cocaine-abusing mothers may also be at risk for intracranial hemorrhage[29,30] or other cerebrovascular events[31,32] including cerebral infarctions,[6-8] cavitary lesions,[7,8] electroencephalograph abnormalities and seizures,[33] and periventricular leukomalacia.[7]

The adverse cerebrovascular effects associated with cocaine use are not always acute; some may occur hours or even days later. Chronic cocaine users have been shown to have areas of defective cerebral blood flow that may persist for up to 10 days after the last usage.[34] As will be discussed later in greater detail, some of the delayed effects attributed to cocaine may in fact be due to its metabolites. Indeed, our laboratories have found that cocaine metabolites can have profound vasoactive effects on cerebral arteries.[35-37]

The cerebrovascular effects of cocaine are not limited to humans. Cocaine has been observed to affect the cerebral circulation in rats,[26,27,38] rabbits,[28] dogs,[27] and cats.[36,37] The similarities between human and animal responses to cocaine allow research studies to be directed toward an understanding of the mechanisms that may be responsible for some of these effects.

To examine the cerebrovascular effects of cocaine in the immature animal, several studies have been performed using chronically instrumented fetal sheep. In our laboratory, cocaine injected intravenously into the awake pregnant ewe at 124 days gestation (term = 147 days) elicited a 31% increase in fetal systemic arterial pressure while decreasing fetal cerebral blood flow 51%, as estimated by a unilateral carotid artery ultrasonic flow transducer (Figure 5.1).[58] Consequently, calculated cerebral vascular resistance increased twelvefold. Within 10 minutes of cocaine injection, a rebound hyperemia was noted with an increase in cerebral blood flow 134% over peak reduction. The cocaine-elicited changes could be attenuated or totally eliminated when studies were performed under general anesthesia.

Our findings differ from those of Gleason and colleagues,[39] who observed increased fetal cerebral blood flow with concomitant fetal hypertension. However, since in their study, the percent increase in fetal systemic arterial pressure was greater than the rise in cerebral blood flow, calculated cerebral vascular resistance actually increased. The differences between our study and that of Gleason et al.[39] likely result from the techniques used to measure cerebral blood flow. The radioactive microsphere assessment used by Gleason et al.[39] allows analysis of only discrete data points, whereas the flow transducers used in our studies allow continuous monitoring. The validity of using flow transducers to measure cerebral blood flow accurately in sheep has been established.[40,41] Thus, in sheep, maternal cocaine injection appears to increase fetal cerebral vascular resistance with sustained fetal hypertension and causes an initial decrease in cerebral blood flow followed by a rebound hyperemia. In vitro studies have confirmed the vasocontractile properties of cocaine on the immature cerebrovasculature.[37,42]

5.1.2 Coronary

Heart attacks occurring immediately[43] and for up to two days after cocaine use[44] have been reported. The coronary artery spasms shown to occur with cocaine use

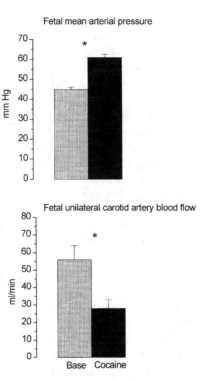

FIGURE 5.1 Maternal cocaine injection (1 mg/kg IV) increased mean arterial pressure and decreased carotid artery blood flow (*p <0.05). (From Covert, R. F., Schreiber, M. D., Tebbett, I. R., and Torgerson, L. J., J. *Pharmacol. Exp. Ther.,* 270, 118, 1994. With permission.)

have been associated with ischemia-produced myocardial infarction.[45,46] That large doses of cocaine are not necessary for myocardial events to occur was demonstrated by Lange et al.,[47] who found that intranasal cocaine administered in doses similar to those used for topical anesthesia caused coronary artery vasoconstriction.

Acutely intoxicated cocaine users may have up to fivefold greater circulating levels of epinephrine and norepinephrine than non-users,[46] and this may be a contributory factor leading to the heart attack. Cocaine may exert an action on the coronary circulation to prevent its normal dilation in response to increased oxygen demand. In one study,[46] coronary artery resistance actually increased despite increased myocardial oxygen demand.

Regular cocaine use seems to induce early arteriosclerotic changes in rabbit blood vessels.[48] The thoracic aorta of cocaine-treated rabbits showed a significant increase in the rate of protein synthesis, which appeared to be a relatively specific response of the blood vessel wall to cocaine since livers from these same animals did not show these changes.[48]

5.1.3 Pulmonary

Although many studies regarding cocaine's physiological effects have concentrated on the cerebral and coronary circulations, there is evidence that cocaine can also affect the pulmonary vasculature. The popularity of smoking "crack" or inhaling free base cocaine has resulted in a spectrum of previously unrecognized pulmonary complications.[49] Among these are an increased incidence of occult pulmonary hemorrhage and pulmonary hypertension.[50] The physiologic effects of inhaling volatilized cocaine are similar to those seen following intravenous administration. These effects are due primarily to the lung's large surface area for absorption and diffusion. However, the euphoria induced by smoking cocaine is of shorter duration than that produced by intravenous use and so more is taken.

Pulmonary symptoms may appear within 1 to 48 hours after drug use. They may resolve rapidly without therapy, resembling transient pulmonary edema, or they may persist with worsening hypoxemia and eventually respiratory failure.[50] It has been hypothesized that smoking cocaine leads to reduced pulmonary diffusing capacity as a consequence of a prolonged cocaine-induced pulmonary vasoconstriction.[50] Such chronic exposure to a vasoconstrictor can eventually produce pulmonary hypertension.[51] Cocaine-induced injury to the pulmonary-capillary membrane is also possible.[52]

Some have suggested,[51,52] that cocaine may have a direct pharmacologic effect on the pulmonary circulation. This may occur regardless of the route of administration, although direct exposure of the smaller pulmonary arteries is more likely when cocaine is smoked.[53] One recent clinical study[51] found abnormalities in small and medium-sized pulmonary arteries from patients whose deaths were cocaine related and where the drug had been ingested by various routes. The abnormalities were not thought to be age-related since the average patient age was 26 years, nor could they be ascribed to adulterants present in street forms of the drug.[49]

5.1.4 Umbilical and Uterine

Many of the fetal complications of *in utero* cocaine exposure, such as intrauterine growth retardation and prematurity, may be attributed to the effect of cocaine on the placental-umbilical circulation. Studies in several laboratories,[54-57] including our own,[58] have demonstrated cocaine-elicited increased uterine vascular resistance and decreased uterine blood flow. This predominantly alpha-adrenergically mediated phenomenon[54] is the primary cause of fetal hypoxemia following maternal cocaine ingestion.[55,56] Clinically, the effects of cocaine on the placental-umbilical circulation are reflected in changes in uterine and umbilical artery flow velocity,[59] with uterine arteries being more sensitive than umbilical arteries.[59-61] The limited effect of cocaine on umbilical arteries is not surprising since they lack adrenergic innervation. The effect of cocaine on human umbilical veins has not been studied. This may be a fertile area for research, because although, as in humans, sheep umbilical arteries do not respond to adrenergic stimulation, ovine umbilical veins are alpha-adrenergic responsive.[62] *In utero* cocaine exposure has also been reported in association with decreased umbilical cord length. Rather than a negative effect on angiogenesis, this effect is likely secondary to cocaine's suppressive effect on fetal movements, a major determinant of umbilical cord length. The association of cocaine and placental abruption and uterine rupture[63,64] is clinically very important, though it is unlikely to be mediated through cocaine-elicited vascular changes. It has been demonstrated that cocaine increases myometrial contractile activity[65] and sensitivity to alpha-adrenergic stimulation[65] and down-regulates myometrial-adrenergic receptors.[67]

5.2 VASCULAR EFFECTS OF COCAINE METABOLITES

5.2.1 Cocaine Metabolism

After ingestion, cocaine is rapidly hydrolyzed to benzoylecgonine. After 24 hours at pH 7.4, almost one half of a cocaine dose may be present as benzoylecgonine.[68] Further metabolism to ecgonine and ecgonine methyl ester occurs through the actions of serum and liver esterases.[68-70] N-demethylation of cocaine produces relatively small amounts of the norcocaine derivatives[68] (Figure 5.2).

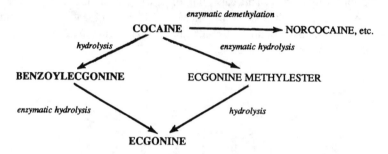

FIGURE 5.2 Metabolic pathways of cocaine, norcocaine, benzoylecgonine, ecgonine, and ecgonine methyl ester. (Reprinted from *Life Sciences,* 47, Madden, J. A. and Powers, R. H., Effect of cocaine and cocaine metabolites on cerebral arteries in vitro, 1109-1114, 1990, with kind permission from Elsevier Science Ltd, The Boulevard, Langford Lane, Kidlington 0X5 1GB, UK.)

While none of the cocaine metabolites has been shown to possess psychotropic activity, they may have vascular effects. Although the elimination half-life for benzoylecgonine in humans has been estimated at 6 to 8 hours,[71] benzoylecgonine has been shown to persist in brain tissue of chronic cocaine users.[69] This finding suggests that some sequestration may take place. Both cocaine and benzoylecgonine have been detected in rat cerebrospinal fluid after intravenous cocaine injection, and there is evidence that intravenous benzoylecgonine can cross into the central nervous system.[72] It has also been suggested that cocaine may remain sequestered in a bodily compartment[73] and be excreted gradually for over 2 weeks after cocaine use.[74]

The perinatal metabolism of cocaine in humans has not been extensively studied. However, studies in pregnant rats suggest that while maternal cocaine concentrations may exceed those of the fetus, the benzoylecgonine concentration in the fetal brain is significantly greater than in the maternal brain.[75,76] Our studies using pregnant sheep[58] suggest that benzoylecgonine does not readily cross the placenta and, thus, the source of fetal benzoylecgonine is fetal cocaine metabolism.

5.2.2 Evidence for Vasoreactivity of the Cocaine Metabolites

Because of the short serum half-life of cocaine, one might expect that the vasoactive effects of the drug would be equally short-lived. There are, however, clinical reports of cerebral and cardiovascular events occurring some time after cocaine inges-tion.[19,21,23,77] Because benzoylecgonine can remain in the body, it may have profound physiological effects such as the persistent, defective cerebral blood flow seen in chronic cocaine users, even after cessation of use.[34] The heart attack reported to occur two days after cocaine use[44] may also have been due to benzoylecgonine or perhaps even to another metabolite.

In our laboratory we investigated the possibility that benzoylecgonine might be responsible for some of the delayed cerebrovascular events previously attributed to cocaine. Isolated, cannulated, and pressurized cat middle cerebral arteries contracted significantly more to benzoylecgonine than to cocaine itself at the same concentration[35] (Figure 5.3). This capability of benzoylecgonine to constrict cerebral arteries by up to as much as 31% may have significant clinical relevance since it has been shown that the amount of smooth muscle contraction required to fully close major cerebral arteries is about 58%.[78]

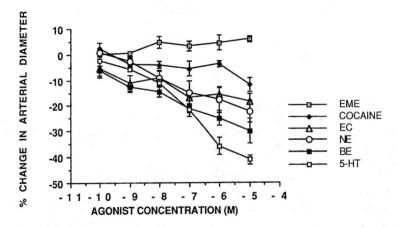

FIGURE 5.3 Percent change in diameter of cat middle cerebral arteries intraluminally perfused with ecgonine methyl ester (EME), cocaine, ecgonine (EC), norepinephrine (NE), benzoylecgonine (BE), and serotonin (5-HT) at doses from 10^{-10} to 10^{-5} M (mean ± SEM; n=5 arteries and 5 different cats). No significant difference in vessel diameter was observed with any compound at 10^{-10} M. With all of the contractile agents, contraction was statistically significant at 10^{-9} M (p<0.05) compared to control and remained so throughout the concentration range for all agents, except cocaine which was not significantly different from control at 10^{-7} and 10^{-6} M. EME caused a slight dilation from 10^{-10} M to 10^{-6} M, which was statistically significant (p <0.05) at only 10^{-5} M. (Reprinted from *Life Sciences*, 47, Madden, J. A. and Powers, R. H., Effect of cocaine and cocaine metabolites on cerebral arteries in vitro, 1109-1114, 1990, with kind permission from Elsevier Science Ltd, The Boulevard, Langford Lane, Kidlington 0X5 1GB, UK.)

In the cerebral vasculature, the vasoreactivity induced by the cocaine metabolites is not restricted to benzoylecgonine. We also found that ecgonine was a potent constrictor, although there was no significant difference in the contractions caused by equivalent maximum molar doses of benzoylecgonine and ecgonine [35] (Figure 5.3). Interestingly, ecgonine methyl ester caused a mild dilation throughout the dose range used (Figure 5.3).

Isolated fetal ovine cerebral arteries were equally responsive to cocaine and benzoylecgonine. However, the fetal sheep was near 100-fold more sensitive to benzoylecgonine (Figure 5.4). In fetal sheep, norcocaine was a weak constrictor, while in adult cats, ecgonine was not vasoactive but ecgonine methyl ester continued to be a weak vasodilator in this preparation. Maternal injection of benzoylecgonine significantly increased fetal cerebral vascular resistance.[58] The contractile response was significantly less than to cocaine, but this likely reflected limited transplacental transfer of benzoylecgonine. Within 30 minutes of maternal cocaine injection, fetal serum cocaine concentration exceeded the maternal concentration by twofold. In contrast, after maternal injection of benzoylecgonine, fetal serum benzoylecgonine concentration never exceeded 7% of maternal serum concentration. Interestingly, benzoylecgonine has limited effects on newborn piglet cerebral arterioles.[42] These differences in cocaine metabolite contractile profiles between fetal sheep, newborn piglets, and adult cats are likely due to maturational, species, and methodological differences.

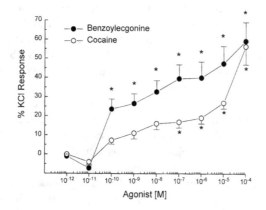

FIGURE 5.4 Concentration-response curves for cocaine and benzoylecgonine. Cocaine (n=19) and benzoylecgonine (n=21) caused statistically significant concentration-dependent vasoconstriction of fetal ovine cerebral artery segments (* $p < 0.05$ vs. 10^{-12} M agonist). (From Schreiber, M. D., Madden, J. A., Covert, R. F., and Torgerson, L. J., *J. Appl. Physiol.*, 77, 834, 1994. With permission.)

The concept that benzoylecgonine could be responsible for some of the later-occurring cardiovascular effects attributed to cocaine has been recently supported by a study in human coronary arteries.[79] The decreased coronary artery diameter 30 minutes after intranasal cocaine was associated with the peak concentration of cocaine in the blood, but a recurrent vasoconstriction 90 minutes later was related to the rising benzoylecgonine concentration. Clinically, it has also been found that up to 4 weeks after cocaine use, people still had silent myocardial ischemia, indicating coronary artery spasm.[80]

The study of the cardiovascular effects of the cocaine metabolites has not been extensive, and it should be kept in mind that the diverse spectrum of effects produced by these metabolites may lead to toxicity when cocaine metabolism is altered due to disease, pregnancy, age, and genetic differences in esterase levels or the degree of tolerance and dependence on the drug.[77]

5.3 MECHANISMS OF ACTION OF COCAINE AND COCAINE METABOLITES ON THE VASCULATURE

5.3.1 Sympathetic

The oldest and most widely accepted hypothesis to explain cocaine's vasoconstrictor action is that the drug blocks a specialized nerve membrane transport system for sympathomimetic amines such as norepinephrine and that this diverts the amine to appropriate tissue receptors and potentiates the response.[81] In guinea pig mesenteric artery, cocaine depolarized the membrane potential and increased membrane resistance in the smooth muscle cells.[82] Cocaine also enhanced norepinephrine but not potassium-induced contractions. Thus cocaine appeared to inhibit the sensitivity of the intrajunctional adrenoceptor and to increase the sensitivity of the extrajunctional adrenoceptor distributed on the post junctional muscle membrane. Cocaine has been shown to potentiate the response to phenylephrine in reserpinized tissues.[83] Cocaine appears to act through both central and peripheral avenues,[84] and there is evidence for a significant central sympathetic stimulation component to its cardiovascular effects.[85] Cocaine can cause direct norepinephrine release[86] and, in the whole animal, result in epinephrine release from the adrenals.[84] Interestingly, Webb and Vanhoutte[86] found that other drugs which also inhibit norepinephrine reuptake did not exert the same actions on the cardiovasculature as cocaine.

In our laboratory we found evidence for an adrenergic component underlying the vasoactive effects of cocaine on isolated cerebral arteries.[36] Destroying adrenergic nerve endings with 6-hydroxydopamine or blocking $alpha_1$ and $alpha_2$ adrenergic receptors inhibited the cocaine-induced constriction (Figures 5.5 and 5.6). There is evidence that $alpha_1$[87,88] but not $alpha_2$ receptors [88] may participate in cocaine-induced vascular responses. Whole animal studies also have provided evidence for $alpha_1$-mediated presser [88,89] and $alpha_2$-mediated stimulant [90] responses. Why denervation with 6-hydroxydopamine resulted in a vasodilatory response to cocaine in the cat cerebral arteries (Figure 5.5) is not known, although it has been shown[91] that extraluminally applied cocaine dilated large and small pial arteries in cats, apparently through a stimulatory effect on beta receptors. This finding was somewhat unusual because while vasodilatory beta receptors are present in cat cerebral arteries, alpha vasoconstrictor effects predominate.[92]

Although the etiology of cocaine-induced heart attack is not known, several studies have suggested that it is due primarily to the increased circulating levels of adrenergic compounds.[46,47,93] In one study,[47] coronary artery vasoconstriction appeared to be mediated by alpha adrenergic stimulation since it was blocked by phentolamine. Egashira et al.[93] found that atherosclerotic porcine coronary arteries showed enhanced vasoreactivity to cocaine *in vivo*. This enhanced reactivity appeared to be mediated by endogenous vasoactive substances rather than a direct action of cocaine on vascular smooth muscle since isolated arterial strips did not

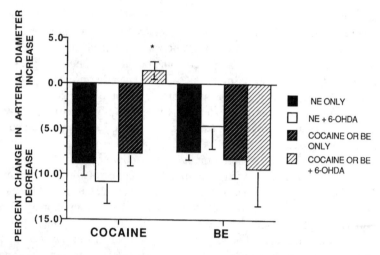

FIGURE 5.5 Percent change in diameter of cat cerebral arteries exposed to norepinephrine (NE; 10^{-6} M), cocaine (10^{-5} M), and benzoylecgonine (BE; 10^{-5} M) before and after denervation with 6-hydroxydopamine (6-OHDA; mean $\pm$ SEM; n=8; *p <0.05 compared to diameter decrease before 6-OHDA). (Reprinted from *Life Sciences,* 56, Madden, J. A., Konkol, R. J., Keller, P. A. and Alvarez, T. A., Cocaine and benzoylecgonine constrict cerebral arteries by different mechanisms, 679-686, 1995, with kind permission from Elsevier Science Ltd, The Boulevard, Langford Lane, Kidlington 0X5 1GB, UK.)

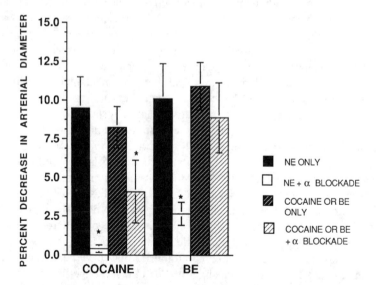

FIGURE 5.6 Percent decrease in diameter of cat cerebral arteries exposed to norepinephrine (NE; 10^{-6} M) and cocaine (10^{-5} M; n=8) and NE and benzoylecgonine (BE; 10^{-5} M; n=10) before and after α blockade with prazosin and yohimbine (10^{-6} M; mean $\pm$ SEM; * p <0.05 compared to decreases in diameter before α blockade). (Reprinted from *Life Sciences,* 56, Madden, J. A., Konkol, R. J., Keller, P. A., and Alvarez, T. A., Cocaine and benzoylecgonine constrict cerebral arteries by different mechanisms, 679-686, 1995, with kind permission from Elsevier Science Ltd, The Boulevard, Langford Lane, Kidlington 0X5 1GB, UK.)

contract directly to cocaine. On the other hand, other investigators have suggested that cocaine's cardiac effects may not be mediated solely through the adrenergic system. Vitullo et al.[94] demonstrated that the cocaine-induced small vessel spasm in isolated rat hearts was prevented by nitrendipine but not by phentolamine. Cocaine-induced coronary artery vasospasm in rats was prevented by nitrendipine but not by phentolamine,[94] but in humans it was prevented by phentolamine.[47]

The pulmonary vasculature is extensively innervated by adrenergic nerves, and it has an extensive system of alpha and beta adrenergic receptors localized on the vascular smooth muscle cells.[95] Cocaine has been shown to accentuate the adrenergic agonists presser responses in the pulmonary circulation.[96] Intrapulmonary arteries are more sensitive to alpha adrenergic stimulation than extrapulmonary segments.[97] Therefore, the effect of cocaine on the pulmonary vasculature might be mediated by the effect on alpha adrenergic receptors. Cocaine-induced pulmonary hypertension associated with decreased left ventricular function may produce pulmonary edema.[96] Cocaine-induced pulmonary edema may result from changes in central adrenergic outflow. Increased adrenergic outflow may cause an increase in pulmonary microvascular pressure that, in turn, could affect pulmonary vascular permeability.[96]

5.3.2 Non-Sympathetic

Mechanisms other than adrenergically-mediated ones have been proposed to account for the vasoactivity induced by cocaine.[87,89,98-104] In isolated bovine coronary arteries norepinephrine did not mediate the cocaine-induced contraction.[100] Evidence for a direct effect of cocaine on vascular smooth muscle is the observation that cocaine alone, without pharmacological pretreatment, augmented tension in human umbilical arteries *in vitro*.[99] Because human umbilical artery segments have no sympathetic innervation, their constriction by cocaine contradicts the traditional concept of cocaine as exclusively potentiating the catecholamine response.

Serotonin, one of the most potent vasoconstrictor amines has been implicated in cocaine-produced vascular effects.[21] Following acute or repeated cocaine injection, concentrations of serotonin and its major metabolite, 5-hydroxyindolacetic acid, decrease,[105] implying depleted serotonin stores. An interactive link between norepinephrine and serotonin has been suggested by several studies.[106,107] At concentrations $>10^{-6}$ M, serotonin acted on alpha adrenergic receptors to release norepinephrine.[107] Lower serotonin concentrations reduced norepinephrine output from sympathetic nerve terminals.[106] The failure of alpha adrenergic antagonists to block electrically-stimulated contraction in isolated cerebral arteries may have been due to a direct serotonin effect.[106] It has also been suggested that the migraine-like headache associated with cocaine use might be attributable to the inhibitory effect of the drug on serotonin reuptake.[20]

Studies have shown that arachidonic acid metabolites may be involved in cocaine-induced effects. Cocaine has been shown to inhibit umbilical artery prostacyclin production,[98] reduce 6- keto PGF_2 alpha production, and increase thromboxane A_2 production.[100] In addition, Perreault et al.[102] proposed that protein kinase C might contribute to cocaine-induced responses in vascular smooth muscle cells.

Some studies[87,99,100] have suggested that cocaine acts directly on vascular smooth muscle. We[36] and others[87,108] have found that the vasoconstrictor action of cocaine did not depend on the vascular endothelium, although this has not been a universal finding.[99,100] In reserpinized aortas[87] there was no norepinephrine supersensitivity and contraction was reduced; contraction was also inhibited by the alpha$_1$ adrenergic receptor antagonist, prazosin.

Cocaine's persistent potentiating effect in the absence of nerve terminals available for reuptake led Egashira et al.[87] to conclude that the drug's potentiating response resulted directly from enhanced calcium flux across cell membranes. How this occurs is not known, but if cocaine augments postsynaptic alpha receptor function then it may follow that the calcium mobilization would be mediated by alpha adrenergic receptors.

5.3.3 The Role of Calcium

The hypothesis that cocaine-induced vasoconstriction may depend on calcium[99,102,104,109] has been strengthened as a result of clinical reports[110-112] showing that calcium channel blockers reduced or eliminated cardiovascular effects linked to cocaine use. In animals, cocaine-induced contractions have been associated directly or indirectly with increased intracellular calcium in ferret thoracic aorta,[87] and cat cerebral arteries,[36] and in cerebral artery smooth muscle cells from dogs, pigs, and sheep.[109] Whether the increased intracellular calcium arises from mobilization of cellular calcium stores or whether it is derived from extracellular calcium influx is not totally settled. Cocaine appeared to exert a constrictor effect in cattle coronary arteries through L-type calcium channels.[104] Blocking voltage-gated calcium channels with low concentrations of verapamil relaxed cocaine-contracted dog basilar arteries.[104] Although dog cerebral arteries were found to be particularly sensitive to calcium antagonists,[113] in our laboratory,[36] treating cat middle cerebral arteries with verapamil before administering cocaine did not block the constriction.

Calcium mobilization from intracellular stores may be equally as important as extracellular calcium influx or it may even be the primary event responsible for cocaine-induced constriction. Cocaine can deplete intracellular magnesium in cerebral artery smooth muscle cells[103] which could potentiate intracellular calcium release. Magnesium applied directly to rat cerebral arteries *in situ* was found to prevent cocaine-induced vasoconstriction.[26] In our laboratory, we found that treating cat isolated middle cerebral arteries with ryanodine before perfusing the vessels with cocaine blocked the vasoconstriction (Figure 5.7). Ryanodine effectively depletes sarcoplasmic reticulum calcium stores by enhancing calcium release and reducing calcium resequestration.[114,115] Constrictor effects induced by alpha adrenergic mechanisms appear to rely heavily on intracellular calcium. Because cocaine seems to exert its vasoconstrictor effects at least partly by elevating plasma catecholamines and potentiating adrenergic activity, it seems logical to hypothesize that the cocaine-induced constrictor responses rely on the availability of cytoplasmic free calcium.

When we applied ryanodine to cat cerebral artery smooth muscle cells, norepineph-rine-stimulated increases in intracellular calcium were significantly reduced.[116] The above hypothesis is further supported by the findings of Greenberg and Innes[117] that cocaine potentiated the response to norepinephrine in isolated spleen strips even in the absence of extracellular calcium.

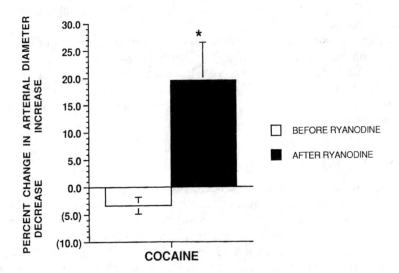

FIGURE 5.7   Percent change in diameter of cat cerebral arteries exposed to cocaine before and after ryanodine (10^{-5} M; mean ± SEM; n=5; *p <0.05 compared to decreased diameter before ryanodine). (Reprinted from *Life Sciences*, 56, Madden, J. A., Konkol, R. J., Keller, P. A., and Alvarez, T. A., Cocaine and benzoylecgonine constrict cerebral arteries by different mechanisms, 679-686, 1995, with kind permission from Elsevier Science Ltd, The Boulevard, Langford Lane, Kidlington 0X5 1GB, UK.)

5.3.4 The Metabolites

Until recently, no mechanism had been proposed to explain the vasoactivity of benzoylecgonine or indeed of any of the metabolites. In our study in adult cats,[36] the benzoylecgonine-induced vasoconstriction did not appear to be adrenergically mediated since neither denervation with 6-hydroxydopamine nor alpha adrenergic receptor blockade had any significant effect on the benzoylecgonine induced con-striction (Figures 5.5 and 5.6). In contrast to these findings, adrenergic stimulation appeared to partially mediate benzoylecgonine-induced constriction in cerebral arter-ies from fetal sheep[37] (Figure 5.8). In neither study, however, could we totally exclude the possibility that dopamine or dopaminergic nerves might play a role. We did determine, however, that in cat cerebral arteries, the vasoconstrictor action of ben-zoylecgonine depended on extracellular calcium influx [36] since verapamil blocked the benzoylecgonine-induced constriction (Figure 5.9). Based on this finding, it seems reasonable to hypothesize that the amelioration by calcium channel blockers of some of the cardiovascular effects attributed to cocaine might be related to effects associated with benzoylecgonine-induced vasoconstriction.

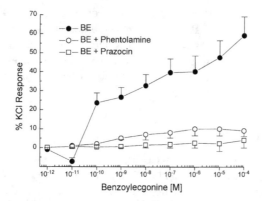

FIGURE 5.8 Effect of α-adrenergic antagonism of benzoylecgonine-induced vasoconstriction. Phentolamine (n=9) and prazosin (n=6; 10^{-5} M) blocked fetal sheep cerebral artery responses to benzoylecgonine. (From Schreiber, M. D., Madden, J. A., Covert, R. F., and Torgerson, L. J., *J. Appl. Physiol.*, 77, 834, 1994. With permission.)

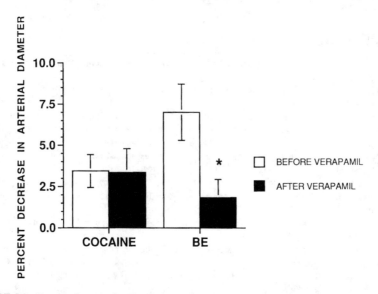

FIGURE 5.9 Percent decrease in diameter of cat cerebral arteries exposed to cocaine (n=9) and benzoylecgonine (BE; n=8) before and after verapamil (10^{-6} M; mean ± SEM; *p <0.05 compared to decreases in diameter before verapamil. (Reprinted from *Life Sciences*, 56, Madden, J. A., Konkol, R. J., Keller, P. A., and Alvarez, T. A., Cocaine and benzoylecgonine constrict cerebral arteries by different mechanisms, 679-686, 1995, with kind permission from Elsevier Science Ltd, The Boulevard, Langford Lane, Kidlington OX5 1GB, UK.)

The vasoreactivity of the cocaine metabolites might be related to their chemical structure. Cocaine, norcocaine, benzoylecgonine, and ecgonine methyl ester are derived from the amphoteric tropane alkaloid, ecgonine. Norcocaine has been shown to produce vasoconstrictor effects similar to those we noted with cocaine.[118] This suggests that the presence or absence of N-methylation has no significant effect on the vasoconstriction. Methyl esterification of the carboxylic function of ecgonine to form ecgonine methyl ester appears to remove or block the contractile effect and ecgonine methyl ester has dilatory effects in cerebral arteries of both cats[35] and fetal sheep.[37] Adding a benzoyl ester to the alcoholic group of ecgonine to form benzoylecgonine enhances the vasocontractile effect, and produces the most potent contractile agent of the group.[35] The methyl ester of benzoylecgonine, cocaine, is a less potent but still active constrictor.

5.4 SUMMARY

Cocaine and its metabolites can have profound physiological effects in various vascular beds of fetal, newborn, and adult humans and animals. The magnitude of the effect may depend on the particular compound, the age, and the metabolic status of the subject. The findings of studies using both cocaine and its metabolites may have implications for the pharmacological management of both acute and subacute vascular events associated with cocaine use. Because both pharmacological and temporal differences may underlie these effects, treatment modalities may have to be designed specifically for individual situations.

REFERENCES

1. Oro, A. S. and Dixon, S. D., Perinatal cocaine and methamphetamine exposure: maternal and neonatal correlates, *J. Pediatr.*, 444, 571, 1987.
2. Hadeed, A. J. and Siegel, S. R., Maternal cocaine use during pregnancy: effect on the newborn infant, *Pediatrics*, 84, 205, 1989.
3. Rosenak, D., Diamant, Y. Z., Yaffe, H., and Hornstein, E., Cocaine: maternal use during pregnancy and its effect on the mother, the fetus, and the infant, *Obstet. Gynecol.*, 45, 348, 1990.
4. Schenker, S., Yang, Y., Johnson, R. F., Downing, J. W., Schenken, R. S., Henderson, G. I., and King, T. S., The transfer of cocaine and its metabolites across the term human placenta, *Clin. Pharmacol. Ther.*, 53, 329, 1993.
5. Dusick, A. M., Covert, R. F., Schreiber, M. D., Yee, G. T., Browne, S. P., Moore, C. M., and Tebbett, I. R., Risk of adverse outcomes after cocaine exposure in a cohort of 323 very-low birthweight babies, *J. Pediatr.*, 122, 438, 1993.
6. Chasnoff, I. and Bussey, M., Perinatal cerebral infarction and maternal cocaine use, *J. Pediatr.*, 108, 457, 1986.
7. Dixon, S. and Bejar, R., Echoencephalographic findings in neonates associated with maternal cocaine and methamphetamine: incidence and clinical correlates, *J. Pediatr.*, 115, 770, 1989.
8. Tenorio, G., Nazvi, M., Bickers, G. H., and Hubbird, R. H., Intrauterine stroke and maternal polydrug abuse, *Clin. Pediatr.*, 27, 565, 1988.
9. Spires, M., Gordon, E., Choudhori, M., Maldonado, E. and Chan, R., Intracranial hemorrhage in a neonate following prenatal cocaine exposure, *Pediatr. Neurol.*, 5, 324, 1989.
10. Hoyme, H. E., Jones, K. L., Dixon, S. D., Jewett, T., Hanson, J. W., Robinson, L. K., Msall, M. E., and Allanson, J. E., Prenatal cocaine exposure and fetal vascular disruption, *Pediatrics*, 85, 743, 1990.
11. Coles, C. D., Platzman, K. A., Smith, I., James, M. E., and Falek, A., Effects of cocaine and alcohol use in pregnancy on neonatal growth and neurobehavioral status, *Neurotoxicol. Teratol.*, 14, 23, 1992.
12. Singer, L.T., Garber, R., and Kliegman, R., Neurobehavioral sequelae of fetal cocaine exposure, *J. Pediatr.*, 119, 667, 1991.
13. Kliegman, R. M., Madura, D., Kiwi, R., Eisenberg, I., and Yamashita, T., Relation of maternal cocaine use to the risks of prematurity and low birth weight, *J. Pediatr.*, 124, 751, 1994.

14. Burkett, G., Yasin, S. Y., Palow, D., LaVoie, L. and Martinez, M., Patterns of cocaine binging: effect on pregnancy, *Am. J. Obstet. Gynecol.*, 171, 372, 1994.

15. Greenfield, S. P., Rutigliano, E., Steinhardt, G., and Elder, J. S., Genitourinary tract malformations and maternal cocaine abuse, *Urology*, 37, 455, 1991.

16. Hannig, V. L. and Phillips, J.A., 3d., Maternal cocaine abuse and fetal anomalies: evidence for teratogenic effects of cocaine, *South Med. J.*, 84, 498, 1991.

17. Levine, S. R., Jefferson, M. F., Kieran, S. N., Moen, M., Feit, H., and Welch K. M. A., "Crack" cocaine-associated stroke, *Neurology*, 37, 1849, 1987.

18. Klonoff, D. C., Andrews, B. T., and Obana, W. G., Stroke associated with cocaine use, *Arch. Neurology*, 46, 989, 1989.

19. Levine, S. R., Brust, J. C. M., Futrell, N., Ho, K-L., Blake, D., Millikan, C. H., Brass, L. M., Fayad, P., Schultz, L.R., Selwa, J. F. and Welch, K. M. A., Cerebrovascular complications of the use of the "crack" form of alkaloidal cocaine, *N. Engl. J. Med.*, 323, 699, 1990.

20. Satel, S. L. and Gawin, F. H., Migrainelike headache and cocaine use, *JAMA*, 261, 2995, 1989.

21. Levine S. R. and Welch K. M. A., Cocaine and stroke, *Stroke*, 22, 25, 1987.

22. Daras, D. M., Tuchman, A. J., Koppel, B. S., Samkoff, L. M., Weitzner, I., and Marc, J., Neurovascular complications of cocaine, *Acta Neurol. Scand.*, 90, 124, 1994.

23. Daras, M., Tuchman, A. J., and Marks, S., Central nervous system infarction related to cocaine abuse, *Stroke*, 22,1320, 1992.

24. Peterson, P. L., Roszler, M., Jacobs, I., and Wilner, H. I., Neurovascular complications of cocaine abuse, *J. Neuropsych.*, 3, 143, 1991.

25. Fredericks, R. K., Lefkowitz, D. S., Challa, V. R., and Troost, B. T., Cerebral vasculitis associated with cocaine abuse, *Stroke*, 22 1437, 1991.

26. Huang, Q. J., Gebrewold, A., Altura, B. T., and Altura, B. M., Cocaine-induced cerebral vascular damage can be ameliorated by Mg^{2+} in rat brain, *Neurosc. Ltrs.*, 109, 113, 1990.

27. Altura, B. M., Altura, B. T., and Gebrewold, A., Cocaine induces spasms of cerebral blood vessels: relation to cerebral vascular accidents, strokes, and hypertension, *Fed. Proc.*, 44, 1637 1985.

28. Snoddy, A. M. and Bohlen, H. G., Cocaine causes constriction of cerebral arteries and arterioles, *FASEB J.*, 2, A1522, 1988.

29. Van de Bor, M., Walther, F. J., and Sims, M. E., Increased cerebral blood flow velocity in infants of mothers who abuse cocaine, *Pediatrics*, 85, 733, 1990.

30. O'Brien, T. P., Gleason, C. A., Jones, M.D., Jr., Cone, E. J., London, E. D., and Traystman, R. J. Cerebral responses to single and multiple cocaine injections in newborn sheep, *Pediatr. Res.*, 35, 339, 1994.

31. Chasnoff, I. J., Burns, K. A., and Burns, W. J., Cocaine use in pregnancy: perinatal morbidity and mortality, *Neurotoxicol. Teratol.*, 9, 291, 1987.

32. Spires, M. C., Gordon, E. F., Choudhuri, M., Maldonado, E., and Chan, R., Intracranial hemorrhage in a neonate following prenatal cocaine exposure, *Pediatr. Neurol.*, 5, 324, 1989.

33. Doberczak, T. M., Shanzer, S., Senie, R. T., and Kandall, S. R., Neonatal neurologic and electroencephalographic effects of intrauterine cocaine exposure, *J. Pediatr.*, 113, 354, 1988.

34. Volkow, N. D., Mullani, N., Gould, K. L., Adler, S., and Krajewski, K., Cerebral blood flow in chronic cocaine users: a study with positron emission tomography, *Br. J. Psych.*, 152, 641, 1988.

35. Madden, J. A. and Powers, R. H., Effect of cocaine and cocaine metabolites on cerebral arteries in vitro, *Life Sci.*, 47, 1109, 1990.

36. Madden, J. A., Konkol, R. J., Keller, P. A., and Alvarez, T. A., Cocaine and benzoylecgonine constrict cerebral arteries by different mechanisms, *Life Sci.*, 56, 679, 1995.

37. Schreiber, M. D., Madden, J. A., Covert, R. F., and Torgerson, L. J., Effect of cocaine, benzoylecgonine and cocaine metabolites on cannulated, pressurized fetal sheep cerebral arteries, *J. Appl. Physiol.*, 77, 834, 1994.

38. Kelly, P. A. T, Ritchie, I. M., Sharkey, J. and McBean, D. E., Alterations in local cerebral blood flow in mature rats following prenatal exposure to cocaine, *Neurosc.*, 60, 183, 1994.

39. Gleason, C. A., Iida, H., OBrien, T. P., Jones, M. D., Jr., and Cone, E. J., Fetal responses to acute maternal cocaine injection in sheep, *Am. J. Physiol.*, 265, H9, 1993.

40. Covert, R. F., Schreiber, M. D., Torgerson, L. J., Torgerson, R. W., and Miletich, D. J., Prediction of cerebral blood flow in anesthetized, exteriorized fetal lambs by a carotid artery ultrasonic flow transducer, *Reprod. Fertil. Dev.,* 8, 157, 1996.
41. van Bel, F., Roman, C., Klautz, C., Teitel, J. M., and Rudolph, A.M., Relationship between brain blood flow and carotid arterial flow in the sheep fetus, *Pediatr, Res,,* 35, 329, 1994.
42. Kurth, C. D., Monitto, C., Albuquerque, M. L., Feuer, P., Anday, E., and Shaw, L., Cocaine and its metabolites constrict cerebral arterioles in newborn pigs, *J. Pharmacol. Exp. Ther.,* 265, 587, 1993.
43. Chiu, Y. C., Brecht, K., Dasgupta, D. S., and Mhoon, E., Myocardial infarction with topical cocaine anesthesia for nasal surgery, *Arch. Otolaryngol. Head Neck Surg.,* 112, 988, 1986.
44. Gubser, R., Goy, J-J., De Torrente, A., Wacker, J., and Humair L., Infarctus du myocarde apres abus de cocaine, *Schweiz. Med. Wschr.,* 118, 1657, 1988.
45. Karch S. B. and Billingham, M. E., The pathology and etiology of cocaine-induced heart disease, *Arch. Pathol. Lab. Med.,* 112, 225, 1988.
46. Wilkerson, R. D., Cardiovascular toxicity of cocaine, in *Cocaine Abuse: New Directions in Treatment and Research,* Spitz, H. I. and Rosecan, J. S., Eds., Brunner/Mazel, New York, 1990, 304.
47. Lange, R. A., Cigarroa, R. G., Yancy, C. W., Willard, J. E., Popma, J. J., Sills, M. N., McBride, W., Kim, A. S. and Hillis, L. D., Cocaine-induced coronary artery vasoconstriction, *N. Engl. J. Med.,* 321, 1557, 1989.
48. Langner, R. O., Bement, C. L. and Perry, L. E., Arteriosclerotic toxicity of cocaine, in *Cocaine Abuse: New Directions in Treatment and Research,* Spitz, H. I. and Rosecan, J. S., Eds., Brunner/Mazel, New York, 1990, 325.
49. Ettinger, N. A. and Albin, R. J., A review of the respiratory effects of smoking cocaine, *Am. J. Med.,* 87, 664, 1989.
50. Forrester, J. M., Steele, A. W., Waldron, J. A., and Parsons, P. E., Crack lung: an acute pulmonary syndrome with a spectrum of clinical and histopathologic findings, *Am. Rev. Respir. Dis.,* 142, 462, 1990.
51. Bergofsky, E. H., Active control of the normal pulmonary circulation, in *Pulmonary Vascular Diseases,* Moser, K. M., Ed., Marcel Dekker, New York, 1979, 248.
52. Tashkin, D. P., Khalsa, M-E., Gorelick, D., Chang, P., Simmons, M. S., Coulson, A. H., and Gong, H. Jr., Pulmonary status of habitual cocaine smokers, *Am. Rev. Respir. Dis.,* 145, 92, 1992.
53. Murray, R. J., Smialek, J. E., Golle, M., and Albin, R. J., Pulmonary artery medial hypertrophy in cocaine users without foreign particle microembolization, *Chest,* 96, 1050, 1989.
54. Dolkart, L. A., Plessinger, M. A., and Woods, J. R., Effect of alpha$_1$ receptor blockade upon maternal and fetal cardiovascular response to cocaine, *Obstet. Gynecol.,* 75, 745,.1990.
55. Moore, T. R., Sorg, J., Miller, L., Key, T. C., and Resnik, R., Hemodynamic effects of intravenous cocaine on the pregnant ewe and fetus, *Am. J. Obstet. Gynecol.,* 155, 883, 1986.
56. Woods, J. R., Plessinger, M. A., and Clark, K. E., Effect of cocaine on uterine blood flow and fetal oxygenation, *JAMA,* 257, 957, 1987.
57. Morgan, M. A., Silavin, S. L., Randolph, M., Payne, G. G., Jr., Sheldon, R. E., Fishburne, J. I. J., Wentworth, R. A., and Nathanielsz, P. W., Effect of intravenous cocaine on uterine blood flow in the gravid baboon, *Am. J. Obstet. Gynecol.,* 164, 1021, 1991.
58. Covert, R. F., Schreiber, M. D., Tebbett, I. R., and Torgerson, L. J., Hemodynamic and cerebral blood flow effects of cocaine, cocaethylene, and benzoylecgonine in conscious and anesthetized fetal lambs, *J. Pharmacol. Exp. Ther.,* 270, 118, 1994.
59. George, K., Smith, J. F., and Curet, L. B., Doppler velocimetry and fetal heart rate pattern observations in acute cocaine intoxication. A case report, *J. Reprod. Med.,* 40, 65, 1995.
60. Cohen, L. S., Sabbagha, R. E., Keith, L. G., and Chasnoff, I. J., Doppler umbilical velocimetry in women with polydrug abuse including cocaine, *Int. J. Gynaecol. Obstet.,* 36, 287, 1991.
61. Hoskins, I. A., Friedman, D. M., Frieden, F. J., Ordorica, S. A., and Young, B. K., Relationship between antepartum cocaine abuse, abnormal umbilical artery Doppler velocimetry, and placental abruption, *Obstet. Gynecol.,* 78, 279, 1991.
62. Zhang, L. and Dyer, D. C., Characterization of alpha-adrenoceptors mediating contraction in isolated ovine umbilical vein, *European J. Pharmacol.,* 197, 63, 1991.

63. Iriye, B. K., Bristow, R. E., Hsu, C. D., Bruni, R., and Johnson, T. R., Uterine rupture associated with recent antepartum cocaine abuse, *Obstet. Gynecol.*, 83, 840, 1994.

64. Hsu, C. D., Chen, S., Feng, T. I., and Johnson, T. R., Rupture of uterine scar with extensive maternal bladder laceration after cocaine abuse, *Am. J. Obstet.. Gynecol.*, 167, 129, 1992.

65. Monga, M., Weisbrodt, N. W., Andres, R. L., and Sanborn B. M., The acute effect of cocaine exposure on pregnant human myometrial contractile activity, *Am. J. Obstet. Gynecol.*, 169, 782, 1993.

66. Hurd, W. W., Robertson, P. A., Riemer, R. K., Goldfien, A., and Roberts, J. M., Cocaine directly augments the alpha-adrenergic contractile response of the pregnant rabbit uterus, *Am. J. Obstet. Gynecol.*, 164, 182, 1991.

67. Smith, Y. R., Dombrowski, M. P., Leach, K. C., and Hurd, W. W., Decrease in myometrial beta-adrenergic receptors with prenatal cocaine use, *Obstet. Gynecol.*, 85, 357, 1995.

68. Stewart, D. J., Inaba, T., Lucassen, M., and Kalow, W., Cocaine metabolism: cocaine and norcocaine hydrolysis by liver and serum esterases, *Clin. Pharmacol. Ther.*, 25, 464, 1979.

69. Spiehler, V. R. and Reed, D., Brain concentrations of cocaine and benzoylecgonine in fatal cases, *J. Forensic Sci.*, 30, 1003, 1985.

70. Van Dyke, C., Cocaine: plasma concentrations after intranasal application in man, *Science*, 91, 859, 1975.

71. Weiss, R. D. and Gawin, F. H., Protracted elimination of cocaine metabolites in long-term, high-dose cocaine abusers, *Am. J. Med.*, 85, 879, 1985.

72. Barbieri, E. J., Ferko, A. P., DiGregorio, G. J., and Ruch, E. K., The presence of cocaine and benzoylecgonine in rat cerebrospinal fluid after the intravenous administration of cocaine, *Life Sci.*, 51, 1739, 1992.

73. Burke, W. M. and Ravi, N. V., Urinary excretion of cocaine. *Ann. Intern. Med.*, 112, 548, 1990.

74. Cone, E. J. and Weddington, W., Jr., Prolonged occurrence of cocaine in human saliva and urine after chronic use, *J. Anal. Toxicol.*, 13, 65, 1989.

75. DeVane, C. L., Simpkins, J. W., Miller, R. L., and Braun, S. B., Tissue distribution of cocaine in the pregnant rat, *Life Sci.*, 45, 1271, 1989.

76. Spear, L. P., Frambes, N. A. and Kirstein, C. L., Fetal and maternal brain plasma levels of cocaine and benzoylecgonine following chronic subcutaneous administration of cocaine during gestation in rats, *Psychopharmacology*, 97, 427, 1989.

77. Erzouki, H. K., Baum, I., Goldberg, S. R., and Schindler, C. W., Comparison of the effects of cocaine and its metabolites on cardiovascular function in anesthetized rats, *J. Cardiovasc. Pharmacol.*, 22, 1993.

78. Walmsley, J. G., Campling, M. R., and Chertkow, H. M., Interrelationships among wall structure, smooth muscle orientation, and contraction in human major cerebral arteries, *Stroke*, 14, 781, 1985.

79. Brogan, W. C., III., Lange, R. A., Glamann, D. B., and Hillis, L. D., Recurrent coronary vasoconstriction caused by intranasal cocaine: possible role for metabolites, *Ann. Intern. Med.*, 116, 556, 1992.

80. Nademanee, K., Myocardial ischemia during cocaine withdrawal, *Ann. Intern. Med.*, 111, 876, 1989.

81. Kalsner, S. and Nickerson, M., Mechanism of cocaine potentiation of responses to amines, *Br. J. Pharmacol.*, 35, 428, 1969.

82. Kuriyama, H. and Suyama, A., Multiple actions of cocaine on neuromuscular transmission and smooth muscle cells of the guinea pig mesenteric artery, *J. Physiol.*, 337, 631, 1983.

83. Bradley, L., Doggrell, S. A., and Edmonds, S. C., Cocaine potentiates the response to methacholine and noradrenalin in the rat vas deferens, *J. Pharm. Pharmacol.*, 37, 369, 1985.

84. Wilkerson, R. D., Cardiovascular effects of cocaine in conscious dogs: importance of full functional autonomic and central nervous systems, *J. Pharmacol. Exp. Ther.*, 246, 466, 1988.

85. Tella, S. R., Schindler, C. W. and Goldberg, S. R., Cardiovascular effects of cocaine in conscious rats: relative significance of central sympathetic stimulation and peripheral neuronal monoamine uptake and release mechanisms, *J. Pharmacol. Exp. Ther.*, 262, 602, 1992.

86. Webb, R. C. and Vanhoutte, P. M., Cocaine-induced release of noradrenaline in rat tail artery, *J. Pharm. Pharmacol.*, 34, 134, 1982.

87. Egashira, K., Morgan, K. G., and Morgan, J. P., Effects of cocaine on excitation-contraction coupling of aortic smooth muscle from the ferret, *J. Clin. Invest.*, 87, 1322, 1991.

88. Schindler, C. W., Tella, S. R., and Goldberg, S.R., Adrenoceptor mechanisms in the cardiovascular effects of cocaine in conscious squirrel monkeys, *Life Sci.*, 51, 653, 1992.

89. Dolkart, L. A., Plessinger, M. A., and Woods, J. R., Effect of alpha$_1$ receptor blockade upon maternal and fetal cardiovascular responses to cocaine, *Obstet. Gynecol.*, 75, 745, 1990.

90. Jackson, H. C., Griffin, I. J., and Nutt, D. J., α_2-adrenoceptor antagonists block the stimulant effects of cocaine in mice, *Life Sci.*, 50, PL-155, 1992.

91. Dohi, S., Jones, M. D., Jr., Hudak, M. L., and Traystman, R. J., Effects of cocaine on pial arterioles in cats, *Stroke*, 32, 1710, 1990.

92. Edvinsson, L. and Owman, C., Pharmacological characterization of adrenergic alpha and beta receptors mediating the vasomotor responses of cerebral arteries in vitro, *Circ. Res.*, 35, 835, 1974.

93. Egashira, K., Pipers, F. S., and Morgan, J. P., Effects of cocaine on epicardial coronary artery reactivity in miniature swine after endothelial injury and high cholesterol feeding: in vivo and in vitro analysis, *J. Clin. Invest.*, 88, 1307, 1991.

94. Vitullo, J. C., Karam, R., Mekhail, N., Wicker, P., Engelmann, G. L., and Khairallah, P.A., Cocaine-induced small vessel spasm in isolated rat hearts, *Am. J. Pathol.*, 135, 85, 1989.

95. Hyman, A. L., Nandiwada, P., Knight, D. S., and Kadowitz, P. J., Pulmonary vasodilator responses to catecholamines and sympathetic nerve stimulation in the cat: evidence that vascular β-2 adrenoreceptors are innervated, *Circ. Res.*, 48, 407, 1981.

96. Lang, S. A. and Maron, M. B., Hemodynamic basis for cocaine-induced pulmonary edema in dogs, *J. Appl. Physiol.*, 71, 1, 1991.

97. Kolbeck, R. C. and Speir, W. A., Jr., Regional contractile responses in pulmonary artery to α- and β-adrenoceptor agonists, *Can. J. Physiol. Pharmacol.*, 65, 1165, 1987.

98. Cejtin, H. E., Parsons, M. T., and Wilson, L., Jr., Cocaine use and its effect on umbilical artery prostacyclin production, *Prostaglandins*, 40, 249, 1990.

99. Isner, J. M. and Chokshi, S. K., Cocaine-related heart disease, *Heart Disease*, 14, 323, 1991.

100. Foy, R. A., Myles, J. L., and Wilkerson, R. D., Contraction of bovine coronary vascular smooth muscle induced by cocaine is not mediated by norepinephrine, *Life Sci.*, 49, 299, 1991.

101. Eichhorn, E. J., Demian, S. E., Alvarez, L. G., Willard, J. E., Molina, S., Bartula, L. L., Prince, M. D., Inman, L. R., Grayburn, P. A., and Myers, S. I., Cocaine-induced alterations in prostaglandin production in rabbit aorta, *J. Am. Coll. Cardiol.*, 19, 696, 1992.

102. Perreault, C. L., Morgan, K. G., and Morgan, J. P., Effects of cocaine on intracellular calcium handling in cardiac and vascular smooth muscle, in *NIDA Research Monograph 108*, Thadani, P. Ed., National Institute on Drug Abuse, Washington D.C., 1991, 139.

103. Altura, B. M., Zhang, A., Cheng, TP-O., and Altura, B. T., Cocaine induces rapid loss of intracellular free Mg^{2+} in cerebral vascular smooth muscle cells, *Euro. J. Pharmacol.*, 246, 299, 1993.

104. Kalsner, S., Cocaine sensitization of coronary artery contractions: mechanism of drug-induced spasm, *J. Pharmacol. Exp. Ther.*, 264, 1132, 1993.

105. Taylor, D. and Ho, B., Neurochemical effects of cocaine following acute and repeated injection, *J. Neurosci. Res.*, 3, 95, 1977.

106. Balfagon, G. and Marin, J., Modulation of noradrenaline release from cat cerebral arteries by presynaptic α_2-adrenoceptors: Effect of chronic treatment with desipramine and cocaine, *Gen. Pharmacol.*, 20, 289, 1989.

107. Mackenzie, E. T., Seylaz, J., and Bes, A., *Neurotransmitters and the Cerebral Circulation*, Raven Press, New York, 1984.

108. Kuhn, F. E., Gillis, R. A., Virmani, R., Visner, M. S., and Schaer, G. L., Cocaine produces coronary artery vasoconstriction independent of an intact endothelium, *Chest*, 102, 581, 1992.

109. He, G-Q., Zhang, A., Altura, B. T., and Altura, B. M., Cocaine-induced cerebrovasospasm and its possible mechanism of action, *J. Pharmacol. Exp. Ther.*, 268, 1532, 1994.

110. Billman, G. E. and Hoskins, R. S., Cocaine-induced ventricular fibrillation: protection afforded by the calcium antagonist verapamil, *FASEB J.*, 2, 2990, 1988.

111. Billman, G. E., Mechanisms responsible for the cardiotoxic effects of cocaine, *FASEB J.*, 4, 2469, 1990.

112. Trouve, R., Nahas, G. G., and Maillet, M., Nitrendipine as an antagonist to the cardiac toxicity of cocaine, *J. Cardiovasc. Pharmacol.,* 9, S49, 1987.

113. Shimizu, K., Ohta, T., and Toda, N., Evidence for greater susceptibility of isolated dog cerebral arteries to Ca antagonists than peripheral arteries, *Stroke,*11, 261, 1980.

114. Iino, M., Kobayashi, T., and Endo, M., Use of ryanodine for functional removal of the calcium store in smooth muscle cells of the guinea-pig, *Biochem. Biophys. Res. Commun.,* 15, 417, 1988.

115. Ashida, T., Schaeffer, J., Goldman,W. F., Wade, J. B., and Blaustein, M. P., Role of sarcoplasmic reticulum in arterial contraction: comparison of ryanodine's effect in a conduit and a muscular artery, *Circ. Res.,* 62, 854, 1988.

116. Vadula, M. S., Kleinman, J. G., and Madden, J. A., Effect of hypoxia and norepinephrine on cytoplasmic free Ca^{2+} in pulmonary and cerebral arterial myocytes, *Am. J. Physiol.,* 265, L591, 1993.

117. Greenberg, R. and Innes, I. R., The role of bound calcium in supersensitivity induced by cocaine, *Br. J. Pharmacol.,* 57, 329, 1976.

118. Chokshi, S. K., Gal, D. and Isner, J. M., Vasospasm caused by cocaine metabolite: a possible explanation for delayed onset of cocaine-related cardiovascular toxicity, *Circulation,* 80, II-351, 1989.

Chapter 6

Behavioral and Convulsive Effects of Cocaine Metabolites: Mechanisms and Implications

Richard J. Konkol, MD, PhD, and Guy Schuelke, PhD

6.0 INTRODUCTION

Many neurological disturbances in newborn infants have been attributed to maternal cocaine use. Such associative observations do not address the question of how maternally derived cocaine causes ill effects in the fetus and infant. Especially perplexing from both a theoretical and clinical view are the often-seen protracted effects lasting more than several days.[1-5] A neonatal withdrawal syndrome is unlikely since there is no established characteristic cocaine withdrawal pattern (see Chapter 7 for discussion). A direct cocaine-toxic effect can only account for a very limited spectrum of clinical changes since the short half-life of cocaine is only about one hour by most estimates.[6-9] Similarly, not all of these subacute behavioral abnormalities can be attributed to a fetopathy since many normalize in the first weeks of life. Therefore, the slowly resolving behavior perturbations are unexplained.

One theory which could account for these disturbances is that the slowly eliminated metabolites of cocaine retain central nervous system biological activity and cause slowly resolving behavioral effects. These more polar metabolites are most certainly derived in the brain from cocaine, which freely penetrates the blood brain barrier (BBB). Because the metabolites are more polar than cocaine they are also retained longer within the brain and eliminated more slowly from the body. For example, chronic adult users continue to eliminate cocaine metabolites for several weeks following cessation of cocaine intake.[10,11] The "active metabolite hypothesis" is consistent with a latency for product accumulation before the emergence of signs and symptoms related to cocaine toxicity.[12-14] The purpose of this chapter is to present the accumulating evidence in favor of a contribution by cocaine metabolites to the total fetal cocaine-associated neurobehavioral pathology and to suggest some mechanisms for their action.

6.1 EXPERIMENTAL STUDIES

Experimental studies are essential in defining the role of metabolites. Seizures and a variety of behavior alterations have been characterized following cocaine administered to animals. Rats display an increase in locomotor activity and stereotyped behaviors on low doses of cocaine. At higher cocaine doses an increased percentage

0-8493-9465-1/96/$0.00+$.50

of animals have seizures and then die. The behavioral activation and seizures can be attenuated by pretreatment with excitatory amino acid antagonists, adrenergic agents and anticonvulsants.[15-18]

6.1.1 Newborn Animal Behavior

Newborn animals whose mothers have received cocaine also display abnormalities of behavior and learning. The differences between cocaine-exposed and noncocaine-treated control animals are most apparent during the first days of life.[19-21] The exposed animals tend to have resolving perturbations of activity. Learning impairments are more subtle and less often reported.[22,23] Recent work indicates that the factors contributing to behavioral and learning defects are complex and include the timing and amount of maternal drug exposure as well as the animal's sex.[24] However, some behavioral deficiencies, although not acutely recognized, may emerge later. (See Chapters 9 and 10 for elaboration on the enduring behavioral effects of transplacental cocaine.)

6.1.2 Metabolite-Induced Effects

A direct method of documenting cocaine (C) metabolite-associated central neurological activity without the confounding effects of the parent compound or additional metabolism is to administer the individual metabolites directly into the brain so as to achieve reliable brain doses. Misra et al.[6] first used this technique to test for central nervous system activity by intracisternal-ventricular space (ICV) administration in adult rats of the metabolites benzoylecgonine (BE), benzoylnorecgonine (NBE), ecgonine (EC), ecgonine methyl ester (EME), and norcocaine (NC). They observed pronounced dose-related increased stimulatory effects after BE, NC, and NBE. Dramatic prolonged running, jumping, and vocalizations were often seen. Russian scientists (translated review) showed in rats that BE, EC, EME, and numerous tropane ring-based compounds, or one of the cocaine fragments, have central stimulatory effects.[25]

6.1.2.1   Behavior and Specific Metabolites

Our group has continued this work with adult and juvenile animals and extended the observations of metabolite effects. The predominant metabolite-related behavioral effects fell into two categories. One consisted of motor activation with myoclonus and tonus following administration of cocaine, BE, NBE, and NC. The other result was characterized by the induction of predominantly sedentary/inhibitory effects observed with EC and EME. After EC and EME animals became quiet, ceased spontaneously moving, and acted as if asleep. When touched they reacted appropriately and then quieted again. The relative dose-response effect of the behavioral activity produced by cocaine and five of its metabolites shows a dose-related order: NBE > BE > C = NC > EC > EME. In the adult, BE and NBE metabolites caused dramatic and dose-related prolonged, well-organized running, bouncing, and vocalization. Signs of sympathetic activation such as pupillary dilation and piloerection accompanied the motor activation. In rats 2 weeks or less in age a more poorly organized nonrhythmic continuous paddling response emerged.

6.1.2.2   Seizures and Mortality

The dramatic behavioral activation pattern most often precedes the appearance of seizures. The seizure-inducing dose-response relationship in the adult rat for cocaine and its major metabolite BE is illustrated in Figure 6.1. When administered intra-ventricularly, BE more often induced seizures than the same amount of cocaine.[28] A similar effect has been found with juveniles.[27,28]

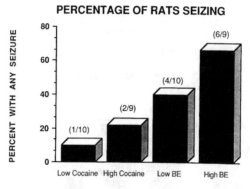

FIGURE 6.1   Incidence of seizures after intraventricular injection of two equimolar doses of cocaine and benzoylecgonine (BE). For each treatment, the number of animals with seizures is shown above the number of rats treated. Chi-square analysis showed a significant difference ($p < 0.02$) between all cocaine- and all BE-injected animals. (From Konkol, R. J., Erickson B. A., Doerr, J. K., Hoffman, R. G., and Madden J. A., Seizures induced by the cocaine metabolite benzoylecgonine in rats, *Epilepsia*, 33, 420, 1992. With permission.)

The main difference between the adult and juvenile responses was a more fragmented, nonrhythmic motor pattern in animals less than 3 weeks of age (Table 6.1). With higher metabolite doses, continuous motor activation preceded death in both age groups. The specific metabolite-related behavioral outcome and the approximate ED 50 dose ranges for juvenile and adult rats are presented in Table 6.2. Results are from two independent laboratories which pooled data only after all experiments were completed.[28] These data demonstrate similar motor activation effects in the two age groups. There was, however, a trend for decreased seizure frequency in older animals given the same dose of NBE (Figure 6.2). This lowered threshold in the younger animals compared to older rats is similar to the lowered threshold motor seizures noted in neonatal animals and man, irrespective of seizure etiology.[29,30]

Table 6.1   BE and NBE Age-Related Behavior Activation Pattern

Rats < 3 weeks of age
Ataxia > Paddling > Clonus > Brief tonus > Myoclonus
Rats > 3 weeks of age
Run > Bounce > Sustained Tonus > Prolonged Hyperactivity

Table 6.2 Relative Activity of Cocaine and Metabolites in Rats

Cocaine/Metabolite	Injected(μg)*	Behavioral Effect
Norbenzoylecgonine**	5–10	Run-Myoclonus-Tonus
Benzoylecgonine	30–50	Run-Myoclonus-Tonus
Cocaine	90–125	Myoclonus-Tonus
Norcocaine	90–125	Myoclonus-Tonus
Ecgonine***	150–250	Myoclonus-Sedation
Ecgonine Methyl Ester	300–800	Sedation

* ICV dose of cocaine and cocaine metabolites producing about a 50% occurrence of behavioral effects. N = 8 to 12/group.
** Tested in juvenile rats only.
***1200 μg dose in adult animals produced brief myoclonus.

(Adapted from Schuelke G. S., Konkol, R. J., Terry L. C., and Madden J. A., Effect of cocaine metabolites on behavior: possible neuroendocrine mechanisms, *Brain Res. Bull.*, 39, 43, 1996. With permission.)

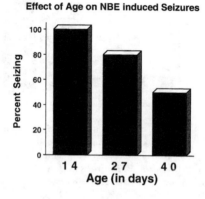

Effect of Age on NBE induced Seizures

FIGURE 6.2 Decreasing frequency of seizures with increasing age. Rats age 14, 27, and 40 days of age had decreasing seizure frequency after each received the same dose of 5 micrograms of norbenzoylecgonine (NBE) intracerebroventricularly (chi-square p <0.05).

Characteristically, the BE and NBE-related motor activation pattern was intermittently interrupted by episodes of tonic seizure, which are identical in appearance to maximal hind limb extension seizures, seen with the electroshock seizure model. These generalized tonic episodes are associated with hippocampal electroencephalographic changes consisting of rhythmic progressively faster frequency hippocampal discharges recorded during the tonic phase of the seizure (Figure 6.3).[26] Thus the data collectively demonstrate that several of the cocaine metabolites, including the most commonly encountered long-lived BE and the NBE species, have epileptogenic effects in both young and old animals. Similarly, Figure 6.4 shows behavioral activation effects occurring in animals that do not seize.

6.1.2.3   Vascular Contraction and Analgesia

Apart from behavior alteration and convulsive effects, BE also has other independent physiological actions. Specific BE-induced cerebral vasoconstriction has been

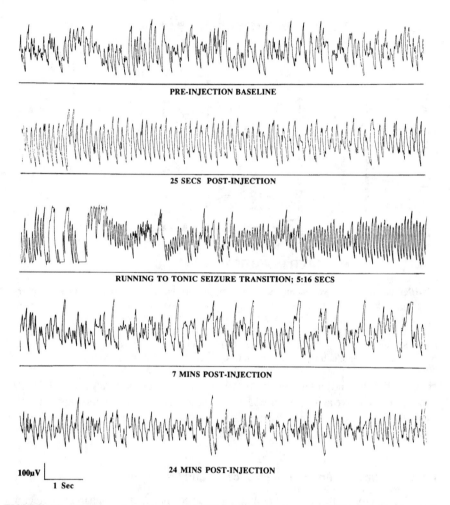

FIGURE 6.3 Hippocampal electrical record of high-dose benzoylecgonine (BE) injected rat. A recording obtained before intraventricular injection showed irregular mixed frequencies. By 25 seconds after injection, a rhythmic synchronization of the background was evident, but the animal showed no clearly recognizable behavioral pattern. After 5 min postinjection, the rat began to run and developed a tonic seizure as the EEG exhibited regular fast frequencies. At 7 minutes postinjection, there was erratic vocalization, biting, and jerking, while high-voltage mixed frequencies were apparent on the EEG. Twenty-four minutes postinjection, the animal was quiet, and the EEG approached that of the preinjection baseline period. (From Konkol, R. J., Erickson, B. A., Doerr, J. K., Hoffman, R. G., and Madden, J. A., Seizures induced by the cocaine metabolite benzoylecgonine in rats, *Epilepsia*, 33, 420, 1992. With permission.)

demonstrated experimentally. There is also some independent clinical data supporting an active vascular action of BE.[31,32] A full discussion of the vascular mechanisms of BE can be found in Chapter 5.

A recently recognized effect of BE is its ability to cause a systemic central analgesia independent of its local anesthetic action. In these experiments the hot plate thermal analgesia assay was used to investigate the molecular components of the cocaine molecule which are required to produce analgesia.[33] These studies

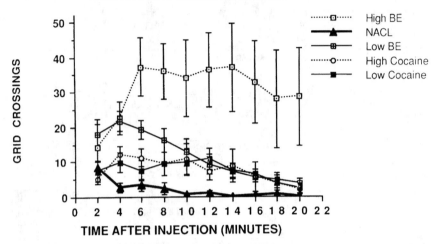

FIGURE 6.4 Activity levels as measured by counts of the quadrants crossed in the test chamber for 2-min intervals after cocaine or benzoylecgonine (BE) injection. Only animals with no seizures were included. A dose-related magnitude of activation of behavior was greater for BE compared to cocaine, and both cocaine and BE were greater than the nonspecific effects of an intraventricular saline injection. (From Konkol, R. J., Erickson, B. A., Doerr, J. K., Hoffman, R. G., and Madden, J. A., Seizures induced by the cocaine metabolite benzoylecgonine in rats, *Epilepsia*, 33, 420, 1992. With permission.)

showed that BE and other tropane-ring-based molecules are analgesic, while EME is not.[33] The relative analgesia of BE, NBE, and EC contrasts with the lack of potency of EME. The data are generally consistent with the earlier report of central effects associated with most tropanoid compounds.[23]

6.1.2.4   Interactions Between Cocaine and Metabolites

The possibility that the relatively long-lived cocaine metabolites may interact was investigated. Potential interactions between compounds producing positive effects (BE, NBE, cocaine) and those producing negative or suppressive effects (EME, EC) were tested. These studies demonstrated that EME inhibited and/or blocked the behavioral activation induced by cocaine and BE. Ecgonine possessed similar properties. In order to be effective, compounds needed to be given in molar excess within several minutes of administration of the test compound. Table 6.3 shows that preinjected EME and/or EC inhibited seizures and/or death produced by subsequently injected cocaine, BE, and pseudococaine. Moreover, we have made an additional observation that EME can inhibit cocaine analgesia when preinjected in molar excess shortly before the cocaine.[33]

6.1.3 Possible Mechanisms of Metabolite Action

6.1.3.1   Ionic/Membrane Effects

Potential mechanisms for seizure induction and anticonvulsive effects have not yet been elucidated. Even less is known about membrane and ionic mechanisms of BE

Table 6.3 Inhibition of Cocaine and Benzoylecgonine Seizures by Ecgonine Methyl Ester (EME) and Ecgonine (EC)

2-Min Pretreatment	Stimulant Drug	p-value
EME (3.7 µM)	Cocaine (2.37 µM)	NS
EME (3.7 µM)	Cocaine (1.78 µM)	0.015
EME (3.7 µM)	Cocaine (1.18 µM)	0.004
EME (3.7 µM)	Pseudococaine (1.23 µM)	0.030
EC (2.26 µM)	Cocaine (1.77 µM)	NS
EC (3.61 µM)	Cocaine (1.77 µM)	0.002
EC (5.41 µM)	Benzoylecgonine (0.57 µM)	0.030*
EC (0.52 µM)	Benzoylecgonine (3.61 µM)	NS

* Indicates inhibition of seizure and death; p value determined by chi-square analysis; n=12–40 rats in each group.

(From Schuelke, G. S., Konkol, R. J., Terry, L. C., Madden, J. A., Effect of cocaine metabolites on behavior: possible neuroendocrine mechanisms, *Brain Res. Bull.*, 39, 43, 1996. With permission.)

and NBE. A strong molecular complex formed between BE and calcium chloride has been described.[34] The functional impact of this complex is unclear. A hint of calcium's importance for BE action on blood vessels was recently described.[35] The voltage-sensitive calcium channel blocker, verapamil, effectively reduced the vascular myogenic effect of BE without altering the response to cocaine. Attempts to generalize this finding from isolated blood vessels to a neuronal membrane mechanism are speculative.

6.1.3.2   Transmitters

In contrast to the catecholamine-related locomotor effects of cocaine,[16-18] a major catecholaminergic (CA) mechanism for metabolite-induced convulsions is considered unlikely for five reasons. First, BE is relatively less effective than cocaine in preventing the uptake of dopamine (DA)[36,37] even though it is more effective in the induction of seizures and behavioral changes.[26] A comparison of relative CA uptake blockade by a variety of cocaine metabolites[36] revealed no correlation with the behavior effects we have reported. Second, the DA receptor blocker haloperidol had no effect in reducing BE-induced seizures (opposite to the effect on cocaine locomotion and stereotyped behaviors).[17,27] Third, selective lesioning of the catecholamine neurons with the neurotoxin 6-hydroxydopamine[38] prior to administration of BE or NBE did not reduce seizure frequency compared to the saline-injected noncatecholamine depleted group (Konkol et al., unpublished data). Fourth, receptor binding affinity studies do not support EC/EME inhibition by competitive binding at dopamine, norepinephrine, serotonin, or sodium channels.[39-41] Molecular isometric restrictions do not seem to be essential for inhibition since EME also inhibited pseudococaine seizures.[42] Fifth, continuous measurement *in vivo* of neurochemical markers of cocaine-related catecholamine release did not correlate with cocaine-induced behavior or electroencephalographic changes.[43]

Noncatecholaminergic transmitter systems, however, appear to be important in the mechanism of seizure production. The BE-induced behavior effects were attenuated by conventional antiepileptic drugs such as phenytoin, phenobarbital, and diazepam, and unaffected by the neuroleptic haloperidol.[27] Diazepam was most effective against the BE-induced syndrome. It also proved effective in reducing the behavioral activation induced by NBE.[44] Similar blocking was seen when the NBE-treated animal was preinjected with the excitatory amino acid blocker, MK801 (Figure 6.5). It therefore appears probable that the NBE- and BE-induced activation involved both GABA-aminergic and excitatory amino acid components.

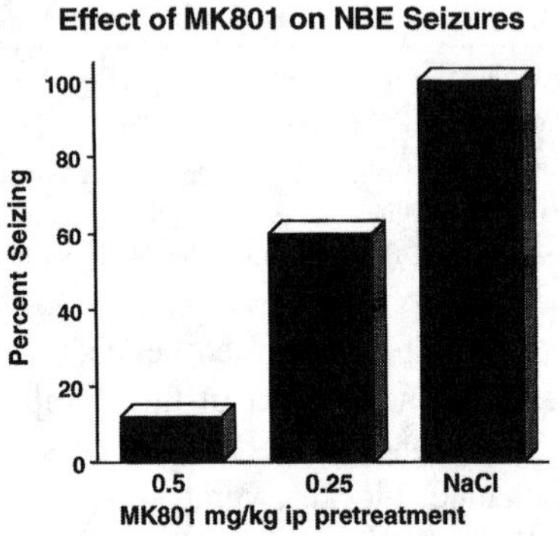

Effect of MK801 on NBE Seizures

FIGURE 6.5 Two-week-old rats were pretreated intraperitoneally with the excitatory amino acid antagonist MK801 15 minutes prior to intracerebroventricular injection with 25 micrograms of norbenzoylecgonine (NBE). An inhibitory effect on the behavior activation and seizure syndrome followed in a dose-related relationship (p <0.01).

6.1.3.3   Neuroendocrine Mechanisms

Enhanced sympathetic catecholaminergic activity due to uptake blockade of transmitter provides one possible means of enhancing behavioral activation. The neuroendocrine axis has also been implicated in the elaboration of behavioral effects of cocaine and other stimulants. These drugs alter corticotropin releasing hormone (CRH) release in wide areas of brain, providing for a mechanism of stimulant sensitization. These CRH behavioral effects are associated with an anxiety-like syndrome which can be suppressed by anti-CRH antibodies.[45,46]

Furthermore, CRH is a potent agent in the induction of seizures.[47,48] Specifically, CRH has also been implicated in the kindling paradigm. In this model a repeated application of an initial innocuous electrical or chemical stimulus results in progressive behavioral and electrographic changes leading to seizures. Therefore, when cocaine was administered once per day it resulted in progressive behavioral activation leading to an epileptogenic state and death. The epileptogenic process and the probability of death due to cocaine is significantly increased in a dose-dependent manner by intraventricular CRH.[49]

We entertained the possibility that the repeated cocaine administrations with the kindling protocol could permit accumulation of cocaine metabolites, as a stimulus for CRH release. To test this hypothesis rats were pretreated ICV with a pharmacological dose (10 micrograms) of CRH and then tested with ICVcocaine metabolites. Table 6.4

shows metabolite interaction under this protocol. There was a profound selective potentiation of BE seizures by CRH. The probable *in vivo* relevance of this finding was indicated by the ability of CRH antagonist (alpha helical CRH) given prior to BE to block the seizure potentiating effects of endogenous CRH. Experimental seizure induction with BE is likely to be potentiated by anxiety-related CRH released due to the necessary handling and restraint of the ICV injection procedure.[50] It may also account for increased mortality,[51] especially for those animals more stressed by the procedures. This mechanism would also be a relevant explanation for the approximately 30% variation of seizure induction between different experimental groups.

Table 6.4   Corticotropin Releasing Hormone (CRH)[a] and Seizures[b]

Treatment	Effect on Seizures
CRH controls	None
Diluent + BE (0.3 µM)	NS***
CRH + BE (0.31 µM)	Enhanced szs*
CRH + Cocaine (1.2 µM)	NS***
CRH + Cocaine (1.8 µM)	NS
CRH + EC (3.4 µM)	NS
CRH + EME (3.4 µM)	NS
alpha-CRH Controls	NS
alpha-CRH + BE (0.31 µM)	Suppressed szs**

[a] All CRH ICV injections were 10 µgs prior to the metabolite or cocaine.

[b] The doses of BE sufficient to produce seizures in a given percentage of animals varied slightly and had to be empirically determined for all test groups. For this batch of rats, the 0.31 µM dose of BE caused seizures in a sufficient number of vehicle control animals (73%) to permit demonstration of seizure inhibition with a limited number of test animals (n=32).

* Enhanced seizures, p = 0.0075.
**Suppressed seizures, p = 0.032.
*** NS = Nonsignificant.
All p values determined by chi-square analysis.

(From Schuelke, G. S., Konkol R. J., Terry L. C., Madden, J. A., Effect of cocaine metabolites on behavior: possible neuroendocrine mechanisms, *Brain Res. Bull.,* 39, 43, 1996. With permission.)

6.2 CLINICAL SIGNIFICANCE OF COCAINE METABOLITES

6.2.1 Metabolites in Infants

The above animal experiments demonstrate specific behavioral effects after administration of several cocaine metabolites. Of these the NBE metabolite is the most potent compound in our test series. When measured in guinea pig fetal tissues, it was found in relatively high amounts, particularly in the amniotic fluids.[52] The clinical relevance of this is unknown since this substance is not usually measured in man because of methodological and sampling limitations. However, when specifically measured, it is found in about two thirds of newborn infants' meconium.[53]

Furthermore, not all of the cocaine catabolic products may be equally relevant because of individual differences in cocaine metabolism. However, most clinical studies emphasize the importance of BE. This is the predominant cocaine metabolite in man.[9,54,55]

Drug usage patterns most certainly contribute to brain cocaine metabolite concentrations. Two weeks after chronic low dose cocaine injections, a significant increase in steady state level of BE was demonstrated in rats.[56] This observation may account for the high relative brain BE/cocaine ratios found in chronic adult abusers.[57]

6.2.2 Metabolism: Risk Factor

Cocaine is degraded by esterases as well as undergoing chemical hydrolysis.[54] Animal and human studies indicate that decreased cholinesterase activity leads to enhanced toxicity. For example, male animals with lower plasma cholinesterase activity required less cocaine to produce cardiovascular toxic signs than females, who had higher cholinesterase activity.[59,60] Accumulation of the BE metabolite has been attributed to low catabolic esterase enzyme activities.[61] It is therefore not surprising that there was a trend for more severe cocaine toxicity in adult patients with reduced plasma pseudocholinesterase activity.[62] More specifically, a statistical correlation was found between severity of cocaine toxicity and a mean 25% reduction of plasma cholinesterase activity.[63] In contrast, one study demonstrated a paradoxical protective effect of experimental pseudocholinesterase inhibition in the rat, suggesting that some enzymatic pathways of cocaine catabolism may enhance toxicity and other pathways suppress or limit toxicity.[64] Different species may have alternate breakdown pathways for cocaine.

Individual and physiological state related factors appear to influence the degree and pathway of cocaine breakdown. In addition to individual genetic variation in serum esterases, pregnancy is associated with depression of endogenous esterases.[65-67] Therefore, newborn infants, in particular, appear more vulnerable for risks related to cocaine metabolites.

Autopsy measurements also point to a higher risk for neonatal regional accumulation of the BE metabolite.[68] BE is found in relatively high levels in amniotic fluid, hair, and meconium.[69-71] In fetal rat brains, BE levels exceed cocaine levels of chronically injected dams. This suggests an increased risk for developmental vulnerability in that fetal brain BE also exceeded maternal brain BE concentration.[58] One human autopsy study[72] demonstrated the highest BE-to-cocaine ratio of about 70:1 in the fetal brain (BE=130µg/g) followed by the kidney (BE=69µg/g); these organs have been said to have an increased frequency of developmental abnormalities in cocaine-exposed infants.[72,73] One factor which may account for the regional difference in levels of cocaine carboxylesterase activity which is ranked: "liver > lung >> heart, kidney, brain, spleen."[59] Thus regional metabolite distribution differences are consistent with organs said to have an increased developmental risk.

6.2.3 Clinical Correlation

Benzoylecgonine's clinical effects and interactions are likely to be the most relevant to the search for an underlying explanation for persistent or late-emerging transient neurobehavioral effects. Prenatal somatic outcomes are correlated with meconium BE levels and reduction of birth head circumference, weight, and length.[74] Residual BE levels may also account for the emergence of seizures, persistent EEG abnormalities, and slowly resolving behavior disturbances in children of chronic cocaine abusers. The metabolite's presence provides a reasonable temporal explanation for a unique and variable clinical syndrome of altered state regulation, motor changes, and jitteriness.[1,2] Animal studies have shown that there is a behavior syndrome even in rats that did not seize after ICV BE (Figure 6.4).

While a cocaine withdrawal syndrome is said to explain some postnatal behaviors, there are no unique markers distinguishing pharmacological toxicity from a possible withdrawal state. Such a marker may emerge from ongoing metabolic studies employing positron emission computed tomography. These studies in adults are tantalizing in demonstrating hyper- and hypometabolic brain areas which distinguish early and protracted cocaine "withdrawal" states.[75]

Clinically late-emerging behavioral changes due to cocaine may be more readily demonstrated in younger children compared to those over 8 years.[76] Children exposed to cocaine smoke experience a high incidence of seizures, consistent with a developmental low seizure threshold for other convulsive agents. Newborns, with a naturally very low seizure threshold, are possibly even more uniquely sensitive to epileptogenic influences.[29,30]

Babies with measurable urinary BE, without detectable cocaine, are more irritable than those that have cocaine in the urine.[67] A previously unexplained syndrome of increased tone and tremors occurring between days 2 and 30 could also be explained by BE.[3] The temporal course of this syndrome is consistent with urinary BE elimination times in adults.[10,11] Brain clearance rates of the more polar "entrapped" metabolites, such as BE, are unknown.

A neonatal toxic syndrome, which may include seizures, is consistent with a subacute perturbation of behavior which resolves as BE clears from the infant brain.[67,77] Therefore, just as BE detection in urine and meconium is a major indicator of cocaine exposure, we propose that it also could be a long-lasting marker for subacute toxic behavioral disturbances. Reports showing a high incidence of BE in those dying of car accidents and homicide raises the question of a psychotropic effect extending into the adult age range.[78-79]

However, cocaine use does not take place in isolation. Other factors such as concomitant use of other drugs and lifestyle factors need to be explored. These may obscure the causal link between cocaine and a clinical syndrome.[80] These factors are further elaborated in Chapter 1. Since most abusers of cocaine also use tobacco and alcohol, cocaine may have an additive toxic role. A recently recognized, notable example is the impact of a toxic ethanol and cocaine condensation breakdown product, cocaethylene. This metabolite is thought to possess even more potent effects than cocaine.[81]

6.2.3.1   Seizures and Electrographic Changes

The temporal conditions associated with neonatal seizures and EEG changes appear to support the "active-metabolite" hypothesis. Kramer et al.[77] found that about half of 16 infants exposed to cocaine *in utero* had seizures within the first two days of life. These and the later seizures largely resolved in weeks to months. Furthermore, infants who did not have seizures but had EEG abnormalities in the immediate postnatal period also normalized in the subsequent weeks.[5,67] Quantitative EEG changes lasting for weeks have been found in chronic adult abusers.[82] In animals EEG desynchronization in the prefrontal cortex is prolonged when drugs which compromise cocaine-metabolizing esterases are given.[43] Case reports of seizures emerging days after cocaine intake also are consistent with the subacute effect of an accumulation and then a slow elimination of biologically active metabolites.[12,13,83]

6.2.3.2   Variability of Behavioral Outcomes

Given the relatively high potential of BE and NBE for inducing seizures, the question can be posed, why is the seizure frequency so low (usually not more than 10% in most larger series) in newborns exposed to cocaine? One possible reason is that metabolite accumulation needed to exceed the seizure threshold is insufficient. However, in our model the levels of metabolite required to induce seizures approximate the levels measured in cocaine abusers.[57,84] See Chapter 7 for a review of actual drug levels found in infants.

Alternatively, metabolite interaction may account for anomalous effects. Because metabolites such as EC and EME can block the activating effects of cocaine, NC, NBE, or BE, the relative proportion of cocaine metabolites is relevant. If there are low levels of excitatory metabolites compared to those with inhibitory properties, the net effect is a cancellation of the behavior activation.

Finally, the possibility of a BE-related refractory period should be considered. Following a CRH-induced seizure there is a prolonged period of about 2 weeks in which cocaine seizures cannot be induced.[49] This mechanism would curtail behavior activation following a covert or overt cocaine-related seizure. However, the significance of CRH's role will remain obscure until the basic neuronal mechanism(s) underlying the behavior activation and seizures due to cocaine metabolites is elucidated.

6.3   CRITERIA FOR DEFINING CLINICAL EFFECT OF SPECIFIC METABOLITES

To define a clinically significant role for a cocaine-derived compound(s) independent of the parent substance, several criteria should be fulfilled. The following lists at least four test conditions which should be satisfied to attribute a specific role to a putative active cocaine metabolite.

6.3.1   Qualitative Effects of the Putative Agent

The effects demonstrated for the putative active metabolite should mimic many or most of the actions attributed to the parent cocaine molecule. Behavioral activation, seizures, vascular constriction, and death have been viewed as cardinal features of cocaine toxicity. These effects all have been reproduced in animals by administration of cocaine metabolite, BE or NBE.[26-28,44,85] Furthermore, evolving and dissimilar clinical signs which emerge after a latency period, may reflect the effects of a changing balance of metabolites with specific central nervous system activating and suppression effects. This interaction may also account for the wide variability and contradictory nature of clinical reports identifying a wide range of characteristics of babies exposed to cocaine *in utero*.

6.3.2 Quantitative Aspects of the Putative Agent in the Brain

The putative compound should be present in sufficient amounts to cause an effect on brain function. As noted above, BE accumulates in relatively high levels in many tissues and fluids of infants. Cocaine abusers have relatively high brain BE/cocaine ratios.[57,84] Similarly, fetal brain has been found to contain significant levels of BE.[22,68,72] Under experimental conditions, the concentration of brain BE (~10 to 30 ng/g) associated with consistent seizure production overlaps that found in chronic cocaine abusers.[27,57] Thus, by these comparisons the cocaine metabolite, BE, approaches satisfying the second criterion.

6.3.3 Exposure Time Course

The time course of the compound within the brain should be consistent with the time course of relevant behavioral parameters. Specifically, the clearance rates of BE from the brain should match the time course of the clinical changes which approximate normalization of function. A BE clearance rate lasting several weeks, as documented in adult abusers,[10,11] and a parallel course for resolution of electrographic and other behavior disturbances in infants and adults generally fit this requirement. Because there are no direct clinical means of measuring metabolite levels in the brain, urine estimations are used as best indirect estimates. However, the critical correlation needed to link behavior changes more precisely to a particular compound await the development of either more sensitive fluid metabolite assays, or an improved means of imaging the effects of the compound in the brain.

6.3.4 Prognosis

The postexposure after-effect of the putative compound should be undetectable unless a separate physiological event, with its own identifiable pathological process, is superimposed.[80] For example if a seizure due to cocaine toxicity occurs, there should be no specific sequelae, such as epilepsy. This observation is supported by experimental data showing that cocaine seizures do not produce specific histological damage.[86] In contrast, after a cocaine-related stroke, the specific focal stroke-related sequelae should be the only remaining residual. For infants, this condition appears to be fulfilled in the vast majority of neonates in that *in utero* exposed neonates escape immediately recognizable sequelae[87] even when a significant number have behavior disturbance and about a 15% incidence of seizures.[4,88] The potential role of confounding variables such as socioeconomic class, other drugs, and the effect of the postnatal environment, all need to be carefully weighed. Caution must be exercised since a variety of neurodevelopmental functions cannot be tested in the neonate and await long-term outcome studies for a final judgment.

6.4   IMPLICATIONS OF THE ROLE OF ACTIVE COCAINE METABOLITES

6.4.1   Clinical Prediction

Conclusions which directly follow from the recognition of the clinical role of cocaine metabolites require a tempering of medical decision making and prognostication. For example, subacute clinical disturbances such as agitation and seizures in cocaine-abusing adults and neonates born to drug-using mothers should be treated symptomatically, and the exposed individual should not be viewed as having enduring drug-induced conditions. The rush to judgment and the pessimistic aura that often envelops healthcare providers and others dealing with drug-exposed newborns may be unfounded if based solely on newborn behavior.[89] Attention to the clinical course will reveal the true nature of the drug effect. Judgments regarding long-term outcome should, therefore, be suspended until the potential toxicity dissipates. If a specific residual is found, the link to cocaine or to covert confounders needs to be weighed.

6.4.2   Mechanisms and Experimental Design

Another theoretical implication extends to interpretation of experimental studies in which chronic cocaine dosing is employed. This consideration necessitates an experimental design accounting for the accumulation of BE. For instance, we speculate that BE accumulation may occur with repeated cocaine doses normally employed in the kindling model of epilepsy. If the brain concentration of BE exceeds the seizure threshold it could account for the "kindling effect" on a pharmacological basis instead of producing the expected reorganization of neuronal activity traditionally ascribed to the kindling process.

If the CRH mechanism is as important in cocaine- and BE-induced seizure production as preliminary studies suggest, controls isolating confounders are required. Arousal and nonpharmacological conditions may indirectly influence CRH availability and subsequent behavioral response threshold. This consideration highlights the role of pretreatment handling and testing conditions which can independently alter the adrenal pituitary axis.

6.4.3   Treatments

The spectrum of clinical effects produced by cocaine metabolites has implications for attempts to treat cocaine abuse and intoxication. Newer methodologies such as the use of antibodies[90,91] and/or enzymes[92] to accelerate cocaine clearance could open a new dimension in specific therapy. More important, some proposed treatments designed to enhance conversion of cocaine to "inactive" metabolites requires reevaluation in light of the potential risk of further clinical compromise incurred by the augmentation of metabolite levels.[93] The specific role of cocaine metabolites needs to be recognized in order to formulate a new safe and effective treatment for cocaine exposure.

Our finding that some cocaine metabolites, such as EC and EME, block the excitatory effects of cocaine, BE, and possibly NBE leads to another testable treatment option. Administration of EC or EME may theoretically shift the balance of cocaine species in favor of those compounds producing behavioral suppressive effects. This speculation, while not yet applicable to man, could lead to experiments assessing the therapeutic value of this hypothesis. However, the full clinical spectrum due to EME or EC is yet to be defined.

Furthermore, if cocaine and possibly BE-induced release of CRH is clinically relevant, then the need to provide an emotionally neutral environment becomes a very important and often overlooked treatment condition. Experimental studies show that the mortality rate of restraint-stressed rats was greatly increased over nonrestraint-stressed animals receiving cocaine. Reduction of anxiety should then indirectly reduce seizures and mortality risk in cocaine toxicity.

6.5 SUMMARY

The effects of cocaine exposure *in utero* are highly complex. However, many disturbances of brain function in the infant are transient. Some of these can be explained as a slowly dissipating toxic state attributable to cocaine metabolites. The best clinically characterized cocaine degradation species is benzoylecgonine. This metabolite has independent behavioral, convulsive, analgesic, vascular, and mortality-related outcomes. Its action and that of the parent cocaine molecule may be modified by other cocaine metabolites, neurotransmitter systems, anticonvulsants, and endocrine mechanisms. Recognition of the clinical impact of cocaine metabolites leads to several practical and theoretical consequences for medical decision making, experimentation, and for the formulation of new options for cocaine toxicity treatment.

REFERENCES

1. Chasnoff, I. J., Burns, W. J., School, S. H., and Burns, K. A., Cocaine use in pregnancy, *N. Engl. J. Med.,* 313, 666, 1985.
2. Chasnoff, I. J., Cocaine, pregnancy and the growing child, *Curr. Prob. Pediatr.,* 22, 302, 1992.
3. LeBlanc, P. E., Parekh A. J., Naso, B., and Glass, L., Effects of intrauterine exposure to alkaloidal cocaine ("crack"), *Am. J. Dis. Child.,* 141, 937, 1987.
4. Konkol, R. J., Tikosfsky, R. S., Wells, R., Hellman, R. S., Nemeth, P., Walsh, D. J., Heimler, R., and Sty, J. R., Normal high-resolution cerebral 99m-Tc-HMPAO SPECT scans in symptomatic neonates exposed to cocaine, *J. Child Neurol.,* 9, 278, 1994.
5. Doberczak, T. M., Shanxer, S., Senine, R. T., and Kandall, S. R., Neonatal neurologic and electroencephalographic effects of intrauterine cocaine exposure, *J. Pediatr.,* 113, 354, 1988.
6. Misra, A. L., Nayak, P. K., Block, R., and Mule, S. J., Estimation and disposition of [3H] benzoylecgonine and pharmacological activity of some cocaine metabolites, *J. Phar. Pharmac.,* 27, 784, 1975.
7. Misra, A. L., Disposition and biotransformation of cocaine, in *Cocaine: Chemical, Biological, Clinical, Social and Treatment Aspects,* Mule, S. J., Ed., Boca Raton, CRC Press, p. 71, 1976.

8. Schuster, L., Pharmacokinetics, metabolism, and disposition of cocaine, in *Cocaine Pharmacology, Physiology, and Clinical Strategies,* Lakoski, J. M., Galloway, M. P., White F. J, Eds., Boca Raton, CRC Press, p. 1, 1992.

9. Karch, S. B., Cocaine disposition in man, in *The Pathology of Drug Abuse,* Karch, S. B., Ed., CRC Press, Boca Raton, p. 29, 1993.

10. Burke W. M. and Ravi, N. V., Urinary excretion of cocaine, *Ann. Intern. Med.,* 112, 548, 1990.

11. Weiss, R. D. and Gawin, F. H., Protracted elimination of cocaine metabolites in long-term high dose cocaine abusers, *Am. J. Med.,* 85, 879, 1988.

12. Peters, A. J., Abrams, R. M., Burchfield, D. J., and Bilmore, R. L., Seizures in a fetal lamb after cocaine exposure: a case report, *Epilepsia,* 33, 1001, 1992.

13. Merriam, A. E., Medaalia, A., and Levine, B., Partial complex status epilepticus associated with cocaine abuse, *Biol. Psychol.,* 22, 515, 1988.

14. Ogunyeni, A. O., Locke, G. E., Kramer, L., and Nelson, L., Complex partial status epilepticus provoked by "crack" cocaine, *Ann. Neurol.,* 26, 785, 1989.

15. Tella, S. R., Korupolu, G. R., Schindler, C. W., and Goldberg, S. R., Pathophysiology and pharmacological mechanisms of acute cocaine toxicity in conscious rats, *J. Pharmacol. Exptl. Ther.,* 262, 936, 1992.

16. Witkin, J. M., Newman, A. H., Nowak, B., and Katz, J. L., Role of dopamine D1 receptors in the lethal effects of cocaine and a quaternary methiodine analog, *J. Pharmacol. Exptl. Ther.,* 267, 266, 1993.

17. Karler, R., Calder, L D., Chaudhry, I.A., and Turkanis, S. A., Blockade of reverse tolerance to cocaine and amphetamine by MK-801, *Life Sci.,* 45, 599, 1989.

18. Karler, R. and Calder, L. D., Excitatory amino acids and the actions of cocaine, *Brain Res.,* 82, 143, 1992.

19. Barron, S. and Irvine, J., Effects of neonatal cocaine exposure on two measures of balance and coordination, *Neurotoxicol. Teratol.,* 16, 89, 1994.

20. Hutching, D. E., Ficco, R. A., and Dow-Edwards, D. L., Prenatal cocaine: Maternal toxicity, fetal effects and locomotor activity in rat offspring, *Neurotoxicol. Teratol.,* 11, 65, 1989.

21. Larerriere, A., Ertung, F., and Moss, I. R., Prenatal cocaine alters open-field in young swine, *Biochem. Pharmacol. Behav.,* 17, 81,1995.

22. Spear, L. P., Kirstein, C. L., Bell, J., Yoottanasumpun, V., Greenbaum, R., O'Shea, J., Hoffman, H., and Spear, N. E., Effects of prenatal cocaine exposure on behavior during the early postnatal period, *Neurotoxicol. Teratol.,* 11, 57, 1989.

23. Kosofsky, B. E., Wilkins, A. S., Bressens, P., and Evarard, P., Transplacental cocaine exposure: a mouse model demonstrating neuroanatomical and behavioral abnormalities, *J. Ped. Neurol.,* 9, 234, 1994.

24. Vorhees, C. V., Reed, T. M., Acuff-Smith, K. D., Schilling, M. A., Cappon, J. E., Fisher, M., and Pu, C., Long-term learning deficits and changes in unlearned behaviors following *in utero* exposure to multiple daily doses of cocaine during different exposure periods and maternal plasma cocaine concentrations, *Neurotoxicol. Teratol.,* 17, 25, 1995.

25. Zakusov, V. V., Kostochka, L. M., and Skoldinov, A. P., Effect of cocaine molecule fragments on the central nervous system, *Biulleten Eksperimentalon, Giolotii i Meditsny,* 86, 435, 1978.

26. Konkol, R. J., Erickson, B. A., Doerr, J. K., and Hoffman, G., Seizures induced by the cocaine metabolite benzoylecgonine in rats, *Epilepsia,* 33, 420, 1992.

27. Konkol, R. J., Doerr, J. K., and Madden, J. A., Effects of benzoylecgonine on the behavior of suckling rats: A preliminary report, *J. Child. Neurol.,* 7, 87, 1992.

28. Schuelke, G. S., Konkol, R. J., Terry, L. C., and Madden, J. A., Inhibition of cocaine-associated seizures, death, analgesia, and self-stimulation by cocaine metabolites and CRH potentiation of benzoylecgonine effects, *Brain Res. Bull.,* 39, 43, 1996.

29. Wasterlain, C. G. and Vert, P., *Neonatal Seizures,* Raven Press, New York, 1990.

30. Moshe, S. L., and Cornblath, M., Developmental aspects of epileptogenesis, in *The Treatment of Epilepsy,* Wyllie, E., Ed., Philadelphia, Lea & Febiger, 1993, 99.

31. Del Aquila, C. D. and Rosman, H., Myocardial infarction during cocaine withdrawal, *Ann. Int. Med.,* 112, 712, 1990.

32. Brogan, W. C., Lange, R. A., Glamann, B., and Hillis, L. D., Recurrent coronary vasoconstriction caused by intranasal cocaine: possible role for metabolites, *Ann. Int. Med.,* 116, 556, 1992.

33. Schuelke, G. S., Terry, L. C., Powers, R. H., Mice, J., and Madden, J. A., Cocaine analgesia: an in vivo structure activity study, *Biochem. Pharmacol. Behav.*, 53, 133, 1996.

34. Misra, A. L. and Mule, S. J., Calcium-binding property of cocaine and some of its metabolites-formation of molecular complexes, *Res. Comm. Chem. Path. Pharmacol.*, 11, 663, 1975.

35. Madden, J. A., Konkol, R. J., Keller, P. A., and Alvarez, T. A., Cocaine and benzoylecgonine constrict cerebral arteries act through different mechanisms, *Life Sci.*, 56, 679, 1995.

36. Williams, N., Clouet, D. M., Misra, A. L., and Mule, S., Cocaine and metabolites: relationship between pharmacological activity and inhibitory action on dopamine uptake into striatal synaptosomes, *Prog. Neuropsychopharmacol.*, 1, 265, 1977.

37. Hawks, R. L., Kopin, I. J., Colburn, R. W., and Thoa, N. B., Norcocaine: A pharmacologically active metabolite of cocaine found in brain, *Life Sci.*, 15, 2189, 1974.

38. Cooper, B. R., Konkol, R. J., and Breese, B. R., Effects of catecholamine depleting drugs and d-Amphetamine on self-stimulation of the substantia nigra and locus coeruleus, *J. Pharm. Exptl. Ther.*, 204, 592, 1978.

39. Ritz, M. C., Cone, E. J., and Kuhar, M. J., Cocaine inhibition of ligand binding at dopamine, norepinephrine and serotonin transporters: a structure-activity study, *Life Sci.*, 46, 635, 1990.

40. Reith, M. E. A., Central and peripheral cocaine binding sites, in *Cocaine Pharmacology, Physiology, and Clinical Strategies,* Lakoski, J. M., Galloway, M. P., White, F. J., Eds., Boca Raton, CRC Press, 1992.

41. Matthews, J. C. and Collins, A., Interactions of cocaine and cocaine congeners with sodium channels, *Biochem. Pharm.*, 32, 455, 1983.

42. Katz, J. L., Tirelli, E., and Witkin, J. M., Stereoselective effects of cocaine, *Behav. Pharmacol.*, 1, 347, 1990.

43. Pan, W. P. T., Chen, M.-H., Lai, Y.-J., and Luoh, H-F., Differential effects of chloral hydrate and pentobarbital sodium on cocaine-induced electroencephalographic desynchronization at the medial prefrontal cortex in rats, *Life Sci.*, 54, 419, 1994.

44. Konkol, R. J., Keskin, S., and Buchhalter, J. R., Neuroactive properties of common long-lasting cocaine metabolite, benzylnorecgonine, *Pediat. Neurol.*, 11, 99, 1994.

45. Kuhn, C. M., and Little, P. J., Neuroendocrine effects of cocaine, in *The Neurobiology of Cocaine, Cellular and Molecular Mechanisms,* Hammer, R. P., Jr., Ed., CRC Press, Boca Raton, 1995, 49.

46. Sarnyai, Z., Biro, E., Gardi, J., Vecsernye's, Julesz, R., and Telegdy G, Brain corticotrophin-releasing factor mediates "anxiety-like" behavior induced by cocaine withdrawal in rats, *Brain Res.*, 675, 899, 1995.

47. Ehlers, C. L., Henriksen, S. J., Wang, M., Rivier, J., Vale, W., and Bloom, F. E., Corticotrophin releasing factor produces increases in brain excitability and convulsive seizures in rats, *Brain Res.*, 278, 332, 1983.

48. Baram, T. Z. and Schultz, L., CRH is a rapid and potent convulsant in the infant rat, *Brain Res.*, 61, 97, 1991.

49. Weiss, S. R. B., Nierenberg, J., Lewis, R., and Post, R. M., Corticotrophin-releasing hormone: potentiation of cocaine-kindled seizures and lethality, *Epilepsia*, 33,248, 1992.

50. Dobrakovova, M., Kvetnansky, R., Oprsalova, Z., and Jezova, D., Specificity of the effect of reported handling on sympathetic adrenomedullary and pituitary-adrenocortical activity in rats, *Psychoneuroendocrinology*, 18, 163, 1995.

51. Pudiak, C. M. and Bozarth, M. A., Cocaine fatalities increased by restrain stress, *Life Sci.*, 55, 378, 1994.

52. Sandberg, J. A. and Olsen, G. D., Cocaine pharmacokinetics in the pregnant guinea pig, *J. Pharmacol. Exp. Ther.*, 258, 477, 1991.

53. Murphy, L. J., Olsen, G. D., and Konkol, R. J., Quantitation of benzoylnorecgonine and other cocaine metabolites in meconium by high-performance liquid chromotology, *J. Chromatogr.*, 613, 330, 1993.

54. Stewart, D. J., Inaba, T., Tang, B. K., Lucassen, M., and Kalow, W., Cocaine metabolism: cocaine and norcocaine hydrolysis by liver and serum esterases, *Clin. Pharmacol. Ther.*, 25, 464, 1979.

55. Isenschmid, D., Fischman, M., Foltin, R., and Caplan, H., Concentration of cocaine and metabolites in plasma of humans following intravenous administration and smoking of cocaine, *J. Analyt. Toxicol.*, 16, 311, 1992.

56. Nahas, G. G., Latour C., Sandouk, P., and Arnaoudov, P. P., Cardiovascular tolerance and plasma cocaine levels after chronic administration of the alkaloid, *Coll. Prob. Drug Depend.*, Abstracts 102, 57th Annual Scientific Meeting (*J. Addict.*), Scottsdale, AZ, June 10-15, 1995.

57. Spiehler, U. R. and Reed, D., Brain concentrations of cocaine and benzoylecgonine in fatal cases, *J. Foren. Sci.*, 30, 1003, 1985.

58. Spear, L. P., Frambes, N. A., and Kirstein, C. L., Fetal and maternal brain and plasma levels of cocaine and benzoylecgonine following chronic subcutaneous administration of cocaine during gestation in rats, *Psychopharmacology*, 97, 427, 1989.

59. Zhang, J., Dean, R. A., Brzezinski, J., Brosron, W. F., Tissue distribution and activity of cocaine carboxylesterase in male and female rats, *FASEB J.*, 9(6), 362, 1995.

60. Morishima, H. O., Massaoka, T., Tsuji, A., and Cooper, T. B, Pregnancy decreases the threshold for cocaine-induced convulsions in the rat, *J. Lab. Clin. Med.*, 122, 748, 1993.

61. Hoffman, R. S., Henry, G. C., Wax, P. M., Weisman, R. S., Howland, M. A., and Goldfrank, R. L., Decreased plasma cholinesterase activity enhances cocaine toxicity in mice; *J. Pharmacol. Exp. Therap.*, 263, 598, 1992.

62. Devenyi, P., Cocaine complications and pseudocholinesterase, *Ann. Int. Med.*, 110, 167, 1989.

63. Hoffman, R. S., Henry, G. C., Weisman, R. S., Howland, M. A, Goldtrank, L. R., Association between plasma cholinesterase activity and cocaine toxicity, *Ann. Emerg. Med.*, 19, 467, 1990.

64. Kambam, J., Naukam, R., Parris, W., Franks, J., and Wright, W., Inhibition of pseudocholinesterase (PCHE) activity protects from cocaine induced cardiorespiratory toxicity (CIC) in rats, *Anesthesiology*, 73, A581, 11990.

65. Shnider, S. M., Serum cholinesterase activity during pregnancy, labor, and the puerperium, *Anesthesiology*, 26, 335, 1995.

66. Pritchard, J. A., Plasma cholinesterase activity in normal pregnancy and in eclamptogenic toxemia, *Am. J. Obstet. Gynecol.*, 70, 1083, 1955.

67. Konkol, R. J., Murphy. L., Ferriero, D. M., Dempsey, D. A., and Olsen, G. D., Cocaine metabolites in the neonate: potential for toxcity, *J. Child. Neurol.*, 9, 242, 1994.

68. Mittleman, R. E., Cofino, J. C., and Hearn, W. L., Tissue distribution of cocaine in a pregnant woman, *J. Foren. Sci.* 34, 481, 1989.

69. Callahan, C. M, Grant, T. M., Phipps, P. et al., Measurement of gestational cocaine exposure; sensitivity of infants' hair, meconium, and urine, *J. Pediatr.*, 120, 763, 1992.

70. Forman, R., Schneiderman, J., Klein, J., Graham, K., Greenwald, M., and Koran, G., Accumulation of cocaine in maternal and fetal hair: the dose response curve, *Life Sci.*, 50, 1333, 1992.

71. Mahone, P. R., Scott, K., Sleggs, G., D'Antoni, T., and Woods, J. R., Cocaine and metabolites in amniotic fluid may prolong fetal drug exposure, *Am J. Obstet. Gynecol.*, 171, 465, 1994.

72. Kline, J., Greenwald, N., Becker L., and Koren, G. Fetal distribution of cocaine: case analysis, *Pediatr. Pathol.*, 12, 463, 1992.

73. Lutinger, B., Graham, K., Einarson, T., and Koren, G., Relationship between gestational cocaine use and pregnancy outcome: a meta-analysis, *Teratology*, 44, 405, 1991.

74. Mirochnick, M., Frank, D. A., Cabral, H., Turner, A., and Zuckerman, B., Relation between meconium concentration of the cocaine metabolite benzoylecgonine and fetal growth, *J. Pediatr.*, 126, 636, 1995.

75. Volkow, N. D., and Fowler, J. S., Brain imaging studies of the cocaine addict: implications for reinforcement and addiction, in *The Neurobiology of Cocaine, Celluar and Molecular Mechanisms*, Hammer, R. J., Jr., Ed., CRC Press, Boca Raton, p. 65, 1995.

76. Mott, S. H., Packer, R. J., and Soldin, S. J., Neurological manifestations of cocaine exposure in childhood, *Pediatrics*, 93, 57, 1994.

77. Kramer, D. L., Locke, G. E., Ogungeni, A., and Nelson, L., Neonatal cocaine-related seizures, *J. Child. Neurol.*, 5, 60, 1990.

78. Marzuk, P. M., Tardiff, K., Leon, A. C., Stajie, M., Morgan, E. B., and Mann J. J., Prevalence of recent cocaine use among motor vehicle fatalities in New York City, *JAMA*, 263, 250, 1990.

79. Hanzlick, R. and Gowitt, G. T., Cocaine metabolite detection in homicide victims, *JAMA*, 265, 760, 1991.

80. Snodgrass, R. S., Cocaine babies: a result of multiple teratogenic influences, *J. Child. Neurol.*, 9, 227, 1994.

81. Hearn, W. L., Rose, S., Wagner J., Ciarlegio, A., and Mash, D. C., Cocaethylene is more potent than cocaine in mediating lethality, *Pharmacol. Biochem. Behav.,* 39, 531, 1991.

82. Noldy, N. E., Santos, C. V., Blair, R. D. G., and Carlen, P. L., Quantitative EEG changes in cocaine withdrawal: evidence for long-term CNS effects, *Neuropsychobiology,* 30, 189, 1994.

83. Merigian, K. S., Park, J. L., Leeper, K. V., Browning, G. G., and Giometi, R., Adrenergic crisis from crack cocaine ingestion: report of five cases, *J. Emerg. Med.,* 12, 485, 1994.

84. Hernandez, A., Andollo, W., and Hearn, W. L., Analysis of cocaine and metabolites in brain using solid phase extraction and full-scanning gas chromatography/ion trap mass spectrometry, *Forens. Sci. Int.,* 65, 149, 1994.

85. Madden, J. A., and Powers, R. H., Effect of cocaine and metabolites on cerebral arteries in vitro, *Life Sci.,* 47, 1109, 1990.

86. Goodman, J. H., and Sloviter R. S., Cocaine neurotoxicity and altered neuropeptide Y immunore-activity in the rat hippocampus: a silver degeneration and immunocytochemical study, *Brain Res.,* 616, 263, 1993.

87. Bateman, D. A., Ng, S. K., Hansen, C. A., and Heagarty, M. C., The effect of intrauterine cocaine exposure in the newborn, *Am. J. Pub. Health,* 83, 190, 1993.

88. Dusick, A. M., Covert, R. F., Schreiber, M. D., Browne, S. P., Moore, C. M., and Tebbett, I. R., Risk of intracranial hemorrhage and other adverse outcomes after cocaine exposure in a cohort of 323 very low birth weight infants, *J. Ped.,* 122, 438, 1993.

89. Zuckerman, B., and Frank, DA., "Crack kids": Not broken, *Pediatrics,* 89:337, 1992.

90. Bagasra, O., Forman, L.J., Howedy, A., and Whittle, P., A potential vaccine for cocaine abuse prophylaxis, *Immunopharmacology,* 23, 173, 1992.

91. Gallacher, G.A., Potential vaccine for cocaine abuse prophylaxis?, *Immunopharmacology,* 27, 79, 1994.

92. Landry, D.W., Zhao, K., Yang, G.X.-Q., Glickman, M., and Georgiadis, T.M., Antibody-catalyzed degradation of cocaine, *Science,* 259, 1899, 1993.

93. Konkol, R. J., and Olsen, G. D., The appropriateness of gastric alkalization in cocaine intoxication, *Ann. Emerg. Med.,* 22: 1238, 1993.

113

Chapter 7

Critical Review of Evidence for Neonatal Cocaine Intoxication and Withdrawal

Delia A. Dempsey, MD, Donna M. Ferriero, MD, and Sarah N. Jacobson

7.0 INTRODUCTION

The usage patterns and possible clinical effects of prenatal cocaine exposure are varied. There is a wide spectrum of maternal cocaine exposure, ranging from very occasional use to frequent binges up to the time of delivery.[1,2] While many neonates are normal, others may be cocaine or metabolite intoxicated, some may develop withdrawal or an abstinence syndrome, and yet another group may have fetopathic effects that manifest themselves later in childhood. Furthermore, some neonates may have a combination of the effects.[3]

The goal of this article is to discuss clinical effects of prenatal cocaine exposure during the newborn period. To conceptualize the mechanisms, a model of neonatal cocaine or metabolite intoxication, withdrawal, and fetopathic effects is presented graphically in Figure 7.1. This model will be developed later in the chapter. This pharmacodynamic model relates the plasma concentration of a drug or metabolite to its clinical effects. Specifically defined, intoxication is a clinical manifestation of the presence of the drug in the body. Withdrawal may develop after the drug is eliminated from the body. Fetopathic effects occur independent of the presence or elimination of a drug and may be evidence of permanent or long-term sequelae of drug exposure. This model has been developed because abnormal behaviors and clinical signs in cocaine-exposed newborns are commonly attributed to withdrawal.[4-11] This may be a costly simplification because clinical markers identifying those newborns at highest risk for later developmental or language disabilities may be dismissed as withdrawal.

It is important to separate intoxication, withdrawal, and fetopathic effects because each may have different predictive values for the long-term effects and for management. The magnitude of the epidemic of prenatal cocaine exposure precludes intensive follow up of all exposed neonates.[12] Time-consuming or expensive procedures such as the Brazelton Neonatal Behavioral Assessment Scale (BNBAS), electroencephalograms, and cry studies, have been used to try to identify the neonates at greatest risk for long-term disability.[8,13-15] To facilitate rational allocation of limited resources, we need to find reliable noninvasive clinical neonatal markers identifying those at risk for long-term disability, markers that separate transient effects from fetopathic effects.[16-18]

0-8493-9465-1/96/$0.00+$.50

115

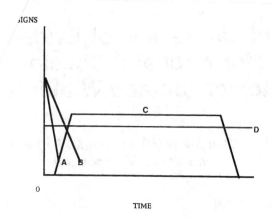

FIGURE 7.1 Model cocaine or metabolite intoxication, withdrawal, and fetopathic effects. (A) Cocaine intoxication, (B) Benzoylecgonine intoxication, (C) Withdrawal, (D) Fetopathic effects.

Cocaine intoxication, withdrawal, and metabolism have been well delineated in adults; these data will first be briefly presented. The limited data in newborns, infants, and young children regarding the metabolism and acute effects of cocaine will be then reviewed in light of what is known in adults. Based on this review, probable signs of newborn cocaine intoxication and withdrawal will be discussed. Finally, new research regarding clinical signs of newborn cocaine intoxication, withdrawal, and fetopathology will be presented. Neonates prenatally exposed to cocaine have a host of confounders that may affect their pre- and postnatal development.[19-21] Some confounders may even have a greater effect upon growth and development than cocaine.[22,23] At this time, the confounders are not incorporated into the model of intoxication, withdrawal, and fetopathic effects. The goal of this review is to demonstrate that there are data to support this model and identify likely signs of intoxication, withdrawal, and fetopathology. When this model is tested, confounders will need to be identified.

7.0.1 A Model of Neonatal Cocaine or Cocaine Metabolite Intoxication and Withdrawal

Cocaine intoxication and/or intoxication from its major metabolite, benzoylecgonine (BE), are manifest at birth or appear shortly after birth in neonates who have cocaine and/or benzoylecgonine in their plasma. These signs wane as the drugs are cleared from the body. Intoxication is graphically represented by lines A and B in Figure 7.1. Intoxication should have little or no predictive value because it is a transient effect.

Cocaine and/or benzoylecgonine withdrawal signs are not initially present in neonates born with measurable plasma drug levels, but then develop as the drugs are eliminated from the body. Newborns chronically exposed to cocaine during the third trimester but free of cocaine or metabolite at birth may exhibit withdrawal signs during the first day of life. Withdrawal may predict long-term sequelae indirectly by identifying high chronic maternal use during the third trimester. If a mother has stopped cocaine use prior to the third trimester, it is difficult from a pharmacologic point of view to attribute abnormal signs in the neonate to withdrawal because it is reasonable to assume that withdrawal would have resolved *in utero* during the third trimester. Withdrawal is represented by line C in Figure 7.1 and should resolve within weeks to months.

Tolerance and withdrawal are interrelated physiologic processes. Tolerance is a general phenomenon noted with many drugs and can involve various mechanisms. Tolerance includes the ability of those chronically exposed to a drug to tolerate doses that would be toxic in a naive user. Barbiturates, opiates, and ethanol are prime examples of drugs that induce tolerance. The mechanism of tolerance may be pharmacodynamic tolerance, where cellular adaptation to the drug takes place. Withdrawal represents the unopposed consequences of the cellular adaptation. The cells have adapted to the presence of the drug, but in the absence of the drug this response is maladaptive. Commonly, the signs and symptoms of withdrawal are the opposite of the pharmacologic effects of the drug. For example, withdrawal from sedative drugs usually produces excitation and agitation, while withdrawal from cocaine produces depression and somnolence.

Fetopathic effects due to cocaine are present on the first day of life and are unaffected by the presence or elimination of cocaine and/or metabolite. These signs persist and may never resolve. Fetopathic effects are represented by line D in Figure 7.1. Animal models have clearly shown that cocaine has a myriad of effects upon the developing nervous system;[18] these are discussed in Chapter 10. Identification of fetopathic effects indicates at risk neonates who need careful follow up and early intervention.[16,17]

7.1 COCAINE INTOXICATION

7.1.1 Adults

Cocaine is a well-recognized sympathomimetic.[24] It primarily blocks the reuptake of catecholamines and indoleamines, and prevents termination of receptor stimulation. Peripherally, it increases the heart rate, myocardial contractility, and peripheral vascular resistance. In the central nervous system, cocaine blocks the reuptake of dopamine, and prolonged dopamine receptor stimulation is thought to be responsible for the euphoria and the rewarding effects of cocaine. The major medical complications of cocaine are hypertension, cardiac arrhythmias, myocardial and other organ ischemia, headaches, agitated delirium, hyperthermia, seizures, strokes, and death.

7.1.2 Infants and Children

The limited data regarding cocaine toxicity in infants and children appear similar to the adult. Based on positive urine screens, the prevalence of cocaine exposure among inner city infants and young children ranged from 2.5 to 5.4%.[25-27] Table 7.1 summarizes 21 case reports and one retrospective review of emergency department charts for pediatric cocaine intoxication. The case reports describe toxicity in young children; most are under 2 years of age. Twelve out of 21 presented with seizures; 5 in status epilepticus. One 9-month-old in status epilepticus, with bizarre arrhythmias and hypertension, had a plasma cocaine level of 190 ng/ml and a

TABLE 7.1   Infants and Children — Cocaine Toxicity

Age	Route	Clinical Description	Reference
Retrospective Reviews of 41 Pediatric Cases			
2 months – 18 years	See comments	Chart review of all 41 children with urine positive for both cocaine and benzoylecgonine out of 1345 pediatric urine screens; 14 excluded because of severe trauma. 19/27 (70%) had neurologic abnormalities. Children under 8 years, predominant route — passive inhalation: seizures (78%); obtundation/ataxia (22%). Children 8 years and older, predominant route — unknown: delirium (40%); drooling (20%); dizziness (10%).	30
Case Reports			
11 weeks	Intranasal	4% cocaine solution (0.6 to 0.7 mg/kg). Signs: tachycardia, hypertension, tachypnea, irritability, inconsolable screaming, rigidity, opisthotonic posturing, tremors, hypertonicity, constant sucking, lip smacking, dilated pupils with deviated upward gaze. Duration — 16 hours.	29
2 weeks	Oral	Signs: Irritability, diarrhea, vomiting, dilated pupils, tremors, increased startle response, poor response to light, hyperactive moro, increased deep tendon reflexes, ankle clonus, high-pitched cry. Time to resolution of signs: 48 hrs.	98
11 days	Oral	Signs: Apnea and status epilepticus.	99
9 months	Oral	Signs: Status epilepticus, apnea, bizarre arrhythmias, and hypertension; full recovery by 4 days; no sequelae. Serum cocaine 190 ng/ml, BE 2360 ng/ml.	28
9 months	Oral	Signs: Status epilepticus, apnea, hyperthermia, mild hypertension.	100
13 months	Oral	Signs: Status epilepticus, severe acidosis.	101
14 months	Trachea	Topical application to tracheal mucosa; dose 30 mg. Signs: Dilated pupils, hyperventilation, continuous movements. Resolved in 18 hours.	102
20 months	Oral	Signs: Apnea, seizures, severe acidosis, hypertension, tachycardia, hyperthermia, dilated pupils. Full recovery in 3 days.	103
15 months	Unknown	Signs: Uncontrollable screaming, irritability, mild tachycardia.	103

TABLE 7.1 Infants and Children — Cocaine Toxicity (continued)

Age	Route	Clinical Description	Reference
15 months	Inhalation	Signs: Seizures.	103
3 months	Inhalation	Signs: Seizure-like activity, hypertonicity, hyperreflexia.	104
2 years	Inhalation	Signs: 20-minute seizure.	104
9 months	Inhalation	Signs: Lethargy and insensitivity to pain associated with a burn.	104
4 years	Inhalation	Signs: Anorexia, nausea, ataxia.	104
6 weeks	Unknown	Signs: None, screen sent because of home environment.	105
2 months	Unknown	Signs: Apnea, listlessness.	105
7 months	Unknown	Signs: Diaphoresis, hypertension, tachycardia, agitation, irritability. Resolved in 8 hours.	105
3 months	Oral	Signs: Seizures.	106
4 months	Unknown	Signs: Seizures, apnea.	106
9 months	Oral	Signs: Status epilepticus, hyperthermia.	106
3 years	Oral	Signs: Multiple seizures.	106

benzoylecgonine level of 2360 ng/ml; this is a relatively low plasma level of cocaine.[28] Tremors, hypertonicity, and hyperreflexia were commonly found in the remaining case reports. Passive inhalation of cocaine smoke and oral ingestion were the predominant routes of exposure. One 11-week-old neonate received 4% nasal cocaine drops (0.6 to 0.7 mg/kg) and developed the classic signs of adult cocaine toxicity, tachycardia, hypertension, and dilated pupils; she also developed opisthotonic posturing, tremors, hypertonicity, and inconsolable screaming which took 16 hours to resolve.[29]

The emergency department charts of all infants and children whose urine was positive for both cocaine and benzoylecgonine were reviewed.[30] The presence of cocaine in the urine indicates recent exposure, and cocaine can be temporally related to clinical events in the emergency department.[24] Among children under 8 years of age whose urine was positive for cocaine and benzoylecgonine, 78% presented with seizures.[30] Although the data compiled in Table 7.1 are limited, they do indicate that the toxicity of cocaine in young children and infants is similar to its toxicity in adults. Based on the high incidence of seizures among the younger subjects and the one case with plasma levels, it appears that the seizure threshold for cocaine-associated seizures may be much lower in infants and children than in adults.

The toxicity of cocaine in the prenatally exposed neonate may not manifest itself as dramatically as it does in the infant or child because of tolerance. Seizures are prominent in the published data in Table 7.1, yet seizures are not commonly reported among exposed newborns (Table 7.2). This may be due to tolerance that has developed from their chronic exposure. This is not to say that neonates will not show signs of cocaine intoxication, but rather it may not be as obvious as it is in a cocaine naive infant or child. There is no reason to assume that neonatal cocaine intoxication is qualitatively different than the infant, child, or adult.

7.1.3 Pharmacologic Activity of Benzoylecgonine

Emerging evidence indicates that BE may have significant pharmacologic properties. In the past, benzoylecgonine was believed to be pharmacologically inactive. The onset of seizures, strokes, and angina in some patients hours after the expected peak concentration of cocaine has raised the possibility of a long-lived, pharmacologically active metabolite of cocaine.[31] Benzoylecgonine is associated with vasoconstriction in human coronary and cat cerebral arteries.[31,32] It also has constrictive properties in both the pregnant ewe and fetus.[33] Furthermore, intrathecally instilled benzoylecgonine causes agitation and seizures in rats in a dose-dependent manner.[34,35] In the rat, the fetal maternal ratio for benzoylecgonine was less than 1, except for the brain where the fetal maternal ratio was 3, indicating that the fetal brain is exposed to high levels of benzoylecgonine relative to the adult.[36] For a detailed discussion of the pharmacologic activity of benzoylecgonine, see Chapters 5 and 6. The data regarding the pharmacologic activity of benzoylecgonine supports the hypothesis that there may be a benzoylecgonine intoxication syndrome.

7.1.4 Fetal Exposure to Benzoylecgonine

Cocaine has a relatively short half-life compared to benzoylecgonine.[24] Benzoylecgonine is a polar metabolite that does not appear to readily cross the human or ewe placenta.[33,37,38] The data indicate that benzoylecgonine is formed *in situ* in the fetus and is not of maternal origin.[33] This is possible because benzoylecgonine formation is partially via nonenzymatic hydrolysis and would not require fetal metabolic capabilities.[39,40] Once formed, it may be trapped on the fetal side of the placenta, resulting in prolonged and/or high fetal concentrations of the metabolite. Amniotic fluid may also be a reservoir for benzoylecgonine.[41] Fetal exposure to cocaine is most likely intermittent even in a chronic maternal user, but the fetal exposure to benzoylecgonine may be continuous and rarely completely cleared between episodes of maternal use. If benzoylecgonine is pharmacologically active in the fetus,[33] then the continuous exposure of the fetus to benzoylecgonine may have the potential to have a profound effect upon the developing fetus.

7.2 COCAINE WITHDRAWAL

7.2.1 Adults

Initially cocaine was believed to be nonaddictive because there is no obvious autonomic syndrome associated with abstinence as there is for opiates. Cocaine withdrawal or abstinence syndrome in adults has been characterized by 3 phases—crash, withdrawal, and extinction.[42] The crash phase is characterized by agitation, anxiety, dysphoria, depression, extreme exhaustion, and hypersomnolence punctuated by periods of wakefulness and hyperphagia, and lasts for several days. Withdrawal begins 12 to 96 hours after cocaine abstinence and may last for 6 to 18 weeks. As the inverse of a cocaine high, it is characterized by decreased energy (anergy), limited interest in the environment, limited ability to experience pleasure (anhedonia), and sleep disturbances. Withdrawal may be punctuated by vivid memories of cocaine highs that lead to intense craving and relapse. Extinction may last for years and is characterized by cue-triggered cravings for cocaine.

7.2.2 Neonates

Adult cocaine withdrawal is essentially a behavioral syndrome, as opposed to an autonomic syndrome. It is extremely difficult to document a behavioral syndrome in a neonate because of their limited repertoire. Yet many caregivers, nurses, and physicians attribute a variety of behaviors and clinical signs to neonatal cocaine withdrawal.[4-11] These behaviors and clinical signs are not universally accepted as evidence of withdrawal, and a number of authors have noted that these effects may be due to the direct effects of the drug.[14,43-45]

Prior to the onset of the cocaine epidemic, maternal opiate addiction and neonatal opiate withdrawal were the dominant illicit drug problems in the nursery.[46,47] Neonatal opiate withdrawal is a profound physiologic syndrome that is poorly tolerated by neonates; if untreated, it can lead to dehydration, metabolic acidosis, seizures, and even death.[48] The syndrome of neonatal opiate withdrawal has been carefully characterized.[48] A standardized scoring system has been developed to monitor the syndrome.[49] Standardized scoring of opiate withdrawal allows for an objective decision as to when to start pharmacologic intervention and prevent further progression of the syndrome.[50]

For years, it has been standard of care in our nursery and in many nurseries to use a single scoring system to monitor all neonates with a history of illicit drug exposure for signs of withdrawal, albeit opiate withdrawal.[51] Table 7.2 lists the studies that have data on abnormal signs or behaviors noted in cocaine-exposed newborns. Many of the abnormal signs given in Table 7.2 are attributed to cocaine withdrawal because of their similarity to neonatal opiate withdrawal, even though cocaine is a sympathomimetic and opiates are sympatholytics. The assignment of most abnormal signs and behaviors in cocaine-exposed neonates to withdrawal comes from the similarity of these signs to opiate withdrawal. However, there are no reports of significant morbidity or mortality associated with neonatal cocaine withdrawal. Cocaine is a stimulant drug, and intoxication is associated with euphoria, tachycardia, hypertension, tachypnea, hyperactivity, anorexia, hyperthermia, seizures, etc. It is possible that some of the signs listed in Table 7.2 are actually signs of cocaine intoxication.

Neurologic or neurobehavioral abnormalities were very frequently reported among the studies in Table 7.2. The most common signs were tremors, hypertonia, and irritability.[7,11,43,44,52-56] Two of these were blinded controlled studies.[54,56] Signs related to the gastrointestinal tract can be prominent with opiate withdrawal but they were uncommon among the cocaine-exposed, except when the cocaine-exposed newborns were grouped with other drug-exposed newborns.[4,11,43,48] Prenatal cocaine exposure does not appear to exacerbate opiate withdrawal.[9] Poor feeding was found in a number of studies, but these were not blinded studies.[7,10,11,43]

Tachycardia, tachypnea, and apnea have also been noted, but mainly in uncontrolled or retrospective studies.[4,6,11,13,44,55,57,58] Two excellent controlled and blinded studies found statistically significant elevations in cardiac output, stroke volume, mean arterial blood pressures, and cerebral artery flow velocities in cocaine-exposed newborns when compared to controls.[59,60] The resolution of these cardiovascular abnormalities by the second day of life is consistent with intoxication. Transient ST segment elevations have also been documented in cocaine-exposed newborns, but the abnormality occurred both in those with positive cocaine screens and those with history of exposure but a negative screen.[61]

Abnormalities of cry and startle have been documented in cocaine-exposed neonates when compared to controls.[8,14,15] One cry study found that the number of cry utterances and the number of short cries among newborns with a positive cocaine screen was twice that of newborns with a history of exposure but a negative screen.[15] In another study, abnormal signs were found among those neonates with a positive urine screen but not among those with a history of exposure only.[55] It was proposed that those with a positive screen were intoxicated, and those with a negative screen were not. Alternatively, the screen could be a marker of the magnitude of cocaine exposure. Newborns with a positive screen may be those with the most frequent exposure throughout gestation, while those whose exposure is known by history only may be the newborns whose mother stopped using, or used intermittently. The

TABLE 7.2 Cocaine Exposed Newborns, Abnormal Clinical Signs or Withdrawal Signs (WD)

Cohort Description	N	% WD Signs	Comments	Reference
a) Cocaine	38	42	Prospective study. Signs: tremulousness, irritability, and muscular rigidity. Median onset of signs – 2 days. Median duration – 3 days.	52
a) Cocaine	39	87	Signs: increased tone, increased DTR, irritability, tremors. Signs peaked on third day of life. EEG study, 17/39 abnormal EEG, all but 1 normalized by year.	53
a) Cocaine	20	80	Fetal ultrasound study with neonatal follow-up. Signs: abnormal state organization (80%) and neurobehavioral abnormalities (50%) as exhibited by tremulousness, tachypnea, hyperresponsiveness, and difficulty in arousal.	44
a) Cocaine	8		No withdrawal symptoms but 1 initially floppy, 1 poor feeding for 24 hours, and 1 jittery but calmed when swaddled.	10
a) Cocaine b) Opiates	32 18	38 6	Apnea density and episodes of periodic breathing exceeded the 95th percentile in 38% cocaine-exposed vs. 6% opiate-exposed infants.	58
a) Cocaine b) Cocaine-poly drug c) Other drugs	66 57 16	26 57 50	Retrospective chart review of newborns born to mothers who admitted use. Signs: seizures, depression, lethargy, feeding problems, hyperactive reflexes, vomiting, diarrhea, high-pitched cry, restlessness, apnea, poor sucking response, neurologic deficits, respiratory symptoms.	4
a) Cocaine b) Control	56 56	13 11	Approximately 10% of both groups had jitteriness. No difference between groups evident in hypotonia, poor feeding, tachypnea, or respiratory distress syndrome. Neurobehavioral symptoms — no statistically significant differences.	64
a) Cocaine b) Poly drug c) Control	50 110 340	190 60	Prospective study, charts reviewed for signs of withdrawal. Signs reported among cocaine-exposed: irritability, abnormal crying, or vigorous suck. No withdrawal signs mentioned for the control group.	5
a) Cocaine Amphetamine b) Opiate c) Control	46 49 45		Cocaine- and amphetamine-exposed neonates combined into 1 cohort: abnormal sleep patterns (81%), tremors (71%), poor feeding (58%), hypertonia (52%), vomiting (51%), sneezing (45%), high-pitched cry (42%), frantic fist sucking (42%), tachypnea (19%), loose stools (16%), fever (16%), yawning (12.9%), hyperreflexia (15%), and excoriation (6%). Stimulant groups had less severe abstinence scores than the opiate cohort. Peak scores on day 2 to 3.	43
a) Cocaine & Opiates b) Opiates c) Control	50 50 50		Prospective study. No significant difference between the exposed populations. Cocaine does not appear to increase the severity of neonatal abstinence symptoms.	9

TABLE 7.2   Cocaine Exposed Newborns, Abnormal Clinical Signs or Withdrawal Signs (WD) (continued)

Cohort Description	N	% WD Signs	Comments	Reference
a) Cocaine b) Control	55 55	38 0	Prospective study, blinded exam. Signs: irritability, tremulousness, and muscular rigidity.	54
a) Cocaine b) Control	53 100	19 2	Prospective unblinded study. Signs: tachycardia (19%), seizures (4%), and hyperresponsiveness (4%).	6
a) Cocaine b) Methamphetamine c) Control	13 28 45		Signs in stimulant- (cocaine or methamphetamine) exposed newborns: abnormal sleep patterns, tremors, hypertonia, high-pitched cry, poor feeding, vomiting, sneezing, frantic sucking, and tachypnea. BNBAS revealed pronounced alteration in visual processing, quality of alertness, tremulousness, startle reflex, and visual processing.	11
a) Cocaine b) Poly drug c) Control	114 24 88	25 54 1	Chart review, universal toxicology screening, exposed cohort — positive screen; control cohort — negative screen and negative history. Signs: tremulousness, irritability, poor feeding, and diarrhea.	7
a) Cocaine b) Cocaine	40 46	12 0	Prospective study of cocaine-exposed newborns. Positive urine screens where newborns were compared with negative urine screen newborns (control). Signs in positive group: high-pitched cry, seizures, sweating, tremulousness, hyperresponsiveness, and tachycardia.	55
a) Cocaine b) Total cohort	140 936	59 44	Prospective blinded study of jitteriness. Differences were not statistically significant ($p = 0.1$). The difference approached statistical significance when there was a positive urine assay postpartum. Jitteriness associated with visual inattention and inconsolability. Jitteriness is not a reliable indicator of drug exposure.	65
a) Cocaine b) Control	14 16		Prospective blinded study. No withdrawal signs found in either group. Significant difference in neurologic exam, hypertonia (86% vs. 33%), plantar extension (46% vs. 19%), coarse tremors (57% vs. 12%), tonic gaze (14% vs. 0%).	56
a) Cocaine b) Control	15 22		Prospective blinded study of cardiovasculature system. On first day of life, statistically significant differences in cardiac output, stroke volume, and mean arterial blood pressure, but no difference in heart rate. Differences resolved by the second day.	59

TABLE 7.2 Cocaine Exposed Newborns, Abnormal Clinical Signs or Withdrawal Signs (WD) (continued)

Cohort Description	N	% WD Signs	Comments	Reference
a) Cocaine b) Control	20 18		Prospective blinded study of cerebral vasculature system. On first day of life, statistically significant differences in heart rate, mean arterial blood pressure, and cerebral artery flow velocities. Differences resolve by second day.	60
a) Cocaine b) Control	21 20	29 5	Holter monitor study within 48 hours of birth. Transient ST segment abnormalities in 3 neonates positive by urine screen and 3 neonates positive by history but with negative screens.	61
a) Cocaine b) Control	50 30	0 0	No withdrawal symptoms noted in either group. BNBAS — both exposed and unexposed neonates scored within the normal range, although there were statistical differences between the exposed and unexposed neonates in the area of autonomic regulation and abnormal reflexes.	1
a) Cocaine b) Control	19 19	16	Prospective study of startle response. Increased eye blink and startle response in exposed cohort (p<0.05). Cocaine-exposed newborns, 16% had signs of withdrawal.	14
a) Cocaine b) Control	80 80		Prospective study of cry characteristics. Two abnormal cry characteristics: 1) "excitable" cry in cocaine-exposed without intrauterine growth retardation, IUGR; 2) "depressed" cry in cocaine-exposed with IUGR. Excitable cry associated with irritability, tremors, jitteriness, and hypertonicity.	8
a) Cocaine b) Control	404 364		Prospective study of cry characteristics and utterances. Exposed cohort: fewer cry utterances (p = 0.001), more short cries (p = 0.02), less crying in hyperphonation mode (p = 0.01). Number of cry utterances and number of short cries in exposed cohort with positive urine screens twice that of exposed cohort with negative screens.	15

effects of prenatal cocaine exposure upon fetal growth have been shown to be correlated with the magnitude of cocaine exposure.[62]

Although the data presented in Table 7.2 indicate that cocaine-exposed newborns are commonly symptomatic, many of the above studies suffer from methodological problems.[45,63] Uncontrolled studies found a very high incidence of withdrawal signs.[44,53] Controlled studies reported much lower rates of abnormal signs.[6,7,54,55] There are 4 controlled studies which could not demonstrate clinically significant differences in "withdrawal" signs between cocaine-exposed and control newborns.[1,5,64,65] Similarly, abnormalities on the Brazelton Neonatal Behavioral Assessment Scale have been inconsistent.[1,11,44,58,66-68]

What might cocaine intoxication or withdrawal look like in a newborn? In adults, cocaine withdrawal is characterized by depression, anxiety, anergy, anhedonia, and sleep disturbances.[42] Transient tachycardia, hypertension, and signs of neurologic stimulation could be consistent with neonatal cocaine intoxication. Only the 2 studies investigating cardiac output, blood pressure, and cerebral blood flow documented plausible abnormalities on the first day of life, which rapidly waned.[59,60] In a neonate, withdrawal might manifest itself in mood and temperament. A withdrawing baby might be a difficult baby with irritability, fussy eating, abnormalities of bonding, and sleep disturbances. It is doubtful these kinds of signs would be detected on a typical inventory of neonatal abstinence signs.[51] Neonatal behavioral abnormalities are very difficult to quantify or study under blinded conditions.

7.3 METABOLISM AND PHARMACOKINETICS OF COCAINE IN ADULTS

7.3.1 Plasma Levels

Cocaine may be ingested, snorted, smoked, or taken intravenously. Average peak venous plasma concentrations range from 200 to 600 ng/ml, while peak arterial concentrations are several times higher than venous after smoking.[24] It is the high arterial concentrations that are presented to the uterus and placenta for tissue uptake of cocaine, while venous plasma levels are reported in the literature. Under controlled situations, euphoria and cardiovascular effects are reported at plasma concentrations above 80 to 100 ng/ml.[69] Among coca leaf chewers, plasma concentrations range from 10 to 150 ng/ml, and clinically are associated with anorexia and a hyper alert state.[70] When intranasal cocaine solutions were used during medical procedures, the peak plasma concentration ranged from 120 to 475 ng/ml.[71] Individual South American cocaine paste smokers maintain their plasma cocaine levels between 250 and 900 ng/ml.[72] In patients presenting with cocaine-associated seizures and strokes, the plasma concentrations ranged from 1 to 1700 ng/ml with a median concentration of 34 ng/ml;[73] seventy-five percent of the patients had plasma cocaine levels below 100 ng/ml. Among chronic cocaine users enrolled in a methadone maintenance program, the average plasma cocaine concentration was 19 ng/ml.[74] Lethal plasma levels of cocaine, inferred from autopsy data, indicate the average plasma concentration of cocaine found in cocaine related deaths is 5300 ng/ml, with a range of 900 to 21,000 ng/ml.[75]

7.3.2 Pharmacokinetics

Cocaine is lipid soluble; it readily crosses the blood brain barrier and the placenta; and it has a volume of distribution of 2 to 3 l/kg.[24] Its major route of elimination is metabolic with less than 5% excreted unchanged in the urine.[24] The elimination half-life ranges from 30 to 90 minutes, although half-lives up to 3.3 hours have been reported in patients presenting with seizures and strokes temporally related to cocaine use.[70,73] The important metabolic elimination pathways of cocaine are illustrated in Figure 7.2. There are at least 11 metabolites of cocaine, but most of them account for only a fraction of cocaine's metabolism.[40] See Chapter 2 on cocaine metabolism for elaboration. Quantitatively, the 2 most important metabolites of cocaine are benzoylecgonine and ecgonine methyl ester.[76,77] Norcocaine is a nonprominent, pharmacologically active metabolite.[78] Cocaethylene is a pharmacologically active metabolite formed in the liver in the presence of ethanol.[39,79]

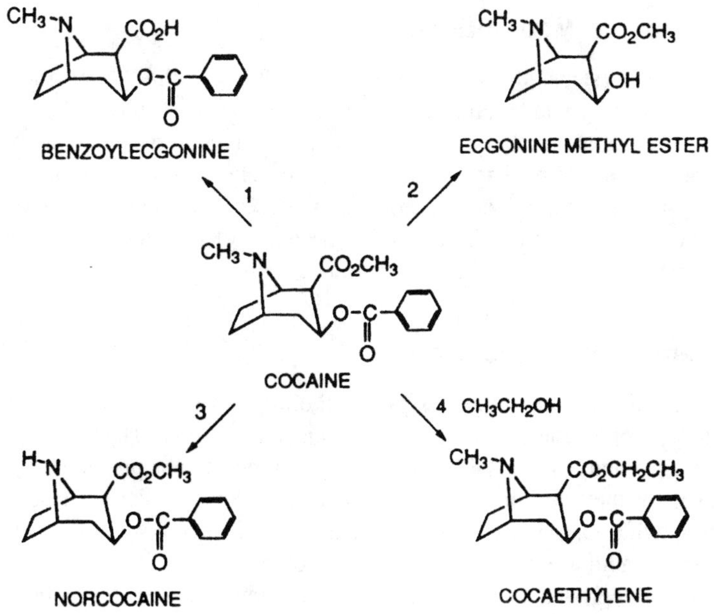

FIGURE 7.2 Cocaine metabolic pathways. (1) Liver carboxylesterase and spontaneous hydrolysis[39,83] (2) Plasma pseudocholinesterase and liver esterase[39,83] (3) Liver demethylase[83] (4) Liver carboxylesterase in the presence of ethanol and cocaine.[39]

7.3.3 Benzoylecgonine

Cocaine is metabolized to benzoylecgonine partially by spontaneous hydrolysis and by a liver carboxyesterase.[39,40] Quantitatively, benzoylecgonine is the most abundant metabolite of cocaine, and is the metabolite tested for in commercial qualitative urine tests.[24] The threshold benzoylecgonine concentration for a positive test on many commercial urine screens is 300 ng/ml, while in a chronic user the urinary concentration can be as high as 350,000 ng/ml.[74] In patients presenting with cocaine-related seizures and strokes, the plasma benzoylecgonine levels ranged from 45 to 15,000 ng/ml with a median of 900 ng/ml.[73] Eighty-seven percent of the samples had benzoylecgonine levels below 4000 ng/ml.[73] Among chronic cocaine users enrolled in a methadone maintenance program, the average plasma benzoylecgonine concentration was 632 ng/ml with a range of 0 to 4770 ng/ml.[74] Benzoylecgonine levels found in the cord blood of newborns range from 70 to 3900 ng/ml; these overlap the above adult plasma levels.[80,81] The half-life of benzoylecgonine is 7.5 hours, and renal excretion accounts for 70% of its elimination.[77,82] The volume of distribution of benzoylecgonine is 0.7 l/kg. This is a quarter to a third of the volume of distribution of cocaine and indicates that benzoylecgonine does not extensively distribute into tissue.[82] Benzoylecgonine is a polar compound that poorly crosses the blood brain barrier, although it is found in cerebral spinal fluid in patients presenting with cocaine-associated stokes and seizures.[34,73]

7.3.4 Ecgonine Methyl Ester

Ecgonine methyl ester is the second most abundant metabolite of cocaine found in the urine.[77] Plasma pseudocholinesterases and liver esterase catalyze the conversion of cocaine to ecgonine methyl ester.[40,83] Neonatal pseudocholinesterase activities are not significantly different than in adults, but they cluster in the low normal adult range and there is great individual variation.[3,84] Based on urinary data, the half-life of ecgonine methyl ester is 4.2 hours.[7] For a review of the pharmacologic activity of ecgonine methyl ester see Chapters 5 and 6.

7.3.5 Sample Preservation

In plasma, cocaine is metabolized by pseudocholinesterase to ecgonine methyl ester, and cocaine spontaneously hydrolyses to benzoylecgonine. These reactions will continue after blood is removed from the body, but they can be prevented by chilling the sample, by the addition of sodium fluoride which inhibits esterases, and by acidification with potassium oxalate which slows spontaneous hydrolysis.[40] Without cooling or the addition of preservatives, approximately 50% of the cocaine in a sample will be degraded during the first 12 to 24 hours, and 80% will be degraded by 48 hours.[40] With death, there is spontaneous acidification of blood, and plasma cholinesterase activity degrades within 24 hours.[40] These two processes limit the post mortem degradation of cocaine. Preservation of samples is routinely done with forensic samples,[85,86] but it is not always done with research samples.[87]

7.4 COCAINE LEVELS AND ELIMINATION IN NEWBORNS, INFANTS, AND CHILDREN

7.4.1 Introduction and Discussion of Confounders

The criteria for intoxication require pharmacologically active plasma levels of cocaine or active metabolites. However, there is no defined pharmacologic threshold level in a neonate. We reviewed the literature for quantitative levels in newborns, infants, and children, but did not find data that correlated drug levels with clinical end points. Tables 7.3 through 7.5 are an annotation of published data regarding quantitative levels in newborns, mothers, infants, and children. Median concentrations were reported because the data were not usually normally distributed, and an outlier would greatly skew the mean.

The quantitative cocaine levels compiled in these tables range from 1 ng/ml to a lethal concentration of 11,900 ng/ml.[88,89] There are confounders to the interpretation of low or not-detected cocaine levels. Samples were not always properly preserved and post collection metabolism and spontaneous hydrolysis were not inhibited.[3,8] The minimum concentration detected by the assay varies from 0.5 to 40 ng/ml.[87,88] This difference in threshold of detection makes it difficult to compare low cocaine levels or interpret "negative" levels. There are 2 problem areas for correlating quantitative levels and mortality. The first is the degradation of cocaine during the time interval between death and the time of sample collection at autopsy.[85] Second, sometimes only the cocaine levels are reported, without metabolite levels.[85] Thus metabolite markers of the magnitude of the exposure, which may reveal the relationship between cocaine and death, are not available.

7.4.2 Cocaine Levels in Infants and Children

There is one case report of a 9-month-old presenting in status epilepticus, with bizarre arrhythmias, and hypertension, who had a plasma cocaine level of 190 ng/ml and a benzoylecgonine level of 2,360 ng/ml.[28] This is a low plasma cocaine level for an adult and suggests that infants may be very sensitive to cocaine. Two children receiving topical cocaine for laceration repair had plasma cocaine levels of 112 ng/ml and 274 ng/ml respectively; they were asymptomatic.[88]

The plasma levels of cocaine associated with stillbirths and infant deaths (Tables 7.3 and 7.4) are within or below the recreational levels reported among adults, and these are substantially lower than adult plasma levels associated with death.[24,75,86,90] Among the stillbirths, only one of 17 had a plasma level in the adult lethal range, 4,200 ng/ml; the second highest cocaine plasma concentration was 490 ng/ml, and the median level was 170 ng/ml.[86] Cocaine degradation could take place during the time from fetal death to delivery, and during the time from delivery to the autopsy. The initial median cocaine concentration among the stillbirths was 170 ng/ml. If we estimate the time from fetal death to autopsy to be 48 hours, then we could expect an 80% drop in the plasma cocaine concentration giving us a possible median plasma cocaine concentration at the time of death of 850 ng/ml. This is still below the lethal range in adults. Therefore, fetal death may be more related to the toxic effects upon the uterus or placenta than to the direct effects upon the fetus.

Among the infant deaths (Table 7.5), cocaine plasma levels ranged from 26 to 300 ng/ml.[85,90] In the majority of cases, the route of exposure was thought to be passive inhalation.[85] Inhaled cocaine enters the arterial circulation as a bolus and would give arterial concentrations of cocaine several times higher than venous levels.[24] Lethal cocaine levels may have degraded prior to autopsy which ranged from 6 to 30 hours after death, (median 22 hours). The median cocaine concentration was 50 ng/ml.[85] If there was an 80% loss of cocaine, the median concentration at death would be 250 ng/ml; 250 ng/ml is in the lower range of plasma concentrations seen in adult users.[24,40] All of these data indicate that infants may be very sensitive to the toxic effects of cocaine and that the lethal plasma concentration of cocaine in the neonate is probably substantially less than in the adult.

TABLE 7.3   Case Reports of Newborns and Fetuses, Quantitative Levels of Cocaine and Benzoylecgonine (BE)

Sample Type	Cocaine ng/ml-ng/g	BE ng/ml-ng/g	Comments	Reference
Neonatal blood	nd	trace	Premature delivery, outcome — lived	107
Umbilical cord	nd	1,200		
Neonatal urine	40	1,950		
Amniotic fluid	70	290		
Neonatal urine		1,240	Perinatal stroke in a neonate.	35
Neonatal urine	130	850	Intoxication via breast milk.	98
Fetal blood	1,000		26-week stillbirth.	57
Maternal blood	5,600	18,700	Maternal death by strangulation, levels	108
Amniotic fluid	3,300	1,600	at autopsy.	
Fetal blood	1,500		Maternal death due to cocaine	109
Maternal blood	13,700		intoxication, 360 g fetus.	
Fetal brain	4,500			
Maternal brain	29.300			
Fetal liver	870			
Maternal liver	1,340			
Fetal kidney	1,370			
Maternal kidney	14,600			
Blood	30	110	250 g neonate, died 45 minutes	110
Brain	20	130	postpartum, death unrelated to	
Scalp	100	100	cocaine, autopsy tissue analysis.	
Liver	150	40		
Kidney	10	70		
Heart	20	50		
Placenta	20	10		

7.4.3 Cocaine Levels in Newborns

The newborn plasma levels are found in Tables 7.3 and 7.4. In one study in which umbilical cord blood samples were preserved with sodium fluoride and potassium oxalate, 40% of the benzoylecgonine samples were also positive for cocaine.[80,81] The peak cocaine level was 88 ng/ml with a benzoylecgonine level of 3880 ng/ml; and a urine sample collected at 27 hours after birth from the same neonate had a cocaine level of 130 ng/ml and a benzoylecgonine level of 41,000 ng/ml. The levels of cocaine in these newborns approximate those of coca leaf chewers and symptomatic emergency department patients.[70,73] Prenatally exposed newborns appear to be tolerant to cocaine compared to cocaine naive infants. Exposed newborns may be

TABLE 7.4 Newborns and Mothers: Quantitative Cocaine and Metabolite Levels

Sample Type (number)	Cocaine ng/ml or ng/g median	maximum	Benzoylecgonine ng/ml or ng/g median	maximum	Comments	Reference
Neonatal urine (20)	145	558	605	26,000	Prospective study, paired maternal /neonatal samples collected within 24 hrs of birth. Ecgonine methyl ester was also assayed.	92
Maternal urine (20)	61	28,680	806	226,000		
Amniotic fluid (3)	173	nd	909	925		
Meconium (19)		2,912		4,798		
Maternal urine (28)	450	2,500	1,300	12,900	Prospective study, hair data included.	111
Meconium (32)	700	5,600	800	4,800		
Neonatal blood (24)			28	252	Blood collected on filter paper for inborn errors of metabolism, n=545, 24/545 positive for BE. Nine maternal and neonatal samples collected up to 72 hours postpartum.	112
Neonatal blood (8)				250		
Maternal blood (9)				525		
Neonatal urine (8)		40	289*	1,950	Prospective study, paired neonatal urine and amniotic fluid samples. Amniotic fluid collected at or near delivery. (* mean)	113
Amniotic fluid (17)		250	1,800	>5,000		
Neonatal blood (11)	nd	<100	200	1,370	Neonatal blood = umbilical cord blood. Norbenzoylecgonine: 7/11 meconium samples with a maximum of 5,100 ng/g; 1/11 cord blood, 90ng/ml.	3
Meconium	>50		450	3,000		
Neonatal blood (18)	35	88	315	3,900	Paired neonatal blood and urine samples. Neonatal blood = umbilical cord blood collected at birth, 33% have BE > 1,000 ng/ml. Neonatal urine collected 24 to 48 hours postpartum.	80, 81
Neonatal urine (16)	73	204	1,373	41,000		
Neonatal urine (15)	36	900	1,536	39,000	Maternal blood collected prior to birth. Urine collected 12 to 48 hours postpartum.	91
Maternal blood (5)	23	421	841	2,254		
Maternal urine (14)	76	720	2,840	81,200		
Fetal blood (17)	170	4,200	1,090	4,300	Coroner's report: 62 consecutive still-births, 19 with obvious cause of demise; 43 without cause, 17/43 positive for BE, 60% have plasma BE > 1,000 ng/ml; 12/17 cocaine positive, second highest plasma cocaine = 490 ng/ml.	86
Liver (5)	180	270	1,790	1,900		
Brain (3)	20	30	500	720		

TABLE 7.5 Infants and Children: Quantitative Cocaine and Metabolite Levels

Sample Type (number)	Cocaine ng/ml – ng/g		Benzoylecgonine ng/ml – ng/g		Comments	Reference
	median	maximum	median	maximum		
Blood (32) a	1.0	112			Topical application of tetracaine, adrenaline, and cocaine (TAC) in children under 16 years old. Plasma collected at 15 to 20 minutes post application in group a, and 45 to 60 minutes in group b, and analyzed for cocaine. 65/72 had levels below 10 ng/ml. 7 had cocaine levels between 10 and 50 ng/ml, 3 had levels between 50 and 100 ng/ml, and 2 had levels above 100 ng/ml.	88
Blood (45) b	2.0	274				
Blood (1)	190		2,360		Case report: Oral ingestion, status epilepticus, bizarre arrhythmias, hypertension, full recovery in 4 days, no sequelae.	28
Blood (23)	nd		12	>600	Topical TAC in children 1 to 14 years. No cocaine was found at a threshold of 40 ng/ml. Ecgonine methyl ester found in 6, median 111 ng/ml, maximum 935 ng/ml.	87
Blood (1)	11,900				Case report: death, 7 months old, excessive TAC used on laceration near mouth, oral exposure. At discharge from hospital, mother noted infant was tense and wide eyed, found dead 3 hours post TAC use.	89
Blood (11)	50	300			Coroner's reports of 16 deaths with detectable cocaine out of 300 infant deaths (5.3%), age 2 weeks to 7 months, all with a history of passive cocaine smoke exposure and no other cause of death was found.	85
Brain (3)	100	100				
Kidney (2)	65	70				
Liver (1)		100				
Blood (1)		26		73	Case report: death, 8 weeks old, levels at autopsy.	90
Brain (1)		19		48		
Liver (1)		24		93		
Blood (1)		94		29	Case report: death, 10 weeks old, levels at autopsy.	90
Brain (1)		40		nd		
Liver (1)		122		nd		

more sensitive to cocaine than adults, and intoxication may occur at much lower concentrations in a tolerant newborn than a tolerant adult.

Some prenatally exposed neonates are born with significant body burdens of cocaine that are similar to those of adult cocaine users. Newborn urine samples collected during the first 48 hours of life had cocaine concentrations as high as 900 ng/ml.[91] In one series of newborns, the median cocaine level in urine was 145 ng/ml.[92] In comparison, the median urine cocaine concentration of adults in a methadone program who use cocaine an average of 14 times per week was 200 ng/ml.[74]

7.4.4 Benzoylecgonine Levels in Newborns

A study that properly preserved umbilical cord blood found that the benzoylecgonine plasma level ranged from 34 to 3900 ng/ml, and a third of the samples had levels above 1000 ng/ml.[80,81] These plasma levels of benzoylecgonine in newborns are similar to those in stillbirths, in pregnant women presenting to labor and delivery, and in adults presenting with cocaine-related seizures and strokes.[73,86,91] In addition, the blood brain barrier of the fetus and newborn is immature, and the fetal and neonatal brain may be exposed to higher concentrations of benzoylecgonine than the adult.[36]

The urine benzoylecgonine data for neonates overlap with adult data, but the peak concentrations are not as high.[74,80,81,92] Newborns are difficult to compare to adults because they have a reduced glomerular filtration rate (2 to 4 ml/minute) which does not reach adult values until 3 to 5 months of age; in addition, other functions such as tubular secretion and the ability to concentrate urine are reduced compared to adults.[93,94] All of this should be considered when comparing peak adult levels with peak neonatal levels.[91,92] The lower peak level in the neonate may not reflect a lesser body burden, but rather a decreased renal ability to excrete the drug.

7.4.5 Half-Life Elimination of Cocaine and Benzoylecgonine in Newborns

We determined the plasma and renal half-life of benzoylecgonine in 12 prenatally exposed newborns. Serial plasma samples were collected during the first 41 hours of life and serial urine samples were collected during the first week of life. The mean plasma elimination half-life of benzoylecgonine was 16 hours with a range of 11 to 22 hours, and the mean renal elimination half-life of benzoylecgonine was 14.6 hours with a range of 10 to 19 hours.[95] These half-lives are in good agreement and are twice as long as the half-life of benzoylecgonine in adults.[77] Given these half-lives, it would take 27 hours for a peak plasma concentration of 4000 ng/ml to drop below 1000 ng/ml and 3 days for it to drop below 100 ng/ml. Therefore, if there is a benzoylecgonine intoxication syndrome in newborns, it might resolve by day 3 to 5 of life.

Renal elimination data for cocaine are available in one newborn.[91] The elimination half-life was 11.6 hours, 10 times longer than the average half-life of cocaine in adults and 3 times longer than the longest reported half-life.[24,73] If this is a representative newborn cocaine half-life, then cocaine intoxication in the newborn may be expected to last 24 to 36 hours.

7.5 CLINICAL SIGNS ASSOCIATED WITH INTOXICATION, WITHDRAWAL, AND FETOPATHOLOGY

7.5.1 Introduction

Cocaine toxicity in infants and children does not appear to be qualitatively different than in adults except that it may occur at plasma concentrations substantially lower than in adults (Tables 7.1 through 7.5). Newborn plasma and urine levels are similar to those in symptomatic adult emergency department patients.[73] Preliminary data indicate that the neonatal elimination of cocaine is substantially longer than in adults and the elimination of benzoylecgonine is twice as long as in adults.[91,95] These data support the hypothesis that some babies could be born cocaine- and/or benzoylecgonine-intoxicated. The theoretical time course for resolution of the intoxication may be as long as 24 to 36 hours for cocaine and 3 to 5 days for benzoylecgonine. The model of intoxication, withdrawal, and fetopathic effects of cocaine represented in Figure 7.1, is based on the pharmacologic and toxicologic data presented above and a retrospective review of withdrawal scoring of prenatally exposed newborns presented below.[96]

7.5.2 Retrospective Review of Withdrawal Scores of High Risk Newborns

San Francisco General Hospital laboratory assayed urine for both cocaine and benzoylecgonine (Table 7.6). Cocaine positive urine toxicology screens were associated with cocaine plasma levels above 40 ng/ml and with plasma benzoylecgonine levels above 1000 ng/ml.[81] We hypothesized that signs of cocaine or benzoylecgonine intoxication would be found among the cohort of neonates whose urine screens were positive for both cocaine and benzoylecgonine. Three cohorts of newborns were defined by their urine toxicology screen results (Table 7.6): Cocaine and benzoylecgonine positive (Coc/BE Cohort); Cocaine negative, BE positive (BE Cohort); and urine toxicology negative (Negative Cohort). The charts of a randomized selection of infants born between 1987 and 1992 were reviewed; and 82 babies were enrolled in the Coc/BE Cohort, 84 babies in the BE Cohort, and 50 babies in the Negative Cohort. Exclusion criteria included intubation or admission to the intensive care nursery, weight less than 2000 grams, urine positive for other drugs of abuse, or absence of a withdrawal scoring sheet.

Nurses maintained withdrawal scoring on newborns with a positive screen and on those with a negative toxicology screen who had a strong history for prenatal drug exposure. During the subjects' first day of life, nurses were blinded to the neonatal urine toxicology results because results were not available until 24 to 48 hours after birth. In 1993, neonatal nurses were surveyed regarding the difference between a cocaine/benzoylecgonine positive urine screen and a cocaine negative/benzoylecgonine positive urine screen. Universally, none had not recognized a

TABLE 7.6 San Francisco General Hospital Newborn Nursery: Yearly Urine Toxicology Statistics

Year	Total tested	Total positive illicit drugs*	Total positive benzoylecgonine**	Positive cocaine & benzoylecgonine
1987***	226	107	91	22
1988	348	136	112	27
1989	399	129	102	17
1990			107	7
1991	362	138	111	19
1992	389	142	111	15

* Excludes cannabinoids.
** Includes newborns positive for cocaine and benzoylecgonine.
*** 9 months of data, April – December.

difference, indicating that the nursing staff was blinded to the two types of positive cocaine urine screens during the study period.

We hypothesized that signs of intoxication would be present on the first day of life in the Coc/BE Cohort, but would be gone by day 3, and that the emergence of signs on or after the second day of life would be consistent with withdrawal. Signs that were static throughout the nursery stay would be consistent with fetopathology. The scores of each individual sign on the withdrawal sheet were computerized for day 1, 3, and 7 of life. The results are shown in Tables 7.7 and 7.8.

TABLE 7.7 Signs with Clinically Significant Differences

Signs	Coc/BE Cohort N=82	BE Cohort N=84	Negative Cohort N=50
	Groups: percent affected		
Lethargy			
Day 1	67%	5%	9%
Day 3	0%	13%	6%
	p=0.002		
Hypertonicity			
Day 1 ·	11%	47%	47%
Day 3	70%	61%	83%
	p=0.05		
No weight gain			
Day 3	30%	9%	17%
Day 7	14%	7%	11%
	NS		
Tachypnea			
Day 1	22%	6%	11%
Day 3	20%	6%	0%
Day 7	0%	7%	0%
	NS		

7.5.3 Results and Discussions

Lethargy and hypertonicity were the 2 signs consistent with the time course of intoxication (Table 7.7). Sixty-seven percent of the Coc/BE Cohort were lethargic on the first day of life, and none were lethargic by the third day of life (p=0.002).

TABLE 7.8   Signs Without Statistically Significant
Differences among Cohorts

Signs with High Incidence Throughout the Nursery Stay

Sign		Range: percent affected
Mental status:	Irritability	45–57%
Neurologic:	Hypertonicity	47–69%
	Tremor	45–57%
	Hyperactive Moro	26–59%
	Increased suck	18–43%

Signs with Low Incidence Throughout the Nursery Stay

Sign		Range: percent affected
Mental status:	Inconsolability	0–12%
	High-pitched cry	5–17%
Neurologic:	Sneezing & yawning	12–27%
	Seizures	0–3%
Gastrointestinal:	Poor feeding	4–6%
	Spitting up & vomiting	0–10%
	Diarrhea	0–9%
Other:	Fever	0–2%
	Respiratory distress	0–6%
	Tachycardia	0%

There was a high incidence of hypertonicity among all three cohorts throughout the nursery stay except for the Coc/BE Cohort on the first day of life, when this incidence was low. On the first day of life, 11% of the Coc/BE Cohort newborns were hypertonic; by day 3, 70% were hypertonic (p=0.05). Irritability also had a low incidence among the Coc/BE cohort on the first day of life and increased over time. The low incidence of irritability on the first day was consistent with the high incidence of lethargy.

There were no statistical differences among the cohorts for the remaining signs (Table 7.8). This lack of differences between the negative and positive cohorts is most likely due to patient selection. Withdrawal scoring sheets were almost universally present in the charts of toxicology screen positive neonates, while nurses maintained withdrawal scoring sheets only on negative newborns with a strong history of exposure. More important, there was no statistically significant change in the incidence of any sign with time, except for the previously discussed lethargy, hypertonicity, and irritability. No signs had a time course consistent with the model of cocaine or metabolite withdrawal (Figure 7.1, line C). Hypertonicity, tremor, hyperactive moro, and increased suck had a high incidence and a static time course among all 3 cohorts; while irritability had a high incidence after the first day of life (Table 7.8). These signs are most consistent with our model of fetopathology. The remaining 10 signs had a low incidence among all 3 cohorts (Table 7.8).

7.6 SUMMARY

This retrospective study has strengths and weaknesses. The withdrawal scoring data from the first day of life is truly blinded because the results of the toxicology screens were unavailable. All newborns in this study were at high risk for a positive urine screen, yet the difference in the incidence of lethargy and lack of hypertonicity in the cocaine cohort was highly statistically significant. The complete resolution of these signs by day 3 is most consistent with cocaine intoxication. The high incidence of neurologic signs such as hypertonicity, tremor, hyperactive Moro, and increased suck among all 3 cohorts and throughout the hospital stay are most consistent with fetopathology. These data agree with previous studies, the most important being the blinded study of Chiriboga et al.[56] Future studies should focus on the neurologic exam, especially tone, as a possible neonatal marker for long-term sequelae. There are reproducible, standardized tone exams developed for the neonate, infant, and young child that are easily administered by a neonatologist or pediatrician.[56,97] Blinded longitudinal studies, which include quantitative cocaine and benzoylecgonine levels, are needed to test the model presented here. It is important to realize that those neonates are at risk, not only socioeconomically but neurodevelopmentally and therefore deserve close neurodevelopmental follow up.

ACKNOWLEDGMENTS

We thank Richard Konkol, MD, PhD, Neal Benowitz, MD, and Peyton Jacob III, PhD, for their contributions, and Cynthia Sedik for her secretarial assistance.

REFERENCES

1. Coles, C. D., Platzman, K. A., Smith, I., James, M. E., and Falek, A., Effects of cocaine and alcohol use in pregnancy on neonatal growth and neurobehavioral status, *Neurotoxicol. Teratol.,* 14, 23, 1992.
2. Burkett, G., Yasin, S. Y., Palow, D., LaVoie, L., and Martinez, M., Patterns of cocaine binging: effect on pregnancy, *Am. J. Obstet. Gynecol.,* 171, 372, 1994.
3. Konkol, R. J., Murphey, L. J., Ferriero, D. M., Dempsey, D. A., and Olsen, G. D., Cocaine metabolites in the neonate: potential for toxicity, *J. Child Neurol.,* 9, 242, 1994.
4. Burkett, G., Yasin, S., and Palow, D., Perinatal implications of cocaine exposure, *J. Reprod. Med.,* 35, 35, 1990.
5. Bingol, N., Fuchs, M., Diaz, V., Stone, R. K., and Gromisch, D. S., Teratogenicity of cocaine in humans, *J. Pediatr.,* 110, 93, 1987.
6. Little, B. B., Snell, L. M., Klein, V. R., and Gilstrap, L. C. D., Cocaine abuse during pregnancy: maternal and fetal implications, *Obstet. Gynecol.,* 73, 157, 1989.
7. Neerhof, M. G., MacGregor, S. N., Retzky, S. S., and Sullivan, T. P., Cocaine abuse during pregnancy: peripartum prevalence and perinatal outcome, *Am. J. Obstet. Gynecol.,* 161, 633, 1989.
8. Lester, B. M., Corwin, M. J., Sepkoski, C., Seifer, R., Peucker, M., McLaughlin, S., and Golub, H. L., Neurobehavioral syndromes in cocaine-exposed newborn infants, *Child Development,* 62, 694, 1991.
9. Ryan, L., Ehrlich, S., and Finnegan, L., Cocaine abuse in pregnancy: effects on the fetus and newborn, *Neurotoxicol. Teratol.,* 9, 295, 1987.
10. Madden, J. D., Payne, T. F., and Miller, S., Maternal cocaine abuse and effect on the newborn, *Pediatrics,* 77, 209, 1986.
11. Dixon, S. D., Effects of transplacental exposure to cocaine and methamphetamine on the neonate, *West. J. Med.,* 150, 436, 1989.
12. Vega, W. A., Kolody, B., Hwang, J., and Noble, A., Prevalence and magnitude of perinatal substance exposures in California, *N. Engl. J. Med.,* 329, 850, 1993.
13. Gingras, J. L., Weese-Mayer, D. E., Hume Jr., R. F., and O'Donnell, K. J., Cocaine and development: mechanisms of fetal toxicity and neonatal consequences of prenatal cocaine exposure, *Early Hum. Dev.,* 31, 1, 1992.

14. Anday, E. K., Cohen, M. E., Kelley, N. E., and Leitner, D. S., Effect of in utero cocaine exposure on startle and its modification, *Dev. Pharmacol. Ther.,* 12, 3, 1989.

15. Corwin, M. J., Lester, B. M., Sepkoski, C., McLaughlin, S., Kayne, H., and Golub, H. L., Effects of in utero cocaine exposure on newborn acoustical cry characteristics, *Pediatrics,* 89, 1199, 1992.

16. Griffith, D. R., Azuma, S. D., and Chasnoff, I. J., Three-year outcome of children exposed prenatally to drugs, *J. Am. Acad. Child and Adol. Psychiatry,* 33, 20, 1994.

17. Angelilli, M. L., Fischer, H., Delaney-Black, V., Rubinstein, M., Ager, J. W., and Sokol, R. J., History of in utero cocaine exposure in language-delayed children, *Clin. Pediatr.,* 33, 514, 1994.

18. Kosofsky, B. E., Wilkins, A. S., Gressens, P., and Evrard, P., Transplacental cocaine exposure: a mouse model demonstrating neuroanatomic and behavioral abnormalities, *J. Child Neurol.,* 9, 234, 1994.

19. Snodgrass, S. R., Cocaine babies: a result of multiple teratogenic influences, *J. Child Neurol.,* 9, 227, 1994.

20. Lutiger, B., Graham, K., Einerson, T. R., and Koren, G., Relationship between gestational cocaine use and pregnancy outcome: a meta-analysis, *Teratology,* 44, 405, 1991.

21. Neuspiel, D. R., Markowitz, M., and Drucker, E., Intrauterine cocaine, lead, and nicotine exposure and fetal growth, *Am. J. Pub. Health,* 84, 1492, 1994.

22. Mayes, L. C., Granger, R. H., Bornstein, M. H., and Zuckerman, B., The problem of prenatal cocaine exposure. A rush to judgement, *JAMA,* 267, 406, 1992.

23. Jacobson, J. L., Jacobson, S. W., Sokol, R. J., Martier, S. S., Ager, J. W., and Shankaran, S., Effects of alcohol use, smoking, and illicit drug use on fetal growth in black infants, *J. Pediatr.,* 124, 757, 1994.

24. Benowitz, N. L., Clinical pharmacology and toxicology of cocaine, *Pharmacol. Toxicol.,* 72, 3, 1993.

25. Kharasch, S., Glotzer, D., Vinci, R., Weitzman, M., and Sargent, J., Unsuspected cocaine exposure in young children, *AJDC,* 145, 204, 1991.

26. Hicks, J. M., Morales, A., and Soldin, S. J., Drugs of abuse in a pediatric outpatient population, *Clin. Chem.,* 36, 1256, 1990.

27. Rosenberg, N. M., Meert, K. L., Knazik, S. R., Yee, H., and Kaufman, R. E., Occult cocaine exposure in children, *AJDC,* 145, 1991.

28. Garland, J. S., Smith, D. S., Rice, T. B., and Siker, D., Accidental cocaine intoxication in a nine-month-old infant: presentation and treatment, *Pediatr. Emerg. Care,* 5, 245, 1989.

29. Schubert, C. J. and Watson, S., Cocaine toxicity in an infant following intranasal instillation of a four percent cocaine solution, *Pediatr. Emerg. Care,* 8, 82, 1992.

30. Mott, S. H., Packer, R. J., and Soldin, S. J., Neurologic manifestations of cocaine exposure in childhood, *Pediatrics,* 94, 557, 1994.

31. Brogan, W. C. I., Lange, R. A., Glamann, D. B., and Hillis, L. D., Recurrent coronary vasoconstriction caused by intranasal cocaine: possible role for metabolites, *Ann. Int. Med.,* 116, 556, 1992.

32. Madden, J. A. and Powers, R. H., Effect of cocaine and cocaine metabolites on cerebral arteries in vitro, *Life Sci.,* 47, 1109, 1990.

33. Covert, R. F., Schreiber, M. D., Tebbett, I. R., and Torgerson, L. J., Hemodynamic and cerebral blood flow effects of cocaine, cocaethylene and benzoylecgonine in conscious and anesthetized fetal lambs, *J. Pharmacol. Expertl. Ther.,* 270, 118, 1994.

34. Misra, A. L., Nayak, P. K., Bloch, K., and Mule, S. J., Estimation and disposition of [3H]benzoylecgonine and pharmacological activity of cocaine metabolites, *J. Pharm. Pharmacol.,* 27, 784, 1975.

35. Konkol, R. J., Erickson, B. A., Doerr, J. K., Hoffman, R. G., and Madden, J. A., Seizures induced by the cocaine metabolite benzoylecgonine in rats, *Epilepsia,* 33, 420, 1992.

36. Spear, L. P., Frambes, N. A., and Kirstein, C. L., Fetal and maternal brain and plasma levels of cocaine and benzoylecgonine following subcutaneous administration of cocaine during gestation in rats, *Psychopharmacology,* 97, 427, 1989.

37. Simone, C., Derewlany, L. D., Oskamp, M., Knie, B., and Koren, G., Transfer of cocaine and benzoylecgonine across the perfused human placental cotyledon, *Am. J. Obstet. Gynecol.,* 170, 1404, 1994.

38. Schenker, S., Yang, Y., Johnson, R. F., Downing, J. W., Schenken, R. S., Henderson, G. I., and King, T. S., The transfer of cocaine and its metabolites across the term human placenta, *Clin. Pharmacol. Ther.,* 53, 329, 1993.

39. Dean, R. A., Christian, C. D., Sample, R. H., and Bosron, W. F., Human liver cocaine esterases: ethanol-mediated formation of ethylcocaine, *FASEB J.,* 5, 2735, 1991.

40. Isenschmid, D. S., A comprehensive study of the stability of cocaine and its metabolites, *J. Anal. Toxicol.,* 13, 250, 1989.

41. Mahone, P. R., Scott, K., Sleggs, G., D'Antoni, T., and Woods, J. R. J., Cocaine and metabolites in amniotic fluid may prolong fetal drug exposure, *Am. J. Obstet. Gynecol.,* 171, 465, 1994.

42. Gawin, F. H. and Ellinwood, E. H. J., Cocaine and other stimulants. Actions, abuse, and treatment, *N. Engl. J. Med.,* 318, 1173, 1988.

43. Oro, A. S. and Dixon, S. D., Perinatal cocaine and methamphetamine exposure: maternal and neonatal correlates, *J. Pediatr.,* 111, 571, 1987.

44. Hume, R. F. J., O'Donnell, K. J., Stranger, C. L., Killam, A. P., and Gingras, J. L., In utero cocaine exposure: observations of fetal behavioral state may predict neonatal outcome, *Am. J. Obstet. Gynecol.,* 161, 685, 1989.

45. Neuspiel, D. R. and Hamel, S. C., Cocaine and infant behavior, *J. Dev. Behav. Pediatr.,* 12, 55, 1991.

46. Pruitt, Neonatal drug withdrawal, *Pediatrics,* 72, 895, 1983.

47. Zelson, C., Rubio, E., and Wasserman, E., Neonatal narcotic addiction: 10 year observation, *Pediatrics,* 48, 178, 1971.

48. Zelson, C., Infant of the addicted mother, *N. Engl. J. Med.,* 288, 1393, 1973.

49. Finnegan, L. P., *Drug dependence in pregnancy: clinical management of mother and child,* U.S. Government Printing Office, Washington, D.C., Rockville, Maryland, 1978.

50. Finnegan, L. P., Neonatal abstinence, in *Current Therapy in Neonatal-Perinatal Medicine,* Nelson, N. M. (Ed.) C.V. Mosby, B.C. Decker, Ontario, Canada, 1984, 262.

51. Pursley, D. M. and Richardson, D. K., Manual of pediatric therapeutics, in *Manual of Pediatric Therapeutics,* 5th Edition, Graef, J. W., Ed., Little Brown & Company, Boston, 1994, 189.

52. LeBlanc, P. E., Parekh, A. J., Naso, B., and Glass, L., Effects of intrauterine exposure to alkaloidal cocaine, *Am. J. Dis. Child.,* 141, 937, 1987.

53. Doberczak, T. M., Shanzer, S., Senie, R. T., and Kandall, S. R., Neonatal neurologic and electro-encephalographic effects of intrauterine cocaine exposure, *J. Pediatr.,* 113, 354, 1988.

54. Cherukuri, R., Minkoff, H., Feldman, J., Parekh, A., and Glass, L., A cohort study of alkaloidal cocaine ("crack") in pregnancy., *Obstet. Gynecol.,* 72, 147, 1988.

55. Mastrogiannis, D. S., Decavalas, G. O., Verma, U., and Tejani, N., Perinatal outcome after recent cocaine usage., *Obstet. Gynecol.,* 76, 8, 1990.

56. Chiriboga, C. A., Bateman, D. A., Brust, J. C., and Hauser, W. A., Neurologic findings in neonates with intrauterine cocaine exposure., *Pediatr. Neurol.,* 9, 115, 1993.

57. Critchley, H. O., Woods, S. M., Barson, A. J., Richardson, T., and Lieberman, B. A., Fetal death in utero and cocaine abuse, *Br. J. Obstet. Gynaecol.,* 95, 195, 1988.

58. Chasnoff, I. J., Hunt, C. E., Kletter, R., and Kaplan, D., Prenatal cocaine exposure is associated with respiratory pattern abnormalities, *Am. J. Dis. Child.,* 143, 583, 1989.

59. Van de Bor, M., Walther, F. J., and Ebrahimi, M., Decreased cardiac output in infants of mothers who abused cocaine, *Pediatrics,* 85, 30, 1990.

60. Van de Bor, M., Walther, F. J., and Sims, M. E., Increased cerebral blood flow velocity in infants of mothers who abuse cocaine, *Pediatrics,* 85, 733, 1990.

61. Mehta, S. K., Finkelhor, R. S., Anderson, R. L., Harcar-Sevcik, R. A., Wasser, T. E., and Bahler, R. C., Transient myocardial ischemia in infants prenatally exposed to cocaine, *J. Pediatr.,* 122, 945, 1993.

62. Mirochnick, M., Frank, D., Cabral, H., Turner, A., and Zuckerman, B., Relation between meconium concentration of the cocaine metabolite benzoylecgonine and fetal growth, *J. Pediatr.,* 126, 636, 1995.

63. Hutchings, D. E., The puzzle of cocaine's effects following maternal use during pregnancy: are there reconcilable differences?, *Neurotoxicol. Teratol.,* 15, 281, 1993.

64. Hadeed, A. J. and Seiqel, S. R., Maternal cocaine use during pregnancy: effect on the newborn infant, *Pediatrics,* 84, 205, 1989.

65. Parker, S., Zuckerman, B., Bauchner, H., Frank, D., Vinci, R., and Cabral, H., Jitteriness in full-term neonates: prevalence and correlates, *Pediatrics*, 85, 17, 1990.

66. Black, M., Schuler, M., and Mair, P., Prenatal drug exposure: neurodevelopmental outcome and parenting environment, *J. Pediatr. Psych.*, 18, 605, 1993.

67. Neuspiel, D. R., Hamel, S. C., Hochberg, E., Greene, J., and Campbell, D., Maternal cocaine use and infant behavior, *Neurotoxicol. Teratol.*, 13, 229, 1991.

68. Mayes, L. C., Granger, R. H., Frank, M. A., Schottenfeld, R., and Bornstein, M. H., Neurobehavioral profiles of neonates exposed to cocaine prenatally, *Pediatrics*, 91, 778, 1993.

69. Javaid, J. I., Fischman, M. W., Schuster, C. R., Dekirmanjian, H., and Davis, J. M., Cocaine plasma concentrations: relation to physiological and subjective effects in humans, *Science*, 202, 227, 1978.

70. Inaba, T., Cocaine: pharmacokinetics and biotransformation in man, *Can. J. Physiol. Pharmacol.*, 67, 1154, 1989.

71. Van Dyke, C., Barash, P. G., Jatlow, P., and Byck, R., Cocaine: plasma concentrations after intranasal application in man, *Science*, 191, 859, 1976.

72. Paly, D., Jatlow, P., Van Dyke, C., Jeri, F. R., and Byck, R., Plasma cocaine concentrations during cocaine paste smoking, *Life Sci.*, 30, 731, 1982.

73. Rowbotham, M. R., Cocaine levels and cocaine elimination in inpatients and outpatients., in *Acute Cocaine Intoxication: Current Methods of Treatment*, H. Sorer, U.S. Government Printing Office, Washington, D C, 1993.

74. Batki, S. L., Manfredi, L. B., Jacob, P. D., and Jones, R. T., Fluoxetine for cocaine dependence in methadone maintenance: quantitative plasma and urine cocaine/benzoylecgonine concentrations, *J. Clin. Psychopharmacol.*, 13, 243, 1993.

75. Baselt, R. C., *Disposition of Toxic Drugs and Chemicals in Man*, 3rd ed., Year Book Medical Publishers, Chicago, 1989.

76. Ambre, J., Fischman, M., and Ruo, T. I., Urinary excretion of ecgonine methyl ester, a major metabolite of cocaine in humans, *J. Anal. Toxicol.*, 8, 23, 1984.

77. Ambre, J., Ruo, T. I., Nelson, J., and Belknap, S., Urinary excretion of cocaine, benzoylecgonine, and ecgonine methyl ester in humans, *J. Anal. Toxicol.*, 12, 301, 1988.

78. Hawks, R. L., Kopin, I. J., Colburn, R. W., and Thoa, N. B., Norcocaine: a pharmacologically active metabolite of cocaine found in brain, *Life Sci.*, 15, 2189, 1974.

79. Hearn, W. L., Flynn, D. D., Hime, G. W., Rose, S., Cofino, J. C., Mantero-Atienza, E., Wetli, C. V., and Mash, D. C., Cocaethylene: a unique cocaine metabolite displays high affinity for the dopamine, *J. Neurochem.*, 56, 698, 1991.

80. Dempsey, D. A., Rowbotham, M. C., Dattel, B. J., and Partridge, J. C., Neonatal blood cocaine concentrations, *Clin. Pharmacol. Ther.*, 53, 150, 1993.

81. Dempsey, D. A., Partridge, J. C., Jones, R. T., and Rowbotham, M. C., Cocaine, nicotine, caffeine, and metabolite plasma concentrations in neonates, unpublished.

82. Hooker, W. D., Jones, R. T., Benowitz, N. L., Stesin, A., and Jacob, P. I., Human pharmacology of benzoylecgonine, unpublished, 1988.

83. Stewart, D. J., Inaba, T., Lucassen, M., and Kalow, W., Cocaine metabolism: cocaine and norcocaine hydrolysis by liver and serum esterases, *Clin. Pharmacol. Ther.*, 25, 464, 1979.

84. de Payster, A., Willis, W. O., and Liebhaber, M., Cholinesterase activity in pregnant women and newborns, *J. Toxicol.*, 32, 683, 1994.

85. Mirchandani, H. G., Mirchandani, I. H., Hellman, F., English-Rider, R., Rosen, S., and Laposata, E. A., Passive inhalation of free-base cocaine (crack) smoke by infants, *Arch. Pathol. Lab. Med.*, 115, 494, 1991.

86. Rogers, C., Hall, J., and Muto, J., Findings in newborns of cocaine-abusing mothers, *J. Forens. Sci.*, 36, 1074, 1991.

87. Fitzmaurice, L. S., Wasserman, G. S., Knapp, J. F., Roberts, D. K., Waeckerle, J. F., and Fox, M., TAC use and absorption of cocaine in a pediatric emergency department, *Ann. Emerg. Med.*, 19, 515, 1990.

88. Terndrup, T. E., Walls, H. C., Mariani, P. J., Gavula, D. P., Madden, C. M., and Cantor, R. M., Plasma cocaine and tetracaine levels following application of topical anesthesia in children, *Ann. Emerg. Med.*, 21, 162, 1992.

89. Dailey, R. H., Fatality secondary to misuse of TAC solution, *Ann. Emerg. Med.*, 17, 159, 1988.

90. Cravey, R. H., Cocaine deaths in infants, *J. Anal. Toxicol.*, 12, 354, 1988.

91. Dempsey, D. A., Unpublished data.
92. Casanova, O. Q., Lombardero, N., Behnke, M., Eyler, F. D., Conlon, M., and Bertholf, R. L., Detection of cocaine exposure in the neonate. Analysis of urine, meconium, and amniotic fluid from mothers and infants exposed to cocaine, *Arch. Pathol. Lab. Med.,* 118, 988, 1994.
93. Reed, M. C. and Besunder, J. B., Developmental pharmacology: ontogenic basis of drug disposition, in *The Pediatric Clinics of North America,* Blumer, J. L. and Reed, M. D., Eds., W.B. Saunders Company, Philadelphia, 1989, 1053.
94. Radde, I. C., Renal function and elimination of drugs during development, in *Pediatric Pharmacology and Therapeutics,* 2nd ed., Radde, I. C. and MacLeod, S. M., Eds., Mosby, Toronto, 1993, 87.
95. Dempsey, D. A., Partridge, J. C., Jones, R. T., and Rowbotham, M. C., Neonatal plasma half-life of benzoylecgonine, a cocaine metabolite. (Abstract), *Clin. Pharmacol. Ther.,* 57, 180, 1995.
96. Dempsey, D., Neonatal cocaine intoxication (abstract), *Ann. Neurol.,* 1995.
97. Amiel-Tison, C. and Grenier, A., *Neurologic Assessment During the First Year of Life,* Oxford University Press, New York, 1986.
98. Chasnoff, I. J., Lewis, D. E., and Squires, L., Cocaine intoxication in a breast-fed infant, *Pediatrics,* 80, 836, 1987.
99. Chaney, N. E., Franke, J., and Wadlington, W. B., Cocaine convulsions in a breast-feeding baby, *J. Pediatr.,* 112, 134, 1988.
100. Rivkin, M. and Gilmore, H. E., Generalized seizures in an infant due to environmentally acquired cocaine, *Pediatrics,* 84, 1100, 1989.
101. Conway, E. E., Mezey, A. P., and Powers, K., Status epilepticus following the oral ingestion of cocaine in an infant, *Pediatr. Emerg. Care,* 6, 189, 1990.
102. Schou, H., Krogh, B., and Knudsen, F., Unexpected cocaine intoxication in a fourteen month old child following topical administration, *Clin. Toxicol.,* 25, 419, 1987.
103. Dinnies, J. D., Darr, C. D., and Saulys, A. J., Cocaine toxicity in toddlers, *Am. J. Dis. Child.,* 144, 743, 1990.
104. Bateman, D. A. and Heagarty, M. C., Passive free-base cocaine (crack) inhalation by infants and toddlers, *Am. J. Dis. Child.,* 143, 25, 1989.
105. Shannon, M., Lacouture, P. G., Roa, J., and Woolf, A., Cocaine exposure among children seen at a pediatric hospital, *Pediatrics,* 83, 337, 1989.
106. Ernst, A. A. and Sanders, W. M., Unexpected cocaine intoxication presenting as seizures in children, *Ann. Emerg. Med.,* 18, 774, 1989.
107. Moore, C. M., Brown, S., Negrusz, A., Tebbett, I., Meyer, W., and Jain, L., Determination of cocaine and its major metabolite, benzoylecgonine, in amniotic fluid, umbilical cord blood, umbilical cord tissue, and neonatal urine: a case study, *J. Anal. Toxicol.,* 17, 62, 1993.
108. Apple, F. S. and Roe, S. J., Cocaine-associated fetal death in utero, *J. Anal. Toxicol.,* 14, 259, 1990.
109. Mittleman, R. E., Cofino, J. C., and Hearn, W. L., Tissue distribution of cocaine in a pregnant woman, *J. Forens. Sci.,* 34, 481, 1989.
110. Klein, J., Greenwald, M., Becker, L., and Koren, G., Fetal distribution of cocaine: case analysis, *Pediatr. Pathol.,* 12, 463, 1992.
111. DeGregorio, G., Ferko, A. P., Barbieri, E. J., Ruch, E. K., Chawla, H., Keohane, D., Rosenstock, R., and Aldano, A., Determination of cocaine usage in pregnant women by a urinary EMIT drug screen and GC-MS analysis, *J. Anal. Toxicol.,* 18, 247, 1994.
112. Henderson, L. O., Powell, M. K., Hannon, W. H., Miller, B. B., Martin, M. L., Hanzlick, R. L., Vroon, D., and Sexson, W. R., Radioimmunoassay screening of dried blood spot materials for benzoylecgonine, *J. Anal. Toxicol.,* 17, 42, 1993.
113. Jain, L., Meyer, W., Moore, C., Tebbett, I., Gauthier, D., and Vidyasagar, D., Detection of fetal cocaine exposure by analysis of amniotic fluid, *Obstet. Gynecol.,* 81, 787, 1993.

Chapter 8

PRENATAL COCAINE EXPOSURE AND THE EYE

William V. Good, MD, Beatrice Latal Hajnal, MD, and Donna M. Ferriero, MD

8.0 INTRODUCTION

Although there is much debate about effects of cocaine on the developing visual system,[1] recent reports have demonstrated that various problems can be seen in some exposed infants.[2-4] The problems with human research in this field are also highlighted in many other chapters.

Briefly, substance-abusing mothers often cannot provide an honest or clear history concerning patterns of abuse. Assays for cocaine exposure can be performed on mothers and babies, but assays for other substances of abuse might be negative if performed more than days after the last episode of substance abuse. This is most obvious in the case of alcohol abuse. It is difficult to obtain accurate data regarding exposure to alcohol, and there is no good measurement of cumulative gestational exposure. Alcohol has been implicated in many of the visual defects seen with cocaine exposure, such as retinal vessel tortuosity and optic nerve hypoplasia.[5,6] Strabismus, microophthalmia, and anterior segment dysgenesis have also been documented.

Another problem is the length of exposure to the substance of abuse. Virtually no data exist on the timing of cocaine abuse vis à vis the development of ocular defects during gestation. For example, optic nerve hypoplasia is a congenital anomaly of the neural retina, which may be due to a primary failure of proper development of retinal ganglion cells. The number of optic nerve axons in the human fetus peaks at 16 to 17 weeks' gestation and then regresses and stabilizes at the age of 31 weeks.[7] Therefore, this defect could occur any time throughout the second or third trimester. When a person abuses cocaine, there is a high likelihood that other substances have been used concomitantly. The likelihood that a mother has only abused cocaine cannot be assured, and the reader may appreciate the difficulty in sorting out the effects of one substance versus another on the developing embryo.

In order to ascertain an increased prevalence of visual abnormalities, appropriate case-control studies have to be performed. Only a few centers have attempted to prospectively look at the question of substance abuse and the effects on the eye, and these centers have encountered difficulty obtaining sufficient patients for followup and appropriate control groups. The results of one study are summarized in Table 8.1.

0-8493-9465-1/96/$0.00+$.50
© 1996 by CRC Press, Inc.

Ophthalmologic Findings in 28 Children Examined*

Finding	Number	GA	Other drugs
ructural:	9		
Optic nerve atrophy	2	Term, term	Opiates, none
Optic nerve hypoplasia	1	Term	Ethanol
Immature retinal vascularization	1	30 wk	Opiates
Retinopathy of prematurity	2	25 wk, 26 wk	None, ethanol/tobacco
Colobomatous microophthalmia	1	Term	Opiates
Increased cup to disk ratio	1	Term	Opiates
Ptosis	2	Term, 34 wk	Opiates, none
Delayed visual maturation	2	Term, term	Ethanol/tobacco, none
Refractive error	2	32 wk, term	Ethanol, none
Periorbital edema	1	Term	Opiates
Normal	16		

(*One patient had more than one eye finding, thus the total number exceeds 28)

(From Tsay, C.H. et al., Neurologic and ophthalmologic findings in children exposed to cocaine in utero, *J. Child Neurol.,* in press, 1996. With permission.)

For many of the reasons listed above, and because the outcome of interest — visual system impairment — is not common, previous research in the area of cocaine abuse failed to show substantial effects of cocaine on the developing eye or visual system.[1] Given that cocaine may a damaging effect on the eyes in less than 3% of cases, an error could be made with sample sizes even as large as 25 or 30 patients. Subsequent reports have suggested the possible adverse effects of prenatal cocaine exposure on the visual system.[2,8,9] In this chapter, we will systematically examine this research and attempt to explore the pathophysiologic mechanisms involved.

8.1 EFFECTS OF COCAINE ON THE DEVELOPING RETINA

Teske and Trese[8] reported a retinopathy of prematurity (ROP) like fundus in one eye and a persistent hyperplastic primary vitreous (PHPV) abnormality in the fellow eye of a baby exposed *in utero* to cocaine. This report suggests that cocaine could play a role in altering ocular development, since PHPV occurs as a result of a failure of regression of primitive hyaloid vasculature. The finding of ROP also suggests that cocaine could alter normal retinal vascular development, particularly during the last trimester of gestation.[10]

However, when we examined a large group of premature babies to determine risk factors for ROP, we could not detect an association between known cocaine exposure and ROP or the severity of ROP (Good, unpublished observations). Despite this study, it has been our impression that some premature babies born with a documented history of cocaine exposure have retinal vascular abnormalities that could have been caused by intrauterine exposure to a vasogenic substance such as cocaine. We have examined a baby who had retinal hemorrhages in a 360° distribution in the mid-periphery of the ocular fundus. Retinal vasculature was developed out to the ora serrata, but we hypothesized that timing of cocaine exposure during gestation could have coincided with partial retinal vasculature development and could have caused these hemorrhages.

In several other cases, we have seen massive retinal hemorrhages, far in excess of what one normally sees after parturition. Occasional blot hemorrhages may be found in as many as 40% of newborn children.[11,12] The finding, massive intraretinal hemorrhaging, may suggest a particularly severe intrauterine, or perinatal, ischemic event.

The consequences of these retinal vascular changes are unknown. The damaging effects of ROP have been clearly determined, but as we noted above, any association between cocaine abuse and ROP is small or nil. Hemorrhaging, on the other hand, normally resolves and leaves no particular visual defect. However, massive hemorrhaging is potentially problematic and can lead to the development of a fibroblastic response with subsequent scarring. Scarring in critical areas of the retina could, in turn, damage visual acuity or visual field.

8.2 DILATED AND TORTUOUS IRIS BLOOD VESSELS

The iris at birth is undergoing developmental changes with the vessels growing in caliber and course. The degree of vascularity is correlated significantly with postnatal age.[13] A report by Isenberg and colleagues demonstrated dilated and tortuous iris blood vessels as a transient finding in cocaine-exposed neonates, but failed to show any serious or long-term damaging effects.[14] A later report by the same authors demonstrated that increased iris vascularity might be found in more sickly infants, regardless of cause.[15] Therefore, the finding of dilated or tortuous iris vessels should not be regarded as pathognomonic for cocaine exposure, and other causes should be considered.

8.3 DELAYED VISUAL MATURATION

Delayed visual maturation (DVM) is diagnosed when a child fails to show normal visual responses and the eye examination is not sufficiently abnormal to explain the poor visual responsiveness. This failure to show visual behavior is seen in the first few weeks and months of life.[16] Delayed visual maturation can be categorized into three types: DVM may occur as an isolated problem, in which case the eye examination is normal, or in conjunction with an optic abnormality, or even in conjunction with neurologic disease. The underlying problem, however, is one of delay in the attainment of maximum vision.

The etiology of DVM remains obscure. In a most recent careful follow-up study, so-called isolated DVM was associated with minor neurologic abnormalities.[17] This association implies that there may be some underlying neurologic defect that causes DVM, but whether DVM is due to a delay in sensory development or a delay in motor fixation is unknown.

When we evaluated all of the children that we had seen with DVM in our pediatric ophthalmology practice, we discovered that over 50% had a clear history of cocaine exposure (Good, unpublished observations). Certainly, this would suggest that drug exposure *in utero* could be a factor in causing DVM. And this association in our practice is reflected in other reports. DVM has been linked to *in utero* cocaine exposure in several previous publications.[4,9] In all cases, visually directed behavior and recovery of vision has occurred.

Mechanisms involved in cocaine-induced DVM are unknown. Cocaine is a potent neurotransmitter and could play a role in affecting neurologic visual development. DVM may simply be a manifestation of the disrupted behavioral states known to occur in cocaine-exposed babies. The problem, DVM, could be a delay in sensory (afferent) reception leading to the behavior, poor visual fixation; or the problem may be efferent (motor) leading to the exact same behavior. In the latter hypothetical etiology, babies would have vision, but would be unable to show the motor response demonstrating that they can see.[17]

8.4 STRUCTURAL DAMAGE TO THE DEVELOPING ANTERIOR VISUAL PATHWAYS

Optic nerve hypoplasia, atrophy, and coloboma have all been reported in children exposed to cocaine *in utero*.[2,9] (Figure 8.1). Optic nerve hypoplasia is a condition in which the optic nerves fail to develop a normal number of axons. The insult that causes this problem can occur early in gestation when axonal development, modeling, and remodeling are known to occur. The mechanisms involved in the development of optic nerve hypoplasia are unknown. Indeed, in the vast majority of cases of optic nerve hypoplasia, no etiology is discovered. Nevertheless, there is some evidence that *in utero* vascular damage affecting the development of midline central nervous system structures could play a role.[18]

Evidence that midline central nervous system damage occurs in conjunction with optic nerve hypoplasia comes from several sources. In the de Morsier syndrome, optic nerve hypoplasia accompanies hypothalamic pituitary insufficiency and agenesis of the septum pellucidum.[19] Other midline CNS structures may be damaged in conjunction with optic nerve hypoplasia. For example, the corpus callosum may be underdeveloped, or holoprosenphaly may occur.[1]

Optic atrophy, on the other hand, occurs with second and third trimester damage. Ordinarily the optic nerves are insensitive to the effects of hypoxia and ischemia, but when events that result in hypoxia are extreme, optic atrophy can accompany diffuse cortical and even brainstem injury. Such was the case in the child reported with optic atrophy after *in utero* cocaine exposure.[9] That baby died shortly after birth.

Ocular colobomas occur in a wide variety of recessive syndromes, as an isolated dominant gene disorder, or in trisomy 13. The relationship of coloboma to *in utero* drug exposure is hypothetical, and the one report to date could represent a real effect of cocaine, or may simply be a coincidence. Further research and follow-up of greater numbers of babies will be helpful in clarifying this issue.

8.5 EYELID EDEMA

The most common abnormality after *in utero* cocaine exposure is the development of periorbital edema. The edema may be transient in the neonatal period but occasionally may last for several months. Edema is presumed to be caused by cocaine-induced ischemic placental insufficiency.[9] Cocaine-exposed babies may be born with

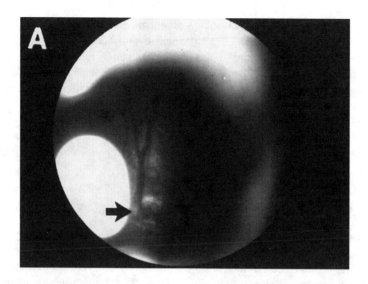

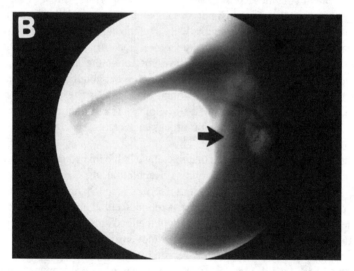

FIGURE 8.1 Unilateral optic nerve hypoplasia seen in an infant with gestational cocaine exposure. A). Arrow indicates hypoplastic disc. B). Normal optic disc in the contralateral eye.

widespread edema (anasarca), but edema will persist periorbitally due to the low pressure in the subcutaneous tissue of this region.

An unfortunate consequence of persistent eyelid edema may be bilateral visual deprivation. In one of our patients, eyelid edema was so massive that eye closure persisted for more than two months. The edema was not amenable to surgery or medical management. Ultimately we resorted to the use of eyelid speculums to keep the eyelids open for an hour or two per day. The edema resolved, and although the baby did not exhibit sensory deprivation nystagmus, the ultimate visual outcome still remains uncertain. In another case, a child presented with nystagmus in the setting of a clear history of prolonged eyelid edema after *in utero* cocaine exposure. In this particular child, cocaine exposure and eyelid edema could have played a pivotal role in leading to failure of a good visual fixation reflex.

Another possible consequence of prolonged eyelid edema with visual deprivation is improper emmetropization. Since a vision-dependent feedback mechanism contributes to the regulation of postnatal eye growth and refraction, prolonged eye closure could result in errors of refraction occurring early in life.

Thus, even though eyelid edema is a transient finding, when it occurs in a critical phase of visual development and persists for prolonged periods of time, it may have profound damaging effects.

8.6 ABNORMALITIES OF REFRACTION

Failure of emmetropization (normalization of refraction of the eyes) may occur in many settings. Both myopia and hyperopia are hereditary in some circumstances, with syndromes that affect collagen or connective tissue development leading to the development of myopia. Recently we have shown that the distribution of refractive errors in prenatal cocaine-exposed babies may be abnormal.[3] Most babies are born mildly hyperopic with astigmatism at an axis of 180°. As the babies age, hyperopia increases and the astigmatism diminishes. By the age of 6, children will show hyperopia of 1–2.5 diopters and this hyperopia gradually resolves through school-age years.[20] Myopia, therefore, usually presents after the age of five. Our recent study investigating the prevalence of ophthalmological abnormalities in a cohort of asymptomatic cocaine-exposed babies found that 26% had refractive errors by the age of one year and 80% of these had myopia.[21] The refraction remained stable, implying that normal emmetropization processes were not available to these particular babies.

What is the disease mechanism that may have led to this abnormality? Dopamine is presumed to play a role in eye growth.[22] Regulation of postnatal eye growth and refraction relies on a vision-dependent feedback mechanism. This mechanism appears to be located, at least in part, in the retina. Retinal amacrine cells containing dopamine seem to be implicated in a negative feedback loop that links ocular growth control to vision.[22] If cocaine interferes with dopamine release or receptors, then it could play a role in affecting visual outcome by changing ocular growth.

Alternatively, eyelid edema seen in the cocaine-exposed neonate may cause partial and temporary occlusion, and this is known to result in myopia. Sixty percent of the children in our study with refractive errors had eyelid edema.[21] Whether delayed visual maturation also plays a role in the development of refractive errors is unknown. Other factors which control refraction, like corneal curvature, anterior chamber depth, and lens thickness, have not been studied adequately to rule out cocaine effect.

8.7 SUMMARY

There is increasing evidence that prenatal cocaine exposure is associated with abnormalities in the development of vision. These abnormalities are both structural (ocular and neurologic) and functional (DVM). There is enough preliminary data linking cocaine to visual defects to warrant the recommendation that cocaine-exposed babies should receive a thorough ophthalmologic examination. In some cases, the defect will be treatable, (e.g., refractive errors, eyelid edema). In others, the patient and family may need to be provided with special vision and social services. Future research should aim to clarify disease mechanisms and exact risks for the development of the various defects described above.

REFERENCES

1. Stafford, J. R., Rosen, T. S., Zaider, M., and Merriam, J. C., Prenatal cocaine exposure and the development of the human eye, *Ophthalmology*, 101, 301, 1994.
2. Dominguez, R., Aguirre Vila-Coro, A., Slopis, J. M., and Bohan, T. P., Brain and ocular abnormalities in infants with in utero exposure to cocaine and other street drugs, *Am. J. Dis. Child.*, 145, 688, 1991.
3. Partridge, J. C., Tsay, C., Good, W. V., and Ferriero, D. M., Neurological and ophthalmological findings in asymptomatic infants with gestational cocaine exposure, *Ann. Neurol.*, 34, 459, 1993.
4. Tsay, C. H., Partridge, J. C., Villarreal, S. F., Good, W. V., and Ferriero, D. M., Neurologic and ophthalmologic findings in children exposed to cocaine in utero, *J. Child Neurol.*, in press.
5. Stromland, K., Ocular involvement in fetal alcohol syndrome, *Surv. Ophthalmol.*, 31, 277, 1987.
6. Cook, C. S., Nowotny, A. Z., and Sulik, K. K., Fetal alcohol syndrome: eye malformations in a mouse model, *Arch. Ophthalmol.*, 105, 1576, 1987.
7. Provis, J. M., Billson, F. A., and Russell, P., Ganglion cell topography in human fetal retina, *Invest. Ophthalmol. Vis. Sci.*, 24, 1316, 1983.
8. Teske, M. P. and Trese, M. T., Retinopathy of prematurity-like fundus and persistent hyperplastic primary vitreous associated with maternal cocaine use, *Am. J. Ophthalmol.*, 103, 719, 1987.
9. Good, W. V., Ferriero, D. M., Golabi, M., and Kobori, J. A., Abnormalities of the visual system in infants exposed to cocaine, *Ophthalmology*, 99, 341, 1992.
10. Torczynski, E., Normal development of the eye and orbit before birth: the development of the eye, in *The Eye in Infancy*, Isenberg, S. J. Ed., Year Book Medical, Chicago, 1989, 9.
11. Schenker, J. G. and Gombos, G. M., Retinal hemorrhage in the newborns, *Obstet. Gynecol.*, 27, 521, 1966.
12. Sezen, F., Retinal haemorrhages in newborn infants, *Br. J. Ophthalmol.*, 55, 248, 1971.
13. Lind, N., Shinebourne, E., and Turner, P., Adrenergic neurone and receptor activity in the iris of the neonate, *Pediatrics*, 47, 105, 1971.
14. Isenberg, S. J., Spierer, A., and Inkelis, S. H., Ocular signs of cocaine intoxication in neonates, *Am. J. Ophthalmol.*, 103, 211, 1987.
15. Spierer, A., Isenberg, S. J., and Inkelis, S. H., Characteristics of the iris in 100 neonates, *J. Pediatr. Ophthalmol. Strabismus*, 26, 28, 1989.
16. Hoyt, C. S., Jastrzebski, G., and Marg, E., Delayed visual maturation in infancy, *Br. J. Ophthalmol.*, 67, 127, 1983.
17. Jan, J. and Good, W., Children with sensory defect nystagmus, normal appearing fundi, and normal electroretinograms, *Dev. Med. Child Neurol.*, in press.
18. Hoyt, C. S. and Good, W. V., Do we really understand the difference between optic nerve hypoplasia and atrophy, *Eye*, 6, 201, 1992.
19. Acers, E. T., Optic nerve hypoplasia: Septooptic pituitary dysplasia syndrome, *Trans. Am. Ophthalmol. Soc.*, 79, 4225, 1981.
20. Banks, M. S., Infant refraction and accommodation, *Int. Ophthalmol. Clin.*, 20, 205, 1980.
21. Latal Hajnal, B., Partridge, J. C., Good, W. V., Tsay, C. H., and Ferriero, D. M., Neurologic and ophthalmologic findings in asymptomatic infants with prenatal cocaine exposure, *Ann. Neurology*, 38, in press.
22. Laties, A. M. and Stone, R. A., Some visual and neurochemical correlates of refractive development, *Vis. Neurosc.*, 7, 125, 1991.

Chapter 9

Transplacental Cocaine Exposure: Behavioral Consequences

Aaron S. Wilkins, Barry E. Kosofsky, MD, PhD,
Anthony G. Romano, PhD, and John A. Harvey, PhD

9.0 INTRODUCTION

An estimated one percent of infants born in America today are exposed to cocaine *in utero*.[1] The children born to women who used cocaine during pregnancy represent a segment of the population that has sustained a unique biologic exposure. This epidemic has captured considerable research interest, including a focus on understanding the behavioral deficits evident in offspring exposed transplacentally to cocaine. Rodent models have been a valuable tool in leading to the characterization of a number of behavioral deficits in cocaine-exposed offspring. In the neonate, these have included studies showing that prenatal cocaine exposure affects simple reflexes,[2,3] motor activity,[2,4-6] and various aspects of learning, including appetitive and aversive classical conditioning tasks.[7-10]

To date, fewer studies have demonstrated persistent behavioral deficits consequent to prenatal cocaine exposure. Church and Overbeck[11] showed that rats administered a high dose of cocaine (100 mg/kg, SC, Embryonic Day [E] E7-20) are deficient in acquiring an active avoidance behavior, but Riley and Foss[12] showed no differences in controls versus animals exposed to a lower dose of cocaine (60 mg/kg, IP, E14-21) in a comparable behavioral test. Bilitzke and Church[13] concluded that prenatal cocaine exposure (80 mg/kg, SC, E7-20) affects behavior in stressful or fearful situations as revealed by impaired performance in the Porsolt swim test. Following prenatal cocaine administration, Peris et al.[14] found hyperactivity resulting from a postnatal cocaine challenge (1 or 3 mg/kg, IV, bid, E7-term; 10 mg/kg, SC, challenge at 3 months of age). Goodwin et al.[10] found a decreased threshold for aggression in cocaine-exposed rats (40 mg/kg, SC, E8-20) when tested as adults. Smith et al.[5] found prenatal cocaine exposure (10 mg/kg, SC, E4-18) affected tail flick and footshock sensitivity in adult animals.

An increasing area of interest has involved the role of prenatal cocaine exposure in affecting adult cognitive performance and attention. Such deficits are clinically evident in a subset of children exposed *in utero* to cocaine, who have been shown to be impaired in mental development[15-18] and attention.[18-20] A number of research teams have used animal models to characterize cognitive and attentional deficits consequent to prenatal toxin exposure, including cocaine, by studying conditioning and discrimination tasks.

Cocaine is known to induce anorexia in humans[21] and in rodents.[22-26] A number of studies in rodents have therefore used pair-fed groups to control for cocaine-induced malnutrition. Malnutrition, both prenatal and early in life, has been documented to affect social behavior,[27] memory,[28,29] learning,[30,31] and discrimination tasks,[32-34] which may subserve attentional processes.

The goal of this manuscript will be to identify the role that prenatal cocaine exposure plays in affecting rodent performance during conditioning and discrimination paradigms that often invoke (or require) attentional processes. Additionally, the effect of cocaine-induced malnutrition in modulating deficits in these tasks will be addressed.

9.1 ANIMAL MODELS OF COGNITION/LEARNING AND ATTENTION

9.1.1 Models of Cognition/Learning

A number of research teams have presented models of retarded cognitive development and learning in rodents following prenatal insults that involve conditioning. For example, Strupp et al.[35] developed a model of cumulative learning that measures adult cognitive ability in the rat. In this cumulative learning paradigm, Strupp investigated an animal's ability to transfer learning across a series of related tasks rather than performance within a single learning task. The training phase was completed when animals successfully made a nose poke to receive a reinforcement; during the testing phase, animals were tested on a sequence of 10 discrimination problems, in which each animal progressed to the next problem in sequence after reaching learning criterion on the previous problem. Strupp et al. found the series of 10 discrimination tests more sensitive than independent discrimination learning tests. For example, animals exposed prenatally to phenylalanine in an animal model of PKU were not deficient on individual learning tests (learning set), but were impaired versus controls in the cumulative learning paradigm. The sensitivity of the cumulative learning task, according to Strupp, may be analogous to an IQ score. Impairments in the cumulative learning paradigm may therefore reflect changes in cognitive ability that single, traditional, behavioral paradigms might not be able to assess. The performance of an animal exposed prenatally to cocaine in a cumulative learning paradigm remains to be determined.

The nictitating membrane response (NMR) has been useful in studying associative learning responses (i.e., classical conditioning) in rabbits.[36,37] The NMR preparation essentially involves an animal's ability to associate a conditioned stimulus (e.g., light, tone) with an unconditioned stimulus (e.g., corneal airpuff). With successful conditioning, the animal will blink when presented with the conditioned stimulus. The response of the nictitating membrane reflects the rabbit's ability to learn in a conditioning paradigm. Marshall-Goodell and Gormezano[38] found that acute cocaine administration to naive adult rabbits (6 mg/kg, IV) significantly increased the number of trials necessary for rabbits to learn the NMR.

9.1.2 Attention

There are several different forms of attention, including selective attention, divided attention, and sustained attention, which includes vigilance.[39] Deficits in mechanisms underlying these forms of attention may result in specific impairments in performance in humans and rodents. In normal humans, treatment with IV clonidine, a noradrenergic alpha$_2$ agonist, impairs attentional performance.[40-43] In rats, Robbins and colleagues found that performance in tasks requiring attention can be disrupted by lesioning the dorsal noradrenergic bundle (DNAB).[44,45] In a visual discrimination task (5-choice serial reaction time task), rats were required to detect brief visual stimuli presented unpredictably at one of five locations and then push a panel paired with the stimulus. Animals with the DNAB lesions displayed deficits in attention in this task when a) loud bursts of white noise were interpolated immediately prior to each visual stimulus,[44] b) the stimuli were presented unpredictably in time,[46] and c) the rats were treated with amphetamine, which caused impulsive and premature responding.[47] Thus the noradrenergic system is believed to be involved in attentional processing.[39,46,48,49] Yet researchers have found that lesions of the dopaminergic,[48] serotonergic,[50] or cholinergic[51] systems also disrupt attention. According to Robbins and Everitt,[49] these systems probably interact in modulating attention.

9.1.3 Models of Attention

One paradigm that evaluates animal attention is latent inhibition (LI). Latent inhibition describes a process by which a series of nonreinforced exposures to a stimulus retards conditioning to that stimulus when it is subsequently paired with a reinforcing event.[52] The preexposed stimulus is called the latent inhibitor, and the resulting retardation of conditioning is called the latent inhibition effect. The animal learns that the preexposed stimulus does not predict an important event, such that when the stimulus is rendered important by being paired with a reinforcing event, the animals must first overcome a learned attentional bias before conditioning can occur.[53] This interpretation of LI is supported by studies showing that LI is an associative process whereby the animal learns to ignore the preexposed stimulus.[54-57]

The blocking paradigm, which was first described by Kamin,[58] is generally accepted as a model of selective attention.[53,59,60] Blocking refers to the phenomenon by which the strength of conditioning to one element of a two-element conditioned stimulus is affected by the organism's prior experience with the other element.[58] If two stimuli are presented as a compound stimulus (AB) from the outset of reinforcement training, either stimulus (A or B) will elicit a strong conditioned response.[61] Blocking occurs when prior conditioning to one stimulus (A) prevents conditioning to a second stimulus (B), of equal associative strength to (A), when the two are subsequently presented together as a compound stimulus (AB). Upon presentation of (AB) following presentation of (A), the animal attends to stimulus (B) on at least the first few presentations of (AB), but ceases attending to it because (B) provides no additional information about the reinforcing event.[53,58,62] The normal animal learns that the second stimulus (B) is redundant and ignores it.

9.2 COCAINE AND IMPAIRMENTS IN COGNITION/LEARNING IN RODENTS

Several groups have demonstrated that prenatal cocaine exposure results in persistent deficits in learning. Levin and Seidler[63] found differential effects in male and female rats (30 mg/kg, SC, bid, E8-20) on radial-arm maze learning performance. Cocaine-exposed females showed impaired choice accuracy during acquisition of radial-arm maze performance when compared with control females. Conversely, the performance of cocaine-exposed males did not differ from that of control males. Smith et al.[5] found cocaine-exposed mice deficient in Differential Reinforcement of Low Rates (DRL) performance, which often reflects hippocampal damage,[64] and in the water maze.

Heyser et al.[65] used a conditioned place preference task (CPP) to evaluate how prenatal cocaine exposure (40 mg/kg, SC, E8-20) affects the rewarding properties of cocaine in adult rats. The CPP consists of repeated pairings of a drug with a highly distinctive context (place). CPP can be construed as a classical conditioning task, in which a drug (cocaine) serves as the unconditioned stimulus and the place serves as the conditioned stimulus. After repeated pairings of the place and the drug, the place becomes associated with the effects of the drug. Heyser et al.[65] demonstrated that rats prenatally exposed to cocaine did not demonstrate place preference, whereas controls did.

9.3 COCAINE AND IMPAIRMENTS IN ATTENTION IN RODENTS AND RABBITS

9.3.1 Cocaine, Discrimination Tasks, and Attention

Heyser et al.[66] assessed rat offspring prenatally exposed to cocaine (40 mg/kg, SC, E8-20) during the acquisition and reversal of a conditional discrimination task, which provides information about performance on a series of tasks that can be viewed as progressively more complex. Animals were initially trained to discriminate between two odors that independently served as cues signaling which of two levers when depressed would result in the delivery of a food reward. After animals learned this discrimination (i.e., an odor paired with a lever), the pairings of odors with levers were reversed and the animals were tested again. Heyser et al. found no effect of prenatal cocaine in altering the ability to acquire the odor aversion. However, cocaine-exposed rats required more sessions to acquire the reversal of the conditional discrimination than did control or pair-fed animals.

Heyser suggests that this performance deficit may represent an alteration in the way information is processed in cocaine-exposed adults. The animals may be slower to adapt to changes in rules and thus persist in a particular response strategy. This deficit may be attentional; in the reversal training, an animal must attend to the odor that will predict the dispensing of food. Initially, animals pay attention to the odor that predicted food in the odor discrimination training session. Yet animals learn to selectively attend to the odor that is not predictive of food (at the expense of the odor no longer relevant in predicting food, which is ignored) because the "old" strategy no longer works. Cocaine-exposed rats may be deficient in their ability to pay attention to or "notice" the other odor since they already learned during the initial training to pay attention to an odor predictive of food. According to Gibson,[67] the training of attention is a primary form of learning that is present in all discrimination tasks.

9.3.2 Cocaine, Discrimination, Attention, and Anterior Cingulate Cortex

Recently, the rabbit has been employed as a model for examining the neurobehavioral effects of prenatal exposure to cocaine.[68] Rabbit dams were treated with cocaine (4 mg/kg, IV, bid) on gestational days 8 through 29. Although intrauterine exposure to cocaine had no effect on the gross physical appearance of offspring in this model, such prenatal cocaine exposure produced an increase in the number of immunoreactive GABA neurons[69] and abnormal dendritic structure of pyramidal cells in the anterior cingulate cortex.[70] A number of cognitive and noncognitive functions have been attributed to cingulate cortex.[71] Two of the cognitive functions associated with this cortical structure are attention and discrimination learning.[72,73] As detailed below, both of these cognitive processes are altered following prenatal exposure to cocaine.

Romano et al.[74] examined classical conditioning of the nictitating membrane response in adult rabbits exposed to cocaine *in utero*. Several effects were noted in the offspring, all of which could be attributed to a dysfunctional anterior cingulate cortex and consequent alteration in attentional processing. Cocaine-exposed rabbits undergoing concurrent acquisition training with tones and lights paired with a corneal airpuff US (unconditioned stimulus) showed a normal rate of acquisition to the light CS (conditional stimulus) and an accelerated rate of acquisition to the tone CS. The accelerated rate of acquisition to a tone CS following prenatal exposure to cocaine was replicated in a second experiment where it was also determined that there was no alteration in the intensity threshold for eliciting CRs (conditioned responses). Thus, a simple alteration in sensory processing of auditory stimuli cannot account for the accelerated rate of learning seen in cocaine-exposed animals. A more subtle mechanism for the accelerated learning appears to be operating. That is, it appears that the neurological effects of intrauterine cocaine exposure functionally increased the associability or attentional value of the tone CS. Such an increase could accelerate the rate of learning without producing a concomitant alteration in the intensity threshold for eliciting CRs, once acquisition is asymptotic.

A number of learning theories have suggested that CSs undergo changes in attentional as well as associative processes and these changes in attentional processes influence the rate of learning. Thus, the attentional value accorded to a CS can (e.g., see Mackintosh[53] for a full discussion) either increase or decrease depending on its current associative strength and its relationship with the US. In the simplest case, a neutral CS paired with a US will undergo an increase in both its attentional and associative values, whereas a neutral CS presented in isolation will undergo a decrease in its attentional value. Animals learn to attend and respond to a CS paired with a US and to ignore and not respond to a CS that has never been paired with a US.

An additional influence on the rate of learning has to do with the salience of the CS. Stimulus salience is directly related to stimulus intensity when comparing stimuli of the same modality. When comparing stimuli of different modalities, stimulus salience has traditionally been defined in terms of the rate of learning associated with a given CS.[75] Given two CSs, the one associated with the faster rate of acquisition is said to be the more salient of the two. For normal rabbits, auditory stimuli tend to be more salient than visual stimuli. Thus, the accelerated rate of acquisition to the tone CS observed in cocaine progeny suggests not only that the tone was more salient than the light but also that the tone received more attentional processing than normal. That is, the difference in salience between the light and tone produced a disproportionate difference in attentional processing for cocaine progeny.

One potential problem in interpreting the preceding results is that lights and tones differ not only in salience but also in modality. In an attempt to separate modality differences from salience differences per se, subsequent experiments examined how altered attentional processing of salient stimuli of the same[76] or different modalities[77] would affect the rate of discrimination learning in cocaine progeny. The first set of experiments employed salient stimuli as the CS+s. Thus, one experiment contrasted a moderate intensity tone as the CS+ (T+) with a flashing light as the CS- (L-). A second experiment contrasted a moderate intensity, 1 kHz tone as the CS+ (loud T+) with an 8 kHz tone of weaker intensity as the CS- (soft T-).

As shown in Figure 9.1, the use of a more salient CS+ versus a less salient CS- had no effect on the rate of CR acquisition in either the cross-modal discrimination paradigm (T+/L-) or the intramodal discrimination paradigm (loud T+/soft T-). Apparently, the increase in task complexity involved in discrimination learning versus simple acquisition interacted with the altered attentional processing in cocaine progeny such that their rate of learning was normalized.

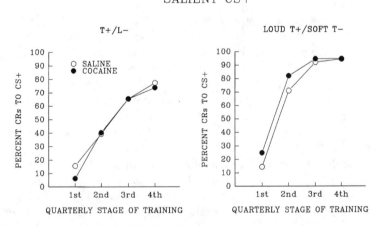

FIGURE 9.1 Mean percentages of conditioned nictitating membrane responses of adult rabbits exposed to cocaine *in utero.* Left panel: Percentage of conditioned responses to a tone CS+ during tone CS+/light CS- discrimination training. Right panel: Percentage of conditioned responses to a loud, 1 kHz tone CS+ during discrimination training between the loud tone and a soft, 8 kHz tone CS-.

Although the use of salient stimuli as CS+s normalized the rate of CR acquisition in cocaine progeny, the use of salient stimuli as CS-s produced very different results. In one experiment,[77] a flashing light served as the CS+ (L+) and a tone served as the CS- (T-); in a second experiment,[76] an 8 kHz weak tone served as the CS+ (soft T+) and a louder 1 kHz tone served as the CS- (loud T-). As shown in Figure 9.2, the use of a less salient CS+ versus a more salient CS- significantly (p<0.025) retarded the rate of CR acquisition in cocaine progeny in both the cross-modal discrimination paradigm (interaction F[3,60]=3.46) and the intramodal discrimination paradigm (interaction F[3,105]=3.15).

SALIENT CS−

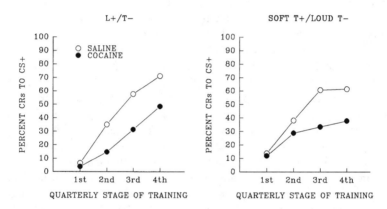

FIGURE 9.2   Mean percentages of conditioned nictitating membrane responses of adult rabbits exposed to cocaine *in utero*. Left panel: Percentage of conditioned responses to a light CS+ during light CS+/tone CS- discrimination training. The interaction between prenatal treatment condition and stage of training was significant [F(3, 105) = 3.15, p <.05]. Right panel: Percentage of conditioned responses to a soft, 8 kHz tone CS+ during discrimination training between the soft tone and a loud, 1 kHz tone CS-. Cocaine progeny were significantly retarded in their ability to acquire CRs to the CS+ in both experiments.

Thus, the modality effects reported here and by Romano et al.[74] are in fact due to differences in stimulus salience rather than to modality *per se*. Moreover, because animals learn to attend and respond to the CS+ and to ignore and not respond to the CS-, the preceding results suggest that when the CS- is the more salient of the two stimuli, cocaine-exposed animals have difficulty in learning to attend to the less salient CS+ such that their rate of CR acquisition to the CS+ is retarded relative to controls. In other words, cocaine progeny have difficulty in preferentially attending to less salient but relevant stimuli when more salient, irrelevant stimuli occur in the same context.

In a conditioned fear paradigm, Selden, Robbins, and Everitt[78] found that DNAB-lesioned animals demonstrated enhanced fear of contextual cues, relative to sham animals, by showing a greater preference for a "safe" environment over the one in which they were shocked. According to Robbins and Everitt, the lesion appears to broaden the rat's attentional span with the result that distal cues are preferentially utilized over proximal cues, even when cues are less predictive of the

US (i.e., shock). Indeed, the cocaine-exposed rabbits' inability to attend to less salient but relevant cues[76,77] is similar to that of the DNAB-lesioned rats. Because the noradrenergic system is functionally impaired in the DNAB-lesioned animals, it may also be deficient in the prenatally cocaine-exposed rabbits.

9.3.3 Cocaine, Impaired Blocking, and Attention

Kosofsky et al.[79] injected pregnant mice with varying doses of cocaine (COC: Cocaine at 40, 20, or 10 mg/kg, SC, bid, E8-E17; or 40 mg/kg, SC, bid from E8-12 or E13-E17). An additional group of animals received phentolamine (5 mg/kg, SC) 15 minutes prior to cocaine administration (P COC 40). Control dams were injected with vehicle (SAL). We utilized pair-fed controls (SPF) and surrogate fostered all pups on P0. Our evaluation of rodent attention was accomplished via the blocking paradigm, which was described above.

On Postnatal Day (P) 50 or P100, mice were assigned to one of three test conditioning groups.[79] One group of animals was simultaneously exposed to a compound conditional stimulus (2 equally salient odors, A and B) paired with footshock. A second group of animals, the unpaired controls, was exposed to odors A and B and footshock separately. A third group of animals, in the blocking group, was first exposed to odor A paired with footshock and then odors A and B paired with footshock. All animals were tested for their preference for odor B or a novel odor. Independent of treatment, animals trained to a compound conditional stimulus spent more time over the novel odor than odor B (Figure 9.3, CCS), which indicates an ability of mice to learn an aversion to an odor when paired with footshock. Animals in group 2, the unpaired control group, displayed no preference for odor B or the novel odor (Figure 9.3, unpaired), demonstrating no intrinsic preference for odor B versus the novel odor.

In the blocking group, animals in the control (SAL) group showed no preference for odor B versus the novel odor (Figure 9.3, blocking, SAL; see also Kosofsky et al.[79]). These animals successfully "blocked" and were able to recognize that odor B was a redundant predictor of footshock when introduced during conditioning. Conversely, mice exposed to 40 mg/kg cocaine from E8-17 (Figure 9.3, blocking, COC 40;[79]) displayed an aversion to odor B as they spent more time over the novel odor than over odor B (p <0.01). Lower doses of cocaine (20 or 10 mg/kg) or early (E8-12) or late (E13-17) gestational exposure did not significantly impair blocking performance (data not shown; see Kosofsky et al.[80]). However, those results demonstrated a correlation between the dose of prenatal cocaine (40 versus 20 versus 10 mg/kg, SC, bid), as well as the degree of prenatal malnutrition (SPF 40 versus 20 versus 10) and performance of adult animals in the blocking paradigm (data not shown; see Kosofsky et al.[80]).

9.3.4 Mechanisms of Cocaine-Induced Brain Injury

The direct effect of cocaine versus the indirect effect of cocaine-induced fetal hypoxia, mediated by uterine artery vasoconstriction,[81,82] in mediating some of the toxic effects

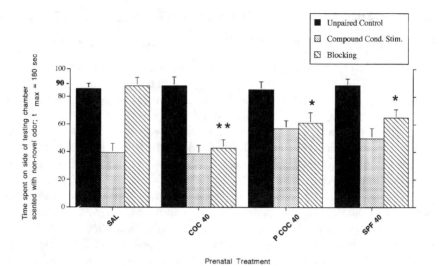

FIGURE 9.3   The relationship between Dam Prenatal Treatment and offspring P50 behavioral test condition. The ability of P50 COC 40, P COC 40, SPF 40, or SAL mice to learn an aversion to a compound conditional stimulus or to selectively attend to a relevant stimulus in a blocking paradigm. Successful blocking is shown in animals spending no less time over the paired side of the testing chamber than animals in the unpaired control group. **p<0.01; *p<0.05: when compared with SAL *ad lib* group (Dunnett t).

of gestational cocaine on developing mouse brain were examined by Kosofsky et al.[83] In acute experiments in pregnant mice, cocaine at 20 or 40 mg/kg, SC, had no effect on mean arterial blood pressure (MAP) measurements in the dams. In chronic experiments, pregnant dams were additionally administered phentolamine (5 mg/kg, SC), a short-acting, reversible alpha-adrenergic antagonist, fifteen minutes prior to administration of cocaine (40 mg/kg, SC, E8-17[83]). When administered independently, phentolamine is likely to decrease uterine blood flow (UBF), as supported in the acute experiment by a decrease in MAP. In acute experiments in sheep[84] utilizing phenoxybenzamine (a non-reversible alpha-adrenergic antagonist), decreased UBF was directly demonstrated with Doppler flow probes. Despite the fact that uterine blood flow was probably compromised following phentolamine pretreatment alone in the chronic experiments, those animals were not growth retarded nor unable to block as adults (data not shown; see Kosofsky et al.[83]). Additionally, P COC 40 animals were impaired in blocking when tested as adults (p<0.05; Figure 9.3). These results imply that:

1. In the mouse model, cocaine's effects on the fetal mouse brain[83] are not due to cocaine-induced maternal hypertension and resulting fetal hypoxia
   - There were no elevations in MAP following cocaine administration, and;
   - Phentolamine alone (with presumed "steal" of blood from the fetus) did not result in compromise of postnatal brain growth or behavior;
2. In the mouse model, α-adrenergic mechanisms are not primarily responsible for mediating the toxic effects of gestational cocaine exposure on developing brain.

9.4 COCAINE-MEDIATED MALNUTRITION AND ATTENTION

9.4.1 Malnutrition, Discrimination Tasks, Attention, and IQ

The relationship between malnutrition and inattention is a problem that has been documented clinically[85-87] and in experimental primate and rodent research.[32-34] Galler et al. demonstrated that children in Barbados malnourished early in life (ages 5-11) had reduced IQ,[87] impaired social skills, poorer physical performance, emotional instability, learning disabilities,[88] and attentional deficits.[87,89] Grade school teachers reported in a questionnaire that malnourished children had shorter attention spans than normally nourished children. These attentional deficits were independent from decrements in IQ.

Galler and Manes[32] used a rat model to compare the effects of malnutrition over many generations with those of malnutrition only during a single generation. Animal performance was evaluated on a Lashley test of visual discrimination, which involves a series of problems of increasing complexity.[90] In the Lashley test, P90-100 animals were required to discriminate between different patterns on backboards in front of 2 windows (black versus white, horizontal versus vertical stripes, circle versus square) and then jump through one or the other window in response to one of these cues. Galler found that deficits in visual discrimination were most severe in males and females with intergenerational malnutrition.[32,91] However, protein deficiency for one generation also impaired visual discrimination.[28,91]

Zimmermann et al.[33] found that monkeys maintained on a low-protein diet after 120 days of life were deficient in reversal learning in a conditional discrimination task (see also Zimmermann,[92]) similar in structure to those utilized by Heyser et al.[66] and Romano and Harvey.[77] Zimmermann trained monkeys to associate a triangle or square, at varying locations within a testing chamber, with a reward. Animals on the low-protein or normal diet were equally adept at acquiring this ability. Monkeys on the low-protein diet were impaired in the reversal task, however, as they showed a decrease in percent correct responses when the shapes were reversed.

Halas and Sandstead[34] found that P100 rats subject to undernutrition throughout lactation were also deficient in a reverse discrimination task. As explained previously, reverse discrimination requires an animal to learn the opposite pairing of an odor with a lever that dispenses food, or in this experiment, a light and lever (e.g., light on + lever = food). When animals were required to learn to press the lever when the light was off during reverse training, malnourished animals initiated fewer correct responses than controls. The malnourished animals may be impaired in their ability to change conditioning strategies or to pay attention to the change in the light and lever pairing.

9.4.2 Malnutrition, Impaired Blocking, and Attention

In the prenatal mouse model, dams whose cocaine-exposed offspring were deficient in blocking (COC 40 mg/kg, SC, E8-17 and phentolamine 5 mg/kg, SC 15 minutes prior to P + COC 40 mg/kg, SC, E8-17) ate less food from E8-16 (Table 9.1), and gained significantly less weight from E8-18 (Table 9.1) than SAL controls (Dunnett t). In addition, animals pair-fed with dams administered cocaine at 40 mg/kg, SC, from E8-17 (SPF 40) also gained less weight than controls. The offspring of these dams were significantly retarded in weight and biparietal diameter (BPD) on P1 and P9 when compared with controls (Table 9.2 and Figures 9.4 and 9.5). By behavioral testing day P50, COC 40-exposed and SPF 40-exposed mice were still smaller in weight, but did not differ from controls in biparietal diameter.

Table 9.1   Summary of Maternal/Litter Data

Variable	COC 40[a]	P COC 40[b]	SPF 40[c]	SAL[d]
Percentage Gestational Weight Gain, E8-E18	25.1*	27.9*	15.8*	37.6
	(1.2)	(5.0)	(1.9)	(0.8)
Total Food Intake (g) E8-E16	157*	134*		205
	(7.4)	(17.1)		(7.6)
Gestational Length (d)	19.0	18.4	18.9	18.3
	(0.2)	(0.2)	(0.2)	(0.2)
Litter Size at P0	11.4	10.9	10.9	12.6
	(0.5)	(0.7)	(0.4)	(0.5)

*p<0.01 when compared to SAL controls (Dunnett t)
( ) indicates SEMs.

[a] Pregnant dams injected with cocaine (COC 40)
[b] Pre-treated with phentolamine and injected with cocaine (P COC 40)
[c] Injected with saline and pair-fed with the cocaine mothers (SPF 40)
[d] Injected with saline and allowed access to food *ad lib* (SAL).

Table 9.2   Summary of Offspring Weight Data[a]

Variable	SAL	COC 40	P COC 40	SPF 40
P1 Wt (g)	1.5	1.2*	1.3*	1.3*
	(.02)	(.02)	(.03)	(.02)
P9 Wt	5.1	4.5*	5.0	4.5*
	(.09)	(0.1)	(0.1)	(0.1)
P50 Wt Male**	34.1	30.1*	33.4	29.9*
	(0.5)	(1.1)	(3.0)	(0.8)
P50 Wt Female	26.2	23.7*	25.8	23.9*
	(0.4)	(0.6)	(0.8)	(0.6)
P1 BPD (in)	.284	.275*	.280*	.276*
	(.001)	(.002)	(.002)	(.002)
P9 BPD	.425	.403*	.409*	.400*
	(.002)	(.002)	(.002)	(.002)
P50 BPD Male**	.529	.529	.533	.540
	(.010)	(.006)	(.007)	(.006)
P50 BPD Female	.518	.509	.525	.504
	(.003)	(.008)	(.002)	(.007)

[a] Summary of offspring weight data (P1, P9, P50) and offspring biparietal diameter data (P1, P9, P50) for pups born to COC 40, P COC 40, SPF 40, and SAL dams. Pups were surrogate-fostered through weaning and separated by sex during the fourth week of life.

( ) indicates SEMs.
* p<0.01; treatment group smaller than SAL controls. (Dunnett t)
** p<0.05; males larger than females.

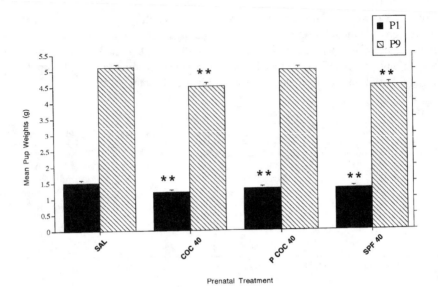

FIGURE 9.4 The effect of dam prenatal treatment on P1 and P9 offspring weight. Mean weights for COC 40, P COC 40, SPF 40, and SAL pups on P1 and P9. ** $p<0.01$; smaller when compared with SAL *ad lib* group on same day (Dunnett t).

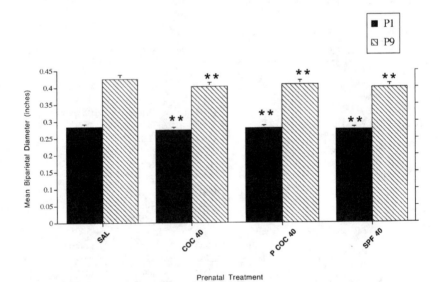

FIGURE 9.5 Males and female means on P1 were collapsed. Error bars indicate SEMs. Mean biparietal diameter for COC 40, P COC 40, SPF 40, and SAL pups on P1 and P9. ** $p<0.01$; smaller when compared with SAL *ad lib* group on same day (Dunnett t). Error bars indicate SEMs.

Of interest, a deficit in blocking was observed in mice pair-fed with COC 40 animals. Yet the impairment seen in performance in SPF 40 mice was not as pronounced as that seen in the COC 40 mice (p <0.05). Whereas roughly 9 of 10 COC 40 mice were deficient in blocking, only 5 of 10 SPF 40 animals showed this deficit.

Offspring of SPF 20 and SPF 10 dams, who were given more food than SPF 40 dams, were successfully able to block (data not shown; see Kosofsky et al.[80]).

9.5 SUMMARY

Transplacental cocaine exposure impairs neonatal and adult behaviors. In adult animals, this includes a consistent deficit across paradigms in impaired performance in conditioning and discrimination tasks. Such deficits may reflect impairments in attentional processes and neural systems subserving attention[79,93] and may have neuropathologic correlates.[94-96] This is consistent with attentional impairments seen in human infants[19,97] and children[18,20,98] exposed *in utero* to cocaine. Cocaine-mediated malnutrition may also affect attention, but this effect may be mediated by another mechanism and have different neuropathological and neurochemical correlates.

The mechanism by which transplacental cocaine impairs cognitive and attentional processes remains to be determined. However, it is highly unlikely that cocaine-induced fetal hypoxia via uterine artery vasoconstriction is the cause of dysmaturation of neuronal systems underlying attentional processes.

Animal models of attention are helpful for identifying deficits caused by transplacental cocaine exposure. It is hoped that studies will lead to an understanding of the mechanisms mediating inattention, which will, in turn, lead to the development of therapeutic agents capable of ameliorating some of the toxicity of cocaine on the developing brain.

REFERENCES

1. *National Pregnancy and Health Survey.* A national institute on drug abuse report. National Institutes of Health, Department of Health and Human Services. Washington, D.C., U.S. Government Printing Office, 1995.
2. Sobrian, S.K., Burton, L.E., Robinson, N.L., Ashe, W.K., Hutchinson, J., Stokes, D.L., and Turner, L.M., Neurobehavioral and immunological effects of prenatal cocaine exposure in rat, *Pharmacol. Biochem. Behav.*, 35, 617, 1989.
3. Foss, J.A. and Riley, E.P., Failure of acute cocaine administration to differentially affect acoustic startle and activity in rats prenatally exposed to cocaine, *Neurotoxicol Teratol*, 13, 547-551, 1991.
4. Hutchings, D.E., Fico, T.A., and Dow-Edwards D.L., Prenatal cocaine: maternal toxicity, fetal effects and locomotor activity in rat offspring, *Neurotoxicol, Teratol,*, 11, 65, 1989.
5. Smith, R.F., Mattran, K.M., Kurkjian, M.F., and Kurtz, S.L., Alterations in offspring behavior induced by chronic prenatal cocaine dosing, *Neurotoxicol. Teratol.*, 11, 35, 1989.
6. Church, M.W., Holmes, P.A., Overbeck, G.W., Tilak, J.P., and Zajac, C.S., Interactive effects of prenatal alcohol and cocaine exposures on postnatal mortality, development and behavior in the Long-Evans rat, *Neurotoxicol. Teratol.*, 13, 377, 1991.
7. Spear L.P., Frambes, N.A., and Kirstein C.L., Fetal and maternal brain and plasma levels of cocaine and benzoylecgonine following chronic subcutaneous administration of cocaine during gestation in rats, *Psychopharmacology*, 97, 427, 1989.
8. Spear, L.P., Kirstein, C.L., Bell, J., Yoottanasumpun, V., Greenbaum, R., O'Shea, J., Hoffman, H., and Spear, N.E., Effects of prenatal cocaine exposure on behavior during the early postnatal period, *Neurotoxicol, Teratol,*, 11, 57, 1989.
9. Heyser, C.J., Chen, W.-J., Miller, J., Spear, N.E., Spear, L.P., Prenatal cocaine exposure induces deficits in Pavlovian conditioning and sensory preconditioning among infant rat pups, *Behav. Neurosci.*, 104, 955, 1990.

10. Goodwin, G.A., Heyser, C.J., Moody, C.A., Rajachandran, L., Molina, V.A., Arnold, H.M., McKinzie, D.L., Spear, N.E., and Spear, L.P., A fostering study of the effects of prenatal cocaine exposure: II. offspring behavioral measures, *Neurotoxicol. Teratol.*, 14, 423, 1992.

11. Church, M.W. and Overbeck, G.W., Prenatal cocaine exposure in the Long-Evans rat: II. dose-dependent effects on offspring behavior, *Neurotoxicol. Teratol.*, 12, 335, 1990.

12. Riley, E.P. and Foss, J.A., The acquisition of passive avoidance, active avoidance, and spatial navigation tasks by animals prenatally exposed to cocaine, *Neurotoxicol. Teratol.*, 13, 559, 1991.

13. Bilitzke, P.J. and Church, M.W., Prenatal cocaine and alcohol exposures affect rat behavior in a stress test (the Porsolt swim test), *Neurotoxicol. Teratol.*, 14, 359, 1992.

14. Peris, J., Coleman-Hardee, M., and Millard W.J., Cocaine in utero enhances the behavioral response to cocaine in adult rats, *Pharmacol. Biochem. Behav.*, 42, 509, 1992.

15. Chasnoff, I.J., Griffith, D.R., Freier, C., and Murray, J., Cocaine/polydrug use in pregnancy: two-year follow-up, *Pediatrics*, 89, 284, 1992.

16. Chiriboga, C.A., Fetal effects, *Neurol. Clin.*, 11, 707, 1993.

17. Azuma, S.D. and Chasnoff, I.J., Outcome of children prenatally exposed to cocaine and other drugs: a path analysis of three-year data, *Pediatrics*, 92, 396, 1993.

18. Griffith, D.R., Azuma, S.C., and Chasnoff I.J., Three-year outcome of children exposed prenatally to drugs, *J. Am. Acad. Child Adol. Psy.*, 33, 20, 1994.

19. Delaney-Black, V., Roumell, N., Shankaran, S., Bedard, M.P., Maternal cocaine use and infant outcome, *Pediatr Res*, 25, 242A, 1990.

20. Mayes, L.C., Granger, R.H., Frank, M.A., Schottenfeld, R., Bornstein, M.H., Neurobehavioral profiles of neonates exposed to cocaine prenatally, *Pediatrics*, 91, 778, 1993.

21. VanRossum, J.M. and Simons F., Locomotor activity and anorexigenic action, *Psychopharmacologia*, 14, 248, 1969.

22. Henderson, M.G. and McMillen, B.A., Effects of prenatal exposure to cocaine or related drugs on rat developmental and neurological indices, *Brain Res. Bull.*, 24, 207, 1990.

23. Church M.W. and Rauch, H.C., Prenatal cocaine exposure in the laboratory mouse: effects on maternal water consumption and offspring outcome, *Neurotoxicol. Teratol.*, 14, 313, 1992.

24. Gressens, P., Kosofsky, B.E., and Evrard, P., Cocaine-induced disturbances of corticogenesis in the developing murine brain, *Neurosci. Lett.*, 140, 113, 1992.

25. Akbari, H.M., Whitaker-Azmitia, P.M., and Azmitia, E.C., Prenatal cocaine decreases the trophic factor S-100*B* and induced microcephaly: reversal by postnatal 5-HT1A receptor agonist, *Neurosci. Lett.*, 170, 141, 1994.

26. Konkol, R.J., Murphey, L.J., Ferriero, D.M., Dempsey, D.A., and Olsen, G.D., Cocaine metabolites in the neonate: potential for toxicity, *J. Child. Neurol.*, 9, 242, 1994.

27. Nelson, S.H., Suresh, M.S., Dehring, D.J., and Johnson, R.L., Relaxation by calcitonin gene-related peptide may involve activation of K+ channels in the human uterine artery, *Eur. J. Pharmacol.*, 242, 255, 1993.

28. Castro, C.A. and Rudy, J.W., Early-life malnutrition impairs the performance of both young and adult rats on visual discrimination learning tasks, *Dev. Psychobiol.*, 22, 15, 1989.

29. Tonkiss, J. and Galler, J.R., Prenatal protein malnutrition and working memory performance in adult rats, *Behav. Brain Res.*, 40, 95, 1990.

30. Giurintano, S.L., Effects of protein-calorie deficiencies on the learning ability of the Wistar rat, *Physiol. Behav.*, 12, 55, 1974.

31. Tonkiss, J., Galler, J.R., Formica, R.N., Shukitt-Hale, B., and Timm, R.R., Fetal protein malnutrition impairs acquisition of a DRL task in adult rats, *Physiol. Behav.*, 48, 73, 1990.

32. Galler, J.R. and Manes, M., Gender differences in visual discrimination by rats in response to malnutrition of varying durations, *Dev. Psychobiol.*, 13, 409, 1980.

33. Zimmermann, R.R., Geist, C.R., Strobel, D.A., and Cleveland, T.J., Attention deficiencies in malnourished monkeys, in *Symposia of the Swedish Nutrition Foundation XII: Early Malnutrition and Mental Development*, Cravioto, J., Hambraeus, L., and Vahlqvist, B., Eds., Almqvist & Wiksell, Uppsala, 1974, 115.

34. Halas, E.S. and Sandstead, H.H., Malnutrition and behavior: the performance versus learning problem revisited, *J. Nutr.*, 110, 1858, 1980.

35. Strupp, B.J., Bunsey, M., Levitsky, D.A., and Hamberger, K., Deficient cumulative learning: an animal model of retarded cognitive development, *Neurotoxicol. Teratol.*, 16, 71, 1994.
36. Gormezano, I., Kehoe, E.J., and Marshall, B.S., Twenty years of classical conditioning research with the rabbit, in *Progress in Psychobiology and Physiological Psychology*, Sprague, J.M. and Epstein A.N., Eds., Academic Press, New York, 1983.
37. Harvey, J.A., Effects of drugs on associative learning, in *Psychopharmacology: The Third Generation of Progress*, Meltzer H.Y., Ed., Raven Press, New York, 1987.
38. Marshall-Goodell, B. and Gormezano, I., Effects of cocaine on conditioning of the rabbit nictitating membrane response, *Pharmacol. Biochem. Behav.*, 39, 503, 1991.
39. Robbins, T.W. and Everitt B.J., Central norepinephrine neurons and behavior, in *Psychopharmacology: The Fourth Generation of Progress*, Bloom F.E. Kupfer, D.J., Eds., Raven Press, New York, 1995, 363.
40. Coull, J.T., Middleton, H.C., Sahakian, B.J., and Robbins, T.W., Noradrenaline in the frontal cortex-attentional and central executive function, *J. Psychopharmacol.*, 95, A24, 1992. (Abstract).
41. Posner, M., Walker, J.A., Friedrich, F.J., and Rafal, R.D., Effects of parietal injury on the covert orienting of visual attention, *J. Neurosci.*, 4, 1863, 1984.
42. Clark, C.R., Geffen, G,M., and Geffen, L.B., Catecholamines and the covert orienting of attention, *Neuropsychologia*, 27, 131, 1989.
43. Frith, C.D., Dowdy, J., Ferrier, N., and Crow, T.J., Selective impairment of paired associate learning after administration of a centrally acting adrenergic agonist (clonidine), *Psychopharmacology*, 87, 490, 1985.
44. Carli, M., Robbins, T.W., Evenden, J.L., and Everitt, B.J., Effects of lesions to ascending noradrenergic neurones on performance of a 5-choice serial reaction time task; implications for theories of dorsal noradrenergic bundle function based on selective attention and arousal, *Behav. Brain Res.*, 9, 361, 1983.
45. Cole, B.J. and Robbins, T.W., Dissociable effects of lesions to the dorsal or ventral noradrenergic bundle on the acquisition, performance, and extinction of aversive conditioning, *Behav. Neurosci.*, 101, 476, 1987.
46. Cole, B.J. and Robbins, T.W., Forebrain norepinephrine: role in controlled information processing in the rat, *Neuropsychopharmacology*, 7, 129, 1992.
47. Cole, B.J. and Robbins T.W., Amphetamine impairs the discriminative performance of rats with dorsal noradrenergic bundle lesions on a 5-choice serial reaction time task: new evidence for central dopaminergic-noradrenergic interactions, *Psychopharmacology*, 91, 458, 1987.
48. Cole, B.J. and Robbins, T.W., Effects of 6-hydroxydopamine lesions of the nucleus accumbens septi on performance of a 5-choice serial reaction time task in rats: implications for theories of selective attention and arousal, *Behav. Brain. Res.*, 33, 165, 1989.
49. Robbins, T.W. and Everitt, B.J., Arousal systems and attention, in *The Cognitive Neurosciences*, Gazzaniga M.S., Ed., The MIT Press, Cambridge, 1995, 703.
50. Harrison, A.A., Muir, J.L., Robbins, T.W., and Everitt, B.J., The effects of forebrain 5-HT depletion on visual attentional performance in the rat, *Psychopharmacology*, 236, A59, 1992. (Abstract)
51. Marston, H.M., West, H.L., Wilkinson, L.S., Everitt, B.J., and Robbins T.W., Effects of excitotoxic lesions of the septum and vertical limb nucleus of the diagonal band on Broca on conditional visual discrimination: relationship between performance and choline acetyltransferase activity in the cingulate cortex, *J. Neurosci.*, 14, 2009, 1994.
52. Lubow, R.E., Latent inhibition, *Psychol. Bull.*, 79, 398, 1973.
53. Mackintosh, N.J., A theory of attention: variations in the associability of stimuli with reinforcement, *Psychol. Rev.*, 82, 276, 1975.
54. Halgren, C.R., Latent inhibition in rats: Associative or non-associative? *J. Comp. Physiol. Psychol.*, 86, 74, 1974.
55. Reiss, S. and Wagner, A.R., CS habituation produces a "latent inhibition effect" but no active conditioned inhibition, *Learning Motivat.*, 3, 237, 1972.
56. Solomon, P.R., Brennan, G., and Moore, J.W., Latent inhibition of the rabbit's nictitating membrane response as a function of CS intensity, *Bull. Psychon. Soc.*, 4, 445, 1974.
57. Solomon, P.R., Kiney, C.A., and Scott, D.S., Disruption of latent inhibition following systemic administration of *p*-chlorophenylalanine (PCPA), *Physiol. Behav.*, 20, 265, 1978.

58. Kamin, L.J., Predictability, surprise, attention and conditioning, in *Punishment and Aversive Behavior*, Campbell B.A. and Church, R.M., Eds., Appleton-Century-Crofts, New York, 1969.

59. Crider, A., Solomon, P.R., and McMahon, M.A., Disruption of selective attention in the rat following chronic *d*-amphetamine administration: relationship to schizophrenic attention disorder, *Biol. Psychiatry*, 17, 351, 1982.

60. Crider ,A., Blockel, L., and Solomon, P.R., A selective attention deficit in the rat following induced dopamine receptor supersensitivity, *Behav. Neurosci.*, 100, 315, 1986.

61. Rescorla, R.A. and Wagner, A.R., A theory of Pavlovian conditioning: variations in the effectiveness of reinforcement and nonreinforcement, in *Classical Conditioning II: Current Research and Theory*, Black, A.H. and Prokasy, W.F., Eds., Appleton-Century-Crofts, New York, 1972.

62. Mackintosh, N.J., Stimulus selection: Learning to ignore stimuli that predict no change in reinforcement, in *Constraints on Learning*, R.A. Hinde, R.A. and Stevenson-Hinde, J. Eds., Academic Press, London, 1973.

63. Levin, E.D. and Seidler, F.J., Sex-related spatial learning differences after prenatal cocaine exposure in the young adult rat, *Neurotoxicology*, 14, 23, 1993.

64. Gray, J.A. and McNaughton, N., Comparison between the behavioural effects of septal and hippocampal lesions: a review, *Neurosci. Biobehav. Rev.*, 7, 119, 1983.

65. Heyser, C.J., Miller, J.S., Spear, N.E., and Spear, L.P., Prenatal exposure to cocaine disrupts cocaine-induced conditioned place preference in rats, *Neurotoxicol. Teratol.*, 14, 57, 1992.

66. Heyser, C.J., Spear, N.E., and Spear, L.P., Effects of prenatal exposure to cocaine on conditional discrimination learning in adult rats, *Behav. Neurosci.*, 106, 837, 1992.

67. Gibson, E.J. *Principles of Perceptual Learning and Development,* Appleton Century Crofts, New York, 1967.

68. Murphy, E.H., Hammer, J.G., Schumann, M.D., Groce, M.Y., Wang X-H., Jones, L., Romano, A.G., and Harvey, J.A., The rabbit as a model for studies of cocaine exposure in utero, *Lab. Animal Sci.*, 45, 163, 1995.

69. Wang, X-H. and Murphy, E.H., Prenatal cocaine exposure results in region specific changes in the development of the GABAergic system in rabbit neocortex, *Society for Neuroscience Abstracts*, 19, 50, 1993.

70. Jones, L., Fischer, I., and Levitt, P., Non-uniform alteration of dendritic development in the cerebral cortex following prenatal cocaine exposure, *Cerebral Cortex*, 1996. (in press)

71. Vogt, B.A. and Gabriel, M. *Neurobiology of Cingulate Cortex and Limbic Thalamus: A Comprehensive Handbook*. Birkhauser, Boston, 1993.

72. Gabriel, M, Functions of anterior and posterior cingulate cortex during avoidance learning in rabbits, in *Progress in Brain Research,* vol. 85, Uylings, H.B.M., Van Eden, C.G., De Bruin, J.P.C., Corner, M.A., and Feenstra, M.G.P., Eds., Elsevier, Amsterdam, 1992, 467.

73. Vogt, B.A., Finch, D.M., and Olson, C.R., Functional heterogeneity in cingulate cortex: the anterior executive and posterior evaluative regions, *Cerebral Cortex*, 2, 435, 1992.

74. Romano, A.G., Kachelries, W.J., Simansky, K.J., and Harvey, J.A., Intrauterine exposure to cocaine produces a modality specific acceleration of classical conditioning in adult rabbits, *Pharmacol. Biochem. Behav.*, 52, 415, 1995.

75. Mackintosh, N.J., *The Psychology of Animal Learning*. Academic Press, New York 1974, 41

76. Romano, A.G. and Harvey, J.A., 1995. (Unpublished observations)

77. Romano, A.G. and Harvey, J.A., Prenatal exposure to cocaine disrupts discrimination learning in adult rabbits, *Pharmacol. Biochem. Behav.*, 1996. (in press)

78. Selden, N.R.W., Robbins, T.W., and Everitt, B.J., Enhanced behavioral conditioning to context and impaired behavioral and neuroendocrine responses to conditioned stimuli following ceruleo-cortical noradrenergic lesions: support for an attentional hypothesis of central noradrenergic function, *J. Neurosci.*, 10, 531, 1990.

79. Kosofsky, B.E., Wilkins, A.S., Genova, L.M., Posten, W., and Hyman, S.E., Transplacental cocaine exposure 1: a rodent model, *Neurotoxicol. Teratol.*, submitted, 1996.

80. Kosofsky, B.E., Wilkins, A.S., and Hyman, S.E., Transplacental cocaine exposure 2: the effects of cocaine dose and gestational timing, *Neurotoxicol. Teratol.*, submitted, 1996.

81. Woods, J.R., Plessinger, M.A., and Clark, K.E., Effect of cocaine on uterine blood flow and fetal oxygenation, *JAMA*, 257, 957, 1987.

82. Volpe, J.J., Effect of cocaine use on the fetus, *N. Engl. J. Med.*, 327, 399, 1992.

83. Kosofsky, B.E., Wilkins, A.S., Marota, J.A., Tabit, E., and Hyman, S.E., Transplacental cocaine exposure 3: mechanisms underlying altered brain development, *Neurotoxicol. Teratol.*, submitted, 1996.

84. Dolkart L.A., Plessinger, M.A., and Woods J.R., Jr., Effect of alpha₁ receptor blockade upon maternal and fetal cardiovascular responses to cocaine, *Obstet. Gynecol.*, 75, 745, 1990.

85. Richardson, S.A., The long-range consequences of malnutrition in infancy: a study of children in Jamaica, West Indies, in *Topics in Pediatrics 2, Nutrition in Childhood*, Warton, B., Ed., Pitman, London, 1980, 163.

86. Richardson, S., Birch, H., Grabie, E., and Yoder, K., The behavior of children in school who were severely malnourished in the first two years of life, *J., Hlth., Soc., Behav.*, 13, 276, 1972.

87. Galler J.R., Ramsey F., Solimano G., and Lowell W.E., The influence of early malnutrition on subsequent behavioral development II. Classroom behavior, *J. Am. Acad. Child. Psych.*, 22, 16, 1983.

88. Galler, J.R., Ramsey, F., and Solimano, G., The influence of early malnutrition on subsequent behavioral development III. Learning disabilities as a sequel to malnutition, *Pediatr. Res.*, 18, 309, 1984.

89. Galler, J.R., Ramsey, F., Solimano, G., Kucharski, L.T., and Harrison, R., The influence of early malnutrition on subsequent behavioral development. IV. Soft neurologic signs, *Pediatr. Res.*, 18, 826, 1984.

90. Lashley K., The mechanism of vision. I.A. methods for rapid analysis of pattern-vision in the rat, *J. Genet. Psychol.*, 37, 453, 1930.

91. Galler, J.A., Fleischer, S.F., Turkewitz, G., and Manes, M., Varying deficits in visual discrimination performance associated with different forms of malnutrition in rats, *J. Nutr.*, 110, 231, 1980.

92. Zimmermann, R.R., Reversal learning in the developing malnurished rhesus monkey, *Behav. Biol.*, 8, 381, 1973.

93. Posner, M.I. and Peterson S.E., The attention system of the human brain, *Ann. Rev. Neuro. Sci.*, 13, 25, 1990.

94. Akbari, H.M. and Azmitia, E.C., Increased tyrosine hydroxylase immunoreactivity in the rat cortex following prenatal cocaine exposure, *Dev. Brain Res.*, 66, 277, 1992.

95. Seidler, F.J., and Slotkin, T.A., Fetal cocaine exposure causes persistent noradrenergic hyperactivity in rat brain regions: effects on neurotransmitter turnover and receptors, *J. Pharmacol. Exp. Ther.*, 263, 413, 1992.

96. Seidler, F.J., Temple, S.W., McCook, E.C., and Slotkin, T.A., Cocaine inhibits central noradrenergic and dopaminergic activity during the critical developmental period in which catacholamines influence cell development, *Dev. Brain Res.*, 85, 48, 1995.

97. Chasnoff, I.J., Griffith, D.R., MacGregor, S., and Dirkes, K., Burns K.A., Temporal patterns of cocaine use in pregnancy, *JAMA*, 261, 1741, 1989.

98. Rodning, C., Beckwith, L., and Howard, J., Prenatal exposure to drugs: behavioral distortions reflecting CNS impairment? *Neurotoxicology*, 10, 629, 1989.

Chapter 10

Neurobehavioral Consequences of Gestational Cocaine Exposure: Studies Using a Rodent Model

Linda Patia Spear, PhD

10.0 INTRODUCTION

As exemplified throughout this volume, numerous research groups have begun to investigate the consequences of gestational cocaine exposure on reproductive outcome and offspring neurobehavioral function in both clinical populations and through investigations using various animal models. Conducting well-controlled clinical studies is exceedingly difficult, and it is often not possible to control completely for potential confounding variables or sampling biases (e.g., see Jacobson and Jacobson[1] for discussion). To the extent that animal models provide data relevant to humans, findings in animal work can be used to confirm and extend clinical studies, to anticipate other potential consequences of early cocaine exposure, and to offer insights into the mechanisms underlying observed behavioral alterations.

10.1 POTENTIAL CLINICAL RELEVANCE OF ANIMAL MODELS OF EARLY DRUG EXPOSURE

When developing animal models of early drug exposure, is it reasonable to expect that data obtained in the animal studies will have any clinical relevance? This question was addressed by a 1989 workshop entitled "Qualitative and Quantitative Comparability of Human and Animal Developmental Neurotoxicity" that was cosponsored by the Environmental Protection Agency and the National Institute on Drug Abuse.[2] The goal of this workshop was to compare behavioral consequences in offspring following exposure to known developmental toxicants in clinical populations with those effects reported in animal studies. Species examined included humans, rodents, and nonhuman primates (where data were available). Substances were chosen for inclusion based on the presence of a sufficiently large database in both clinical and animal studies to allow for across-species comparisons; focus substances included ethanol, phenytoin, methylmercury, lead, polychlorinated biphenyls, and ionizing radiation. Offspring outcomes were classified into five categories of functional effects (sensory, motivational/arousal, cognitive, motor, and social). Each of these categories of functional effects could be assessed across species, although the specific tests used often varied markedly from species to species. For example, IQ tests or evaluation of language performance typically were used to

0-8493-9465-1/96/$0.00+$.50
© 1996 by CRC Press, Inc.

assess cognitive function in humans, whereas assessment of learning or retention of classical or operant conditioning tasks often was examined in rodents. After the effects of each developmental toxicant were systematically characterized within each species, this large database was examined to determine comparability of the data across species. In this analysis, a remarkable degree of across-species comparability was observed: "At the level of functional category, close agreement was found across species for all the neurotoxic agents reviewed at this Workshop. If a particular agent produced, for example, cognitive or motor deficits in humans, corresponding deficits were also evident in laboratory animals. This was true even when the specific endpoints used to assess these functions were often operationally quite different across species."[3]

However, on one dimension the data were not very comparable across species — that is, in terms of administered dose levels (i.e., the amount per kilogram body weight of the substance necessary to produce a given effect). As discussed by Rees et al.,[4] often 100 to 10,000-fold greater dose levels of the substances on a delivered dose level were required in rodents to produce similar effects to those observed in humans. This perhaps should not be surprising given that the metabolic rate of rodents is substantially greater than that of humans. Indeed, if the data are expressed in terms of internal dose levels (i.e., in terms of blood concentrations or estimated brain levels, to the extent that these data are available in humans), the dose comparisons across species are very similar, with effective doses based on internal doses being of the same magnitude across species.[4]

From these across-species comparisons, it would be predicted that studies of early cocaine exposure in rats are likely to yield data of relevance to human cocaine-exposed offspring, although for comparability of dose levels across species, internal dose levels need to be considered rather than delivered dose levels. This does not mean, of course, that it can be concluded with absolute certainty that the effects of cocaine observed in animal models will necessarily mirror perfectly the effects observed in humans, but that it would be highly atypical if good comparability across species also was not evident when assessing the developmental toxicology of cocaine.

10.2 NEUROBEHAVIORAL CONSEQUENCES OF GESTATIONAL COCAINE EXPOSURE

Numerous animal models of gestational cocaine exposure have been developed. It is not the intent of this presentation to provide a comprehensive review of this rapidly growing database (for such a review, see reference 5), but rather to highlight our basic research findings to date examining the effects of early cocaine exposure on offspring neurobehavioral function in the rat.

In this work, the offspring examined were generally those of Sprague-Dawley rat dams exposed to 10, 20, and/or 40 mg/kg cocaine HCl subcutaneously (SC) from gestational days 8 to 20 (C40), pair-fed dams (PF) SC injected daily with saline and whose food intake was matched to that of the C40 dams, and nontreated control dams (LC). These doses and route of administration produce dose-dependent and clinically relevant plasma cocaine levels.[6] Given that we have found some residual effects of prior cocaine exposure during pregnancy on later maternal behavior of the dams[7] and subsequently on behavioral functioning in the offspring they rear,[8] offspring were fostered by litter to surrogate dams on the day after birth (postnatal day 1 = P1). All of the testing procedures were conducted by experimenters who were "blind" to prenatal treatment condition and other independent variables whenever possible.

10.2.1 Neural Alterations

As outlined below, we have seen a variety of neural alterations in offspring prenatally exposed to cocaine. Although cocaine is predominantly a dopamine (DA) uptake inhibitor, these neural alterations are evident not only in the DA system, but in other neural systems as well. Neural alterations are long lasting and can be detected in adulthood, although compensatory processes may at least partially mask these effects under basal test conditions.

10.2.1.1   Alterations in the DA system

Alterations in the DA system following prenatal cocaine exposure are seen with some response measures, but not others. Using a number of approaches, we have obtained evidence to suggest that DA functioning may be attenuated following prenatal cocaine exposure. For instance, C40 offspring were observed to exhibit a reduction in footshock-precipitated wall climbing at P12; given that wall climbing previously has been shown to be strongly related to levels of catecholamine activity at this age, this finding supports the suggestion that gestational cocaine exposure may result in an attenuation in catecholamine function.[9] Further data consistent with this hypothesis were provided by the observations that C40 offspring exhibit an attenuated psychopharmacological response to the DA agonist apomorphine (P12 test) along with a conversely accentuated behavioral response to the DA antagonist haloperidol (P8 test).[10] Electrophysiological data collected in collaboration with the laboratory of Rex Wang provided strong support for the notion that dopamine function was attenuated in these offspring. In this study, adult male offspring exposed gestationally to cocaine were found to have significantly fewer spontaneously active DA cells than control offspring, particularly in the A10 (ventral tegmental area) brain region (Figure 10.1); interestingly, this decrease in electrophysiological activity does not appear to be related to an alteration in DA somatodendritic autoreceptor sensitivity as these D2 autoreceptors displayed normal responsivity to apomorphine.[11] If there is an attenuation in DA activity following gestational cocaine exposure, it might be expected that there might be a compensatory increase in sensitivity of one or more DA receptor subtypes. Indeed, we observed a significant increase in D2 binding, associated with an increase in ligand affinity, in striatum in weanling offspring exposed gestationally to cocaine.[12] This increase, although modest (18%), may be of functional significance in that C40 offspring of this age exhibit an increased responsiveness to the D2 receptor agonist quinpirole, as reflected by a shift to the left in the dose-response curve for a number of quinpirole-induced behaviors.[13]

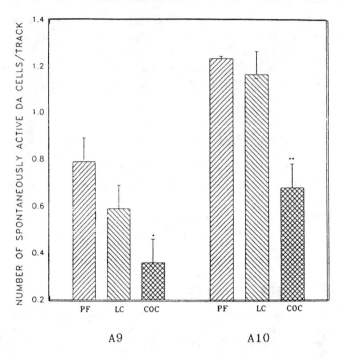

FIGURE 10.1 The number of spontaneously active DA cells/track in the substantia nigra (A9 region) and ventral tegmental area (A10 region) obtained from adult male offspring exposed prenatally to cocaine (COC) as well as their pair-fed (PF) and untreated Lab Chow-fed (LC) controls. Each bar represents the mean number of DA cells/track ± SEM. COC offspring exhibited a decrease in the number of spontaneously active DA neurons in the A9 region relative to PF controls (*p<0.05), and in the A10 region relative to both LC and PF controls (**p<0.01). (Reprinted from *Brain Research, 586,* Minabe, Y., Ashby, C.R. Jr., Heyser, C., Spear, L.P., Wang, R.Y., The effects of prenatal cocaine exposure on spontaneously active midbrain dopamine neurons in adult male offspring: an electrophysiological study. 152–156, copyright 1992, with kind permission from Elsevier Science Ltd, The Boulevard, Langford Lane, Kidlington 0X5 1GB, UK.)

Despite this clear evidence for an attenuation in DA activity in terms of electrophysiological activity,[11] we have had difficulty detecting this neurochemically through estimates of DA turnover rates obtained in nucleus accumbens or striatum either from the decline in DA levels after synthesis inhibition[10] or by ratios of DA metabolites to DA.[14,15] The lack of notable alterations in terms of neurochemical measures of DA functioning despite electrophysiological evidence for a decrease in the number of spontaneously active DA neurons suggests the possibility that, although there may be an underlying deficit in DA functioning in cocaine-exposed offspring, compensatory processes may functionally counter this apparent attenuation in DA activity under basal test conditions. However, challenging or stressing the organism may reveal latent deficits in DA function that may not be evident under baseline testing conditions. This notion is not a new one. For instance, Cabib et al.[16] concluded that "the effects of early experiences on brain DA functioning may not be evident in basal conditions and (may) be revealed only under environmental pressure."

10.2.1.2   Alterations in Other Neural Systems

Although cocaine is predominantly a DA uptake inhibitor, alterations are seen not only in the DA system but in other neural systems as well. For instance, in work conducted in collaboration with the laboratory of Ron Hammer, increases were seen in opiate receptor binding (labeled with [³H]naloxone) in numerous forebrain regions in weanling C40 offspring relative to PF and LC controls (Figure 10.2), although few differences were evident in diencephalon or brainstem.[17,18] These increases in opiate binding appear to be of functional significance in that young C40 offspring exhibit a greater sensitivity to morphine and the mu opiate agonist DAMGO in terms of opiate agonist-induced decreases in ultrasound production, but not in terms of opiate-induced analgesia, which is presumably mediated by brainstem regions.[19] In work conducted in collaboration with the laboratory of Efrain Azmitia, gestational cocaine exposure was observed to result in a transient delay in the development of the serotonergic system,[20] and in collaborative work with Ken Leskawa, a transient increase in brain levels of gangliosides and neutral glycolipids was seen in C40 neonates at P1 that returned to control levels by P11.[21] Thus, the effects of prenatal cocaine exposure do not appear to be limited to the DA system, findings consistent with other emerging data in the literature. (See Spear[5] for further discussion and references.)

10.2.2 Behavioral Alterations

We have observed a variety of different behavioral alterations in offspring following gestational cocaine exposure. For instance, in terms of social behaviors, alterations in play behavior were evident, with prenatal cocaine exposure affecting play primarily by altering the responses that the drug-exposed animals elicit from normal playmates.[22] Studies examining additional aspects of social behavior in these offspring are ongoing.

Other behavioral alterations observed in these offspring include alterations in performance on tests of cognitive functioning, and in their behavioral responsivity to stress. Cocaine-exposed offspring also exhibit alterations in their later sensitivity to the discriminative stimulus properties and reinforcing efficacy of cocaine, findings that may have significant implications with regard to later drug abuse liability. These alterations in cognitive, stress, and drug responsivity appear to be particularly characteristic of these offspring and will be discussed in the following sections.

10.2.2.1   Alterations in Cognitive Functioning

Deficits in classical conditioning are seen in young cocaine-exposed offspring. For instance, following prenatal cocaine exposure P7-8 rat pups failed to develop a preference for an odor that was paired with intraoral milk infusions, a preference that was strongly evident in control offspring.[9] Cocaine-exposed offspring at this age also exhibit classical conditioning deficits using an aversive US (unconditioned stimulus, in this case footshock), failing to avoid an odor that was previously paired with footshock.[8,23] This deficit in aversive classical conditioning was not related to a decreased sensitivity to the footshock US, as C40 offspring did not differ from controls in shock-sensitivity thresholds in either infancy[9] or adulthood.[8]

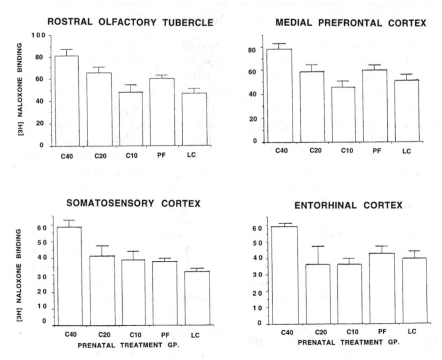

FIGURE 10.2 Opiate receptor binding in selected brain regions of P21 male offspring treated during gestation with 40, 20 or 10 mg/kg cocaine (COC 40, COC 20, COC 10, respectively) relative to pair-fed (to COC 40 dams) and untreated, Lab Chow-fed controls. Each bar represents the mean binding (fmol/mg) ± SEM obtained from autoradiographs of 2.5 nM [^{3}H]naloxone binding. As illustrated by these sample histograms, COC 40 offspring exhibited an increase in tritiated naloxone binding in dopaminergic terminal regions such as the rostral olfactory tubercle and the medial prefrontal cortex as well as other limbic and cortical regions (e.g., somatosensory cortex; entorhinal cortex). (Data compiled and reprinted from *Developmental Brain Research, 59,* Clow, D.W., Hammer, R.P. Jr., Kirstein, C.L., & Spear, L.P. Gestational cocaine exposure increases opiate receptor binding in weanling offspring. 179–185, copyright 1991, with kind permission from Elsevier Science Ltd, The Boulevard, Langford Lane, Kidlington 0X5 1GB, UK.)

It is not the case, however, that young cocaine-exposed offspring are incapable of learning classical conditioning tasks. Rather, they appear to require more training to exhibit significant conditioning relative to control age-mates. For instance, although cocaine-exposed offspring at P7-8 do not show evidence of classical conditioning when only two training trials are given,[23] these offspring can exhibit conditioning when the amount of training is increased. Number of training trials was varied in a study by Goodwin et al.[8] where the effects of fostering condition were also assessed. Foster and LC control offspring under all rearing conditions exhibited a significant aversion to the odor paired with footshock following as few as 2 training trials. In contrast, C40 offspring reared by foster dams (FOS/C40) required 4 training trials to demonstrate conditioning, and C40 pups reared by their own dams (C40/C40) did not exhibit conditioning even after 4 training trials (Figure 10.3). Thus, given sufficient training, young cocaine-exposed pups do appear to be capable of demonstrating simple classical conditioning.

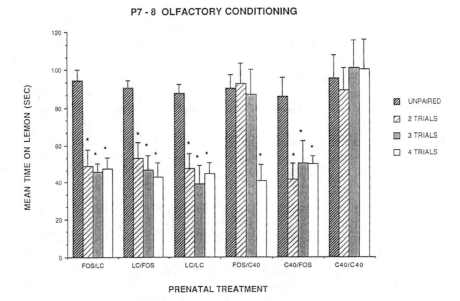

FIGURE 10.3   Mean time spent (± SEM) over the lemon odor by P7-8 animals from the various prenatal treatment/rearing conditions following pairings of lemon with footshock for 2, 3, or 4 training trials or following explicitly unpaired exposures to both the lemon odor and footshock. FOS = Foster; LC = Saline injected controls; C40 = animals exposed to 40 mg/kg cocaine during gestation. Groups are designated by maternal treatment and pup origin (e.g., FOS/C40 reflects C40 pups reared by FOS dams). *Evidence for conditioning as indicated by values significantly different from corresponding UP controls, p<0.05. Whereas LC and FOS offspring, regardless of rearing condition, exhibited significant conditioning after 2 training trials, C40 pups reared by FOS dams required 4 training trials to exhibit significant conditioning, and C40 pups reared by their own dams did not exhibit conditioning even after 4 trials. (Reprinted from *Physiology and Behavior, 55,* Molina, V.A., Wagner, J.M., and Spear, L. P., The behavioral response to stress is altered in adult rats exposed prenatally to cocaine. 941–945, copyright 1994, with kind permission from Elsevier Science Ltd, The Boulevard, Langford Lane, Kidlington 0X5 1GB, UK.)

Another factor that should be considered is that task difficulty/complexity may be an important factor in revealing conditioning deficits in cocaine-treated offspring, and this may in turn vary with age. Whereas C40 pups given 2 training trials did not exhibit odor/footshock conditioning at P7-8,[8,23] C40 pups given similar training at P12 or P21 did exhibit significant conditioning,[23] and at P18 these offspring exhibited a significant odor/footshock aversion following only one training trial.[8] However, when task complexity is increased, cognitive deficits are often evident in older C40 offspring. For instance, as discussed below, deficits in higher order conditioning have been observed in C40 pups at P12 using a sensory preconditioning task, and alterations in cognitive function are also seen in adulthood.

The conditioning deficits seen early in life following prenatal cocaine exposure do not appear to be related merely to a delay in cognitive development. Using typical learning situations where task performance improves during ontogeny, it is difficult to assess the possibility that conditioning deficits seen early in life are related to a delay in cognitive development. There are some tasks, however, that show a dissociation between age and performance. One such task is sensory preconditioning, a task readily learned by young rat pups in the age range from P7-18, but not by weanling (P21) animals.[24] If cocaine-exposed animals exhibit a delay in cognitive development, then it would be anticipated that at P21 they should perform like younger animals, and hence exhibit better performance on this task than same-age controls. To examine this possibility, we assessed sensory preconditioning in C40 and LC offspring at P8, 12, and 21.[23] C40 offspring did not exhibit sensory preconditioning at any age tested, whereas significant conditioning in this task was observed in LC control offspring at P8 and 12, but not P21, confirming previous reports of an ontogenetic decline in performance on this task.[24] These data support the suggestion that conditioning deficits seen early in life in C40 offspring are not related simply to a delay in cognitive development but rather reflect a fundamental alteration in cognitive performance.

If the cognitive deficits seen in young cocaine-exposed offspring are not related to a delay in cognitive development, it would be expected that deficits should also be evident in adulthood in tasks that are sufficiently cognitively challenging. Indeed, although early exposure to cocaine may not always result in impaired cognitive function, alterations in cognitive performance can be detected in adulthood on some tasks, such as reversal performance. In Heyser et al.,[25] adult male offspring were trained on an operant conditional discrimination task where odor cues were used to indicate which of two levers was correct on a given test day. After animals reached criterion on the initial discrimination, the contingency of the odor discrimination was reversed and number of trials to reach criterion on the reversal assessed. Whereas there were no differences among the prenatal treatment groups in the number of sessions to criterion on the initial odor discrimination, C40 offspring required more sessions to acquire the reversal response than control offspring (Figure 10.4). We have recently observed a similar deficit in reversal performance in adult male C40 offspring tested in a Morris water maze.[26] Thus, in adulthood, offspring prenatally exposed to cocaine seemingly persist in their behavior and appear to have trouble modifying their behavior in response to the cognitive challenge of a rule change.

10.2.2.2   Responsivity to Stressors

Cocaine-exposed offspring are notably different from controls in their behavioral response to stressors. Adult rats, when exposed to an inescapable stressor typically exhibit escape responses for a period of time, followed by the development of immobility; this increase in immobility is seen not only during exposure to the stressor, but also frequently after the stressor when confronted with a novel situation.[27] We examined stress-induced immobility in adult male C40, PF, and LC offspring.[28] Animals were given either a 5-minute forced swim (25°C), 10-minute exposure to intermittent footshock (20 footshocks of 1 mA, 1 second duration), or were not exposed to either acute stressor. One day later, all animals were given a 5-minute open field test. As can be seen in Figure 10.5, C40 offspring exhibited less immobility than control animals during exposure to either acute stressor and did not exhibit the stress-induced increase in open field immobility that was seen in PF and LC offspring following prior footshock exposure. These findings essentially replicate and extend those of Bilitzke and Church,[29] who reported that male offspring exposed

NUMBER OF SESSIONS TO CRITERION

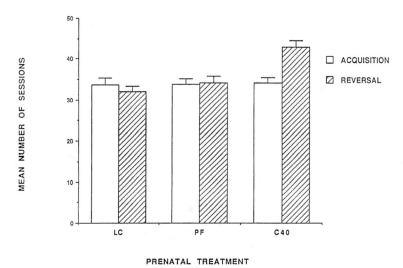

FIGURE 10.4 Mean number (± SEM) of sessions to criterion for acquisition and reversal of an operant conditional discrimination response in adult male offspring from the various prenatal treatment groups (LC = nontreated control group; PF = pair-fed control group; C40 = animals exposed to 40 mg/kg cocaine during gestation). Criterion for both acquisition and reversal was defined as >80% correct in the first 10 responses and >90% correct responses over the entire session for 5 consecutive days. Whereas none of the groups differed in the rate of acquisition of the original conditional discrimination response, C40 offspring were significantly slower than all other groups to learn the reversal response (*, p<0.05, C40 relative to all other groups). (Data from Heyser, C.J., Spear, N.E., and Spear, L.P., Effects of prenatal exposure to cocaine on conditional discrimination learning in adult rats, 106, 837, 1992. Courtesy of the American Psychological Association.)

prenatally to cocaine exhibited less immobility than controls in the Porsolt version of the swim test.

In other work in our laboratory that used slightly different procedures,[22] we obtained similar findings in periadolescent (P30-36) male and female offspring. In this study, the periadolescents were exposed to a different stressor every other day: P30 – 5-minute intermittent footshock (1mA, 1-second shock on a FI 60-second schedule); P32 – 4-minute forced swim; P34 – 1-hour white noise stress; P36 – 5-minute footshock. While there were no differences among the prenatal treatment groups in amount of shock-induced immobility during the brief (5 minute) initial footshock exposure, C40 offspring exhibited less immobility during the last footshock exposure, failing to show the increase in immobility from the first to last shock session that was evident in LC and PF offspring. Thus, prenatal cocaine exposure results in a robust and reliable decrease in stress-induced immobility, findings that have been replicated both intra- and inter-laboratory. Immobility has been construed as an adaptive response to stress that serves to conserve energy output until escape is possible.[30] (See Porsolt et al.[31] for an alternative view.) Thus, the decrease in immobility seen in cocaine-exposed offspring potentially could reflect an attenuation in their ability to successfully cope with stress.

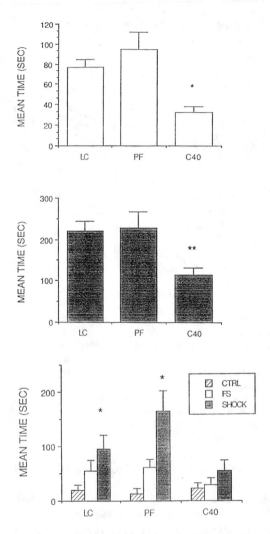

FIGURE 10.5   Mean time (in seconds ± SEM) spent in immobility during a forced swim (top panel) and a footshock session (middle panel), and during an open field test 24 hours following either no stressor (CTRL) or exposure to the forced swim (FS) or footshock (SHOCK) (bottom panel) by animals from the various prenatal treatment conditions. LC = nontreated control; PF = pair-fed control; C40 = animals exposed to 40 mg/kg cocaine during gestation. C40 animals exhibited less immobility during both the forced swim and footshock sessions, and failed to exhibit the increase in immobility in the open field induced by prior exposure to footshock that was evident in PF and LC control animals (*p<0.05; **p<0.001 for these comparisons). (Reprinted from *Physiology and Behavior, 55,* Molina, V. A., Wagner, J.M., and Spear, L.P., The behavioral response to stress is altered in adult rats exposed prenatally to cocaine 941–945, copyright 1994, with kind permission from Elsevier Science Ltd, The Boulevard, Langford Lane, Kidlington 0X5 1GB, UK.)

10.2.2.3   Alterations in Later Responsiveness to Cocaine Challenges

Cocaine-exposed offspring appear to exhibit a decreased sensitivity to the discriminative stimulus and reinforcing properties of cocaine. We observed that C40 offspring exhibited attenuated cocaine-induced odor preferences in infancy[32] and cocaine-induced conditioned place preferences (CPP) in adulthood.[33] The attenuated ability of the C40 animals to develop a preference for stimuli previously associated with cocaine could potentially reflect a general impairment in learning, given the conditioning deficits seen in these offspring, as discussed earlier. However, this possibility appears unlikely, at least in the adult CPP testing, given that adult C40 offspring have been observed to exhibit normal acquisition of a conditional discrimination response,[25] and hence they should be at least as capable of acquiring the basic discrimination necessary for CPP conditioning. The lack of observable CPP in adult C40 offspring also does not appear to be related simply to pharmacokinetic factors. The prenatal treatment groups did not differ in brain cocaine levels at any time point examined following exposure to a challenge dose of 10 mg/kg cocaine given intraperitoneally (IP) in adulthood, nor did they differ in responsivity to the locomotor stimulant effects of cocaine measured in the open field following administration of challenge doses of 2 and 5 mg/kg IP.[34]

Adult (male) C40 offspring also were observed to exhibit a reduced sensitivity to the discriminative stimulus effects of cocaine as evidenced by a significant shift to the right in the dose response curve for cocaine discrimination.[34] Thus, prenatal cocaine exposure appears to reduce the sensitivity of offspring to both the discriminative stimulus and reinforcing properties of cocaine. This potential reduction in the later reinforcing efficacy of cocaine induced by gestational cocaine exposure may be related to long-term alterations in the DA system (see above), given that mesolimbic DA regions have been implicated in the reward mechanisms of cocaine.[35,36] The possible implications of this potential reduction in reward efficacy are significant. At least with respect to ethanol, animals that exhibit greater ethanol ingestion due to genetic background[37,38] or chronic heavy metal exposure[39] show a reduced sensitivity to ethanol, including the reinforcing efficacy of ethanol.[39] This raises the possibility that, to the extent that exposure to cocaine during gestation attenuates the reinforcing efficacy of cocaine, exposed offspring may exhibit higher rates of cocaine self-administration in adulthood. This hypothesis is being tested directly in current work.

10.3 SUMMARY

Using an animal model of gestational cocaine exposure, we have obtained clear evidence for a variety of neurobehavioral alterations in these offspring. One should not gain the impression, however, that these effects are all pervasive. Although neural effects are evident early in life and in adulthood, these alterations sometimes may be masked by compensatory processes under basal test conditions. Behaviorally, deficits are not always seen, with alterations most likely to be evident in situations that are either stressful or cognitively challenging. The picture that is gradually emerging is that exposure to cocaine during gestation does induce long-lasting neurobehavioral alterations in the offspring, although these alterations are sometimes rather subtle and may be most evident under increasing environmental demands when the organism is cognitively challenged, or subjected to stressors or other adversities.

ACKNOWLEDGMENTS

The research from Dr. Spear's laboratory discussed in this chapter was supported by National Institute on Drug Abuse Grants R01 DA04478 and K02 DA00140.

REFERENCES

1. Jacobson, J. L. and Jacobson, S. W., Methodological issues in human behavioral teratology, in *Advances in Infancy Research*, Vol. 6, Rovee-Collier, C. and Lipsitt, L. P., Eds., Ablex, Norwood, NJ, 1990, 111.
2. Kimmell, C. A., Rees, D. C., and Francis, E. Z., Eds., Qualitative and quantitative comparability of human and animal developmental neurotoxicity [Special Issue], *Neurotoxicol. Teratol.*, 12, (Whole Issue), 1990.
3. Stanton, M.E. and Spear, L. P., Workshop on the qualitative and quantitative comparability of human and animal developmental neurotoxicity, Work Group I Report: Comparability of measures of developmental neurotoxicity in humans and laboratory animals, *Neurotoxicol. Teratol.*, 12, 261, 1990.
4. Rees, D. C., Francis, E. Z., and Kimmel, C. A., Qualitative and quantitative comparability of human and animal developmental neurotoxicants: a workshop summary, *Neurotoxicology*, 11, 257, 1990.
5. Spear, L. P., Neurobehavioral consequences of gestational cocaine exposure: a comparative analysis, in *Advances in Infancy Research*, Vol. 9, Rovee-Collier, C. and Lipsitt, L. P., Eds., Ablex, Norwood, NJ, 1995, 55.
6. Spear, L. P., Frambes, N. A., and Kirstein, C. L., Fetal and maternal brain and plasma levels of cocaine and benzoylecgonine following chronic subcutaneous administration of cocaine during gestation in rats, *Psychopharmacology*, 97, 427, 1989.
7. Heyser, C. J., Molina, V. A., and Spear, L. P., A fostering study of the effects of prenatal cocaine exposure: I. Maternal behaviors, *Neurotoxicol. Teratol.*, 14, 415, 1992.
8. Goodwin, G. A., Heyser, C. J., Moody, C. A., Rajachandran, L., Molina, V. A., Arnold, H. M., McKinzie, D. L., Spear, N. E., and Spear, L. P., A fostering study of the effects of prenatal cocaine exposure: II. Offspring behavioral measures, *Neurotoxicol. Teratol.*, 14, 423, 1992.
9. Spear, L. P., Kirstein, C. L., Bell, J., Yoottanasumpun, V., Greenbaum, R., O'Shea, J., Hoffmann, H., and Spear, N. E., Effects of prenatal cocaine exposure on behavior during the early postnatal period, *Neurotoxicol. Teratol.*, 11, 57, 1989.
10. Spear, L. P., Kirstein, C. L., and Frambes, N. A., Cocaine effects on the developing central nervous system: behavioral, psychopharmacological and neurochemical studies, *Ann. N. Y. Acad. Sci.*, 562, 290, 1989.
11. Minabe, Y., Ashby, C. R., Jr., Heyser, C., Spear, L. P., and Wang, R. Y., The effects of prenatal cocaine exposure on spontaneously active midbrain dopamine neurons in adult male offspring: an electrophysiological study, *Brain Res.*, 586, 152, 1992.
12. Scalzo, F. M., Ali, S. F., Frambes, N. A., and Spear, L. P., Weanling rats exposed prenatally to cocaine exhibit an increase in striatal D2 dopamine binding associated with an increase in ligand affinity, *Pharmacol. Biochem. Behav.*, 37, 371, 1990.
13. Moody, C. A., Frambes, N. A., and Spear, L. P., Psychopharmacological responsiveness to the dopamine agonist quinpirole in normal weanlings and in weanling offspring exposed gestationally to cocaine, *Psychopharmacology*, 108, 256, 1992.
14. Spear, L. P., Kirstein, C. L., Frambes, N. A., and Moody, C. A., Neurobehavioral teratogenicity of gestational cocaine exposure, *NIDA Research Monograph (Problems of Drug Dependence, 1989)*, 95, 232, 1990.
15. Goodwin, G. A., Rajachandran, L., Moody, C. A., Francis, R., Kuhn, C. M., and Spear, L. P., Effects of prenatal cocaine exposure on haloperidol-induced increases in prolactin release and dopamine turnover in weanling, periadolescent, and adult offspring, *Neurotoxicol. Teratol.*, 17, 507, 1995.
16. Cabib, S., Puglisi-Allegra, S., and D'Amato, F. R., Effects of postnatal stress on dopamine mesolimbic system responses to aversive experiences in adult life, *Brain Res.*, 604, 232, 1993.

17. Clow, D. W., Hammer, R. P., Jr., Kirstein, C. L., and Spear, L. P., Gestational cocaine exposure increases opiate receptor binding in weanling offspring, *Dev. Brain Res.*, 59, 179, 1991.

18. Hammer, R. P., Jr., Clow, D. W., and Spear, L. P., Opioid involvement in the rewarding effects of chronic cocaine, *NIDA Research Monograph (Problems of Drug Dependence, 1990)*, 105, 182, 1991.

19. Goodwin, G. A., Moody, C. A., and Spear, L. P., Prenatal cocaine exposure increases the behavioral sensitivity of neonatal rat pups to ligands active at opiate receptors, *Neurotoxicol. Teratol.*, 15, 425, 1993.

20. Akbari, H. M., Kramer, H. K., Whitaker-Azmitia, P. M., Spear, L. P., and Azmitia, E. C., Prenatal cocaine exposure disrupts the development of the serotonergic system, *Brain Res.*, 572, 57, 1992.

21. Leskawa, K. C., Jackson, G. H., Moody, C. A., and Spear, L. P., Cocaine exposure during pregnancy affects rat neonate and maternal brain glycosphingolipids, *Brain Res. Bull.*, 33, 195, 1994.

22. Wood, R. D., Molina, V. A., Wagner, J. M., and Spear, L. P., Play behavior and stress responsivity in periadolescent offspring exposed prenatally to cocaine, *Pharmacol., Biochem. Behav.*, 52, 367, 1995.

23. Heyser, C. J., Chen, W. J., Miller, J., Spear, N. E., and Spear, L. P., Prenatal cocaine exposure induces deficits in Pavlovian conditioning and sensory preconditioning among infant rat pups, *Behav. Neurosci.*, 104, 955, 1990.

24. Chen, W. J., Lariviere, N. A., Heyser, C. J., Spear, L. P., and Spear, N. E., Age-related differences in sensory conditioning in rats, *Dev. Psychobiol.*, 24, 307, 1991.

25. Heyser, C. J., Spear, N. E., and Spear, L. P., Effects of prenatal exposure to cocaine on conditional discrimination learning in adult rats, *Behav. Neurosci.*, 106, 837, 1992.

26. Heyser, C. J., Spear, N. E., and Spear, L. P., The effects of prenatal exposure to cocaine on Morris water maze performance in adult rats, *Behav. Neurosci.*, 109, 734, 1995.

27. Armario, A., Gil, M., Marti, J., Pol, O., and Balasch, J., Influence of various acute stressors on the activity of adult male rats in a holeboard & in the forced swim test, *Pharmacol., Biochem. Behav.*, 39, 373, 1991.

28. Molina, V. A., Wagner, J. M., and Spear, L. P., The behavioral response to stress is altered in adult rats exposed prenatally to cocaine, *Physiol. Behav.*, 55, 941, 1994.

29. Bilitzke, P. J. and Church, M. W., Prenatal cocaine & alcohol exposures affect rat behavior in a stress test (The Porsolt Swim Test), *Neurotoxicol. Teratol.*, 14, 359, 1992.

30. Abel, E. L. and Bilitzke, P. J., A possible alarm substance in the forced swimming test, *Physiol. Behav.*, 48, 233, 1990.

31. Porsolt, R. D., Anton, G., Blavet, N., and Jalfre, M., Behavioural despair in rats: A new model sensitive to antidepressant treatments, *Eur. J. Pharmacol.*, 47, 379, 1978.

32. Heyser, C. J., Goodwin, G. A., Moody, C. A., and Spear, L. P., Prenatal cocaine exposure attenuates cocaine-induced odor preference in infant rats, *Pharmacol. Biochem. Behav.*, 42, 169, 1992.

33. Heyser, C. J., Miller, J. S., Spear, N. E., and Spear, L. P., Prenatal exposure to cocaine disrupts cocaine-induced conditioned place preference in rats, *Neurotoxicol. Teratol.*, 14, 57, 1992.

34. Heyser, C. J., Rajachandran, L., Spear, N. E., and Spear, L. P., Responsiveness to cocaine challenge in adult rats following prenatal exposure to cocaine, *Psychopharmacology*, 116, 45, 1994.

35. Wise, R. A., The role of reward pathways in the development of drug dependence, *Pharmacol. Therap.*, 35, 227, 1987.

36. Koob, G. R. and Goeders, N. E., Neuroanatomical substrates of drug self-administration, in *The Neuropharmacological Basis of Reward*, Liebman, J. M. and Cooper, S. J., Eds., Oxford University Press, New York, 1989, 214.

37. Randall, C. L. and Lester, D., Differential effects of ethanol and pentobarbital on sleep time in C57BL and BALB mice, *J. Pharmacol. Exp. Ther.*, 188, 27, 1974.

38. Lumeng, L., Waller, M. B., McBride, W. J., and Li, T. K., Different sensitivities to ethanol in alcohol-preferring and nonpreferring rats, *Pharmacol., Biochem. Behav.*, 16, 125, 1982.

39. Grover, C. A., Nation, J. R., Reynolds, K. M., Benzick, A. E., Bratton, G. R., and Rowe, L. D., The effects of cadmium on ethanol self-administration using a sucrose-fading procedure, *Neurotoxicology*, 12, 235, 1991.

Chapter 11

Positron Emission Tomography (PET) in Substance-Abuse Exposed Infants: A Preliminary Report

Harry T. Chugani, MD

11.0 TECHNICAL CONSIDERATIONS

The PET (positron emission tomography) is a noninvasive imaging technique that can be used to measure local chemical functions in various body organs.[1] This technique resembles computed tomography (CT) in its use of reconstruction algorithms to produce an image, but unlike CT, the source of radiation is in the form of an administered chemical compound labeled with a positron emitting isotope, rather than an external X-ray beam. In the brain, PET has been applied in the study of local glucose and oxygen utilization, blood flow, protein synthesis, neurotransmitter uptake and binding, and various other biochemical and physiological processes.[2]

In a typical PET study of cerebral glucose metabolism, the child is fasted for four hours prior to administration of the tracer 2-deoxy-2-[^{18}F]fluoro-D-glucose (FDG). Venous access is obtained in either a hand or foot, and electroencephalogram (EEG) electrodes are placed on the scalp if EEG monitoring is desired during the FDG uptake period (first 30 minutes after FDG injection) of the PET study, as is often the case in patients with epilepsy. The dose of FDG injected intravenously as a bolus is usually 0.143 mCi/kg. It is important to minimize environmental effects on the distribution of glucose consumption in the brain, and therefore, during the FDG uptake period, the child is kept awake, with minimal parent-child interaction. The lights in the room are dimmed and visual, auditory, and other sensory stimuli are kept to a minimum. After 30 minutes, EEG monitoring (if performed) is stopped and sedation may be used if required since sedation or natural sleep at this late period will no longer affect the cerebral distribution of the tracer. Forty minutes after the FDG injection, scanning of the brain is performed and lasts about 30 minutes. The tomographic images usually are oriented parallel to the canthomeatal plane, but any desired plane may be used. Furthermore, currently available software allows PET data to be resliced in any plane, and to be registered with the CT or MRI scans.

In order to calculate the absolute rates of local cerebral glucose metabolism (LCMRglc), it was required previously to collect arterial or arterialized (through hand warming in a small heated chamber) blood samples during the PET study and define the arterial input function to the brain.[3] Recent advances allow this arterial input function to be defined based on dynamic imaging of the myocardium

0-8493-9465-1/96/$0.00+$.50
© 1996 by CRC Press, Inc.

for 20 minutes following FDG administration and the collection of three small blood samples (1 ml each) toward the end of the procedure from a different venous source than the one used for FDG injection (unpublished data). This approach has made quantification in the PET procedure far less invasive and cumbersome than previously, and therefore easier to accomplish in young children.

11.1 NORMAL BRAIN DEVELOPMENT

Studies of local cerebral glucose metabolism in infants and children using PET have provided important information on human brain functional development. We have found that the pattern of glucose metabolism in the human neonate is markedly different from that of adults; typically, four brain regions are metabolically prominent: sensorimotor cortex, thalamus, brainstem, and cerebellar vermis. Phylogenetically, these are relatively old structures which dominate the behavior and primitive intrinsic reflexes of newborns. During the first year, the ontogeny of cerebral glucose metabolism proceeds in phylogenetic order, correlating well with behavioral maturation of the infant. By 1 year, glucose metabolic patterns qualitatively resemble those of normal young adults.[4]

Quantitative analysis of LCMRglc revealed that the brain follows a protracted glucose metabolic maturational course. Neonatal LCMRglc values, which are about 30% lower than adult rates, rapidly increase to exceed adult values by 2 to 3 years in the cerebral cortex and remain at these high levels until about 8 to 10 years, when LCMRglc declines to reach adult rates by 16 to 18 years.[5]

We have postulated that the ascending portion of rapid LCMRglc increase corresponds to the period of rapid overproduction of synapses and nerve terminals known to occur in the developing human brain. The plateau period during which LCMRglc exceeds adult values corresponds to the period of increased cerebral energy demand as a result of transient exuberant connectivity. That segment of the metabolic maturational curve describing the LCMRglc decline corresponds to the period of selective elimination or "pruning" of excessive connectivity, and marks the time when developmental plasticity markedly diminishes in humans.[6]

In studies designed to test these hypotheses, we have measured LCMRglc in the developing kitten. As in humans, the kitten brain also goes through a protracted period of metabolic maturation, including a phase when LCMRglc exceeds values for the adult cat. Furthermore, the ascending portion of the LCMRglc maturational curve for kitten visual cortex, seen between 3 weeks and 3 months, corresponds to the critical period and period of rapid synaptogenesis for this structure in the cat.[7] Similarly, there is a correspondence between the period of excessive cerebral glucose utilization in the rhesus monkey (2 to 6 months postnatally) and the period of synaptic exuberance in rhesus cortex.[8]

This basic knowledge of metabolic maturation in the human brain serves as a basis for comparisons with children exposed to substances of abuse *in utero* in order to assess developmental abnormalities resulting from exposure.

11.2 PET STUDIES IN CHILDREN WITH *IN UTERO* EXPOSURE TO COCAINE

In a pilot study, we have performed PET studies of cerebral glucose metabolism in 6 children with a history of drug exposure *in utero*.[9] The subjects selected for this study were preschool-aged youngsters (4 to 6 years) who had participated in a larger study of 36 full-term children. All were from an inner city population. The children were identified for the larger study at birth, based on a positive urine toxicology screen for phencyclidine (PCP) in either the infant or the mother. However, the mothers reported polysubstance abuse, with cocaine being the most predominant substance used. All participated in a home-based intervention program from birth to 2 years of age. Children were selected for the present pilot study to represent the range of developmental function within the larger group of full-term infants.

Visual inspection of the 6 PET studies showed that 3 children had evidence of relative right frontal cortical hypometabolism (Figure 11.1), extending from the superior prefrontal region interiorly to the orbitofrontal area. Correlation with the developmental data revealed that the 3 children with relative right frontal hypometabolism had head circumference measurements in the normal range but had attention deficit disorder (ADD) with Gesell Developmental Quotients in the normal range.

In contrast, the 3 children with no evidence of focal glucose abnormality on visual inspection had a head circumference at or below the 5th percentile. Two of these 3 children had microcephaly and were mentally retarded, whereas the one whose head circumference was at the 5th percentile had a normal Gesell Developmental Quotient.

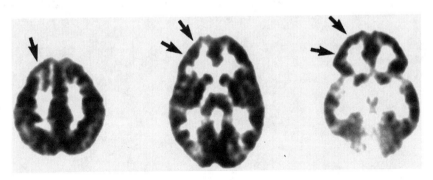

FIGURE 11.1 PET scan of cerebral glucose metabolism in a five-year-old boy who was exposed to cocaine *in utero*. Note the glucose hypometabolism in the right frontal cortex (arrows).

Although preliminary, these data are exciting and emphasize the need for a larger study, in which strict criteria for study entry should be employed. The finding of right frontal hypometabolism in the 3 subjects is particularly relevant in light of previous PET findings of Zametkin et al.[10] and Volkow and Fowler.[11] Without quantitative PET data, it is impossible to ascertain whether cerebral glucose metabolism was normal in the 3 subjects without focal hypometabolism, or whether a diffuse global hypometabolism was present. The latter is more likely to be the case because of the presence of mental retardation in 2 of these 3 children. Future quantitative PET studies will address these issues.

REFERENCES

1. Phelps, M. E., Mazziotta, J. C., and Schelbert, H. R., *Positron Emission Tomography and Autoradiography,* Raven Press, New York, 1986.
2. Phelps, M. E. and Mazziotta, J. C., Positron emission tomography: human brain function and biochemistry, *Science,* 228, 799, 1985.
3. Phelps, M.E., Huang, S.C., Hoffman, E.J., Selin, C.E., Sokoloff, L, and Kuhl, D.E., Tomographic measurement of local cerebral glucose metabolic rate in humans with (18-F)2-fluoro-2-deoxyglucose: validation of method, *Ann. Neurol.,* 6, 371, 1979.
4. Chugani, H. T. and Phelps, M. E., Maturational changes in cerebral function in infants determined by 18-FDG positron emission tomography, *Science,* 231, 840, 1986.
5. Chugani, H. T., Phelps, M. E., and Mazziotta, J. C., Positron emission tomography study of human brain functional development, *Ann. Neurol.,* 22, 487, 1987.
6. Chugani, H. T., Development of regional brain glucose metabolism in relation to behavior and plasticity in *Human Behavior and the Developing Brain,* Dawson, G. and Fischer, K.W. Eds., Guilford, New York, 1994, 153.
7. Chugani, H., Hovda, D., Villablanca, J., Phelps, M., and Xu, W., Metabolic maturation of the brain: a study of local cerebral glucose utilization in the cat, *J. Cereb. Blood Flow Metab.,* 11, 35, 1991.
8. Jacobs, B., Chugani, H., Allada, V., Chen, S., Phelps, M., Pollack, D., and Raleigh, M., Metabolic brain development in rhesus macaques and vervet monkeys: a positron emission tomography study, *Cerebral Cortex,* 5, 222, 1995.
9. Tyler, R., Chugani, H.T., and Howard, J., A pilot study of cerebral glucose utilization in children with prenatal drug exposure, *Ann. Neurol.,* 34, 460, 1993. (Abstract)
10. Zametkin, A. J., Nordahl, T. E., Gross, M., King, A. C., Semple, W. E. Rumsey, J., Hamburger, S., and Cohen, R. M., Cerebral glucose metabolism in adults with hyperactivity of childhood onset, *N. Engl. J. Med.,* 323, 1361, 1990.
11. Volkow, N.D. and Fowler, J.S., Neuropsychiatric disorders: investigation of schizophrenia and substance abuse, *Sem. Nucl. Med.,* 22, 254, 1992.

Index

A

Abruption, placental, 39
Abscesses, brain, 6
Adrenergic receptors
  alpha$_1$, 41
  alpha$_2$, 41
  beta$_1$, 41
  in rabbit uterus, 41–42
Alcohol, 8
  IUGR and, 10
Amniotic fluid, 25
  benzoylecgonine in, 51, 104, 131
  cocaine and, 50–51, 131
  ecgonine methyl ester in, 51
  norcocaine in, 51
Anesthesia, CNS and, 42–43
Angina, 120
Animal models, 169
Anomalies, fetal, 39–41
  atresias, 40
  intracranial, 41
Anterior cingulate cortex, 155–158
Apnea, 13, 116, 117
Appetite, cocaine suppression of, 7
Arachidonic acid metabolites, 84
Attention, 151, 153
  catecholaminergic systems and, 153
  cholinergic systems and, 153
  malnutrition and, 158
  models of, 153
  selective, 153
    blocking paradigm as model of, 153
    model of, 153
  serotonergic systems and, 153
Attention deficit disorder, 15
Autism, 14

B

Baboons, 44
Behavior, 15–16
  deficits, 151
    malnutrition and, 152
    persistent, 151
    variability of, 106
  play, 173
  types of, 96
Benzoylecgonine, 24, 35
  accumulation of, 108
  in amniotic fluid, 50, 104
  analgesia and, central, 99
  anesthetic action of, 99–100

behavioral effects of, 96–97
beta receptor binding and, 59
brain levels of, 107
  fetal, 104, 120
calcium ion chelation and, 26
cardiovascular activity of, 53
central stimulatory effects of, 96–98
  mechanism for, 100–103
    ionic/membrane effects as, 100–101
    neuroendocrine, 102–103
    transmitter, 101–102
  neonatal, 104
  refractory period associated with, 106
chemical structure of, 36
  vasoreactivity and, 87
clearance rates of, 107
clinical effects of, 107
CNS effects of, 98–99
cocaine vs., 98, 121
coronary arteries and, 81
CRH and, 103
cytotoxic effects of, 28
dopamine uptake and, 101
dose response of, 98
ecgonine and, 101
elimination of, 133–134
in fetal brain, 104, 120
fetal cerebral arteries and, 81
fetal exposure to, 121
hair levels of, 104
half-life of, 121
  neonatal, 133–134
hippocampal electrical record of, 99
hypertension and, 53
meconium levels of, 104
pharmacologic activity of, 120
plasma levels of, 120, 128
  in fetuses, 131
  in newborns, 131
renal elimination of, 133–134
strokes and, 120
urine levels of, 131
urine screens for, 127
vasoconstriction and, cerebral, 98–99
withdrawal, 116
Benzoylecgonine intoxication syndrome, 120
Benzoylnorecgonine, 24
  anesthetic action of, 100
  calcium ion chelation and, 26
  central stimulatory effects of, 96–98
  chemical structure of, 36
  dose response of, 98